IRA ALDRIDGE
The Negro Tragedian

KU-329-772

1. Ira Aldridge as Othello. An oil painting by an unknown artist in the Bakhrushin State Central Theatrical Museum, Moscow.

IRA ALDRIDGE

The Negro Tragedian

by

HERBERT MARSHALL

and

MILDRED STOCK

SALISBURY SQUARE · LONDON

©
BY HERBERT MARSHALL AND MILDRED STOCK
1958

KING ALFRED'S COLLEGE
WINCHESTER ·

792.92
ALD   36275

MADE AND PRINTED IN GREAT BRITAIN BY
THE CAMELOT PRESS LTD., LONDON AND SOUTHAMPTON

Contents

NOTE

Superior figures in the text refer to the section "References" at the end of the book.

List of Illustrations

CHAPTER I

Prologue: It Came to Pass

ON 23rd April 1932, the birthday of William Shakespeare, the new Memorial Theatre at Stratford-upon-Avon was officially opened by Edward, Prince of Wales, in the presence of representatives of many nations, who had gathered to pay homage to the genius that Stratford had produced, but who belonged to the world.

After the old theatre burned to the ground in 1926, a worldwide campaign for funds was initiated, and nearly a quarter of a million pounds was raised, almost half coming from America. On behalf of the Shakespeare Memorial Society, the Prince received from the late Dr. James Weldon Johnson* a gift from the Negroes of the United States, and today one of the seats in the Shakespeare Memorial Theatre bears a bronze plate with the simple inscription—IRA ALDRIDGE. This is one of thirty-three such chairs in memory of the greatest names in world drama—Burbage, Garrick, Mrs. Siddons, the Kembles, Kean, Macready, Phelps, Forrest, Irving, Ellen Terry, and others.

Thus did Ira Aldridge take his place beside the most celebrated Shakespearean actors of the past, yet how many people today know that he ever existed? How many people who sit in that very chair in the fourth row of the stalls are aware of its significance? The world has forgotten, but Dr. Johnson and the others who fought against racial discrimination and for the advancement of their people knew that symbolic of that struggle was this American-born Negro, who, 100 years before, had achieved distinction as one of the great interpreters of Shakespeare, who was the first Negro to play white roles, including the greatest in world drama—Macbeth, Shylock, King Lear—who had received

* Author of *Black Manhattan*, for many years secretary of the National Association for the Advancement of Colored People.

from crowned heads and learned and artistic societies honours and decorations unheard of for an actor either before or since his time and who, above all, had been a living refutation of the unscientific notion that genius is confined to one race.

One wonders how it is, then, that in all these years a proper biography has not been published either in the land of his birth or of his adoption. It is only within the last fifteen years or so that a handful of individuals in different countries, at first unknown to each other, began delving into the life of this "famous unknown" actor, among them being the authors of this book.

With Herbert Marshall the idea took root before the war, when he directed Paul Robeson in the little London Unity Theatre in *Plant in the Sun*, a play by an American writer, Ben Bengal. The part was intended for a white character, but was equally suitable for a Negro without altering a word! Robeson took this part after refusing a lucrative offer to star in Basil Dean's production, *The Sun Never Sets*, at Drury Lane, making a public statement that he would no longer play jingoistic melodrama in which he portrayed "the noble savage". He then appeared in *The Proud Valley*, a film based on an original story written for him by Herbert Marshall and Fredda Brilliant, produced by Ealing Studios, London. In it he took the part of an ordinary worker, a coal-miner in Wales, where, incidentally, his singing was even more highly appreciated than anywhere else in the United Kingdom. In the search that followed for film subjects of a new kind for Robeson, the characters of Toussaint L'Ouverture and Ira Aldridge came up for consideration. About L'Ouverture much had been written, but about Aldridge—nothing. When the war broke out, this project had to be shelved, but in 1946, after Robeson's return to England, the question once more arose of a film based on the life of Ira Aldridge. Work was begun on a script, in the course of which it was learned that in 1930, when he was preparing for his first appearance as Othello in London, Robeson had studied voice and diction with Ira Aldridge's younger daughter, Miss Amanda Ira Aldridge. Thus, it may be said, did the mantle of Ira Aldridge fall in direct succession on to the shoulders of one who may rightly be designated "The Ira Aldridge of Today"! Among Miss Aldridge's possessions at the time of her death was a photograph of Robeson inscribed:

To Miss Aldridge—With many thanks for the fresh inspiration received from all the reports of her father's greatness. I realize that I can only carry on in the "tradition of Aldridge".

The film, unfortunately, did not materialize, because Robeson, after returning to the United States, was not permitted to leave again.

In 1945, on a visit to Paris, Marshall met Gordon Craig and began telling him about his work on "a fascinating Negro Shakespearean actor of the last century". Craig interrupted with "Oh, you mean Ira Aldridge!" and immediately put him in contact with Dr. Michel Kovatchévitch, a Yugoslav actor and Shakespearean scholar living in Paris, who had spent the war years making an intensive study of Aldridge, simultaneously with his war work for the Allies. Dr. Kovatchévitch's article, "Shakespeare in Serbia" (in which he brings out Aldridge's role in the development of Shakespearean production in Serbia), is dealt with later in this book, and his forthcoming biography of Aldridge in French will undoubtedly be a major contribution to theatre history. Now the picture began to reveal much more than had at first been realized, for here was a Negro actor whose activities extended into practically every country in Europe, including Tsarist Russia. Marshall began accumulating original material—playbills, leaflets, newscuttings, portraits—until it became obvious that the facts of Aldridge's work far exceeded anything previously known, and cried out for a biography, particularly now, in the context of the re-emergence of the coloured peoples on the world arena, the final struggle for equality by the American Negro, and the upsurge in Africa. So we see that things had begun to move in England and France.

In the United States, Mildred Stock, a native New Yorker, first heard the name of Ira Aldridge from a Negro actor who was studying the role of Othello. "Ira Aldridge did this a hundred years ago", he remarked.

"And who was Ira Aldridge?" she politely asked, little dreaming where this innocent question would lead her. But her informant knew little more than that he was an American-born Negro actor who had to leave his country for an opportunity to pursue his art, and that he settled in England, where he ranked with the greatest Shakespearean actors of his time, playing not only coloured, but *white roles*. Now this was getting interesting, and worth a little investigation.

A visit to the Theatre Collection of the New York Public Library produced a number of scrap-books on Aldridge, containing a variety of playbills, newspaper and magazine cuttings, photographs, and odds and ends of biographical notes, but these last were so fragmentary and contradictory that it was impossible to be certain even where he was born, or when. The Schomburg Collection of Negro History and Literature in Harlem (the Countee Cullen Branch of the New York Public Library), had additional interesting information and a large collection of playbills which the late A. A. Schomburg, the Curator, had personally collected. Still a connected story failed to emerge, and on his origin and personal life there was no consistent or documented information. The only point on which there was agreement was that he was a great actor, a great interpreter of Shakespeare, had great versatility, and here and there one came upon the word "genius". Well, if he was as good as that, there must be more definite information about him somewhere.

The search for this information took Miss Stock on a tour of the major Negro university libraries in the Southern states and the Folger Shakespeare Library in Washington, all of which she ransacked, and, although ending up with a wealth of fascinating material, including photographs, autograph letters and other rare documents, what she had was a gigantic jig-saw puzzle with big pieces missing in such strategic places that it seemed hopeless even to attempt to put it together.

In the course of this work, Jean Blackwell, Curator of the Schomburg Collection, put her in touch with Owen C. Mortimer, a graduate student at Northwestern University in Illinois, who had been making a serious study of the life and art of Ira Aldridge since 1949. They entered into correspondence and, in a spirit of friendly competition, many ideas and "scoops" were exchanged. Through his collection of illustrative material, "The Ira Aldridge Memorial Collection", and the talks he has given in connection with it, many hundreds learned about Ira Aldridge for the first time. One of the developments of this work in the United States was the formation of the Ira Aldridge Society, which has as its main purpose the restoration of the forgotten name of this great actor to its rightful place in theatre history. So on the East Coast and in the Middle West of the United States things were also stirring.

In the spring of 1955 Miss Stock sailed for London to continue her research and to visit Aldridge's only surviving child. Before leaving, she learned from Frederick O'Neal, a leading Negro actor from the Anna Lucasta Company, that Herbert Marshall had a special interest in Ira Aldridge and was planning a book on him. So, after comparing notes and finding that their interest in Ira Aldridge and their approach to the presentation of his story were in harmony, they decided to work together on a biography, factual, documented, definitive.

Many questions remained to be answered. Where was he born? Senegal claimed him, New York claimed him, and Maryland claimed him. When was he born? Anywhere from 1804 to 1820! Had he really descended from a line of African kings? Was his first wife really the daughter of a Member of Parliament? What was her maiden name and where in England did the marriage take place? Was his second wife really a Swedish baroness? If his first wife died shortly after the marriage in 1825, as some accounts stated, and his second wife was not born until 1834 (as established by her obituary notice), who was the mother of the son born to Aldridge in 1847? Maybe his second wife was in reality his third wife! Was he valet to Edmund Kean when that great English actor came to New York, or was he Henry Wallack's dresser at the Chatham Theatre? Was it Edmund Kean, Henry Wallack, or his brother, James Wallack, who took young Ira to England and gave him his first "break"? Did he return to the United States in the 1830s and play "unsuccessfully at the Mud Theatre in Baltimore"? Did he study for eighteen months at Glasgow University and receive "several premiums in Latin composition"? All these statements, and many more, were made in one place or another—all haphazard, all undocumented.

They had many meetings with eighty-nine-year-old Amanda Ira Aldridge, who was an infant when her father died in 1867, and while she was most gratified to learn of the newly revived interest in her illustrious father and was as co-operative as she could be, she was unable to supply all the missing pieces, particularly those relating to his first wife, whose origin was shrouded in mystery, and to the son born in 1847. The few remaining mementoes of her father's rich collection she very proudly exhibited to the authors.

Followed months of intensive work, ploughing through many volumes of old playbills, theatrical journals, and provincial newspapers in the British Museum, the Gabrielle Enthoven Collection at the Victoria and Albert Museum, the Shakespeare Memorial Library, the Raymond Mander and Joe Mitchenson Theatre Collection, the Garrick Club and local libraries having theatre collections; visits to old theatres, bookshops, libraries, museums in the many towns and cities of the British Isles where Aldridge had played, following up every clue, however remote, visiting descendants of individuals said to have known Aldridge— all of which helped to fill in some of the gaps.

Edward Scobie of London, a Negro journalist and close friend of Miss Aldridge for several years before her death in March 1956, co-operated by passing on whatever information he had about the family. He had written several articles about Miss Aldridge and her father in the *Chicago Defender* and other publications, and had arranged a number of radio broadcasts and public appearances for Miss Aldridge in the last few years. But despite the wonderful co-operation of individuals, of town and county clerks, archivists, curators, and librarians throughout England, some of whom were given a difficult time in this desperate and tenacious search for the facts, there still remained some missing links, but the authors felt that the story, though not complete in all its aspects, was sufficiently interesting and important to be placed before the public.

In order to reconstruct the story of his life and career, much reliance had to be placed on the writings of Aldridge's contemporaries. Appeals for information were sent to the European capitals which he had visited. Poland, France, Germany, and the U.S.S.R. responded by forwarding much valuable information in their original language, a study of which gave a clear, but none the less second-hand glimpse of the actor in motion. It might, of course, have been possible to give play to one's creativeness and imagination to fill in the gaps and to present the story as though the authors had personally known Aldridge and seen his performances, but such an orientation, it was felt, is for the novelist. The serious biographer, especially in the first modern work on a subject about whom very little authentic information has been recorded, must base himself on the word of contemporaries. This may seem to be merely a matter of scissors and paste—a montage of news-cuttings and the like—but it was an essential part of this biography to condense and synthesize the mass of material scattered around the world and to present it as fully as possible, even at the risk of being repetitious and tiresome in spots. At least the basic record would be there, at the disposal of future students, writers, historians, actors, and others who might wish to develop some special phase of the Aldridge story.

⋆   ⋆   ⋆

Despite his unique and undeniable contribution to the art of the theatre, there has been what amounts to a systematic exclusion of Ira Aldridge from the works of theatre historians. Such reputable dramatic historians as Dutton Cook and Laurence Hutton do include him in their works and on the whole give a fairly unbiased presentation, but their general attitude toward a Negro actor is such that Cook includes him in a chapter headed "Strange Players",[1] and Hutton finds a place for him in his *Curiosities of the American Stage* in a chapter on the American stage Negro.[2] A study of the career of Ira Aldridge shows that he was neither a strange player nor a curiosity. Despite a conspiracy of silence in certain spheres, so great was Aldridge's success as an actor and appeal as a man that references to him have found their way into a large number of miscellaneous publications—encyclopedias, biographical dictionaries, magazines, newspaper editorials, books, essays, dramatic reminiscences, and the like. These have been published over a span of more than a hundred years in a variety of countries and languages, but they all have one thing in common: they are replete with error, contradiction and confusion, though many were written with the best of intentions. Thirty-four lines are devoted to Aldridge in the first volume of *Enciclopedia Dello Spettacolo*, published in Rome in 1954, and a fictionalized biography was written in Hungary in 1932 by Erno Ligeti, *Az Idegen Csillag: Ira Aldridge, Regenyes Elete*, (Strange Star: Ira Aldridge's Romantic Life). The *Encyclopaedia Britannica* makes no mention of him, though many other less important reference works do. A typical item is the one

7

in the *New Century Cyclopedia of Names*, published by Appleton-Century-Crofts, Inc., New York, 1954:

> Aldridge, Ira Frederick (called the African Roscius), b. probably at New York, *c.* 1805; d. Lodz, Poland, August 10, 1867. American Negro tragedian, a protégé of Edmund Kean, whose valet he probably was for a time. Made his debut (1826) as Othello at the Royal Theatre, London. He was poorly received at Baltimore (*c.* 1830). He played successfully at London (1833 *et seq.*) and met with considerable acclaim in Europe (1853-6, 1858, 1867), particularly for Shakespearean roles, such as Othello, Lear, Aaron, and Macbeth. He was honoured by the governments of Prussia, Austria, Russia, and others.

The errors in this piece will be apparent to the reader by the time he has finished this book. Aldridge is mentioned briefly and with error in such books as *A Dictionary of the Drama*, by W. Davenport Adams, the *Oxford Companion to the Theatre*, *A History of the Theatre*, by George Freedley and John A. Reeves, *The Negro in the American Theatre*, by Edith J. R. Isaacs, to mention only a few serious and reputable works. One can have no quarrel with the well-intentioned but ill-informed writer and historian for the errors, misconceptions and legends which have persisted through the years. Yet he died only some ninety years ago! No one had undertaken the time-consuming and often frustrating task of sorting out the mass of bits and pieces with a view to separating the real from the legendary, the fact from the fiction, and setting the record straight once and for all time.

There is, however, another group, well-informed but ill-intentioned, who have played a role in keeping the name of Ira Aldridge and his work in oblivion. One instance of the glaring, and one must conclude deliberate, omission of Aldridge from an otherwise exhaustive work was revealed by W. Napoleon Rivers, Jr., a Negro student, who had come across a most important review of Aldridge's performances in St. Petersburg in 1858 written by the great French writer and dramatic critic, Theophile Gautier. In an article in *The Crisis* (New York) of January 1932, Mr. Rivers said:

> ... My work on a doctoral thesis in Romance Languages here at Cornell brought me in contact with it. My discovery of this

unbiased criticism, so complimentary to Aldridge, led me to make a page-for-page and line-for-line comparison between the French text and the 24-volume English translation of Gautier's work by Professor F. A. deSumichrast of the French Department of Harvard University.[3] To my surprise, it was omitted. De Sumichrast translates beautifully enough up to this passage on Aldridge, makes an abrupt halt, then takes a leap and continues his translation one paragraph beyond!

I then investigated with extreme care the doctoral dissertation of Helen Patch, Bryn Mawr, 1922, bearing the title, *The Dramatic Criticism of Theophile Gautier*. Mention of the criticism on Aldridge could not have been found within its covers. Louise Bulkley Dillingham, writing another doctoral dissertation on Gautier at Bryn Mawr five years later, does not touch upon the subject. Thus we see that this tribute to Aldridge has been denied an available or permanent forum in English.

Another of the many sins of omission was committed by Henry Saxe Wyndham in his two-volume work, *The Annals of Covent Garden Theatre*,[4] in which he gives an elaborate account of events at that theatre, bringing the reader up to 25th March 1833, when Edmund Kean was stricken on the stage in his last performance of *Othello*, then skipping to 24th April, omitting all mention of Aldridge's epoch-making appearances on 10th and 12th April, when he too played *Othello* with the same cast and the same Desdemona with whom Kean had played a fortnight before. Evidently a Negro actor appearing at Covent Garden for the first time in the history of that great theatre was not of sufficient importance or significance to be included in Wyndham's history. Or could there have been some other reason for this omission?

One could go on with instances of omission of this kind which would explain, at least in part, why the name of the world's greatest Negro actor is virtually unknown today. He does get a mention in the autobiography of a contemporary, that of John Coleman,[5] who refers to him as "an obese buck-nigger".

Then there are such pin-pricks as the article in the *New Yorker* of 22nd January 1944, which contains the incredible statement: "Aldridge's interpretation [of Othello] was, to judge by the contemporary critiques, nothing much!" What is amazing about this statement is that the writer had at his disposal Gautier's critique of 1858, from which he quotes, "He smothered Desdemona in the most considerate manner and roared with decorum", and, further basing himself on this critique, he remarks that Gautier was fascinated by the fact that Aldridge "made up" as a white man, except for his hands. But the writer sees fit to withhold from the *New Yorker* readers all reference to the rest of Gautier's critique, in which he says: ". . . His first entry was magnificent, he was Othello himself, as created by Shakespeare, his eyes half-closed as though dazzled by an Afric sun . . . acts wisely and restrainedly in a majestically classical style much resembling that of Macready. He produced a great performance which drew forth endless applause."* Perhaps the writer based his statement on other "contemporary critiques", such as the one by Eliza O'Neill (Lady Wrixon Becher), an actress of the highest calibre in Great Britain, who wrote to a friend: ". . . I have seen him [Aldridge] in Cheltenham and Cork, and during my professional as well as private life I never saw so correct a portraiture of Othello amidst the principal luminaries of my age." Perhaps the *New Yorker* writer thought that the King of Prussia, H.M. Frederick IV, was mad when he presented Aldridge with the medal for Art and Science after seeing him perform Othello, or that the Russian actors and actresses of the Imperial Theatre did not know what they were about when, accompanied by their leading stars and Shakespearean scholars, they attended his performances as though they were lessons in dramatic art.

It becomes indisputable, as one goes deeper into the subject, that there has been a deliberate exclusion of Ira Aldridge from the works of many writers, and a distortion of the facts by others, and the conclusion is forced upon one that the basic reason for this treatment of a great artist is that he was a Negro. Interestingly, this neglect is in inverse ratio to the distance one travels from the country of his birth. One finds that he is better known, his genius more publicly acknowledged, articles and reviews of his performances grow in size, depth, and analytical thoroughness as one moves East—to England, to Germany, to Poland, to Russia. Indeed, the most serious and thorough analyses of his Shakespearean roles are to be found in old Tsarist Russia, and the only

* This critique is given in full in Chapter XII.

authoritative book about him in the last hundred years was published in Moscow in 1940!

Three published items have been used as basic source material and will be constantly referred to throughout this book. The first is a small book entitled *Memoir and Theatrical Career of Ira Aldridge, the African Roscius*, published anonymously in 1849 in London by J. Onwhyn. The fly-leaf has a quotation from the *Merchant of Venice*, Act II, Scene 1, when the Prince of Morocco introduces himself,

> Mislike me not for my complexion,
> The shadowed livery of the burnished sun,

and is "Dedicated to Sir Edward Lytton Bulwer Lytton, Bart., M.P., Distinguished philanthropist, Author and Friend of the Drama". Bulwer Lytton was a patron of Ira Aldridge, and his name appears with many others on a playbill of 21st June 1841. This source, which will be referred to as the *1849 Memoir*, or simply the *Memoir*, is considered of primary importance because it was published during Aldridge's lifetime and is obviously based on material and information supplied by Aldridge himself. Since he was ever conscious of the value of publicity and took an active part in that direction, it is not unreasonable to suppose that it was written at his suggestion and with his active co-operation. He may even have been the author!* There is evidence that he was personally responsible for its translation into German,[6] Polish,[7] Swedish,[8] Russian,[9] and French.[10]

The second item of basic source material is an article in the *Anglo-African Magazine* of January 1860, the only known piece of printed matter dealing with Aldridge's early life, and the correctness of which is confirmed by his own statement in a letter to the author some months after its publication. It was written by Dr. James McCune Smith, a schoolmate of Aldridge at the African Free School in New York. Dr. Smith studied at the University of Glasgow, receiving his B.A. in 1832, his M.A. in 1833, and his M.D. in 1834, and became an important figure in the medical profession in New York as well as a scientific writer of note. This article will be referred to as the *1860 Chronicle*.

---

* See playbill of 1838 on pp. 147-8, where he gives a dramatic reading from "A Memoir of the African (written by himself . . .)".

The third source used extensively in those sections dealing with Aldridge's Russian tours is the book by Sergei Durylin, *Ira Aldridge*, published by the State Publishing House, Moscow-Leningrad, 1940. This is a highly documented work (in Russian), with detailed information about his performances in Tsarist Russia, culled mainly from contemporary newspapers and magazines. As Durylin showed a slight tendency in his otherwise excellent work to emphasize the favourable criticisms of Aldridge, a tendency which was commented on by the late Professor Morozov, the leading Soviet specialist on Shakespeare, the authors have made it a point to refer back, wherever possible, to Durylin's original sources. The All Union Theatrical Society of Moscow supplied more than a hundred typed pages of material in Russian, consisting of extracts from contemporary newspapers, magazines, and books dealing with Aldridge, all of which was translated by Marshall. This material helped in presenting a well-balanced and faithful picture of Aldridge's reception in Tsarist Russia.

Occasional reference will be made to the unpublished manuscript of the late Cyril Bruyn Andrews, an English writer who had met Miss Amanda Aldridge when they were neighbours in Henley-on-Thames in the 1930s, and became so interested in the story of her father that he undertook to write his biography, basing himself mainly on material furnished by Miss Aldridge. In this project he worked jointly with J. A. Orr-Ewing, with whom he had co-edited *Victorian Swansdown* (extracts from the early travel diaries of John Orlando Parry), and of the *Torrington Diaries*, both published by Messrs. Eyre and Spottiswoode of London. According to correspondence exchanged in the mid-thirties between Andrews and A. A. Schomburg, then Curator of the Schomburg Collection, plans had been completed for the same publishers to produce the Aldridge biography, but this did not in fact materialize. Interestingly, Miss Aldridge spent the last few years of her life with Mr. Andrews's daughter, Fanny Andrews, to whom the authors are indebted for putting at their disposal her father's notes, which contained the text of many letters and documents which might not otherwise have been available to them.

★　　　★　　　★

A biography of Ira Aldridge is long overdue. This book, with its many limitations, is offered with humility as a beginning of what is hoped will be a rebirth of interest in the life and art of Ira Aldridge. The authors hope that it will serve to stimulate others to pick up where they leave off, until this great man is given his rightful place in theatrical history, and until the fascinating story of a unique representative of the Negro people becomes known to the world.

HERBERT MARSHALL.
MILDRED STOCK.

CHAPTER II

Descendant of a Princely Line?

IRA ALDRIDGE was born in the era following two great
revolutions, the French and the American, and the first successful
slave revolt in history, the Haitian Revolution, which ended in
1804, three years before Aldridge was born.

With the advent of the American Revolution the hopes and
aspirations of the Negro slaves for freedom and equality were
raised. The Legislature of New York passed an Act granting
freedom to all slaves who served in the Army for three years or
until honourably discharged, and a Bill was passed providing for
two Negro regiments. Coloured men of New York formed a
good proportion of the nearly 4,000 Negroes who fought in the
Colonial Army. But their dreams were to remain dreams for
many years to come, for "the American Revolution was not
directed against Colonial laws and institutions, but against over-
seas pretensions to direct Colonial life and business. Colonial
government, society, industry, religion, and education largely
persisted through the war and became the basis of the free State
which followed. When all the factors are taken into account, the
American Revolution was, on the whole, not an extremely
radical movement. Except for sundering ties with the British
Empire, old usages were not torn up by the roots. Under the high-
sounding phrases of the day, the old civilization with its blessings
and its evils was carried over into the new era to be changed as
exigencies demanded in the years ahead."[1]

Despite the aspirations of the Negro, especially those who
fought in the war, and the hopes of the more enlightened and
idealistic sections of the white population, the number of slaves,
instead of decreasing after the War of Independence, actually
increased. The invention of the cotton gin and textile machinery
in the Colonies as well as in England created larger markets for
cotton-planters who found themselves in need of more land and

more free labour. From 700,000 in Washington's time the number of slaves rose to 3,000,000 by 1850. The bulk of them came,
of course, from the land of Aldridge's forebears.

Among the 50 per cent. that survived their capture and
passage from Africa to America were the ancestors of Ira Aldridge.
There is no available information on which to base even a guess
as to when they arrived in the New World, nor is there any
evidence that Aldridge's father, Daniel Aldridge, was at any time
a slave. Our main sources regarding his ancestry are the *1849
Memoir* and the information contained in the mass of playbills,
handbills, biographical sketches, theatre announcements, Press
notices, and other publicity material obviously supplied by
Aldridge himself. Both these sources are for the most part in
agreement, except for the vital point of Aldridge's birthplace,
which in the *Memoir* is given as Senegal and in the other material
as New York.

Since the legend of Aldridge's royal birth in Senegal has
persisted through the years, causing considerable confusion, we
quote that part of the *Memoir* which deals with it:

His forefathers were princes of the Fulah tribe, whose dominions
were Senegal, on the banks of the river of that name, on the
West Coast of Africa, to which shore one of our early missionaries
found his way, taking charge of the father of Mr. Aldridge, in
order to qualify him for the work of civilizing his countrymen.
From what we can gather, his grandfather was more enlightened
than his subjects, probably through the instruction of the kind
missionary, and proposed that his prisoners taken in battle should
be exchanged and not, as was the custom, sold for slaves. This
wish interfered with the notions and perquisites of his tribe,
especially his principal chiefs, and a civil war waged among the
people. During these differences, the father of Mr. Aldridge, then
a promising youth, was taken to America by the missionary and
sent to Schenectady College, near New York, to receive the
advantages of a Christian education. Three days after his departure, the revolutionary storm which was brewing broke out
openly and the advocate of humanity, the reforming prince, was,
together with his whole family and personal attendants and
connexions, savagely butchered; the missionary escaped with his
young charge just in time to avoid a similar fate.

Mr. Aldridge's father remained in America until the death of
the rebellious chief who had headed the conspiracy and reigned

instead of the murdered prince. During the interval he had become a minister of the gospel and was regarded by all classes as a man of uncommon abilities. He was, however, desirous of establishing himself at the head of his tribe, possess himself of his birthright, and advance the cause of Christianity among his countrymen. For this purpose he returned to his native country, taking with him a young wife, one of his own colour, whom he had but just married in America. To this step he was prompted by the advice of his white friends, who doubtless looked forward to his reign as one calculated to encourage the growth of those "gospel seeds" which religious zeal had planted among the children of the Fulah tribe. Their pious hopes and intentions were frustrated. Mr. Aldridge senior no sooner appeared among the people of his slaughtered father than old disagreements revived, and two opposition parties were formed. Civil war again broke out, and in the struggle of contending chiefs the enlighted African was defeated, barely escaping from the scene of strife with his life, and for some time unable to quit the country, which was watched by numerous enemies anxious for his capture.

During the first month of the arrival of Mr. Aldridge's parents he, the subject of this memoir, was born; but nine years elapsed before the proscribed family escaped to America. All this time they were concealed in the neighbourhood of his foes, during vicissitudes and hardships that can well be imagined, but need not be described. As is always the case under such circumstances, for all men more or less dependent upon one another, there was a faithful adherent whose services mainly helped to save the lives of the rejected prince and his wife and son. He accompanied those whom he so served to America, and there Mr. Aldridge senior returned to his ministerial duties, influencing aright the minds of people of his own complexion in that country instead of his own.

The present Mr. Aldridge recollects that when a child some eight years old, playing at the door of a hut where he resided, some warriors belonging to his father's enemies were passing that way and noticed his resemblance to their fugitive chief, who was then, unknown to them, in the neighbourhood. Upon their making inquiries about the boy, the woman of the hut, without betraying alarm, claimed him as her daughter's child, and he was unmolested. A narrow escape for the future African Roscius! Thus was he saved in his infancy to vindicate in his manhood the cause of his whole race; thus was he snatched from, after participation in, or falling a victim to, the tragedies of real life practised by his countrymen, that he may among more civilized people, and

16

better applauded members, revel in mimic strife! The Negro boy of Senegal, whose life was so in jeopardy, had a strange career before him!

The parallel between this and Othello's story was evidently too good to be missed by an actor with imagination. "I am a descendant of a princely line", said Aldridge-Othello on the stage, and off-stage his forefathers were princes of the Fulah tribe! Nor could he resist a little embellishment when others "question'd me the story of my life, from year to year, the battles, sieges, fortune, that I have pass'd. I ran it through, even from my boyish days, to the very moment that he bade me tell it: Wherein I spake of most disastrous chances, of moving accidents by flood and field; of hair-breadth 'scapes i' the imminent deadly breach; of my redemption thence, and portance in my travel's history. . . ." But, however Aldridge may have romanticized, there is no reason to doubt that he descended from the Fulah people.

Senegal is a colony of French West Africa. Its possession by the French had two interruptions—from 1758 to 1783 and from 1800 to 1817, when it was in British hands. There are various theories among historians, some of them contradictory, about the origin of the Fulah people, their tribal customs and physical characteristics, but there appears to be agreement that they were in a somewhat higher category of people than those they conquered and, says the *Encyclopaedia Britannica*, "taken as a whole, the Fulah race is distinguished by great intelligence, frankness and strength of character".

The first British missionaries were the Society for the Propagation of the Gospel in 1752. The Society had many branches in North America and was particularly interested in proselytizing the Negro slaves coming to America. If, as the *Memoir* asserts, the missionaries had succeeded in converting a ruling prince of the Fulah tribe, it must have been a great achievement, because the Fulahs are, generally, Muslims, and the records show that the major successes in conversion were among primitive pagan tribes of Central and southern Africa and not among the Muslims of North Africa.

Let us analyse the *Memoir's* story. We are told that one of the early English missionaries took Daniel Aldridge, "then a promising youth", to America, but are given no clue as to the date. It may be assumed that if it occurred at all it was during one of the periods when Senegal was in British hands. Daniel Aldridge was born in 1772, according to his death certificate, so the first period of British occupation (1758-83) appears to be too early. At the opening of the second period (1800-17), Daniel is twenty-eight years old, hardly "a promising youth". He is taken to America; he studies at Schenectady College (of which we could obtain no proof, but that does not rule out the possibility); he becomes a preacher; he returns to Senegal with his young wife, and one month after their arrival Ira is born. This would be in July 1807. "But nine years elapsed before the proscribed family escaped to America." So this time they apparently get no help from the British missionaries, but escape to America on their own. It would be interesting to know how they "escaped" in an era when the only way in which a Negro crossed the Atlantic was in chains, and why they chose to escape to a country which held the Negro in chattel slavery, unless they were still protected members of a missionary society sent to proselytize their own people in America. And where is Ira's older brother, Joshua, all this time? There is not a word about him, although the *Memoir* does tell us later on that "Ira's mother died in 1818, leaving but two surviving children out of a numerous family. One of these, Mr. Aldridge's brother, was murdered at New Orleans some few years ago, having incurred the anger of some whites in a quarrel." Yet as late as 1860 we find Aldridge inquiring of Dr. Smith about this brother, Joshua.

Even a casual perusal of the *Memoir's* account of Aldridge's origin leads to the conclusion that it is but a story—romantic and interesting, but quite unacceptable as fact. We deal with it in such detail in the hope that the points we make, in addition to the copious documentary evidence produced, will establish once and for all time that New York was Ira Aldridge's birthplace, despite the reluctance in some quarters even today to give up the romantic version. A person in Aldridge's position was as unlikely as the theatrical promoter of today to be a stickler for accuracy in matters of publicity. African royal birth would go over with the public, so African royal birth it was. But in his private correspondence and official documents, "my native country" was always the United States. We do not, however, rule out the possibility of his forebears having been African princes. It did not take much to be a prince in Africa in those days. One need only own a village or two, some animals, and half a dozen wives.

An interesting question arises at this point—that of the name "Aldridge". If Daniel Aldridge were indeed the princely son of an African ruler, how did he come by that name? "Daniel", of course, is a Biblical name, but it is doubtful that an infant born in Senegal would have been so named. "Ira" is neither Biblical nor African. "Aldridge" is an English name. There is a village in Staffordshire so called. It was a common practice to identify Negro slaves in the United States by the surname of their master or the estate to which they belonged. Dr. James McCune Smith tells us that Ira Aldridge's father was a native of Baltimore and his mother of North Carolina. If so, it is possible that they were slaves and that, like so many thousands of others, they made their way to free territory, or perhaps Daniel Aldridge obtained his freedom when he began serving as a preacher. Or it may be—and this is the greater likelihood—that Daniel's father, Ira's grandfather, had been brought over from Africa as a slave and dubbed "Aldridge". Throughout Aldridge's career we find the Press making comments on the name, such as: "Mr. Ira Aldridge, or so this gentleman calls himself . . ." and "The tragedy of *Othello* was performed, the part of the Moor by an individual of Negro origin, as his features sufficiently testify, who calls himself Aldridge."

Dr. Smith ends his chronicle by saying: "Mr. Aldridge is so nearly a pure Negro that there is probably not one thirty-second portion of white blood in his face. His complexion is black, and yet of that shade through which the red blood may be seen glowing beneath. His hair is woolly. His features, of that Negroe'd [*sic*] type which we see in the Egyptian Sphynxes. He is above the middle height, athletic, and of noble presence." How is one to interpret the observation that there is *probably not* one thirty-second portion of white blood in his face? Did Dr. Smith know of *any* white blood? If so, that would point to a slave relationship somewhere along the line, since it was not uncommon for slave-holders to father the children of their beautiful young slaves. One can only speculate as to Dr. Smith's cryptic remark.

Daniel Aldridge died in New York on 27th September 1840. His death certificate gives his age as sixty-eight, and "place of nativity" as New York. Since this is the only documentary evidence obtainable, we must accept the fact that he was born in New York in 1772, at the same time bearing in mind that it may have been expedient for him and his children, in pre-Civil War United States, to have it recorded that he was born not only in America but in a northern state.

The following notice of his death appeared in a New York newspaper:

At New York, on the 27th of September, the Reverend Daniel Aldridge, father of Mr. Ira F. Aldridge, celebrated African Roscius. There are few individuals who have been generally more useful than the Reverend Mr. Aldridge, and whose loss will be more severely felt in New York among his coloured brethren, to whom he was endeared by his faithful discharge of the duties incumbent on him as a Christian minister.

Daniel Aldridge was buried in St. Philip's Cemetery in lower Manhattan.

Dr. Smith, writing in 1860, makes no reference to the romantic story of the *1849 Memoir*, but says:

The father of Ira Aldridge was Daniel Aldridge, a straw-vendor in the city of New York. Mr. Aldridge was a strict member, in high standing, in "Old Zion". We well remember the old gentleman—short in stature, with a tall, broad-brimmed white hat, mounted on a high cart filled with his merchandise, and dolefully crying, "Straw, s-t-r-a-w!" through the streets, especially on Saturday nights. He was a native of Baltimore, and his wife [Ira's mother] of North Carolina; so that the great actor himself hails from the region which has produced so many distinguished colored Americans.

Now we have three places claiming Daniel Aldridge—Senegal, New York, and Baltimore!

It will be noted that Dr. Smith does not say that Daniel Aldridge was a minister or a reverend, but that he was a member in high standing in "Old Zion". The *Memoir* remarks: "There may be something suggestive of ridicule in the thought of a black preacher, and heaven knows there have been enough burlesques written and drawn to associate the idea with preposterously absurd notions of 'nigger' eloquence and theology; be that as it may, it should be remembered that sterling merit ought to be measured by the means possessed for working good, rather than by the amount obtained, and Mr. Aldridge's father did not live in vain."

It may be that Daniel Aldridge was a lay preacher in those early years to which Dr. Smith refers, and that at the time of his death he was a reverend and a minister.* It is doubtful that in the earlier period a Negro community, however devout, could support a full-time minister. This may have been possible after the abolition of slavery in New York State in 1827, when the Negroes began earning money as labourers, handicraftsmen, and even small businessmen, and could make contributions to their church.

The religious profession was the first that any Negro could aspire to, and even in the South a talented Negro slave might, by becoming a preacher, have his freedom bought for him by the missionaries, who found that proselytizing was more successful when the preacher was of the same race as those they sought to convert.

As long as the law in the Colonies decreed that a Christian could not be held as a slave, the slave-owners were violently opposed to the religious education of the Negro, but after the Colonists secured, through legislation by their assemblies and a formal declaration of the Bishop of London, the abrogation of this law, then the slave-holders welcomed this religion of passive submission. On this point Dr. W. E. B. DuBois says:

> The long system of repression and degradation of the Negro tended to emphasize the elements in his character which made him a valuable chattel: courtesy became humility, moral strength degenerated into submission, and the exquisite native appreciation of the beautiful became an infinite capacity for dumb suffering. The Negro, losing the joy of this world, eagerly seized upon the offered conceptions of the next; the avenging Spirit of the Lord enjoining patience in this world, under sorrow and tribulation, until the Great Day when He should lead His dark children home —this became his comforting dream. His preacher repeated the prophecy, and his bards sang, "Children, we all shall be free when the Lord shall appear!"[2]

* On the certificate of his second marriage on 20th April 1865, Aldridge gives his father's "rank or profession" as "clerk".

21

This deep religious fatalism, so vividly expressed in *Uncle Tom's Cabin*, and which we later find in some of the melodramas in which Ira Aldridge played, was agreeable and profitable to the slave-holder. But the beginning of the Abolitionist movement and the gradual development of a class of free Negroes brought about a change. The free Negro produced a new kind of leader who chose not to wait for freedom "when the Lord shall appear", but to fight for it here and now. The black bards caught new notes and sometimes even dared to sing:

> O Freedom, O Freedom, O Freedom over me,
> Before I'll be a slave
> I'll be buried in my grave,
> And go home to my Lord and be free.

And years later, after performing one of the great master-pieces of world drama and acknowledging the thunderous applause of the audience in some European capital, Aldridge would take up his guitar and with humility and simplicity sing an anti-slavery song, "Dear Heart, What a Terrible Life am I Led", or the Negro dancing song, "Let Me, When My Heart a-Sinking, Hear the Sweet Guitar a-Clinking" (both from the ballad opera, *The Padlock*), or the Negro comic song, "Opossum Up a Gum Tree", thus expressing in his own inimitable way his identity with his people and their protest against slavery. And a century later we hear Paul Robeson sing out "Let My People Go" until the whole world hears him, and he changes the submissive and fatalistic "Old Man River" into a song of protest and courage, and "I'm tired of living and fear'd of dying" becomes "I must keep on fighting until I'm dying. . . ."

This, then, was the atmosphere in which the Reverend Daniel Aldridge served his flock and in which his son was born and spent his childhood.

CHAPTER III

The African Free School

THE date of Ira Aldridge's birth has been given variously as 1804, 1805, 1807, 1808, 1810, and even 1820—five years before he appears in his first starring role in a London theatre! It can now be stated on the following evidence that Ira Aldridge was born in New York on 24th July 1807: first, his British Naturalization Certificate, an official document, the text of which appears elsewhere in this book; second, the biographical and publicity material mentioned in the preceding chapter; third, New York is given as place of birth on Aldridge's death certificate issued in Lodz, Poland, in August 1867 (although his age is given as fifty-nine instead of sixty); and, finally, the statement of Dr. Smith in the *1860 Chronicle*: "Ira Aldridge was born in Chapel Street, now West Broadway, in 1808." The error in Dr. Smith's date may be explained by the fact that, although a schoolmate, he was several years younger than Ira, and would not necessarily know the exact year of his birth. It is clear that he obtained some of his information from Ira's older brother, Joshua, who might understandably, in 1860, have been mistaken by one year in the date, but would be most unlikely to err as to place of birth, having no doubt himself been born in the same place. The month and day—24th July—are further attested to by an entry in Aldridge's diary on 24th July 1854 in Switzerland: "My birthday, celebrated by the Troupe, serenaded in the morning with Dr. DuNegal a barrel of beer enveloped in grape vine."

The *1860 Chronicle* continues:

> At the time of the existence of Brown's Theatre, he attended the African School in Mulberry Street, on the site now occupied by Colored Ward School No. 1. He was among the big boys of our schoolmates, yet we do not recollect, nor do others of his schoolmates, that he especially distinguished himself in any direction. . . . He lost his mother while yet a child, and being of a

23

roving disposition only remained at home a few months after the father's second marriage; he shipped on a brig and sailed South. While in a port in North Carolina he attracted the attention of a slave dealer, who offered the captain $500 for him; but the captain, who happened to be a Christian man, refused the offer, saying that the boy had trusted to his honor to carry him back to New York.

Today on West Broadway (formerly Chapel Street) in lower Manhattan, New York, there still stand several rows of very old, crumbling wooden shacks no longer habitable. It may be that the house in which Ira was born is among them, but precise identification is no longer possible.

Ira must have done his share of hauling water from one of the wooden pumps located on every fourth street corner, and helping with other family chores necessary to make life bearable in the days when wood was the only available fuel and oil lamps the only illumination. His activities outside of school were probably not different from those of the average boy of old New York, except that he must have been required to attend church and Sunday school with more than ordinary regularity, his father being "a strict member of Old Zion". Since he was "among the big boys" and, we are told in the *Memoir*, he was awarded prizes for declamation at school, it is not surprising that his father considered him good material for the ministry and decided on that for his career. But Ira, who had very early developed a passion for the theatre, had other ideas, although there is nothing to show that he ever openly opposed his father in the matter of career. Like most poor children, he probably did odd jobs in the neighbourhood to earn a few cents for a bottle of mead or spruce and some cakes or, more important, for admission to Brown's Tea-garden to derive inspiration from the Negro actor, James Hewlett (of whom we shall read in the next chapter), or for a ticket to the fourth gallery of the Park Theatre.

*　　　*　　　*

Since Aldridge was a product of the African Free School, which was attended by many other Negro children who distinguished themselves in later life in various spheres, let us see what manner of school it was, and consider briefly the general question of the education of Negro children in New York during that period.

The education of the Negro in New York really stemmed from the War of Independence, and specifically from the formation in January 1785 of the Society for the Promotion of the Manumission of Slaves and Protecting Such of Them As Have Been or May Be Liberated. Among the aims of this Society was the defence of the rights of the blacks, and their education.

The first Afro-America Free School was established in New York in 1787 by the Manumission Society. It opened in a single room with forty pupils. The teacher was Cornelius Davis, who had given up a school for white children to take care of the black. The first separate building for the school was erected in Cliff Street in 1796. It is interesting that the establishment of the African Free School gave the black children of New York a free school some years before there was free education for white children.

The Cliff Street building was burnt down in 1814, and the Corporation of New York City made a grant to the Society of a lot on William Street, near Duane, where a "commodious brick building" was erected and opened in 1815. This was African Free School No. 1, at No. 245 William Street.

African Free School No. 2, with accommodation for 500 pupils, was built on Mulberry Street, near Grand, in 1820. The boys were taught reading, writing, arithmetic, English grammar, composition, geography, astronomy, use of the globe, and map and linear drawing.

Charles C. Andrews, an Englishman, was the Principal for many years, and in 1830 he published a *History of the African Free Schools*.[1] In it he gives an account of an examination held on 7th May 1824, upon which a report was made to the Common Council of the City of New York by a committee appointed by that body. Ira Aldridge may have been among those who took that very examination, and it may, in fact, have been his final one before leaving school, for before the year is over he is already in England. As the African School No. 2 on Mulberry Street was erected in 1820, and as Dr. Smith states specifically that Ira was a pupil there, it would seem that he had been to school for only four years, from 1820 to 1824, although it is possible that he started in School No. 1 and then transferred to the new one.

According to Joshua, Ira ran away from home a few months after his father's second marriage, the date of which we do not know, but since their mother died in 1818, the second marriage could have taken place any time between 1818 and 1820, when Ira went into the new school. As the *Chronicle* says that he was "among the big boys", he may have been twelve or thirteen years old when he started school. In the original school records* it is stated that scholars attaining the age limit of fifteen were dismissed, but some were permitted to remain a short time longer. This would suggest that he may have stayed on until 1823 or 1824, when he would have been sixteen or seventeen.

That the African Free School was an extraordinary institution for its time is borne out by various official documents. A member of The Committee of the British and Foreign School Society, a Mr. Shaw, visiting New York in 1817, wrote a report to the Society in which he remarked upon a school for the children of Africans in New York, saying, *inter alia*: "Never was anyone more highly gratified than myself on visiting the school. Whether the unusual sight of three hundred Africans in an improved and improving mental state made me look with partiality on them, I know not, but I can conceive that there was more order there, and more strict attention paid to the system† than in any school which I had visited. In one corner was an African prince attentively copying the alphabet. A young lad about fourteen years of age was reciting passages from the best authors, suiting the action to the words; another was working difficult questions in geography, etc. In fact, let the enemies of those neglected children of men perform a pilgrimage to New York and confess that the prior despised African is as capable of every intellectual improvement as themselves." That was the African Free School in 1817, when Ira was ten years old.

The foundation of Aldridge's education was such as to encourage every talent and inclination of the young Negro student, perhaps more so than in later years, when the African schools were taken over by the New York Board of Education and

---

*In the Manuscript Division, Library of the New York Historical Society.

† The Lancasterian, or Monitorial, System devised by Joseph Lancaster in England "for the eduction of poor children and the training of masters for country schools". It was basically a means for the more economical use of personnel, books, and other necessary material.

merged with other coloured and white schools "open for the education of pupils for whom admission is sought without regard to race or color".

The African Free Schools helped to create a Negro intelligentsia which later participated actively in the leadership of the Abolitionist movement, in the fight for equal rights and against segregation, and which proved by its own example that, given the same opportunity, the potentialities of Negro and white are the same.

CHAPTER IV

The African Theatre

IN dealing with the next period of Aldridge's life, from the time he left the African Free School until he departed for England, we will consider the New York theatre of the time, its influence upon him, and his participation in it.

From the *1860 Chronicle* we learn that in 1821 or 1822 Brown's Theatre was opened on Mercer Street, and "Ira and his brother Joshua took to the stage, but their father, finding it out, took them away from the theatre". The *1849 Memoir* says: "Mr. Ira Aldridge was intended by his father for the Church . . . the son, however, began betimes to show his early preference and ultimate passion. At school he was awarded prizes for declamation, in which he excelled, and there his curiosity was excited by what he heard at theatrical representations—representations, he was told, which embodied all the fine ideas shadowed forth in the language he read and committed to memory. It became the wish of his heart to witness one of these performances, and that wish he soon contrived to gratify."

This would be the moment when young Ira would first come up against the colour bar, for "In one theatre [the Park]," continues the *Memoir*, "an obscure portion of a higher gallery is set apart for people of colour, and there may be seen a dark mass of shining ebony faces, relieved by the ivory teeth shown upon every slight incitement to risibility. Here the most respectable are expected to herd with sweeps and pickpockets. No other places must they occupy. So young Aldridge was cut off from witnessing the best performances, and, in common with many of his colour, felt severely the distinction which unjustly marked the difference which God's hand had made, and no mortal endeavour could remove."

The Park Theatre, opened in 1798 in New York, fronting on City Hall Park, was a great advance in theatre architecture. It was a large stone building, in contrast to the old John Street Theatre, which had been of wood, and its three tiers of boxes, a gallery, and a pit gave it a seating capacity of about 2,000. The gallery was set aside for Negroes and the third tier of boxes was reserved for prostitutes! The doors opened at half-past six and at seven the programme began. It usually consisted of two pieces, a tragedy and comedy, and sometimes even three, with a comic song or dance in between. The atmosphere in the theatre and the behaviour of the audience is described (as of 1802) by Washington Irving in his *Jonathan Oldstyle Letters*:

> I was much amused with the waggery and humour of the gallery which, by the way, is kept in *excellent* order by the constables who are stationed there. The noise in this part of the house is somewhat similar to that which prevailed in Noah's Ark; for we have an imitation of the whistles and yells of every kind of animal. This, in some measure, compensates for the want of music, as the gentlemen of our orchestra are very economic of their favours. Somehow or other, the anger of the gods seemed to be aroused all of a sudden, and they commenced a discharge of apples, nuts and gingerbread on the heads of the honest folks in the pit, who had no possibility of retreating from this new kind of thunder-bolts. I can't say but I was a little irritated at being saluted aside of my head with a rotten pippin; and was going to shake my cane at them, but was prevented by a decent-looking man behind me, who informed me that it was useless to threaten or expostulate. "They are only *amusing themselves* a little at our expense," said he; "sit down quietly and bend your back to it."

Who were the actors and what were the plays that young Ira could have seen from his perch high up in the Park gallery? The very earliest theatre companies were, of course, English, but the year 1767 found the first independent American company playing in the John Street Theatre. In 1805 the Park Theatre was put under the management of a well-established English actor, Thomas Abthorp Cooper, who had played Hamlet, Macbeth, and other major roles at Covent Garden Theatre and had emigrated to the United States in 1796. He was the first of many English actors who adopted the United States as their homeland.

In 1818, when Ira was eleven years old, there appeared an English actor who, together with his brother, was to play an important part in the life of Ira Aldridge. This was James William

Wallack (1791-1864) and Henry Wallack (1790-1870). The Wallacks are inseparably connected with the development of the New York theatre and the theatres they built and which bore their name existed in lower Manhattan for many years. James made his first appearance in New York on 7th September 1818 as Macbeth, and thereafter played a wide variety of roles, including Richard III, Romeo, Hamlet, Coriolanus, Henry V, Brutus, Don Felix, Bertram, and Rolla. Incidentally, the role of Rolla in Kotzebue's *Pizarro* is the first, as far as we know, that Aldridge played in the African Theatre. James made many trips to England throughout his entire career.

Henry Wallack first came to the States in 1819, but did not appear in New York until 9th May 1821 at the Anthony Street Theatre, the Park having been destroyed by fire the previous year and was not reopened until September 1821. Here he performed a part that Aldridge was to act many years later—Rob Roy, in a play adapted from Scott's novel. He did not appear again in New York until 25th May 1824, when he became leading man at the Chatham Garden Theatre, doing such roles as Shylock and Othello. Lafayette attended one of his performances on 8th July 1825.

Then in 1820 appeared the renowned tragedian, Edmund Kean, who excelled in Richard III, Macbeth, Othello, Hamlet, King Lear, Shylock and Sir Giles Overreach. He was at the Anthony Street Theatre from 29th November until 28th December, then went on tour, returning to New York for March and April 1821.

Ira might also have seen Junius Brutus Booth (1796-1852), who opened in *Richard III* on 5th October 1821, later doing Brutus, Lear, Othello and Hamlet. From then until his death, except for two short engagements at Drury Lane, he was constantly seen on the American stage, and was the founder of the Booth family of actors, one of whom went down in history as the assassin of Abraham Lincoln.

In the autumn of 1822 Charles Mathews (1776-1835), the most famous of English comedians and monologists, appeared at the Park as Goldfinch in *The Road to Ruin*. His engagement lasted until May 1823, during which period he gathered material for his series of sketches, *A Trip to America*, in which he parodied what he claimed was a performance of Ira Aldridge at the African Theatre, as we shall see.

The new Park Theatre opened on 1st September 1821 with a seating capacity of 2,500, and revolutionary lighting consisting of new patent oil lamps hung in three chandeliers, each containing fifteen lights, a wonder of the age. Its manager since 1809 had been the avaricious, boastful and unpopular Stephen Price (1783–1840), who was dubbed "Stephen Half-Price" when he was lessee for a time of Drury Lane Theatre in London. English theatre managers complained that "he lured away to the shores of America every performer of distinction (and what is of equal importance, utility) whom gold could tempt or speculation seduce." Had Ira Aldridge not been a Negro, he would not have gone in the opposite direction.

This, in brief, was the New York theatre in the period when Ira Aldridge was growing up, and which inspired the free Negroes to start their own African Theatre about 1820. A very interesting account of its origin is given by Dr. Smith in the *1860 Chronicle*:

In 1816-17 Mr. Brown, steward of a Liverpool liner, gave up following the sea and hired a house on the north side of Thomas Street, nearly opposite that since made famous by the Helen Jewett tragedy,* and fitted up a tea-garden in the rear of the lot. In the evening he made the garden attractive by vocal and instrumental music. His brother stewards and their wives, and the colored population generally, gave him a full share of patronage. Among his *artistes* were Miss Ann Johnson, since Mrs. Allen, the mother of an excellent *cantatrice* of the present time, and James Hewlett. These evening entertainments were not dry affairs; brandy and gin-toddies, wine-negus, porter and strong ale, with cakes and meats, enabled the audience to gratify several senses and appetites at the same time. James Hewlett was quite a character in his line; a very fine singer for the times, he added by degrees, dramatic exhibitions to the entertainments. His off-nights were invariably spent in the gallery of the old Park Theatre, and spent not in vain, for he soon became celebrated for the talent and versatility which enabled him—anticipating Mathews, we believe—to perform several widely differing characters, very perfectly, at one exhibition. He followed the fashionable world to Saratoga, and in the height of the season, when rival singers

* A young woman was brutally hacked to death by her lover at 41 Thomas Street in 1836, and by a strange coincidence this was the very building in which Daniel Aldridge died in 1840.

would scatter their paper announcements through the hotels, there would appear, thickly scattered around, tastily printed on white satin:

JAMES HEWLETT,
Vocalist, and Shakespeare's proud
Representative
Will Give an Entertainment
in Singing and Acting
in the large room of the United States Hotel,
etc., etc.

Hewlett was a mulatto of middle height, with sharp features, and a well-set, coal-black eye. He was a native of one of the West Indian islands.

So great was Mr. Brown's success with his tea-garden that in four or five years he built a theatre in Mercer Street, above Prince, then, of course, well up-town. The edifice was of wood, roughly built, and having capacity for an audience of 300 or 400. The enterprise was quite successful, the audience being composed largely of laughter-loving young clerks who came to see the sport, but invariably paid their quarter for admission.

This appears to have been the beginning of the Negro theatre in the United States, and if, like the African Free School, it had been allowed to grow, perhaps fine Negro theatre companies might have flourished fifty or even 100 years before they actually came into their own.

So popular became Brown's Theatre that white people began to attend, and eventually a portion of the African Theatre was set aside for whites!! How the white community reacted to this phenomenon may be seen from various items in the New York Press. The *National Advocate* of 3rd August 1821 editorialized:

Among the number of ice cream gardens in this city, there was none in which the sable race could find admission and refreshment. Their modicum of pleasure was taken on Sunday evening, when the black dandies and dandizettes, after attending meeting, occupied the sidewalks in Broadway, and slowly lounged towards their different homes. As their number increased, and their consequence strengthened, partly from high wages, high living, and the elective franchise, it was considered necessary to have a place of amusement for them exclusively. Accordingly, a garden has been opened somewhere back of the hospital called the

African Grove; not spicy as those of Arabia (but let that pass), at which the ebony lads and lasses could obtain ice cream, ice punch, and hear music from the big drum and clarionet. The little boxes of this garden were filled with black beauties "making night hideous" and it was not an uninteresting sight to observe the entree of a happy pair. The gentleman, with his wool nicely combed, and his face shining through a coat of sweet oil, borrowed from the castors; cravat tight to suffocation, having the double faculty of widening the mouth and giving a remarkable protuberance to the eyes; blue coat, fashionably cut; red ribbon and a bunch of pinch-beck seals; white pantaloons, shining boots, gloves, and a tippy rattan. The lady, with her pink kid slippers; her fine Leghorn, cambric dress with open work; corsets well fitted; reticule hanging on her arm. Thus accoutred and caparisoned, these black fashionables saunter up and down the garden, in all the pride of liberty and unconscious of want. In their dress, salutations, familiar phrases, and compliments, their imitative faculties are best exhibited. . . .

The following month, on 21st September, the same newspaper again wrote at length:

African Amusements: We noticed some time ago the opening of a tea-garden and evening serenades for the amusement of our black gentry; it appears that some of the neighbors, not relishing the jocund nightly sarabands of these sable fashionables, actually complained to the Police, and the avenues of African Grove were closed by authority; and thus were many of our ebony friends excluded from a participation in those innocent recreations to which they are entitled, by virtue of the great charter that declares "all men are equal". These imitative inmates of the kitchen and pantries, not relishing the strong arm of the law thus rudely exercised, were determined to have some kind of amusement; and after several nightly caucuses, they resolved to set up a *play*, and the upper apartments of the neglected African Grove were pitched upon for the purpose. *Richard III*, after mature deliberation, was agreed upon, and a little dapper, woolly-headed waiter at the City Hotel personated the royal Plantagenet. As may be supposed, some difficulties occurred in the cast of characters and suitable costumes. Richard III had some robes made up from discarded merino curtains of the ball-rooms; and from a paucity of actors, some doublets occurred, as these: King Henry and the Duchess Dowager were represented by one and the same person, while Lady Ann and Catesby were sustained by another. The room was decorated with some taste, and chairs were placed by the wings for two clarionets.

If any proofs are wanting of the native genius and vigor of thought of our colored fellow citizens, surely their conception of Shakespeare will be sufficient, and how delighted would the Bard of Avon have been to see his Richard performed by a fellow as black as the ace of spades. However, let us review the performance according to the best and most equitable rules of criticism.

The person of Richard was on the whole not amiss; it was perceived that the actor had made the King hump-backed instead of crooked back, having literally a hump behind his neck little less than a camel's. Shaping "the legs of unequal size" was also difficult, but was overcome by placing false calves before, and wearing a high-heeled shoe. The entrance of Richard was greeted with loud applause and shaking of handkerchiefs by the black ladies in the front seats and many whispers went around of "How well he looks." . . . Several fashionable songs, sung with no mean taste, concluded the evening's amusement, and the sable audience retired peaceably to their homes. Richard and Catesby were unfortunately taken up by the watch [i.e. they were arrested].

James Hewlett had his benefit on 1st October 1821, and the playbill announcing it declared: "Mr. Brown has spared neither time nor expense in rendering this Entertainment agreeable to the Ladies and Gentlemen of Color." On 27th October the *National Advocate* informed its readers that "The gentlemen of color announce another play at their Pantheon, corner of Bleecker and Mercer Streets on Monday evening. . . . They have graciously made a partition at the back of their house for the accommodation of the whites." The tables are turned, indeed! The theatre historian, George C. D. Odell, makes the following remark on this unique procedure: "This partition erected by a race so long segregated in the Negro gallery of playhouses strikes me as pathetic and ominous. The inroad of whites, out for a lark and bringing disorder and wanton mischief, led to a closing of the concern, as we learn from the *American* of 10th January 1822."[1]

Odell was right in his use of the word "ominous", but we do not agree that "the closing of the concern" was caused by the whites who "were out for a lark". It will be seen from the item in the *American* which we quote in full below that the alarm was

34

sounded when "it appears that the sable managers, not satisfied with a small share of the profit and a great portion of fame, determined to rival the great Park Theatre". When the blacks begin to be dissatisfied with a small share of the profit, then something must be done:

HUNG BE THE HEAVENS WITH BLACK—SHAKESPEARE

We have heretofore noticed the performances of a black corps dramatique in this city, at their theatre, the corner of Bleecker and Mercer Streets. It appears that the sable managers, not satisfied with a small share of the profit and a great portion of fame, determined to rival the great Park Theatre, belonging to Messrs. Beekman and Astor, and accordingly hired the Hotel next door to the theatre, where they announced their performances. The audiences were generally of a riotous character, and amused themselves by throwing crackers on the stage, and cracking their jokes with the actors, until danger from fire and civil discord rendered it necessary to break up the establishment. The ebony-colored wags were notified by the police that they must announce their last performance, but they, defying the public authority, went on and acted nightly. It was at length considered necessary to interpose the arm of authority, and on Monday evening a dozen watchmen made part of the audience. The play was *Richard*. The watchmen interrupted the royal Plantagenet in one of his soliloquies with, "Hello, you—there—come along with me."

Richard replied with a real tragic grin, "Fellow begone—I'm not at leisure."

"Not at leisure?" says the watchman. "We'll find time for you, so come along."

Several immediately ascended the stage and arrested His Majesty. "Where am I going?" says he. "To de tower?"

"No; to the watch house," said the Knights of the Lantern.

So forthwith Richard, Richmond, Lady Ann, the dead King Henry, Queen Elizabeth, and the two young princes were escorted in their tinselled robes, to the watch house, into which they marched with royal contempt and defiance. King Richard dropped his character and assumed Macbeth, and, on his entrance, broke out:

> "How now you black and secret
> Midnight hags—what are you about?"

"Come, come," said the watch; "none of your play-acting airs—into the black hole with you." The sable corps were thrust in one green room together where, for some time, they were loud and theatrical; ever and anon, one would thrust his head through a circular hole to survey the grim visages of the watchmen. Finally they plead so hard in blank verse, and *promised never to act Shakespeare again* (emphasis added), that the Police Magistrates released them at a very late hour.

"One Stephen Price", says the *1849 Memoir*, "a manager of some repute, became actually jealous of the success of the 'real Ethiopian' and emissaries were employed to put them down. They attracted considerable notice; and people who went to ridicule remained to admire, albeit there must have been ample scope for the suggestion of the ridiculous. Riots ensued, and destruction fell upon the little theatre. Of course, there was no protection or redress to be obtained from the magistracy (for, unhappily, they were whites), and the company dissolved, much to the chagrin of the Juliet elect, who declared that nothing but envy prevented the blacks from putting the whites completely out of countenance."

But there are records to show that the group did not stay dissolved very long. They were soon back in business and everyone was again at liberty to heap ridicule on them.

Laurence Hutton, in his *Curiosities of the American Stage*, tells of a playbill he saw announcing that on 20th and 21st June 1823 the performers of the African Company were giving a benefit to their manager, Mr. Brown, and the piece chosen was "*The Drama of King Shotaway*, founded on facts, taken from the Insurrection of the Caravs on the Island of St. Vincent. Written from experience by Mr. Brown". Hewlett played King Shotaway.

This is the last we hear of the African Company, and it is in keeping with the general outlook of the group that it went out, not with a whimper, but with a bang—a Negro insurrection, with which Mr. Brown had some experience. Maybe this first Negro drama of revolt was the last straw for the authorities, who now felt more than ever impelled to close down the African Theatre for good. And, as Brown was having a benefit, it may well be that he was giving up his efforts to keep an African Theatre going. Thereafter, Hewlett appears in other theatres, and one year later Ira Aldridge "ships for Old England".

Growing reaction throughout the country and the hardening of white prejudice against the blacks carried with it the demise of the Negro theatre, but curiously, it was at this very time (1823) that the white actor, Edwin Forrest, "represented on the stage the Southern plantation Negro with all his peculiarities of dress gait, accent, dialect, and manners". So the genuine Negro performers in America were forced out to make way for the white "nigger ministrels", and in 1828 an American actor, Thomas Dartmouth Rice (1806-60) created the character of Jim Crow, based on an original character whom he had heard sing an authentic Negro ditty, with a shuffling accompaniment of his feet:

> Wheel about and turn about and do jis' so,
> Ev'ry time I wheel about I jump Jim Crow.

Hewlett went on to perform in other theatres, and an advertisement in the *American* of 27th April 1825 signed "A Friend to Merit", declared that Mr. Hewlett "will again appear at the Spruce Street Theatre, No. 11, on 28th April, when the admirers of talent will have another opportunity of witnessing one of the most astonishing phenomena of the age, a young man who, notwithstanding the thousand obstacles which the circumstances of complexion must have thrown in the way of improvement has, by the mere dint of natural genius and self-strengthened assiduity, risen to a successful competition with some of the first actors of the day". On 15th December Hewlett is again announced at the Assembly Room, Military Garden, giving "A Grand Entertainment prior to his return to London, to fill his engagement at the Coburg Theatre". The Coburg was the original name of the Old Vic of today, and was the theatre in which Ira Aldridge made his first major appearance in England in October 1825, but so far we have been unable to find evidence that Hewlett actually appeared on its boards. The only proof we have that Hewlett was in England in 1825 is contained in a letter from Charles Mathews to his wife written from Liverpool on 13th January 1825, in which he says, "Mr. Hannibal Hewlet* has been here, and gave an 'At Home', and actually applied to Lewis for an engagement. He went to London, as he said, to challenge me for ridiculing him in a part he never played. I cannot find anybody

* Original footnote in the printed version of this letter: "The black Roscius of a minor theatre in New York."

who saw him; but he performed here two or three nights."[2]

Lewis was manager of the Theatre Royal, Liverpool, and Mathews obviously considered it impudent of "Hannibal" Hewlett to apply to him for an engagement. It appears that Hewlett went on performing his imitations of Kean's Richard III, Cooper's Bertram, Kemble's Rolla, and Mathews's *At Home*, and the last we hear of him is in connection with "a farewell performance" on 22nd September 1831 at the Columbian Hall (New York), with "Mrs. Hewlett presiding at the piano".

Aldridge must have been inspired by Hewlett and encouraged by his rise in the theatre at that time. The *Star* of 22nd December 1825 made special mention of Hewlett, saying: "A native of our own dear Island of Nassau, and Rockaway is said to have been his place of birth.* He is of lighter color than ordinary mulattoes. His histrionic education took place under those celebrated masters Cooke and Cooper, whom he followed as a servant boy and stole their actions and attitudes. Hewlett, however, must have had a natural talent for theatrical performances, and an excellent voice, or he could never have surmounted his early difficulties. His songs were excellent, and his style, taste, voice and action such as would have done credit to any stage. His imitations of Kean, Mathews, and others were recognized as correct, and evinced a nice discrimination of tact . . . which ought to recommend him to every lover of pure acting. Hewlett is yet young enough to receive some of the advantages of education, and we should advise him to persevere in the way his genius seems to direct."

However, though Hewlett persevered and seemed to be going the way Ira Aldridge eventually went via the Coburg Theatre, it is strange that the last we hear of him is in New York in 1830-1 at the Chatham Theatre. "The first week in March", Odell tells us, "brought no less a celebrity than the Negro Hewlett. . . . Listed in the *American* as 'the celebrated tragedian', and in the *Post* as 'the Star of the West—the Aboriginal Ecce Homo'. In July, Shakespeare's proud representative—Hewlett, to wit—gave imitations and took exhilarating gas. . . . Herein lurks a real tragedy of Negroes' thwarted ambition." Odell does not elaborate on this, but that tragedy did enter into the life of the first American Negro tragedian, James Hewlett, there can be no

* Elsewhere his birthplace is given as one of the islands of the West Indies.

doubt, for at that point he disappears from history. In a letter to Dr. Smith in 1860, remarking on the inaccuracies of many published references to him, Aldridge says: "They confuse me with poor Jim Hewlett." Thus far, searches into the records of the Coburg Theatre produce no trace of Hewlett's appearance in London, but of Aldridge there is much evidence of his "perseverance in the way his genius seems to direct".

★   ★   ★

So we see that Aldridge had the opportunity of at least getting into the fourth tier of the Park Theatre and seeing the great American and English actors, and of getting into Brown's Theatre as an equal. Brown's Theatre opened in 1820-1, and it is reasonable to suppose that Aldridge acted there during the time James Hewlett was the star attraction. From the *Memoir* we learn that "he fell to work and studied the part of Rolla in the play of *Pizarro*, and in that character he made his first appearance on any stage. This was at a private theatre, where he was singularly successful, and all his fellow-performers were of his own complexion; and to use his own words, 'the gentle Cora was *very* black, requiring no small quantity of whiting, yellow ochre, and vermilion to bring her cheeks to the hue of roses and lilies', such a face as Sheridan describes in the text."

Pizarro was adapted by Richard Brinsley Sheridan from the German original of Kotzebue, a prolific writer of romantic, "Gothic" dramas. It was produced at Drury Lane in 1799 and for the next sixty years Rolla was one of the great roles, ranking with Macbeth, Richard III and Sir Giles Overreach, and was performed in the Park Theatre by James Wallack, George Frederick Cooke, and Thomas Abthorpe Cooper. Aldridge may have chosen Rolla for his first role because its "purple passages" were filled with passionate patriotism, wherein the Peruvian defends his country against the Spanish invaders, and Aldridge must have identified the conquered Peruvians with his own conquered and enslaved people.

Then came the next great step. Why not tackle Shakespeare, as James Hewlett was doing? Turning again to the *Memoir*, "But fancy a black Juliet! And why not? May there not be an Ethiopian Juliet to an Ethiopian Romeo? So reasoned and *felt* the coloured members of the amateur corps when Mr. Aldridge undertook to perform the lovesick swain in a sable countenance. Certain Yankees, with a degree of illiberality peculiar to some 'Liberals', had no notion of such indulgences being allowed to Negroes, whose 'tarnation conceit and considerable effrontery licked natur' slick outright'."

With the outbreak of yellow fever in New York, the new Park Theatre was closed for a time in 1822, and reopened in November of that year with the appearance of Charles Mathews, one of Charles Dickens's circle, who performed in his own sketches and popular comedies.

It was during this trip to New York that Mathews visited the African Theatre and saw some of their first amateur performances, which he later parodied in his sketch, *A Trip to America*, and to which Aldridge alluded some years later. We reprint here a page or two from *Mr. Mathews at Home*, published in London in 1824, dealing with this visit:

While in New York, Mathews stayed at Mrs. Bradish's boarding house. While residing at Mrs. Bradish's, Mr. Mathews takes an opportunity of visiting the Niggers (or Negroes) Theatre. The black population being, in the national theatres, under certain restrictions have, to be at their ease, a theatre of their own. Here he sees a black tragedian (the Kentucky Roscius) perform the character of Hamlet, and hears him deliver the soliloquy, "To be or not to be, dat is him question, whether him nobler in de mind to suffer or lift up him arms against a sea of hubble bubble and by opossum (oppose 'em) end 'em." At the word Opossum, the whole audience burst forth into one general cry of "Opossum, Opossum, Opossum". On enquiring into the cause of this, Mr. Mathews was informed that "Opossum Up a Gum Tree" was the national air, or sort of "God Save the King" of the Negroes, and that being reminded of it by Hamlet's pronunciation of "oppose 'em," there was no doubt but that they would have it sung. "The opossum," continued Mr. Mathews informally, "is addicted to climbing up the gum tree, thinking no one can follow him; but the racoon hides himself in the hollow of the tree, and as poor opossum goes up, pulls him down by the tail, and that is the plot." The cries of "Opossum, opossum" increasing, the sable tragedian comes forward, and addressing the audience, informs them that he will sing their favourite melody, with him greatest pleasure, and accordingly sings it. The following is a translation from the original Indian:

3. James Wallack in *The Brigand*, 1829. From an engraving in the Raymond Mander and Joe Mitchenson Theatre Collection.

2. James Hewlett as Richard III, 1821. From an engraving in the Raymond Mander and Joe Mitchenson Theatre Collection.

Royal Coburg Theatre.

First Night of the celebrated AMERICAN TRAGEDIAN
Of a New and most effective Melo-Dramatic Romance.
Third Week of the Spy of the Neutral Ground, which Nightly encreases in Attraction

MONDAY, October 10th, 1825, and DURING the WEEK, at Half-past Six o'Clock precisely,
Will be produced, a Grand West Indian Melo-Drama, founded on Interesting and Pathetic Facts, to be Called, The

Revolt of Surinam
OR A SLAVE's REVENGE.

This Piece exhibiting a most faithful Portrait of the horrors that arise out of that dreadful traffic, which it is the proudest boast of Britain to use her best efforts towards suppressing, must receive an immense portion of additional interest from being supported in its principal Character by a *Man of Colour*, one of the very race whose wrongs it professes to record; being the first instance in which one of that Complexion has displayed a striking degree of Histrionic Talent, and which has secured him the rapturous Approbation of an enlightened Public on the other side of the Atlantic.

Oroonoko, - - the Royal Slave, - - Mr. KEENE,
Tragedian of Colour, from the African Theatre, New York.

Aboan, (First Time,) Mr. BENGOUGH. Governor of Surinam, Mr. YOUNG. Blandford, Mr. HEMMINGS. Capt. Driver, Mr. GOLDSMITH. Hotman, Mr. BRADLEY. Stanmore, Mr. HOWARD. 1st. Planter, Mr. SAUNDERS. 2d. Planter, Mr. GEORGE. 3d. Planter, Mr. SMITH. Sambo, Mr. ELSGOOD. Loto, Mr. THOMPSON. Kalu, Mr. WILLIAMS. Imoinda, Mrs. BRETTON. Widow Lackit, Mrs. WESTON. Female Slaves, Mesdis. Bradley, Gough, Pharoah, Denn, Bennett, &c. &c.

The Piece will exhibit a Variety of CHARACTERISTIC WEST INDIAN SCENERY.
Peculiarities in the mode of Government of the Slaves, and the Terrific Effect of an injured African's Vengeance

After which will be Performed, *for the First Time*, a New Romantic Sicilian Melo-Drama, founded on a Popular Romance, and replete with intense Interest and peculiar Effects, to be Entitled, The

Mysterious Stranger;
Or, The CAVE of St. CATALDO.

The Music entirely New by Mr T. Hughes.—The Scenery by Messrs. Jones, Danson, Morris and Assistants.—The Machinery by Mr. Burroughs—The Dresses by Mr. Hood and Mrs. Follett—The Properties by Mr. Elliott.

Count Beraldi, Mr. LEWIS. —the Mysterious Stranger, Mr. COBHAM. Montenero, *Captain of Banditti*, Mr. HEMMINGS.
Geraldo, / Mr. YOUNG.
Gaspar, } Members of his Band, { Mr. VILLIERS.
Donato, / Mr. ELSGOOD.
Leonardo, *Servant to the Count*, Mr. HOWARD.
Jeremiah Flux, (*Nephew to Mr. Flux, Pawnbroker and Silversmith, No. 19 and a 0, Norton Fulgate*,) Mr. BUCKSTONE. Alberto, Master MEYERS.
Countess Beraldi, Mrs. BRETTON. Barbarina, Mrs. DAVIDGE. Attendants, Villagers, Soldiers, Robbers, &c. &c.

AMONGST THE NEW SCENERY, PAINTED EXPRESSLY FOR THIS PIECE, WILL BE FOUND,
A BEAUTIFUL VIEW of the COUNTY of CATANEA, in SICILY, WITH DISTANT VIEW OF
THE VOLCANO ETNA,
And the Vine Farm of St. Cataldo.
THE COURT YARD OF THE CASTLE OF BERALDI,
Attack of the Banditti Capt. Conflagration of Building, the Child of Beraldi saved by the Heroic interference of the Mysterious Stranger.
INTERIOR OF THE STUPENDOUS CAVERNS OF ST. CATALDO.
Treachery of the Banditti Capt. punished by the Stranger, who is elected Capt. of the Band, & engages them to submit to Legitimate Authority.
Splendid Gothic Hall in the Castle of Darazzo, prepared for the Mysterious Banquet, Triumph of the Stranger and his Associates.

The whole to conclude with an entirely New Melo-Drama, founded on certain occurrences which took place during the American War, & pourtraying American Scenery and Manners, which has been long in Preparation, and is now produced with New Local Scenery and appropriate Decorations, Called, The

Spy of the Neutral Ground;
OR THE
AMERICAN WAR OF 1780.

BRITISH.—Colonel Wellmere, Mr. HOWARD. Captain Henry Wharton, Mr. HEMMINGS. Sentinel, Mr. GEORGE. Officers, Soldiers, &c.
AMERICANS.—Mr. Harper, Mr. LEWIS. Mr. Wharton, Mr. LEWIS.
Colonel Singleton, / Mr. GOLDSMITH.
Major Dunwoodie, } ....*Officers of the American Army*, { Mr. COBHAM.
Captain Lawton, / Mr. VILLIERS.
Captain of a Band of Skinners, or Forest Banditti, *Fighting under the American Colours*, Mr. BRADLEY. First Skinner, Mr. SMITH.
Serjeant Hollister, Mr. ELSGOOD. Old Birch, Mr. YOUNG. Harvey Birch, *the Spy of the Neutral Ground*, Mr. DAVIDGE.
Corporal, Mr. JONES. Mr. Cæsar Thompson, *Negro Servant to Mr. Wharton*, Mr. BUCKSTONE.
Miss Peyton, *Sister to Mr. Wharton*, Mrs. BRETTON. Frances, *Daughter of Mr. Wharton*, Mrs. DAVIDGE.
Mrs. Elizabeth Flannigan, Mrs. WESTON. Katy Haynes, Mrs. BRADLEY.

On MONDAY Next will be Produced a peculiar Drama, to be Called,
Grim, the Collier of Croydon, or the Fatal Shaft.
With a Variety of New Entertainments,
And in the course of the Evening several New Performers will make their 1st Appearance
BEING FOR THE BENEFIT OF MR. DAVIDGE.

Boxes 4s. & 3s. Pit 2s. Gal. 1s. Doors open Half-past 5, begin Half-past 6. Second Price Half-past 8. Romney, Pr. Lambeth. Places and Private Boxes Nightly or for the Season, and Free Admissions to be had of Mr. A. R. BOWES, at the New Box Office in the Grand Marine Saloon.

4. Playbill for Aldridge's first appearance in London, Coburg Theatre, 1825. In the British Museum.

Opossum up a gum tree,
　Tinkey none can follow:
Him damn quite mistaken,
　Racoon in de hollow.
Opossum him creep softly,
　Racoon him lay mum,
Pull him by de long tail,
　Down opossum come.
Jinkum, jankum, beaugash,
　Twist 'em, twine 'em, run;
Oh de poor opossum,
　Oh, de sly racoon.

Opossum up a gum tree,
　Racoon pull him down;
Tink him got him snugly,
　Oh, de poor racoon.
Racoon in de hollow,
　Nigger down below,
Pull opossum's long tail,
　Racoon let him go.
Jinkum, jankum, beaugash,
　Twist 'em, twine 'em, run,
Oh de cunning nigger,
　Oh, de poor racoon.

Opossum up a gum tree,
　Racoon in de hollow;
No beat cunning nigger,
　Though him cannot follow.
Nigger him so clever,
　Him so sly and rum,
Pull him by de long tail,
　Down opossum come.
Jinkum, Jankum, etc.

Finishing his song, this versatile genius, retiring up the stage, is strutting down with one arm akimbo, and the other spouting out in front, just for all the world like a black teapot, bellowing out—"Now is de winter of our discontent made de glorous summer by de sun of New York." And on a person in the boxes telling him he should play Hamlet and not Richard III, replies, "Yes, him know dat, but him tought of New York den and could not help talking about it."

"Possum Up a Gum Tree" was later published, with entirely different words from those quoted above, now bringing in the treatment of the Negro as a slave. Since Aldridge was later to include it in his performances, to the exquisite pleasure of his audiences, we give the published version as well. The title page reads:

Possum Up a Gum Tree,
A South Carolinian Negro Air,
as sung by Mr. Mathews, in his Entertainment called
A TRIP TO AMERICA
and Arranged Expressly for him by
T. Philipps

from the Original Negro Melody, of which this is the only correct copy extant, and is the property of the publishers, I. Willis & Co., 55 St. James's Street, London.

The burden of this little Ballad is founded on a Circumstance in Zoology reported by Naturalists. The Opossum climbs a Tree, the hollow of which is occupied by the Racoon. He seizes the tail of the Opossum as he ascends, who loudly exclaims against this unjust invasion of his property, but is notwithstanding too slothful to quit the vicinity of his Oppressor.

Possum up a Gum Tree
  Up he go, up he go,
Racoon in the hollow
  Down below, down below.
Him pull him by him long tail
  Pully hawl, pully hawl,
Then how him whoop and hallow,
  Scream and bawl, scream and bawl.
Possum up a Gum Tree
  Racoon in the hollow,
Him pull him by hims long tail,
  Then how him whoop and hallow.

Massa send we Negro Boy
  Board a ship, board a ship,
There we work and cry "Ye hoy"
  Cowskin whip, cowskin whip,
Negro he work all de day,
  Night get groggy, night get groggy,
But if Negro he go play

Massa floggy, Massa floggy,
Possum up a Gum Tree, etc.

Caesar steal him Massa's boots
  Last Whitsunday, Whitsunday,
'Cause him marry Polly Cootes,
  Look fine and gay, fine and gay.
Caesar all day walk in pain
  Boot so tight, boot so tight,
He no get them off again
  All de night, all de night,
Possum up a Gum Tree, etc.

Miss Polly say, "You nasty brute,
  Get out of bed, get out of bed,
If you come near me wid de boot
  I break your head, I break your head."
Caesar he no more entreats him,
  He quite dummy, he quite dummy,
Massa see his boots and beat him
  All to mummy, all to mummy,
Possum up a Gum Tree, etc.

Mathews continued to include this skit in his entertainments in England until his death in 1834, sometimes in the same season and very theatre in which Aldridge appeared. It was natural for the theatre public to assume that it was an imitation of Aldridge, especially since early playbills had styled him "The Celebrated Tragedian of Colour from the African Theatre, New York". Mathews saw no reason to correct this impression. In *Mr. Mathews at Home*, the Negro actor in question is referred to as the "Kentucky Roscius", which could not have been Aldridge. Hewlett also, as we have seen, indignantly disclaimed any connection with the story, but let us see what Aldridge himself had to say about this at a public dinner, as quoted in the *Memoir*:

Mr. Mathews paid a visit to the theatre on one of the evenings of my performance, and this occurrence he has made the vehicle for one of the most amusing anecdotes in his well-known *Trip to America*. There is certainly a good deal more in the manner of his telling the story than in the matter, and he has embellished the whole circumstances with a great many fictitious variations, not the less amusing because untrue, but which are pardonable enough in such a work as Mr. Mathews, the materials of which are acknowledged to have been made up as much of fiction as of truth. He says that on the occasion alluded to, I played Hamlet, and in the celebrated soliloquy, "To be or not to be" the similarity of the sound of the words reminding the audience of the Negro melody, "Opossum Up a Gum Tree", they loudly called for it, and this polite request Mr. Mathews makes me accede to in the following language: "Well, den, ladies and gemmen, you like 'Opossum Up a Gum Tree' better den you like *Hamlet*? Me sing him to you", which I, according to the anecdote, did three or four times, much to the exquisite edification of my black hearers, and then resumed my part of the pensive prince. The truth, however, is that I never attempted the character of Hamlet in my life,* and I need not say that the whole of the ludicrous scene so well and so humorously described by Mr. Mathews never occurred at all.

Despite this denial, the song, via Mathews's impersonation, became fathered on to Aldridge who, willy-nilly, included it in his repertoire, it being demanded by managers and the public. A playbill of the Theatre Royal, Bristol, of 26th March 1830, says: "The celebrated Mathews, having alluded to a Comic Incident in the Career of the African Roscius, and founded on it one of his most whimsical hits, the public are respectfully informed that (by the particular desire of numerous parties), the African Roscius will sing (in Character) the Celebrated Negro Medley of 'Opossum Up a Gum Tree'."

"As both a tragic and a comic actor," said the *Memoir*, "Mr. Aldridge's talents are undeniably great. In tragedy he has a solemn intensity of style, bursting occasionally to a blaze of fierce invective or passionate declamation, while the dark shades of his face become doubly sombre in their thoughtful aspect; a night-like gloom is spread over them, and an expression more terrible than paler lineaments can readily assume. In farce he is exceedingly amusing; the ebony becomes polished; the coal emits sparks. His face is the faithful index of his mind; and, as there is not a darker frown than his, there is not a broader grin. The ecstasy of his long, shrill note in 'Opossum Up a Gum Tree' can only be equalled by the agony of his cry of despair over the body of Desdemona."

From eyewitness accounts of the early days of the African

* Aldridge did give several performances of Hamlet, but many years later.

Theatre, though from a prejudiced, white point of view, there is
no doubt that there was much that was ludicrous, and the
temptation to exaggerate is one that few actors would resist.
However, even these amateurish attempts at Shakespeare by
Negroes aroused enough jealousy and anger in their "superiors"
to lead to the eventual suppression of the African theatre.

The only recourse for a serious, determined and aspiring young
Negro actor was to emigrate. There are several factors which influenced Aldridge in this decision. For one thing, it is undoubtedly
true, as Fountain Peyton[3] says, that he was advised by friendly
white persons who recognized his talent, that there were no pros-
pects for a Negro actor in the United States. Then there was the
example of James Hewlett, who, according to the announcements,
was "returning to London to fill his engagement at the Coburg
Theatre". This was proof that a coloured actor was accepted
in London and could actually play in a "Royal" theatre. Finally,
there were the Wallacks.

"He had a schoolfellow", says the *Memoir*, "who was in the
habit of taking Mr. Henry Wallack's dresses to the Chatham
Theatre, and the acquaintance of this boy he assiduously cultivated. With a little contrivance and the assistance of this
privileged individual, young Aldridge obtained an introduction
to the mysteries of the Stage. The boy soon after died of the
yellow fever, and the coloured aspirant eagerly tendered his
services, and obtained the wished-for entry to 'behind the scenes'
by becoming the bearer of the leading actor's dresses, and making
himself generally useful in the way of running to and fro. This
employment, if known to his father, was not that in which he
wished to see his son engaged; but amply was that son repaid for
his services, by being permitted to gaze upon the scenes which
presented themselves."

Since Henry and James Wallack were brothers as well as
actors, often appearing together in the New York theatres, it is
difficult to identify their individual relationship with Ira Aldridge
in those early days, but that there was such a relationship there is
no doubt. It may be assumed, though, from the above reference
in the *Memoir* and from the fact that "He brought with him to
London a letter of recommendation from Henry Wallack", that
it was Henry who originally befriended him. But, according to
the *1860 Chronicle*, Joshua Aldridge said that James Wallack

engaged Ira as his personal attendant while on the passage to Liverpool, so that it would appear that James, too, took an interest in the young actor. Afterwards, in England, it was not unusual to find interwoven in reviews of Aldridge's work such statements as "Mr. Keene [Aldridge], it is whispered, was a servant to Wallack",[4] and "The sceptical alleged that the so-called prince had been James Wallack's dresser in New York".[5] And the Yankee, Mr. Elliott, went even further when he protested to Calcraft, Manager of the Theatre Royal, Dublin, in 1833, at the mere possibility of his wife, Madame Celeste, acting in the same theatre with a "nigger", and, among other things, said to Calcraft, "You oughtn't to have engaged this fellow. He's a thief. He robbed Wallack when he was his servant."

The *Memoir continues*:

> The young Roscius hung about the wings receiving intoxicating pleasure, listening with rapture to the wildest rant, and strengthening his hopes of emulating the most admired actors who presented themselves. But a sudden termination was put to his nightly enjoyment; through the interest of Bishops Brenton and Milner, he was entered at Schenectady College, near New York, in order to prepare himself for the ministry; and here for a while he entered into theological studies. Notwithstanding the progress he made in learning, he lacked advancement in his chief profession. No qualities of the mind could compensate in the eyes of Americans for the dark hue of his skin; the prevailing prejudice, so strong among all classes, was against him, and it was deemed advisable to send him to Great Britain. He was accordingly shipped for the Old Country.

Inquiries both at Schenectady (Union College) and with appropriate religious authorities in New York produced no evidence of either Aldridge or his father having studied there. We have, however, traced the Rev. James Milnor, D.D., in a Directory of New York for 1834, showing him as the head of St. George's Church (Episcopal), one of the Vice-Presidents of the Educational and Missionary Society of the Protestant Episcopal Church of the State of New York, a trustee of the Protestant Episcopal Society for Promoting Religion and Learning in the State of New York, and Vice-President of the Colonization Society of the City of New York. It is likely that Daniel Aldridge, on taking Ira away from the theatre, made him stay by his side in the Church he served, with the intention of sending him to a theological school, and that the bishops in question used their influence in that direction, but by now young Aldridge had decided on his life's work.

He had already served on a ship, as we have seen; Brown, who ran the African Theatre, was a retired steward, and his tea-garden and theatre were frequented by sea-going coloured folk; New York was a great port from which packet ships to Liverpool sailed weekly—all of which makes the next step obvious. When Ira learns that one of the Wallacks is embarking for England, he does the most natural thing—he ships as a steward on the same boat. This is borne out by Joshua's statement in the *1860 Chronicle* that "some time after this [i.e. his father taking him away from the theatre], Ira again shipped, this time as a steward in a vessel bound for Liverpool. It happened that James Wallack, the actor, was passenger in the same vessel. Mr. Wallack engaged Ira as his personal attendant while on the passage, and on the arrival of the vessel in Liverpool, Aldridge left her with that view [i.e. to become an actor]. He has not since returned to the United States."

J. J. Sheahan of Hull, England, a close friend of Aldridge for many years, wrote in *Notes and Queries* of 17th August 1872:

Our youthful Thespian managed to scrape an acquaintance with the late James Wallack, then manager of a theatre at New York, and when that gentleman resolved upon returning to England, he conceived the idea of introducing young Aldridge to his fellow country people, and thus making money by him. Arrived at Liverpool, Wallack was silly enough to state that his *protégé* had been his servant in America; a rupture and a newspaper war ensued, and the "Child of the Sun" was left to his own resources in a strange land, and without much money in his purse.

CHAPTER V

First Year in England

THE exact date of Aldridge's arrival in England is not known. The year 1825 appears to be generally accepted, but the evidence points to 1824, when he was seventeen years old. His application for British naturalization in 1863 gives the duration of his residence in England as thirty-nine years. In October 1825 he begins an engagement at the Coburg Theatre in London. It must have taken him the better part of a year to gain sufficient foothold in the theatre world to have obtained such an engagement.

He arrived at the very turning-point of the Industrial Revolution, at the beginning of a new era. Steam engines were replacing water power; industries were being carried on by new, modern methods. It was a period of rapid growth in population and of increasing desire for education, of interest in science and art by the radical middle class and of the upsurge of large provincial towns, where entertainment had to be provided for the new "operatives". Trade unions were legalized in 1824; the workers were becoming class-conscious, and waged militant struggles, sometimes together with the middle class, for basic democratic rights.

These were the audiences that went to see and applaud the Negro actor from America, who represented to them a people also fighting for equality.

The *Memoir* gives 1825 as the year of his arrival, and says that in the same year "he entered Glasgow University where, under Professor Sanford, he obtained several premiums and the medal for Latin composition. Here he remained about eighteen months, when he broke entirely from the scholastic thraldom imposed upon him."

It has thus far not been possible to obtain proof of Ira's attendance at the University of Glasgow, nor does the following letter from that University establish anything definite:

On three separate occasions prolonged searches of the University records have revealed no trace of the name—Ira Frederick Aldridge. Mr. Aldridge is not shown in our list of graduates, nor does the name appear in our list of matriculated students covering the period 1728-1858. Unfortunately, matriculation or official registration as a student of this University was compulsory only for "Gown" students in the Faculty of Arts. It was optional in the case of all other students, and as the "Gown" classes embraced only Latin, Greek, logic, ethics, and physics, it will be seen that a large field—mathematics, medicine, law, and theology was left untraversed. In view of this, the fact that Mr. Aldridge was not a matriculated student and therefore does not appear in our records obviously does not preclude him from having been in attendance at this University, but unfortunately we are not in a position to quote records showing his attendance. . . . The search through our University records has been particularly exhaustive, because, for one thing, Sir Daniel Sandford was in fact Professor of Greek in this University from 1821-37. Furthermore, enquiries have been received from two other sources asking for similar confirmation of the attendance of Ira Aldridge at this University.

In those days the University was noted for its liberal outlook, and many Negroes who were barred from colleges in the United States went to Glasgow, including Dr. James McCune Smith. Although at this writing the date and circumstances are undetermined, it is our considered opinion that Ira Aldridge did attend the University of Glasgow. While he may, for the sake of interesting publicity, and perhaps at the prompting of theatre managers, have given out a romantic story of royal birth—and who could gainsay it—it is doubtful that he would have issued a statement about this attendance at Glasgow that could have been disproved at the time.

Wilson Armistead, in *A Tribute to the Negro*, gives an interesting account of another young Negro, Thomas Jenkins, who, in the early part of the nineteenth century, had been sent by an African ruler to study in England, and who found himself stranded on his arrival owing to the sudden death of the ship's captain, into whose care he had been entrusted. After a period of struggle and self-education in Latin and Greek, he went to the University of Edinburgh and "applied to the Professor of Latin for a ticket to his class", which was granted. Perhaps Ira Aldridge did the same at Glasgow, taking extra-mural courses in specific subjects. If he had been at the University at that time, he might very well have been a member of the Athenaeum Debating Society, which met in the Ethic Class Room on Friday evenings, and have participated in such debates as "Whether the Crusades have been attended with any Benefit to Europe" and "Whether it be probable that Britain will ever relapse into a State of Barbarism". Our readers will be pleased to learn from *The Collegian* of 13th December 1826 that, after much discussion, the latter question was decided in the negative!

With the growth of democracy and of the population, together with the linking of the new outlying towns with the metropolis through gradually improving locomotion, went the growth and development of the theatre. At the beginning of the nineteenth century there were ten theatres in London, only one of which, the Haymarket, was open in the summer. Of these ten, only the two patent houses, Drury Lane and Covent Garden, were permitted to present legitimate drama. After the breaking of the monopoly in 1843, by the middle of the century there were twenty-two theatres, over half of which presented plays that previously could be performed only at the patent theatres.

"By far the most important point of contact between the stage and the life of the city was the subjection of the drama to the rising tide of democracy", writes Ernest Bradlee Watson. "At the turn of the century the theatres succumbed to the rabble as a weakened constitution might to a virulent disease. The infection was immediate and complete. The theatres seemed to invite the masses as never before, and the masses had soon made the theatres almost exclusively their own; for the aristocracy and the intellectuals gradually withdrew as the populace advanced. One of the most constant grievances of the managers throughout the first half of the century was that only their pits and galleries were filled, for only on rare occasions could the aristocracy be induced to attend."[1]

Though they ceased to attend, they still kept the heavy hand of censorship on the theatre, influencing the kind of play produced. Herein lies the basic reason why this era was one of great acting rather than great drama. It was an era of political upheaval, of revolutions, revolt, hunger, and poverty, but little of this was reflected in the drama of the period.

Bulwer Lytton, in his Preface to the 1841 edition of his plays, deplored the fact that he had to conduct a play in the period following the French Revolution without being political or talking about a republic. Fear of the revolution, fear of the Chartists, and fear of the working masses was reflected in the determination to portray nothing on the stage that might promote such ideas and movements. That the Press was very sensitive to this viewpoint is seen, for instance, from a remark in one periodical following a performance of Aldridge in Schiller's *Fiesco*: "The audience do not expect a long-drawn speech in favour of Republicanism."[2] Despite these restrictions, the basic urge for reality, for realism, continued and grew, and since it could not express itself overtly in the dialogue or plot of the drama, it did so in the growing realism of the acting and the production.

A new actor, however talented, arriving on the scene at this moment would not necessarily have created any special flurry in the theatre world. But, interestingly, what had been a "liability" to Aldridge in the United States was his greatest asset when he landed in England. For slavery and the Negro people were very much in the public consciousness and were perhaps the leading topics of the times, arousing great intensity of feeling in the free-born Englishman.

About his early theatrical activities, the *Memoir* says: "Mr. Aldridge commenced at the Royalty, at the East End, under the management of Mr. Dunn, where he first felt the British pulse, and found it favourable to his pretensions. This was in 1826, soon after his arrival from Glasgow. He made his début in *Othello*, in which he was highly successful. Thus encouraged and strengthened, he procured an engagement at the Coburg, where Messrs. Leclercq, Davidge, Hornblower, and Bengough were the managers; here he played Oroonoko, Gambia, Zarambo, and obtained great applause." This we now know is not accurate, because there are playbills showing that he opened at the Coburg in October 1825. He must therefore have been at the Royalty before then, but nothing in the form of playbills or newspaper cuttings has thus far been found, nor is there any record of a Mr. Dunn as manager of the Royalty (which burned down in 1826 and in 1816 had changed its name to the East London Theatre). We do find, however, that Dunn and Jones built the Coburg Theatre in 1816, so possibly the writer of the *Memoir* confused the Royal Coburg with the Royalty, though the

Coburg was definitely not in the East End of London. The Coburg Theatre, having been built under the patronage of Princess Charlotte (heiress presumptive to the Throne) and her husband, Prince Leopold of Saxe-Coburg, though not a theatre royal (patent theatre) was allowed to use "royal" before its name. Many other minor theatres, both in London and the provinces, adopted this practice, but without warrant. Fountain Peyton says, "He made his début in *Othello* at the Royal Theatre, London, 1826, with Stuart, the greatest living Iago, to support him", but we have been unable to find any verification of this, although Stuart did play Iago to Aldridge's Othello in Northampton in 1831.

The statement about his making his début at the Royalty in the East End in 1826 is repeated in miscellaneous books, magazine articles, and other writings, and no doubt their main source was the *Memoir*, but the Coburg playbill herein reproduced proves conclusively that he appeared in a starring role a year before his so-called début in 1826. It is possible that he made a first trial performance at the Royalty before his Coburg engagement, but it is manifestly impossible for him to have studied for eighteen months at Glasgow before the date of his opening at the Coburg, unless he arrived in Scotland very early in 1824, before he was seventeen years old.

*　　　*　　　*

The monopoly of the two patent theatres, Drury Lane and Covent Garden, to present the legitimate drama dates originally from Restoration times. Later the Haymarket was given a charter to open during the summer months when the other two theatres were closed. Gradually the demand for entertainment, particularly in the outlying districts, caused numerous theatres to arise where managers attempted to defy the patent theatres and present the spoken drama. Sometimes they were successful and the patent theatres did not pursue their rights, but whenever any of these theatres found an actor or an attraction who drew their audiences away, they at once invoked the law and caused the offending playhouse to be closed. Eventually some legal protection was given to these minor theatres by the issuing of a burletta licence, which permitted them to perform plays provided they included music and a specified number of songs. Immediately, the plays of Shakespeare and other dramas officially the property of the patent theatres were adapted into versions which would conform to the burletta licence. This state of affairs was not remedied until the monopoly was broken by the Theatres Act of 1843. The minor theatres of London catered for the vast working-class audience that had arisen in the outskirts of London. Although the patent theatres had been forced to lower their standards, the minors presented full-blooded, penny-plain and tuppence-coloured productions suited to the taste of their audiences. Often actors from the West End were able to alter their style sufficiently to please this public, but more often than not their local favourites were preferred.

Ira Aldridge's first engagement with top billing in London, to our knowledge, was at the Coburg Theatre, beginning Monday, 10th October 1825.

One may wonder at this point how it was possible for Aldridge, so soon after his arrival, to be playing leading roles in a London theatre, albeit a minor one. Of his activities prior to this engagement we have, as has been indicated, only vague and contradictory shreds of information, and can therefore do no more than speculate about them. It is likely that the letter of recommendation from Wallack, an actor of high standing, helped in making his initial contacts in theatrical circles. In fact, theatre announcements show that Wallack was in London playing Rolla at Drury Lane on the very evening Aldridge opened at the Coburg. A more important factor was that the social and political climate, even the trend of fashion, were in his favour. But all these circumstances were, at best, only contributing factors to his success. The decisive elements lay within Ira Aldridge himself, as we shall see as our story progresses.

The theatre column of *The Times* of 10th October 1825 carried this announcement:

ROYAL COBURG THEATRE

This evening at half-past six o'clock precisely will be produced a grand West Indian Melodrama, called *The Revolt of Surinam, or A Slave's Revenge*. After which a new romantic Sicilian melodrama called *The Mysterious Stranger, or The Cave of St. Cataldo*. The whole to conclude with an entirely new melodrama called *The Spy of the Neutral Ground, or the American War of 1780*.

The text of the first playbill begins as follows:

ROYAL COBURG THEATRE

First night of the celebrated AMERICAN TRAGEDIAN of a new and most effective Melo-Dramatic Romance.

MONDAY, October 10th, 1825 and During the Week, at Half-past Six O'clock precisely, will be produced a Grand West Indian Melo-Drama, founded on Interesting and Pathetic Facts, to be Called the

REVOLT OF SURINAM
or A Slave's Revenge

This Piece exhibiting a most faithful Portrait of the horrors that arise out of that dreadful traffic, which it is the proudest boast of Britain to use her best efforts towards suppressing, must receive an immense portion of additional interest from being supported in its principal character by a *Man of Colour*, and one of the very race whose wrongs it professes to record; being the first instance in which one of that Complexion has displayed a striking degree of Histrionic Talent, and which has secured him the rapturous Approbation of an enlightened Public on the other side of the Atlantic.

OROONOKO   THE ROYAL SLAVE   MR. KEENE

Tragedian of Colour, from the African Theatre, New York.

There are several points of interest in this part of the playbill. First, it stresses what must have been the theatre's trump card for novelty appeal—"a Man of Colour" in the principal character. Secondly, the reference to "the first instance in which one of that Complexion has displayed a striking degree of Histrionic Talent" leaves unsubstantiated James Hewlett's claim in December 1825 that he was soon to "return to London to fill his engagement at the Coburg Theatre", unless on his previous visit he had not "displayed a striking degree of Histrionic Talent". The fact is that neither Hewlett nor Aldridge was the first man of colour to appear on the English stage, for in the 1760s Ignatius Sancho, an ex-slave and former attendant to the Fourth Earl of Montague, acted Oroonoko, the very role in which Aldridge made his London début, and also in *Othello*. But Sancho's articulation was poor: apparently he lisped and, intelligent though he was, he did not succeed.

Aldridge is presented as "MR. KEENE, Tragedian of Colour". He used the name "Mr. Keene" in the very early years. It is not uncommon practice in the theatre even of today to attract attention by the use of a name similar, if not identical, to that of a famous star. We see a playbill of 1814 headed "Mr. Keane of Theatre Royal, Exeter" and a bill of 1827 headed "Mr. Keene of Theatre Royal, Newcastle", the former referring to Edmund Kean (the final "e" being a misprint), the latter referring to Ira Aldridge. By 1827 Aldridge is billed as "the Celebrated Mr. Keene, the African Roscius" (playbill of Theatre Royal, Newcastle, 12th March 1827). By 1831 he is calling himself "F. W. Keene Aldridge, the African Roscius",* as seen in *A Critique of the Performance of Othello*, written and published by John Cole of Scarborough, which will be quoted later. By 10th April 1833, the date of his Covent Garden appearance, he is "Mr. Aldridge (A Native of Senegal) known by the appellation of The African Roscius". Thereafter he is either "The Celebrated African Roscius, Mr. Ira Aldridge" or "The Celebrated African Tragedian" or just "The African Roscius". The name "Keene" appears to have been dropped completely between 1831 and 1833.

The first playbill, it will be noted, is headed "FIRST NIGHT OF THE CELEBRATED AMERICAN TRAGEDIAN", with "a Man of Colour" in small type. A week later, on 17th October, the bill announces the "UNPRECEDENTED SUCCESS OF THE AFRICAN TRAGEDIAN!!!" He is never again billed as "American". He has become the "African Tragedian" or the "African Roscius", whose forefathers came from Senegal. From the playbill it will be seen that the cast of characters is set in a uniform small type, except for the star—MR. KEENE.

The Revolt of Surinam, or A Slave's Revenge, the play in which Aldridge made his first appearance, was an adaptation of Thomas Southerne's play, *Oroonoko*. As the play was the property of the patent theatres, at the Coburg it naturally had to be performed in a version to conform with the regulations.

The original Oroonoko was an African prince who, through the treachery of the captain of a slave ship, was kidnapped, together with a group of his own slaves, and brought to Surinam in the West Indies. His story was recounted in a novel, *Oroonoko, or The Royal Slave—A True Story*, written by Aphra Behn

---

* After the great Roman actor, Quintus Roscius Gallus (*c.* 126-62 B.C.)

55

(1640-99) and published in 1688. Mrs. Behn asserted that the book was based on her first-hand knowledge of Oroonoko and his life, gained while she was living in Surinam. In the Epistle Dedicatory addressed to the Right Honourable the Lord Maitland, the author declared: "This is a true story of a man gallant enough to merit your protection; and had he always been so fortunate he had not made so inglorious an end; the Royal Slave I had the honour to know in my travels to the other world, and though I had none above me in that country, yet I wanted power to preserve this great man."*

Aldridge opened on 10th October, and continued in the title role for the rest of that week. During the week beginning 17th October he played *The Ethiopian, or the Quadroon of the Mango Grove* (*The Slave*), followed by *The Libertine Defeated, or African Ingratitude* beginning the week of 24th October, and on 31st October the playbill announces: "For the first time an entirely new West Indian Romance . . . constructed expressly for the purpose of displaying the powerful talent of the African Tragedian and to be called *The Negro's Curse, or the Foulah Son*. The piece was written by H. M. Milner." On 7th November we are told that "The success of Mr. Keene, the African Tragedian, in the first original character ever written for him, has transcended all his previous efforts and imparted to the melodrama of *The Negro's Curse* a degree of interest which calls for its repetition until further notice".

* Today *Oroonoko* is never performed, but before Aldridge made his début in it, many great actors had essayed this popular tragedy, including Pope, Cooke, Kemble, Edmund Kean, and the elder Booth, and it held the stage for about 150 years. But, of course, they were all white men.

Its contrast to the plays of slavery that followed is seen, not only in its treatment of the slave as a truly noble tragic character, but being written only eighty years after Shakespeare's death it still bore the marks of blank verse tragedy, now, however, stilted and artificial, but with moments of passion and protest shining through. The author really loved and mourned her character, for he had been a living man she had known. Again, in contrast to later melodramas, Oroonoko and all the participants of the tragic elements spoke in blank verse, the comic participants in prose. Neither Oroonoko nor any of the Negroes spoke in any accent or phraseology of the West Indies or U.S.A., as in the melodramas of the nineteenth century.

The gulf between these characters and those in later melodramas reflects the early attitude to slavery and then, over a gap of 125 years, how it hardened with economic necessity and the brave, proud but tragic, noble figure becomes a pitiful servile humble "nigger", and finally a "nigger-minstrel".

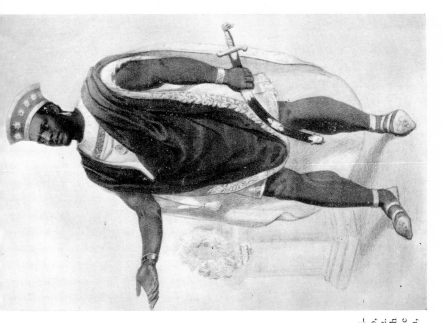

5. *Left:* Ira Aldridge. A lithograph by Barabas, 1853, in the Bakhrushin State Central Theatrical Museum, Moscow.

6. *Right:* Ira Aldridge as Othello, Frankfurt, 1852. From a lithograph by S. Bühler in the Theatre Museum, Munich.

Theatre Royal, Covent-Garden.

COMPLETE SUCCESS!!!

THE NEW SERIO-COMIC LEGENDARY FAIRY TALE, called

The ELFIN SPRITE,
AND

The Grim Grey Woman,

was received on its 2d representation with roars of laughter and applause.—The SPLENDID SCENERY and MACHINERY were honored throughout with enthusiastic approbation. This HIGHLY SUCCESSFUL NOVELTY will therefore be repeated

Every Evening until further notice.

This present WEDNESDAY, April 10, 1833,

Will be performed SHAKSPEARE's Tragedy of

OTHELLO.

The Duke of Venice, Mr. RANSFORD,
Brabantio, Mr. DIDDEAR, Gratiano, Mr. TURNOUR,
Lodovico, Mr. PAYNE, Montano, Mr. HAINES,
Othello by Mr. ALDRIDGE,
(A NATIVE OF SENEGAL,)
Known by the appellation of the AFRICAN ROSCIUS.
who has been received with great applause at the Theatres Royal, Dublin, Edinburgh, Bath, and most of the principal provincial Theatres.
His First Appearance on this Stage.
Cassio, Mr. ABBOTT,
Iago, Mr. WARDE,
Roderigo, Mr. FORESTER, Antonio, Mr. IRWIN, Julio, Mr. Matthews
Giovanni, Mr. J. COOPER, Luca, Mr. BRADY, Lorenzo Mr. Bender
Messenger Mr MEARS, Marco Mr Collet, Cosmo Mr Heath, Paolo Mr Stanley
Desdemona, - Miss E. TREE,
Emilia, Mrs. LOVELL.

To which will be added, (3d time) a New SERIO-COMIC LEGENDARY FAIRY TALE, called The

Elfin Sprite;
AND THE

Grim Grey Woman.

The Scenery, Machinery, Dresses and Decorations are entirely new.
The Overture and Music composed and selected by Mr. G. STANSBURY
The Scenery painted by Mr. GRIEVE, Mr. T. GRIEVE, & Mr. W. GRIEVE.
Assisted by Messrs. PUGIN, THORN, MORRIS, &c.
The Tricks, Decorations, Changes & Transformations by Mr. W. BRADWELL
The Machinery by Mr. SLOMAN.——The Dresses by Mr. HEAD & Mrs. BALDING.
The whole arranged and produced by Mr. FARLEY.

The ELFIN GLEN,
In the DRACKENFIELDT.
Elfin Moth, (the Elfin Sprite,) Miss POOLE
The Grim Grey Woman, Mr. W. H. PAYNE, Principal Elfin, Master W. MITCHINSON
Elfins, Sprites, and Fairies, Masters Platt, Melvin, Mears, Norman, Daly, Stansbury, Waite, Addison, Burton, Erwood, Flowers, Wells, W. Wells, Simpson, Ball, G. Matthews, Girard, Packer, Cross, Clark, May, Alger.

A FERRY across the RHINE,
Sir Joddril's Chateau in the distance.
Julian of Hilldersheim, Mrs. VINING,
Vintagers, Messrs. RANSFORD, HENRY, IRWIN, Butler, Guichard, May, Newcomb, Shegog, S. Tett, C. Tett, Willing, &c.
Vintage Girls, Mesdames Davis, Ryalls, Blaire, Fairbrother, Jones, Hall, Hill, Payne, Vials, Wells, &c.

INTERIOR of JULIAN's COTTAGE.

Grand Tapestry Chamber,
In the CHATEAU of HILLDERSHEIM.
Sir Joddril, of Hilldersheim, Mr. KEELEY,
Glibbert, (his Steward) Mr. F. MATTHEWS,
Michael and Martin, Mr. T. MATTHEWS and Mr. BENDER,
Tailor, Mr. ADDISON, Hatter, Mr. STANLEY, Bootmaker, Mr. LEG,
Agatha, (Confidant to Lady Blanch) Mrs. KEELEY.

7. Playbill for Ald first appearance at C Garden, 1833.

For the two weeks beginning 14th November and 21st November he acts in *The Death of Christophe, King of Hayti*, and the playbill says: "The forcible manner in which the Public attention has, by recent occurrences been called to the affairs of the *Newly recognized kingdom of Hayti*, the anxiety with which the present situation of that State is universally viewed, and the probability which exists that it may shortly again become the Theatre of those terrible commotions which attended its first organization as an Independent Nation, cannot but attach a peculiar Interest to those events which accompanied the last struggle made by a Negro Population for a municipal Freedom, and which are so powerfully illustrated in the above Popular Drama. This Interest cannot but be considerably heightened by the Personation of the principal Character by an Actor of the same race and complexion as the sable hero himself, and under these combined circumstances the Managers feel confident that the piece will now be revived with a degree of favor at least equal to that with which it was honored on its first Production."*

Unfortunately, we have been unable to locate the text of *The Death of Christophe, King of Hayti*, a piece written by J. H. Amherst, but from the real life of Christophe, on which the play was based, we know that, like Oroonoko, he was a tragic figure and a rebel. But in the character of Gambia in *The Slave*, by Thomas Morton (on the Coburg playbill it is called *The Ethiopian, or the Quadroon of the Mango Grove*), we have a character entirely different from Oroonoko. The place is the same, Surinam, but Gambia is the sentimental, super-patriotic colonial slave, servile to his masters, fighting his master's enemies, his own coloured brothers who dared to revolt and fight for freedom. He not only rescues his enslavers, but also his rival in love! The villain has a deathbed repentance, won over by the noble slave!

The first playbill announcing Aldridge as Oroonoko says, by way of description, "The Piece will exhibit a Variety of CHARAC-TERISTIC WEST INDIAN SCENERY". The playbill of the following week, however, goes into great detail in listing the scenery used in Aldridge's next play, *The Ethiopian, or the Quadroon of the Mango Grove*. This is the name under which *The Slave* was produced and which Aldridge had in his repertoire throughout

* The American spelling of certain words suggests that Aldridge prepared the copy himself.

his whole career. This musical drama (sometimes called an opera) by Thomas Morton, with music by Henry Bishop, was first produced at Covent Garden in 1816, when the part of Gambia was played by Macready. It became a popular item in the repertoire of both patent theatres. It is interesting that Macready played Gambia again for only one performance on 31st May at Drury Lane in the same year as Aldridge's London début. Here is the text of the playbill for 17th October 1825:

ROYAL COBURG THEATRE
Unprecedented Success of the AFRICAN TRAGEDIAN! ! !

TO THE PUBLIC

It was the decided Intention of the Managers to have produced, on this Evening, an entirely New and peculiar Drama, under the Title of "GRIM WILL, the COLLIER of CROYDON; or The Death of the Red King", for which Piece the most extensive Preparations, in Scenery and Machinery, were completed, but the *very powerful Sensation* excited by the brilliant success and astonishing Talent of Mr. KEENE, the TRAGEDIAN of COLOUR, the rapturous Applause which has attended each of his Performances, and the encreasing *anxious demand for Places* to witness this Royal and Interesting display of Histrionic Art, have determined them to gratify the Public Curiosity, by introducing this unexpected Acquisition to the Theatrical Talent of the Establishment, in a New Character eminently calculated for the display of his peculiar Powers; in consequence of which, all other Novelty is for the present postponed.

MONDAY, October 17th, 1825, and DURING THE WEEK will be Presented a Grand West Indian Musical Melo-Drama in Three Acts, with New Scenery and Decorations, Called The
ETHIOPIAN
Or, The Quadroon of the Mango Grove

to Music by Mr. H. R. Bishop—The Scenery by Messrs. Jones & Danson—The Dresses by Mr. Saunders and Mrs. Pollett—The Properties by Mr. Elliott—The Machinery by Mr. Burroughs.

The Governor of Surinam, Mr. GOLDSMITH.
Captain Clifton, Mr. WILSON, his First Appearance at this Theatre.
Colonel Lindenburg, in the Dutch Service, Mr. YOUNG.
Matthew Sharpset, Mr. HEMMINGS.
Fogrum, a Londoner on his Travels, Mr. DAVIDGE.
Sam Sharpset, a Yorkshireman, his Mentor, Mr. LEWIS.

Somerdyke, Agent to Lindenburg, Mr. VILLIERS.
First Planter, Mr. HOWARD.
Second Planter, Mr. GEORGE.

    GAMBIA   An Ethiopian Slave   Mr. KEENE
    The Celebrated Tragedian of Colour from the
African Theatre, New York, his Seventh Appearance

Officer, Mr. ALMAR.
Jailer, Mr. BUCKSTONE.
Mrs. Lindenburg, Mrs. COBHAM.
Stella Clifton, Miss POOLE from the Theatre Royal, Drury Lane,
    her First Appearance.
Zelinda, a Quadroon Slave, Miss JOHNSTON, Her First Appearance
    at this Theatre these Two Years.
Provost, Mr. ELSGOOD.
Clifton's Child, Master MEYERS.
Miss Von Frump, Mrs. WESTON.

IN THE COURSE OF THE PIECE

Will be exhibited the following New Local and Picturesque
SCENERY, painted expressly for this occasion. View of a Sea Port
in the West Indies, with Fortifications, etc. Anxious expectation
of the Inhabitants of Succours from England, to quell a Revolt
of the Negro Slaves—Arrival of the British Fleet, with the New
Governor and a numerous Force.

FOREST OF TROPICAL TREES

Bridal Procession of African Slaves
Attack of the Rebel Negroes on the Plantation—Heroism of
Gambia—his Rival rescued by his intrepidity from impending
death.

A SUGAR PLANTATION

Entry of the Victorious Troops—the valour of Gambia rewarded
with Freedom.

A PRISON

Clifton by the treachery of Lindenburg thrown into prison—
Rescued by the noble generosity of Gambia, who sacrifices his
newly acquired freedom, and again sells himself for a Slave, to
procure the release of Clifton from his Bond.

THE MANGO GROVE BY MOONLIGHT

Prepared for a Nuptial Festival, Pavilion and Ornamental Waters.

ARRIVAL OF THE GOVERNOR, ETC. IN BARGES

Lindenburg recognized by Clifton as a Gambler and Sharper,
whose life he had spared in Combat, and who had robbed him of

the money intended to redeem his Wife and Child—the Villain exults in calling them his Slaves, refuses to sell them, and proceeds to acts of appalling severity—Agony of the Father and Mother at this cruel separation, assuaged by the promises of Gambia.

AN APARTMENT IN A WEST INDIAN VILLA

The honour of Zelinda threatened by the Villain Lindenburg, she is preserved by the interference of Gambia, who secures the person of Lindenburg, whilst Zelinda effects her escape.

PICTURESQUE LANDSCAPE, WITH WATERFALL AND HANGING BRIDGE

suspended by Ropes from Trees which cross the Torrent. The escape of Zelinda and Clifton effected by the resolution of Gambia. Destruction of the Bridge. The Child about to be plunged into the Torrent by the Pursuers, wonderfully rescued by Gambia, & restored to his Mother's arms.

LINDENBURG'S APARTMENT

Gambia brought before him Prisoner, condemned to a Death of Torture, for attacking his Master, having discovered on Lindenburg's breast the BRAND OF GUILT, his knowledge of that secret secures him from his resentment. Generosity of the Slave in swearing to preserve silence.

GENERAL VIEW OF THE ISLAND

Lindenburg's obduracy being conquered by the magnanimity of Gambia, he is, together with

ZELINDA AND HER CHILD RESTORED TO FREEDOM

This detailed synopsis of the action and the scenery suggests that Mr. Burroughs's "machinery" was quite necessary and complicated to bring about the required transformation. The playbill also lists the musical items: "In the course of the Piece will be introduced the following songs, duets, choruses, etc.:

Opening Glee and Chorus, "Blow Gentle Gales"
Song, "My Highland Home"—Mr. Bedford
Song, the "Mocking Bird"—Miss Johnston
Finale—Messrs. Bedford, Wilson, Miss Johnston and Chorus
Song, "Up Lads and At Them!"—Mr. Wilson
Song, the "Wonders of London Town"—Mr. Lewis
Finale, "Strike the Oar"
Song, "A Highland Laddie"—Mr. Bedford
Song, "Sons of Freedom"—Miss Johnston
Finale, All the characters

Only two of the songs appear to have some relevancy, "Strike the Oar" and "Sons of Freedom". The latter is sung by Zelinda, the Quadroon Slave, whom Gambia surrenders to his English captain:

> Sons of Freedom! hear my story,
>   Mercy well becomes the brave:
> Humanity is Briton's glory—
>   Pity, and protect the Slave!
>
> Free-born daughters, who possessing
>   Eyes that conquer, hearts that save;
> Greet me with a sister's blessing,
>   Oh! Pity and protect the Slave!

To give a complete picture of the reaction of the audience and the critics to the phenomenon of a Negro actor in their white theatre, we quote all the reviews we have found, beginning with the august *Times* (London) 11th October, 1825:

The appetite for theatrical novelty seems to have spread rapidly, and because at this time of the year the managers have the play-houses pretty nearly to themselves, they are resolved to "foot it to the top of their bent". At Drury Lane they have Mr. Booth; at Covent Garden Mr. Warde; at the Surrey Theatre a man who plays a monkey in the most natural manner possible,* and at the Coburg (not to be behind their neighbours) they have brought out what Mr. Doubikins† calls "a *genuine* nigger" to act *Oroonoko*. It is extremely difficult to criticize a black actor, on account of the novelty of the spectacle, however, excepting Prince Anamabao, who was engaged by the late Stephen Kemble to exhibit the true method of eating raw beef-steaks, we never remember to have heard of any sable candidate for histrionic distinction in England. It is true that his Royal Highness Prince Anamabao turned out to be a Jew, who usually got his bread by selling sealing wax; yet he nevertheless ate the undressed beef-steaks as well as a natural-born savage; that, however, was a mere accomplishment, and can

---

* This is a reference to Monsieur Gouffé, a man of extraordinary agility, who was brought out by Charles Dibdin the Younger. He was essentially an acrobat, performing astonishing feats of balancing, leaps, suspensions, etc.

† Jonathan W. Doubikin, the central character in a farce by Peake called *Jonathan in England*, which character Charles Mathews included in his sketch, *A Real Yankee*.

never entitle him to be considered as the predecessor of Mr. Keene, the African Roscius, who last evening made his first appearance before an enlightened audience at the Coburg Theatre. This gentleman is in complexion of the colour of a new half-penny, barring the brightness; his hair is woolly, and his features, although they possess much of the African character, are considerably humanized. His figure is unlucky for the stage; he is baker-knee'd and narrow-chested; and owing to the shape of his lips it is utterly impossible for him to pronounce English in such a manner as to satisfy even the unfastidious ears of the gallery. He played the part of Oroonoko probably as well as was necessary, because it is full of bombast and affectation. The audience wondered and laughed at him all through the play until he stabbed his wife, and then they applauded him loudly; but it was not until he killed himself that their delight grew outrageous. Then indeed they seemed perfectly delighted. It appears from the playbills (and who can doubt them?) that this gentleman is one of the principal ornaments of the African Theatre at New York, and for his own sake we regret that he did not stay there; not that he is worse than the ordinary run of such actors as are to be seen at the Coburg Theatre, but that there are so many of them that his merits will hardly distinguish him; and excepting by his colour, he will not be known from the rest of the *corps*. In the meantime, as a mere wonder, the exhibition of this Mr. Keene is not likely to turn out very well. After the managers had been at the trouble of getting a starveling out of a parish workhouse to rival the *Anatomic Vivante*, and had succeeded so well, they might, if they were bent upon having a blackamoor, have procured one whose complexion was more *fonce*—the man who sweeps the crossings at the end of Fleet-Market, for example; they would then have spared the gentlemen in the gallery, who looked for nothing lighter than a chimney sweeper on May-Day, the disappointment which they experienced on the first appearance of the African Mr. Keene. If, however, the managers mean to continue the African Roscius, we beseech them to change the black worsted stockings which the heroic Aboan wears, because as he is the countryman of Oroonoko, it is not fit that their complexions should present so striking a contrast as they do at present, the one being but little darker than the dun cow, the other as black as a pair of new boots on which all the glories of Day and Martin* have been shed.

* A boot polish.

62

The *Globe* (11th October, 1825):

Curiosity led us last night to see the black tragedian from the African Theatre at New York, and of whom we had already heard something, in the humorous but exaggerated description given by Mr. Mathews of the "genuine Nigger". Whatever other merits this place of amusement may possess, the circle of novelties which it is constantly purveying for the public gratification is not one of the least conspicuous and characteristic features. Their importation of Mr. Keene from the African Theatre seems to be a lucky hit, and free from all the objections which sometimes attach to their novelties. This is, we believe, the only case in which one of "Afric's swarthy sons" has in Europe aspired to the honours of the buskin. Had Mr. Keene appeared on the boards of one of the minor theatres merely as a provincial performer and an Englishman, he would have merited considerable applause, but considering he has attained his eminence under all the disadvantages of the present state of American society, his claims must belong to a much higher grade. The part of Oroonoko, which Mr. Keene performed last night, is so characterized by rant and affectation, that whatever may be the taste and feeling of the performer, it is almost impossible for him to avoid falling more or less into these defects. We should say, however, on the whole that his conception of the character was very judicious and that he rarely "overstepped the modesty of nature". Several of his touches in the last scene were impressive and notwithstanding a very evident disposition among the audience to indulge the risible faculty brought down spontaneous plaudits. His enunciation is distinct and sonorous, though his voice is deficient in modulation and flexibility; his features appear too hard and firm to admit of outwardly exhibiting the darker passions and most embittered sufferings of the heart. But he looks his character.

Two days later the *Globe* ran the following little item:

Keene *v*. Kean. The African votary of Thespis, yclept Mr. Keene, goes on triumphantly at the Coburg. Two sons, they say, cannot shine in the same hemisphere, and the new and the Old World have done well to exchange luminaries.*

The *Morning Advertiser* (11th October, 1825):

Royal Coburg Theatre: A very novel performance excited much attention last night at this theatre. *The Revolt of Surinam, or A*

* The reference is to Edmund Kean, who was then on an American tour.

Slave's Revenge was brought forward to introduce Mr. Keene, an African, in the character of Oroonoko. He has repeatedly performed in the African Theatre in New York, and is evidently a man of much observation, and had a very excellent conception of the character, which he performed in a manner so as to receive the approbation of a numerous audience.

The *Drama*, November 1825:

THE BLACK ROSCIUS AT THE COBURG

. . . Finally they have a real *bona-fide* black man, and he plays tragedy. He was indeed a black draught to us, still there are worse actors. Mr. Keene, it is whispered, was a servant to Wallack. He is tall and tolerably well-proportioned—his features are not very Negroish; but he has a method of thrusting out his chin, and throwing back his brow which makes him look silly. He gabbles apace, but has no particular brogue—his action is not ungraceful but altogether unmeaning—his voice is weak, so is his conception. Theatricals we suspect will never be profitable to him.

It will be seen that these reviews contain varied and often contradictory opinions, and there is obvious hostility in at least a section of the Press. *The Times* reviewer proclaims that it is utterly impossible for him to pronounce English properly owing to the shape of his lips! The *Globe*, however, finds his enunciation distinct and sonorous. Aldridge, of course, did not speak Oxford English, but Maurice Lenihan, who knew him well, said: "He spoke English with a good accent, yet not entirely divested of the peculiarity which is attached by his countrymen to the pronunciation of certain syllables."[3] Whether the "peculiarity" refers to American or Negro speech is not clear.

In the hundreds of reviews, descriptions and photographs which were studied in the preparation of this work, there is nothing to indicate that Aldridge was "baker-knee'd" or that his figure was "unlucky for the stage". On the contrary, he was generally described as tall, well built, noble, graceful, and portraits and photographs of him in his early years bear this out; later, towards middle age, he grew a little stocky.

The main conclusion that emerges from the criticisms of this period is that he lacks training and experience. We must remember that at this time he is only eighteen years old, and, as the

Globe remarks, the merits he has are to be more highly praised than if he had been an Englishman in his own country.

✱   ✱   ✱

Apparently the audiences at the Coburg were not as disappointed as *The Times* reviewer would have us think, as the following week's playbill announces the continuation of Aldridge's engagement for four weeks because of the "very powerful sensation excited by the brilliant success and astonishing talent of Mr. Keene, the Tragedian of Colour, the rapturous applause which has attended each of his performances, and the increasing anxious demand for places". In one point only do we agree with *The Times* critic, and that is in his observation that "as a mere wonder, the exhibition of this Mr. Keene is not likely to turn out very well". If Aldridge had been nothing but "a mere wonder", the management would have cashed in quickly, he would never have been heard of again, and *The Collier of Croydon* would have been presented as scheduled. But not only did they continue with Aldridge for six more weeks, but H. M. Milner was commissioned to write a special play for him.

And a week after that, on 7th November: "The success of Mr. Keene, the African Tragedian, in the first original character ever written for him, has transcended all his previous efforts and imparted to the melodrama of *The Negro's Curse* a degree of interest which calls for its repetition until further notice." We have been unable to trace a manuscript of this play, which was either not published or is a version of a play bearing a different title, but be it noted that it is about the very people from whom Aldridge declared his descent, and may have had some special interest for that reason, but the fact that it is not retained by Aldridge rather suggests that it was not a suitable vehicle for him.

Despite his success at the Coburg and his enthusiastic reception by the theatre-going public, the hostile, anti-Negro attitude of the Press, representing as it did the most powerful section of London society, had its effect, and prevented Aldridge from establishing himself firmly in London. He therefore went into the provinces, where he continued to grow in popularity with the provincial public and to develop his art throughout the next quarter of a century, culminating in his European apotheosis.

✱   ✱   ✱

It was during this Coburg engagement, after his performance of Gambia, that he met the woman he married—"an English lady of respectability and superior accomplishments", we are told in the *Memoir*. He had been invited to a private box to receive the congratulations of a group who had expressed a desire to meet him, among them being the lady in question. Six weeks later they were married. It has been impossible to ascertain the date and place of the marriage, but if we are to accept the above account given in the *Memoir*, it took place at the very end of the year, either in London or in Brighton, where he proceeded to fill an engagement immediately following his run at the Coburg.

We next hear of him at the Theatre Royal, Brighton, his very first provincial engagement, on 13th December in *Oroonoko*, and we quote the first review of a serious and unprejudiced kind from the *Brighton Gazette* of 15th December:

> . . . We repaired to the house in full expectation of beholding a mere burlesque of tragedy, and were therefore not a little surprised to find in the "Roscius" an actor of real and undoubted talent. He exhibited an acquaintance with the stage, a justness of conception, and force of execution that not only would not have shamed the tragedians of our own country, but were such as, with few exceptions, are not to be found amongst us in the present day. His points were almost invariably made with accuracy, and we scarcely remember an instance of their having failed; and what is perhaps still more calculated to excite surprise, although his voice was loud and energetic, his style was perfectly free from extravagance; his action being on the contrary chaste, and his attitudes generally appropriate and graceful. He was received with great applause and on the fall of the curtain the shouts of "Bravo!" were kept up for a considerable time. It is really a curious and an interesting spectacle to behold a representation of such a character as Oroonoko by an African; and one well calculated to awaken a trend of deep reflections, as we view the emanations of that "untutored mind" which we have been taught to consider on a level with the brute creation, and incapable of raising itself to the common range of humanity.

The following week, the *Brighton Gazette*, (presumably the same critic), wrote: "Mr. Keene, the African Roscius, performed Oroonoko and Othello on Friday and Saturday last, but in the latter part he was less successful than in Oroonoko; the drama of

Shakespeare is evidently beyond his reach, and in the dignified, although fierce passion of the noble Moor, he fell far short of the force and propriety which marked his delineation of the sable prince."

From these two reviews we have a clear and sympathetic statement of the weakness as well as the strength of Aldridge at the start of his career.

In Porter's *Theatres of Brighton*[4] we find this terse note: "The African Roscius, Keene (Ira Aldridge), enacted Oroonoko on the 13th; Othello 17th, but created no special furore." The critic who was present wrote about the great applause and the shouts of "Bravo!" but Porter, writing almost twenty years after Aldridge's death, gives a different impression. This variance between the actual facts and their later presentation will be seen to run throughout the whole of our study.

Reviewing the same performance, the London *Morning Post* said:

Mr. Keene, the African Roscius, made his appearance at the Brighton Theatre last night as Othello. He was not so much at home in the character, however, as he had previously been in that of Oroonoko, but he evinced a talent sufficient to bring down frequent peals of applause. In the third act, on releasing, Iago whom, in his anger and frenzy, he had seized, after the words, "For nothing canst thou to damnation add greater than that," appeared so exhausted by the energy of his efforts, that he staggered, fell, and continued motionless on the stage. Iago, Mr. Barry, and ably was the character embodied, not suspecting that any matter but what had previously *been planned* by Othello had occurred, went on with his part until, not receiving the expected reply from the prostrate Moor, he approached and partially raised him—but he seemed lifeless, and the drop scene soon after hid him from the audience. In about fifteen minutes, however, the play was renewed at the breaking-off point, and without any symptom of remaining disorder in Mr. Keene who, if he had had recourse to the strategem mentioned to produce effect, had been completely disappointed in the result, for the audience neither bestowed on it censure nor applause—or who, if actual indisposition had overcome and rendered him powerless, had been visited by one of the most sudden and entire recoveries that ever visited illness, and put all right again. In the intellectual ability which Mr. Keene, however, has manifested in his several personations here, much good perhaps, may result to the sable brethren, inasmuch as they have afforded a powerful illustration that blacks as well as whites may be equally fashioned by education—and that to education, principally, is to be ascribed that mental superiority which the latter have too often endeavoured to persuade themselves that they exclusively enjoy.

As to Aldridge's alleged illness on the stage, the London critic is a little more sceptical than the local critic, who wrote at the end of his review: "While performing Othello, Mr. Keene fell down in a fit upon the stage, but medical assistance being at hand, he was promptly restored, and the play was scarcely interrupted for a moment. He is, we understand, subject to fits of this kind." We hear nothing more of attacks of this kind at any time in Aldridge's life, and it may be that the London critic came nearer the truth about it. It must be remembered that Aldridge is still very young and inexperienced, and it is possible that he is following through the character of Othello, who was subject to fits of this kind. The Folio Edition indicates in Act IV, Scene 1:

> *Falls in a trance* and Iago says:
>   My lord is fall'n into an epilepsy:
>   This is his second fit; he had one yesterday.

And we see that Aldridge fell into his trance after the lines,

> For nothing can'st thou to damnation add
> Greater than that,

in which it was usual business for Othello to attack Iago, and it is permissible for this to be the fit which Iago had in mind when he says, "He had one yesterday." It is conceivable, therefore, that Aldridge, in working up the passion of Othello to the point where he will lose control of himself (as here), and later fall into a fit, might have lost control of himself as the actor—which, of course, should never happen. On the other hand it may be, as the London critic suspects, that Aldridge deliberately "had recourse to the strategem mentioned, to produce effect", but overdid it, and it did not come off. Whatever the explanation, we do not find that it ever occurred again. In fact, though the realism of his passion sometimes terrified his Desdemona, much as Kean had terrified his brother actors, we have testimony that Aldridge was in complete control of his faculties at all times, and followed out the instructions of the master, "for in the very torrent, tempest, and as I may say, the whirlwind of passion, you must acquire and beget a temperance that may give it smoothness".

★   ★   ★

Thus ends the first year of Aldridge's life in England, and when he set foot on the shores of that land he might well have expressed his sentiments as did his character Gambia when he said, "England! shall I behold thee? Talk of fabled land or magic power! But what land, that poet ever sung, or enchanter swayed, can equal that which, when the Slave's foot touches, he becomes free!—his prisoned soul starts forth, his swelling nerves burst the chain that enthrall'd him, and, in his own strength he stands as the rock he treads on, majestic and secure."

In this year he had achieved fame as a star attraction at the Coburg Theatre, he had found a Desdemona of his own, and before him was time and the world.

We do not hear of him now for more than a year. What happened from the time he left Brighton until we hear of him again in Sheffield on 11th January 1827 we do not know. Perhaps in view of his unpreparedness for Shakespeare he decided to study at Glasgow, as is stated in the *Memoir*. Perhaps he was ill. Whatever the case may be, according to our records he made no public appearances in the year 1826, but bursts once more into success in the Midlands and the North in 1827.

CHAPTER VI

Early Provincial Tours

IN 1827 we find Aldridge touring the provinces, appearing in Sheffield, Halifax, Manchester, Newcastle, Edinburgh, Lancaster, Liverpool, and Sunderland. The *Memoir* tells us that after the Coburg and Brighton engagements, "having, one may say, felt his way thus far in comparative obscurity, he withdrew into the provinces, the better to fit himself for a great trial in the metropolis. He accordingly took a country tour . . . returning to London after a lapse of seven years, an apprenticeship which he had turned to good account. During this time Mr. Aldridge had studied deeply and laboured hard at his profession." His basic repertoire was *Othello, Oroonoko, The Slave, The Castle Spectre, The Padlock,* and *The Revenge.*

The Revenge, by Edward Young, was first produced at Drury Lane in April 1721. The play is a mixture of *Othello* and Aphra Behn's *Abdelazar, or the Moor's Revenge* (1671), which in turn came from Marlowe's *Lust's Dominion.* The character of Zanga the Moor, a fine acting part, helped to keep the play alive well into the nineteenth century (Kean revived it in 1815). It was an excellent choice for Aldridge. A commentator on the play, writing in 1833, says of Zanga: "Dark and malevolent as he is represented, some sympathy is excited for him by the remembrance that his lofty and impatient spirit has been irritated by his father's death, his own conquest, captivity, loss of his crown, and the indignity of a blow—all from the same person; against whom, an open and honourable atonement being impossible, he employs a subtle and secret vengeance. No wonder it appealed to the African Roscius."

It was during this period that we first hear of Aldridge as a singer. At the Coburg, Shakespearean plays and the legitimate dramas had perforce to include music to make them permissible in a minor theatre. It may therefore have occurred to the enterprising manager or, more likely, to Aldridge himself that he should attempt a singing part, and in the search for a play or ballad opera with a Negro part the obvious choice was *The Padlock*, by Isaac Bickerstaff, with music by Charles Dibdin (the original creator of the role of Mungo). Or it may have been that in the search for parts to suit "the only actor of colour", Mungo in *The Padlock* was suggested, and only then was it discovered that Aldridge had a fine singing voice.

The Padlock was first acted in Drury Lane on 3rd October 1768, and was one of the best musical entertainments of the time. Bickerstaff wrote it at the suggestion of an actor, John Moody, who had been in Barbados and studied the dialect and manners of the Negroes, but Moody did not eventually create the part. The plot was taken from Cervantes' *The Jealous Husband*, but Mungo, the slave of a West Indian planter, is a character based on reality.

The Padlock bears a similarity to Molière's *School for Wives* (1662) and Beaumarchais's *Barber of Seville* (1775). Don Diego, an ageing and very rich West Indian planter (a type of Dr. Bartholo), wants to marry Leonora (counterpart of Rosine), a young woman of great beauty and poor parents. It is agreed by all concerned that Leonora should live under Don Diego's roof, carefully guarded by her faithful *duenna*, for a period sufficient to test her virtue and their compatibility for marriage. When Don Diego is about to leave to make known to Leonora's parents his decision to marry their daughter, he leaves Mungo (an obvious Figaro), his Negro slave and house servant, in charge of the house, with strict injunctions to permit no one to enter. Leander, a young student in a nearby school, is in love with Leonora and she with him, and by serenading Mungo, who loves music, with his guitar and with a bottle of wine, Leander gains entry into the house and, by flattering the *duenna*, reaches Leonora's room.

Mungo, though a slave, is not the usual abject, servile creation of the nineteenth-century melodramas. He is a man of spirit, protesting against his ill-treatment, and daring to voice his protests even to his master, though it may lead to still more flogging. Here is a typical scene between Mungo and Don Diego. Mungo is lugging a hamper down the stairs:

MUNGO: Go, get you down, you damn hamper, you carry me now. (*Sits on the hamper.*) Curse my old Massa, sending me always here and dere, for one something to make me tire like a mule—curse him imperance—and him damn insurance.

DIEGO: How, now?

MUNGO: Ah, Massa, bless your heart.

DIEGO: What's that you are muttering, sirrah?

MUNGO: Not'ing, Massa, only me say, you very good Massa.

DIEGO: What do you leave your load down there for?

MUNGO: Massa, me lilly tire.

DIEGO: Take it up, rascal.

MUNGO: Yes, bless your heart, Massa.

DIEGO: No, lay it down: now I think on't, come hither.

MUNGO: What you say, Massa?

DIEGO: Can you be honest?

MUNGO: Me no savee, Massa, you never ax me before.

DIEGO: Can you tell truth?

MUNGO: What you give me, Massa?

DIEGO: There's a pistreen for you; now tell me, do you know of any ill going on in my house?

MUNGO: Ah, Massa, a damn deal.

DIEGO: How! That I'm a stranger to?

MUNGO: No, Massa, you lick me other day with your rattan: I'm sure, Massa, that's mischief enough for poor Neger man.

DIEGO: So, so.

MUNGO: La, Massa, how could you have a heart to lick poor Neger man, as you lick me last Thursday?

DIEGO: If you have not a mind I should chastise you now, hold your tongue.

MUNGO: Yes, Massa, if you no lick me again.

DIEGO: Listen to me, I say.

MUNGO: You know, Massa, me very good servant.

DIEGO: Then you will go on?

MUNGO: And ought to be use kine.

DIEGO: If you utter another syllable——

MUNGO: And I am sure, Massa, you can't deny that I worky worky—I dress a victuals, and run a errands, and wash a house, and make a beds, and scrub a shoes, and wait a table——

DIEGO: Take that—now will you listen to me?

MUNGO: La, Massa, if ever I saw——

DIEGO: I am going abroad and shall not return till tomorrow morning. During this night I charge you not to sleep a wink, but be watchful as a lynx, and keep walking up and down the entry, that if you hear the least noise you may alarm the family.

MUNGO: So I must be stay in a cold all night, and have no sleep,

and get no tanks, neither; then him call me tief, and rogue, and
rascal, to temp me.

DIEGO: Stay here, perverse animal, and take care that nobody
approaches the door; I am going in and shall be out again in a
moment. (*He exits.*)

Mungo sings:

> Dear heart, what a terrible life am I led!
> A dog has a better, that's sheltered and fed;
> > Night and day 'tis de same,
> > My pain is dere game,
> Me wish to de Lord me was dead.

> What e'er's to be done
> Poor black must run,
> > Mungo here, Mungo dere,
> > Mungo everywhere;
> > Above and below,
> > Sirrah come, sirrah go,
> > Do so and do so,
> > O! O!
> Me wish to de Lord me was dead.

The master puts a great padlock on the door and leaves. Mungo
gets his own back by letting in the lover to see the girl his master
is so carefully guarding, and as he leaves them alone to prepare a
meal he says, "Me get supper ready, and now me go to de cellar—
but I say, Massa, ax de old man now, what good him watching do,
him bolts, and him bars, him walls and him padlock." Then
Mungo sings a merry song, "Let Me, When My Heart a-Sinking",
which expresses the natural musical aspirations of the Negro in
his most typical form, with a guitar, of which Aldridge was a
master. But even this merry song has a sting in the tail, another
expression of revolt:

> Let me, when my heart a-sinking,
> Hear de sweet guitar a-clinking;
> > When a string speak,
> > Such music he make,
> Me soon am cured of tinking.

> Wid de toot, toot, toot,
> Of a merry flute

And cymbalo,
And tymbalo
To boot,
We dance and we sing
Till we make a house ring,
And, tyed in his garters,
Old Massa may swing.

Finally "old Massa" comes home, saying, "Good Heavens! what a wonderful deal of uneasiness may mortals avoid by a little prudence! I doubt not now, there are some men who would have gone out in my situation; and, trusting to the goodness of Fortune, left their house and their honour in the care of an unexperienced girl, or the discretion of a mercenary servant. While he is abroad, he is tormented with fears and jealousies; and when he returns home, he probably finds disorder, and perhaps shame. But what do I do—I put a padlock on my door, and all is safe." He unlocks the padlock and enters, when Mungo appears from the cellar, drunk, with a flask in one hand and a candle in the other:

DIEGO: Heaven and earth, what do I see!
MUNGO: Where are you, young Massa, and Missy? Here wine for supper.
DIEGO: I'm thunderstruck!
MUNGO: My old Massa little tink we be so merry—hic-hic—— What's the matter with me, the room turn round.
DIEGO: Wretch, do you know me?
MUNGO: Know you—damn you.
DIEGO: Horrid creature! What makes you here at this time of night; is it with a design to surprise the innocents in their beds, and murder them sleeping?
MUNGO: Hush, hush—make no noise—hic-hic.
DIEGO: The slave is intoxicated.
MUNGO: Make no noise, I say; dere's young gentleman wid young lady; he play on guitar, and she like him better dan she like you. Fal, lal, lal.
DIEGO: Monster, I'll make an example of you.
MUNGO: What you call me names for, you old dog?
DIEGO: Does the villain dare to lift his hand against me!
MUNGO: Will you fight?
DIEGO: He's mad.

Diego, in a rage, rushes off to confront the pair, and finally has to surrender to youth.

Such scenes as the above gave Aldridge the scope and opportunity to develop the character of a simple, apparently stupid, slave into a rebel against slavery. Yet at the same time it was linked with the utmost comicality. It is regrettable that even here, with his most-repeated and popular play, one can find no detailed analysis in the British Press. The *Cambrian* (Swansea) of 27th July 1833 merely says, "His farce parts, particularly Mungo, are perfect" and the *Northern Whig* (Belfast) of 14th April 1846 says, "He convulsed the house by his comic talents." Two years later the *Morning Advertiser* (21st March 1848) says, "In the farce of *The Padlock*, his performance of the part of Mungo was equal to anything we ever witnessed; he displayed his humour and histrionic art in setting forth the salient points of that very facetious specimen of sable servants. The greatest applause accompanied his efforts", and the *Douglas Jerrold Newspaper* at that same time said: "He performed Mungo with so much humour, and with such characteristic songs that it gave universal satisfaction, and it is doubtful if his *forte* be not rather comedy than tragedy. . . . He was enthusiastically received by a very excellent house." The *Cambridge Chronicle* of 14th September 1850 thought "Mungo and Ginger Blue are the most laugh-moving impersonations that can be conceived".

The *Era* of 25th October 1846 devotes a whole article on Ira Aldridge, in which the writer says, in part: "The versatility of Garrick himself, who played Richard and Abel Drugger, Macbeth and Jerry Sneak on the same night, appears at any rate to attach to the African Roscius who in the same evening achieves his Othello or his Zanga with his Mungo and his Ginger Blue. The sock and the buskin appear, by provincial criticism, to fit him equally; the tear or the horse-laugh being alike at his command."

Ginger Blue, a character in the *Virginian Mummy*, was a role in which his audiences found him as hilariously funny as in Mungo, but Mungo took first place with him. Ginger Blue is described in the playbills as "an independent nigger, head waiter, always absent when wanted, yet mindful of his perquisites, remarkably familiar, bursting with fun and laughter, very industrious (by deputy), receiving all gratuities in person, a most accommodating appetite; love of money induces him to become a mummy". Dr. Galen has compounded an elixir possessing the extraordinary quality of restoring life after being extinct 3,000 years. He demonstrates it and brings the "mummy" to life! The situations and Aldridge's acting are extremely funny, but the piece does not have the content of *The Padlock*, nor does it offer the same scope. It does not appear to have been performed outside of England, and our last record of it is in Glagow in November 1860. *The Padlock* remained in his repertoire until the very end, and was performed on the Continent with regularity. A German critic who saw it wrote:

> He played like Pierrot in the wonderful, grotesque style of old comedy. It is impossible to describe the song he sang with a bottle in his hand, so amusingly swaying and dancing: with his merriment he could shake even the most venerable pyramids, until they caught hold of their sides with laughter.[1]

And an interesting detail comes from a Russian critic, who thought he was particularly funny in the drunken scene:

> Holding in one hand a bottle of rum and in the other a lighted candle, Mungo, instead of the bottle, put the lighted candle in his mouth, after which he spat it out, laughing, grinning with all his white teeth, rolled his eyes and sang and danced.[2]

> Before this ballad opera he gave us *Othello*, and all those who cried, watching Aldridge-Othello, laughed to the very depths of their being at Aldridge-Mungo. How sympathetic he is in that role! What truth, what unfeigned merriment, what comedy![3]

And Durylin sums it up by saying: "This little playlet satisfied his need to be an actor-Negro, playing a simple, ordinary Negro-servant, like thousands of others, in that country of slaves. And it was not for nothing that Aldridge linked this play with *Othello*; it seemed to him that here were two truths: a mighty truth and a tiny truth about one man—a black."

And it is the one role, apart from Othello, that he played the whole of his life, without a break, and he never failed to bring the house down.

The *Manchester Courier* of 24th February 1827 announces Aldridge's benefit for that evening and hopes "that a generous public will show their liberality to this descendant of the suffering sons of Africa. It need not be said that worth and merit are confined to no country. The African Roscius in those characters for which his complexion is peculiarly adapted, approaches closer to nature than any European actor we ever saw."

The playbill of the Theatre Royal, Newcastle, of March 12th shows him still performing as Mr. Keene, the African Roscius, and says: "He has been acting with great success at the Theatres Royal, Liverpool, Manchester, Bath, Bristol, etc., and is engaged to act at the Theatre Royal, Covent Garden, during this season." The reference to Covent Garden may have been a mere puff, or there may have been negotiations in progress for his appearance at that great theatre, but, as we shall see, that did not materialize until April 1833.

In April he is in Edinburgh and from the local Press we see that while sympathy for the slaves of Africa was great, the working population of Britain was starving, and that members of the theatrical profession were giving a benefit performance to raise funds for the "relief of the distressed operatives" of Edinburgh.

The benefit system, by which the whole or a part of the receipts was given to the actor or a specified charity, had commenced in the early days of the theatre, and continued well into the second half of the nineteenth century. This made the actor dependent on the goodwill of his admirers for part of his income, and became an important item in theatrical negotiations. Aldridge, for instance, writes to Mr. Maxfield, theatre manager of Southampton, in August 1834: "I will come for fourths and a half benefit", meaning one-fourth of the net receipts and one-half of a benefit night. Some idea of the amounts involved may be had from the memorandum on p. 78.

After Aldridge became a Freemason in Ireland, he canvassed his benefit by sending out a printed note to his fellow members in the area of the theatre:

SIR AND BROTHER,—In enclosing a Programme of the Entertainments for my Benefit, permit me very respectfully to solicit a share of the Patronage which has ever been as cordially awarded to the Stranger as to the resident Brother.

I have the honour to be,
Faithfully and Fraternally yours,
IRA F. ALDRIDGE, C.R.A., M.G.L.I.

77

As benefits became more common, often special efforts were made to give them a special flavour, either by the actor playing an unusual part, a friendly author writing a special after-piece or an epilogue, or the actor giving an address to the audience. Aldridge soon made good use of these occasions, for on a playbill of the New Theatre, Kendal, 20th August 1830, we read: "Each person entering the theatre will be presented with a biographical memoir of the African Roscius and also copies of his Farewell Address. Last appearance but one previous to his departure for his native country."

The cry of "Farewell appearance" was, of course, bait to bring in the audience, and the announcements that went with it were often only pious hopes. On 5th October 1827, at the Theatre

BENEFIT OF THE AFRICAN ROSCIUS
Theatre Royal, Bath, Saturday, Jan. 21, 1832

Boxes, 1st Act	.	.	.	.	£47 0 0	
Pit	.	.	.	.	17 16 0	
Gallery	.	.	.	.	9 9 6	
					£74 5 6	
Boxes, 2nd Act	.	.	.	£8 15 6		
Pit	.	.	.	5 14 6		
Gallery	.	.	.	2 12 6	17 2 6	
					91 8 0	
African Roscius half Benefit	.	.	.	.	45 14 0	
Dr. to 10 Box Tickets, 17 Pit, 2 Gallery	.	.			4 15 6	
Balance	.	.	.	.	.	.	£40 18 6

Royal, Lancaster, Aldridge is announced as Othello "for the Benefit of the African Roscius, positively the last night of his appearance, as his engagement at the Theatre Royal, Covent Garden, obliges him to proceed to London immediately". But six days later he begins a two-week run at the Theatre Royal, Liverpool! During the Liverpool engagement he goes through his familiar roles—Othello, Zanga, Gambia, Hassan, Mungo—but there is an important development in his career. For the first time he plays with another star. The playbill announcing the

re-engagement of the African Roscius for three nights also announces that on Monday John Vandenhoff will perform *Macbeth*
and on Tuesday he will play Iago to Aldridge's Othello. John
Vandenhoff (1790-1861) was a favourite with the audiences of
Liverpool, Manchester, and other big provincial towns. In 1820
he had played Lear and Iago at Covent Garden, the latter being
considered one of his best parts. For more than eighteen years he
played leads in London, but, lacking pathos and passion, he became a sort of minor Kemble and failed to reach a commanding
position, particularly with Kean at his height. Still, it was a
feather in the cap of the twenty-year-old Ira Aldridge that
Vandenhoff supported him in the role of Iago and of Earl
Osmond in *The Castle Spectre*. They played together again in
Dublin in December 1832, as we shall see.

That Aldridge planned to return to the United States is seen
from a more reliable source than theatre announcements—a
letter written in his own hand on 15th August 1834 from Hull to
the Manager of the Southampton Theatre, in which he stated
that he was available to act a few nights, "being on the eve of
returning to my native country". But the evidence is incon-
testable that, in fact, he never did return. The *Dictionary of American Biography*, in its brief sketch of Aldridge, says: "After 1830—
date unknown—Aldridge appeared unsuccessfully at the Mud
Theatre in Baltimore." In his letter to Dr. James McCune Smith
of June 1860, Aldridge remarks specifically on the incorrectness
of this biographical reference and ends by saying, "I never was in
Baltimore." The likelihood is that after his early success in the
provinces and his inability to get important London engagements,
he may have considered tackling his native country once more, or
he may have considered it again after he had been commended
by Edmund Kean and had appeared at the Theatre Royal,
Covent Garden, but we have no record of any negotiations for
such a tour until 1867.

On 2nd December 1827 Ira Aldridge received his first official
recognition. The Government of the Republic of Haiti, at a
session in its capital, honoured "the first man of colour in the
theatre" with a commission in the Army of Haiti, in the 17th
Regiment of the Grenadier Guards of the President of the Republic, Boyer. It will be recalled that Aldridge played the role of
Christophe in *The Death of Christophe* during his first Coburg

engagement, and the denouement of the play is the taking over of power by President General Boyer. Maurice Lenihan, the Irish critic who knew Aldridge personally, wrote in the *Clonmel Advertiser* in January 1833: "... Among other high compliments that have been paid him, the House of Representatives of St. Domingo passed a unanimous vote in 1828 complimenting him on his successful progress in contradicting the assertion that his race is incapable of mental culture, and bestowed upon him a commission, with the rank of Captain, and Aide-de-Camp Extraordinary to His Excellency the [then] President Boyer. This honour was delivered to Mr. Aldridge through the Consul in London."

Nothing could be more appropriate than that the first State honour of the African Roscius should come from the first Negro Republic, from the slaves who fought against the greatest military genius of the age, Napoleon, and won; from the black people who produced such great men of world history as Toussaint L'Ouverture, Dessalines, and Christophe. In honouring a Negro actor thousands of miles away they were honouring a Negro who was fighting a lone battle, as they had fought, and was winning, as they had won.

The last appearance of Aldridge before receiving recognition from the black republic was in Liverpool, the greatest centre of the slave trade in the United Kingdom, where only three years before he had landed as an unknown, penniless stranger. One can imagine the feelings of the pro-slavery elements at the presumption of this Negro to appear in anti-slavery plays like *Oroonoko*, *The Revenge* and *The Padlock*, and furthermore to see a well-known star like Vandenhoff playing his Iago and a white woman, Miss F. H. Kelly, playing his Desdemona! Such a leap in so short a time was indeed something unparalleled in theatre history, as well as a unique challenge to racial superiority.

Once again we lose track of Aldridge—from 20th October 1827 to February 1829. It is possible that he was still touring the provinces, but that playbills and notices have not come to light thus far. The records in our possession are by no means complete. Inquiries made of the Haitian Government produced a reply which opens up the possibility, however remote, that Aldridge was in Haiti some time during this period. A letter from the Director of the National Archives of the Republic, Port au

Prince, date 11th January 1954, states in part: "It is of particular pleasure to me to inform you that Ira Aldridge, tragedian of great renown, effectively belonged to the Army of Haiti under the BOYER Government, according to certain documents. We have found his name in the list of soldiers of the 17th Regiment of Grenadiers who were present at the parade of 2nd December 1827." Whether he was there in person, or whether "effectively" means that he was represented by name only, we do not know. The last theatre playbill we have for 1827 places him at the Theatre Royal, Liverpool, on 20th October. He could have taken a ship for Haiti from that port and arrived in time to be present at the parade of 2nd December. In February 1829 we know that he is in England. It is hoped that this gap will one day be filled.

A King's Lynn (England) theatre playbill of 18th March 1829 announces:

Much disappointment having been occasioned by the sudden and unfortunate indisposition of the African Roscius on Saturday evening, and many persons having expressed a desire of witnessing his performance in *The Savage of the Desert* it is respectfully announced that he will have the honour of appearing (for this night only) in the character of KALKANCO.

This is followed by the usual note about Mathews's allusion to the African Theatre incident, and that Aldridge will sing "Opossum Up a Gum Tree" in character. We are told that *The Savage of the Desert* is an "entire new melodrama (in two acts) written expressly for the African Roscius by W. Roberds, Esq., interspersed with marches, dances, etc." Captain Welford, a shipwrecked mariner, is played by Mr. Hughes, Kalkanco, an African but formerly in the British Navy, played by the African Roscius, "positively his last appearance", and that "this piece abounds with interest, as each scene depicts that warmth of feeling and fidelity so often evinced by that species of beings who have been so dreadfully persecuted by despotic power".

After King's Lynn we find him in places as far apart as Norwich, Yarmouth, Bury, Hull, Richmond, and Belfast. It is in Belfast that he reaches the next important stage of his career, for here he plays with Charles Kean, the son of Edmund Kean. The elder

Kean was also fulfilling an engagement in Belfast at this time, and Aldridge must have made it a point to see him in the characters of Shylock, Othello, and Brutus, which he played in this city.

The local Press[4] carried the following advertisement:

THEATRE, BELFAST

For the Benefit of Mr. Kean, Jun., and last night of his performance, on which occasion the

AFRICAN ROSCIUS

will positively make his last appearance in Belfast and (by particular desire) will sing "Opossum Up a Gum Tree".

This present evening (Friday, July 10) will be presented (for the first time this season) the Comedy of

TOWN AND COUNTRY

Reuben Glenroy: Mr. Kean, Jun.

End of the Comedy, a dance by Miss Fairbrother, after which the musical after-piece (compressed into one act) of

THE PADLOCK

Mungo by the African Roscius, in which character he will sing the Negro's Lament, "Dear Heart, What a Terrible Life am I Led" and the dancing song, "Let Me, When My Heart a-Sinking".

Charles Kean had made his début at Drury Lane as Young Norval on 1st October 1827; a year later he had acted in Glasgow with his famous father and now, in 1829 in Belfast, he plays Iago to Aldridge's Othello, and Aldridge plays Aboan to Kean's Oroonoko—the slight, elegant, Eton-educated, classical actor with the weak voice and the speech defect, and the big, broad-shouldered, earthy, romantic Negro, self-educated (who, it was whispered, had been a servant to Wallack), with the rich, melodious voice and natural speech and action. Charles Kean did not play with Aldridge again.

On 9th July the Belfast playbill refers to Charles Mathews's parody of the African Theatre in New York:

THE CELEBRATED MATHEWS

having alluded to a Comic Incident in the career of the AFRICAN ROSCIUS, and founded on it one of his most whimsical Hits in his TRIP TO AMERICA, the Public are respectfully informed that (by particular desire of numerous Parties) the AFRICAN ROSCIUS will sing (in Character) the Celebrated Negro Melody of

OPOSSUM UP A GUM TREE

In the Course of the Evening the AFRICAN ROSCIUS will also sing an entire New Song entitled

THE NEGRO BOY

written expressly for him by J. Bisset, Esq., of Leamington Spa.

We have been unable to trace a copy of "The Negro Boy". James Bisset (1761-1832) was a prolific writer of verse, and the Leamington Spa Library possesses many manuscript notebooks of his numerous poems, ballads, reminiscences, and the like, but the song in question is not among them.

Two months later, a Mr. Gray tries to steal a bit of Aldridge's thunder. He (Mr. Gray) is having a busy season at the theatre in Scarborough, and on his benefit night, 29th September 1829, the playbill announces that he "will give an imitation of sketch of Mr. Mathews's TRIP TO AMERICA, comprising the most laughable of the stories, characters and adventures, including three original comic songs", of which one was "Opossum Up a Gum Tree". This is the only instance, to our knowledge, of another actor attempting this sketch, but how successful Mr. Gray was with it we do not know.

At about the time that these songs were introduced into his repertoire, Aldridge begins to deliver a "farewell address" on the last night of his engagement, in which he speaks directly to the audience, driving home even more directly than in many of his plays the plight of the slave and his hope of freedom.

Until his appearance in Dublin in 1831, when he was seen by Edmund Kean, he toured principally the northern circuits. In June 1829 we find him playing in Hull with Samuel Phelps (1804-78), who was to become one of the outstanding producers and actors of Shakespeare in the nineteenth century, then starting his career. We have two reviews of Aldridge's performances in Hull:

Theatre Royal: Mr. Butler appears to be determined, by providing a succession of novelties, to deserve well of his patrons. This week Mr. Keene, the African Roscius, has appeared in a succession of characters and, we are informed, with considerable success. The only opportunity we had of seeing him was on Wednesday evening as Zanga in Dr. Young's tragedy of *The Revenge*. The house was thin. The piece at all times drags on heavily, and on this occasion its want of interest in many scenes was increased by the inefficiency of some of the performers; but in spite of the disadvantages, Mr. Keene's performance, as a whole, did him great credit, and at least reached the level, if it did not rise above the ordinary standard. Perhaps he hardly gave sufficient prominence to the cool, calculating, diabolical malignity of the revengeful Moor. Indeed, there is no tendency to exaggeration—no rant or stage trick—observable in his actions or play. His person is tolerable, his face expressive, and his voice powerful and well-modulated; but his attitudes want grace and variety. The only other performers worthy of mention are Mr. Phelps as Don Alonzo and Mrs. Angel as Leonora.[5]

Mr. Keene, the African Roscius, is performing Oroonoko, Zanga, and Mungo here. We consider Mr. Keene to be an actor of great talent. We attended the theatre under the impression that the playing of Othello by a native African or, at least, one born of African parents and bearing an African complexion of the purest and deepest tint would turn out to be what is sometimes called in theatrical parlance "a gag". We were agreeably disappointed. Mr. Keene, though positively a Negro, is a gentleman and a man of education and could not have portrayed the character in a manner more intellectual if his face had been "as white as unsunned snow". There was not an individual present who did not honour his performance, long and even tedious as the tragedy is in parts, with most breathless attention. The applause was on several occasions given in reiterated peals. Mr. Keene's bursts of deep and impassioned feeling were at times completely electric. His voice and person are good and his action easy and graceful; the expression of his features is in keeping with the language he utters, and which he evidently feels as far as passion is concerned.[6]

An important aspect of Aldridge's acting emerges from these reviews—his style is more realistic than the general trend. He does not rant or exaggerate, he plays no stage tricks, and, despite the tediousness of parts of the play, which both critics point out, and the poor support of the other players, he holds the audience in "most breathless attention". Clearly, he believed in what he was doing, and thus gave reality to his role. Realism evolved on the English stage through its actors far in advance of realism in the drama, as was so brilliantly shown by Edmund Kean, and here Aldridge shows that he, too, can breathe life even into dry bones.

Continuously on the search for parts he could play as a coloured actor, Aldridge ransacked the whole repertoire of English theatre and spurned no play, however melodramatic, but eventually the number of such plays came to an end and he had to switch to parts not so coloured! Authors, on their part, introduced Negroes into plays because of their box-office appeal in those years of intense Abolitionist activity. One such was *The Castle Spectre*, by Mathew Gregory Lewis, which was first performed at Drury Lane in 1797. It epitomizes the Gothic drama and the features of the literature of the German romantic school. The author was fully aware of the puerility of much of his writing, and frankly admitted that he wrote for the box-office. In his Address to the Reader in the published *The Castle Spectre* in 1798, he said: "That Osmond is attended by Negroes is an anachronism, I allow; but from the great applause which Mr. Dowton constantly received in Hassan (a character which he played extremely well), I am inclined to think that the audience was not greatly offended at the impropriety. For my own part, I by no means repent the introduction of my Africans; I thought it would give a pleasing variety to the characters and dresses if I made my servants black; and could I have produced the same effect by making my heroine blue, blue I should have made her." It is obvious, however, that he chose black because of the sympathy of the English people toward the slave, and this may account for the "great applause" which Hassan constantly received.

The Castle Spectre is typical of the plays of that period in so far as it was a composite of many plays and characters. One character is based on Juliet's nurse, another on Sheridan's Father Paul; one scene is from the *Castle of Otranto*, another from Schiller's *The Robbers*, and so on! Today such a procedure would not be tolerated. "The pieces of Lewis", said Charles Rice, "are all of a meagre cast, the characters are monotonous, the language is forced, and a general sameness pervades the whole of the drama." Such was *The Castle Spectre*, the kind of play that could be made palatable only by the acting. Rice further remarks: "When a play of perfect construction is performed by inferior artists it palls upon the sense, and it stands to reason that when mediocrity is the standard of both play and player, the tediousness must be of double force."[7]

The role played by Aldridge in this romantic drama was that of Hassan, one of four African slaves captured by Osmond years before. At the time of the action of the play, the slaves serve Osmond as castle guards. Hassan is the most articulate of the Africans, and in several speeches throughout the play he gives voice to the sorrows and atrocities of slavery. These are spoken in confidence to his comrade, the slave, Saib, as the two stand watch in the torch-lit corridors of the grim castle. In one of these speeches Hassan bitterly recalls his happy youth in remote Africa. There he had been born, grown to manhood, worked and dreamed, until his seizure by the slave-traders and the violent separation from his wife, Samba:

> My heart once was gentle, once was good; but sorrows have broken it, insults have made it hard. I have been dragged from my native land; from a wife who was everything to me, to whom I was everything! Twenty years have elapsed since these Christians tore me away; they trampled upon my heart, mocked my despair, and when in frantic terms I raved of Samba, laughed, and wondered how a Negro's soul could feel. In that moment, when the last point of Africa faded from my views—when, as I stood on the vessel's deck, I felt that all I loved was to me lost for ever— in that bitter moment did I banish humanity from my breast. I tore from my arm the bracelet of Samba's hair; I gave to the waves that precious token; and while the high waves swift bore it from me, vowed aloud endless hatred to mankind. I have kept my oath; I will keep it.

Hassan describes the terrible ostracism which the Negro slave suffers in the white world:

> Am I not branded with scorn? Am I not marked out for dishonour? Was I not free, and am I not a slave? Was I not once beloved, and am I not now despised? What man, did I tender my service, would accept the Negro's friendship? What woman, did I talk of affection, would not turn from the Negro with disgust? Yet, in my own dear land, my friendship was courted, my love was returned. I had parents, children, wife! Bitter thought! In one moment all were lost to me! Can I remember this, and not hate these white men? Can I think how cruelly they have wronged me, and not rejoice when I see them suffer?

For "ill-starred Hassan", as his comrades call him, the only answer to the slave's suffering is to nurture an implacable passion for vengeance upon the oppressors. When he utters the words of vengeance, we hear an echo of Shylock, the Jew, a role Aldridge was soon to portray with equal realism.

Another of Aldridge's vehicles was *Paul and Virginia*, a musical drama by James Cobb, with music by Mazzinghi and Reeve, in which all the characters, including the slave, Alambra, played by Aldridge, have singing parts. It was written in 1800 and is typical of the many musical pieces and dramas in which the adventures of the hero and heroine were interwoven with anti-slavery sentiments. Alambra is a runaway slave who appeals for aid from the hero and heroine, Paul and Virginia. They intercede for him, and after the usual adventures the slave sets out to rescue both his rescuers in a thrilling last scene in which their ship is not only hurled on to the rocks by a tropical storm, but catches fire as well! Of course, everyone is saved and all join with Alambra in a song of rejoicing as a beautiful rainbow appears in the sky! The part added nothing to the development of Aldridge's acting.

He is now beginning to exhaust the number of Negro characters in existing dramatic literature, and the question arises: What next? What roles other than black can he attempt? So comes to mind the first play in which he ever took part—*Pizarro*—in which he had played the role of Rolla, a Peruvian hero, in the African Theatre with a full Negro company. According to our records, Aldridge's first performance of Rolla in England took place on 3rd October 1827 at the Theatre Royal, Lancaster.

This is the most revolutionary step taken by Aldridge so far in his career—indeed, by the black man in his advance into "white" culture.

Genest says: "Never was a speech better calculated to entrap applause than Rolla's address to the soldiers. Its primary object was evidently to reprobate the principles of the French Revolution, yet nothing is said that might not be addressed to the Peruvians with propriety."[8] Its opening performance at Drury Lane in 1799 had indeed a galaxy of stars: John Philip Kemble played Rolla, Charles Kemble was Alonzo, Mrs. Jordan, Alonzo's wife, Cora, Mr. Barrymore, Pizarro, leader of the Spaniards, and Mrs. Siddons, Elvira, his mistress.

The story is based on the struggle of the Peruvian people against the Spanish invaders led by Pizarro. Rolla is the army commander who leads the defending Peruvians into battle. The selection of this revolutionary role for Aldridge's first amateur performance in New York is significant. Rolla's rousing orations to his oppressed people are a foreshadowing of his future career in Europe—the voice of a people crying out, demanding, challenging, uncompromising.

It is in Kendal, on 23rd August 1830, that Aldridge essays his first white *European* role, that of Captain Dirk Hatteraick in *Guy Mannering*, adapted from Sir Walter Scott's novel by Daniel Terry in collaboration with the author. This was the first of Scott's novels to be dramatized. The growing demand for novelty and dramatic material had already, in the second half of the seventeenth century, started the dramatization of novels, but it was not until Scott's time that the whole field of fiction was eagerly and systematically ransacked, as Nicoll points out in his *History of English Drama*. *Rob Roy* was perhaps the most popular of these adaptations, a part which Aldridge also plays later on.

"With a countenance bronzed by a thousand conflicts with the north east wind", Hatteraick is a Dutch sea Captain, "prodigiously muscular, strong and thick-set". He commands a lugger named the *Yungfrauw Hagenslaapen*, which is engaged in smuggling contraband goods into Scotland. Confidante of the rugged Captain is the dark-skinned gipsy woman, Meg Merrilies, said to be a notorious witch. Together they outwit the Customs officials. Through a series of adventures, Hatteraick flaunts his lawlessness, singing Dutch sea chanties all the while, and laughing heartily and fearlessly. He finally cheats the law of his execution by committing suicide in jail. The role is a rollicking one, somewhat grim and brutal, but it will be noticed that it is a role into which Aldridge can once more inject defiance, gusto, and power, as well as that comic richness and natural expression in song that is his Negro heritage. This version was interspersed with verses by Burns and Wordsworth, and the whole set to music by Bishop.

We have no reviews of this, his first white part, but he has clearly chosen with care a role in which to display his talents. We learn from later accounts that in playing white parts he used

white make-up and a wig, possibly a beard in this case, that completely transformed the black into white. Being a Dutch character, any faults of English diction which he may still have had
would not have been too apparent. As far as we know, this role
did not become a regular part of his repertoire.

From the northern circuits, Aldridge now went, in March
1830, to the west and played at the Theatre Royal, Bristol, that
lovely Georgian theatre, now the home of the Bristol Old Vic.
Here is included another West Indian melodrama, *Obi, or Three-
fingered Jack*, which had also been in the repertoire of the African
Theatre and which was long to remain in Aldridge's repertoire.
From a Northampton playbill we get the following information
about this production:

> A new and beautiful Melodrama, founded on fact, and written
> expressly for the African Roscius by J. Murray, Esq. . . . This
> interesting melodrama is founded on an actual occurrence in the
> West Indies. Jack, or Karfa, which was his real name, became the
> terror of the Negroes, and there were many white people who
> believed him to be possessed of supernatural powers. Allured by
> the rewards offered by the Governor, Dalling, in a proclamation
> dated December 12, 1780, two Negroes named Sam and Quashee
> went in search of him, taking with them a little boy of good
> spirit, and surprised Jack while roasting plantains in his cave or
> hut. The moment was awful, but after a desperate struggle in
> which Jack, getting the better of Quashee, was about to give him
> his death wound, the boy shot him, and Sam, perceiving him
> still able for mischief, finally dispatched him.

So much for the playbill. In point of fact, the play is a melodrama version of a pantomimic drama written by John Fawcett
long before Aldridge and J. Murray! It is said that while reading
a *Treatise on Sugar* he was inspired by a tale of Jamaica to compose
Obi for the Haymarket Theatre, where it was first performed on
2nd July 1800. For some reason, Jack's mother, named on the bill
as the "Obi Woman", was always played by a man. Willson
Disher says: "The Obi Woman caused one actor who played her
to be known as 'O. Smith' all his life and after . . . and Jack, a
ferocious, fugitive slave thirsting for revenge against the killers of
his wife and children in Africa, was so much more credible than
any Gothic Blue Beard that he begat a line of villains with a

justifiable hatred of humanity."[9] What is not apparent on the playbill is here explained—again the Rebel with a Cause, as against, say, Bertram, a Gothic Blue Beard.

The next full-length play in his repertoire is the Reverend R. C. Maturin's *Bertram, or the Castle of St. Aldobrand*, another European role, first performed by Aldridge, to our knowledge, at the Theatre Royal, Derby, on 9th May 1831. This play was recommended by Lord Byron to Drury Lane, where it was produced on 9th May 1816 with Edmund Kean in the title role. The hero is a count who, after the machinations of his enemy, St. Aldobrand, becomes a pirate. In his absence his beloved, Imogine, marries St. Aldobrand to save her sire from ruin. Bertram, the outcast, is wrecked near the castle of the wedded pair; the erstwhile lovers meet, Imogine forgets duty to her husband, allows herself to be seduced by Bertram, who kills St. Aldobrand, whereupon Imogine goes mad and dies, whereupon Bertram kills himself!

It may seem strange to us today that such works could have been highly praised, and that high hopes were held out for the dramatists who wrote them. However, some critics were aware of the weaknesses of *Bertram*, as may be seen, for example, from the following review in the *Devonport Telegraph* some fifteen years later, and which also serves to show how Aldridge managed to make acceptable the horror and frenzy of such a "Gothic tragedy":

> Maturin's play of *Bertram* was performed on Monday night and introduced the African Roscius to us in a new light. If possible his genius shone more conspicuously than ever. The character of Bertram is a terrific exemplification of human passion, and it is only in the hands of such a person as Mr. Aldridge that it could be at all tolerated by a discriminating audience—because the dialogues do not possess the power of exciting either sympathy or regret; and the author appears to gloat solely on the dark and malignant side of the human character. But the African Roscius, as well as the immortal Kean, has made the piece somewhat acceptable, by the true representation he has given of the revengeful and despairing Bertram. We particularly refer to the dialogue between the Prior and Bertram, when he learns from him that he is in the neighbourhood of his mortal enemy, St. Aldobrand:
>
> > Oh! that I could but mate him in his might,
> > Oh! that we were on the dark wave together,

With but one plank between us and destruction,
That I might grasp him in these desperate arms,
And plunge with him among the weltering billows,
And view him grasp for life—and—
Ha, ha, I see him struggling,
I see him—ha, ha, ha!

The demoniac manner in which he delivered these lines caused a thrill of horror in the house, and such a terrible sensation, that we forgot for a moment that all was delusion. And, in the last act, when he is closeted with the corpse of his victim, Aldobrand, whom he murdered, in reply to the Prior he says—

I am the murderer. Wherefore are you come;
Wist you whence I come!
The tomb—where dwell the dead—and I dwell with him,
Till sense of life devolved away with me.
I am amazed to see ye living men,
I deemed that when I struck the final blow
Mankind expired, and we were left alone—
The corpse and I were left alone together,
The only tenants of a blasted world.

He exceeded, in the delivery of these lines all the great actors of the day. We can never sufficiently give that meed of praise to this great man to which his merits entitle him; for we could not witness him in a single scene in the play without feeling a shuddering horror creep along the veins. We congratulate Mr. Doel for his enterprise in securing this most extraordinary auxiliary.

Here we have the first clear statement by a critic of Aldridge's growing power and ability to terrify an audience with his realism which later, like with Kean, affected even his fellow-actors.

In August 1831 he is playing in Scarborough, and at this time is published, for the first time in pamphlet form, a commentary on his acting, the title page of which reads:

A CRITIQUE
of the
PERFORMANCE OF OTHELLO
by
F. W. KEENE ALDRIDGE,
The African Roscius

—"Mislike me not for my complexion
I' the shadow'd liv'ry of the burnish'd sun."*

SHAKESPEARE

By the Author of "The Talents of Edmund Kean
Delineated"; "Biographical Account of Master Herbert,
the Infant Roscius," &c.

SCARBOROUGH
Printed (only 30 copies) for John Cole
1831

John Cole was celebrated in his day as the historian and anti-
quarian of Scarborough, as well as its chief librarian, publisher,
and dramatic critic. We give the full text of this pamphlet:†

On Friday evening we were called upon to witness a perfect
novelty in the department of theatricals, for such may be considered the acting of a man of colour, whether good or otherwise,
but the African Roscius is certainly an actor of genius. His complexion is deeply tinctured with Afric's ray of shade; his figure is
tall, manly and muscular; and he is in the very vigour of manhood,
being only in his 25th year. His pronunciation of the English
language is as perfectly correct as that of a native, and his voice
possesses great power, with intonations of an intuitive order,
and which genius only can display; indeed, it is our opinion,
that for every variety of intonation and inflection of the voice,
there cannot be rules given, for the orator of true genius can
throw out from the feelings of the soul such refrangibility of
reflection (if we may be allowed to use these optical allusions) as
beggars the rules of art. The tragedy selected for performance on
Friday evening was Shakespeare's *Othello*: the hero by the African
Roscius. Novel, imposing, and sublime was the first sight of the
Moor, personated as he was by the sable African. So effective was
the commencement before a word was spoken. The intonations
of deep and sweet melody were however soon added to the
grandeur of his personal appearance, and every trait of the noble-
minded and generous Moor was afterward presented in appropriate and conspicuous style. His second *entre* was princely, and the
immediate interview with Desdemona peculiarly attractive; the

* The first use of this quotation (here slightly misquoted!) in connection
with Aldridge, which later was used in the *Memoir* and other printed matter.
† Source: the British Museum.

tone of love was tenderly uttered, and here the African Roscius met with judicious support from his Desdemona, Mrs. Edwards. His acting during the brawl was animated; and the subsequent risings of jealousy were defined in a masterly manner; the dashed and hurried spirits being troublously portrayed. His next meeting with Desdemona was of a heart-rending description, and his exit from the scene most piteous.

> "Farewell the plumed troop"

was pathetically delivered, and the whole of that portion of the tragedy in which this beautiful soliloquy occurs strikingly impassioned. The scene in which arises the contention respecting the handkerchief was acted by the African Roscius in a highly embittered tone of jealous "well-painted passion". The internal commotions of despair, displayed in the last act of the tragedy, with the occasional accompanying "fury of words", were pictured with great force and feeling; and upon the whole we consider *Othello*, as played by the African Roscius, a performance enriched with the brilliancy of genius. We must not in justice omit to observe that the Emilia of Mrs. Brooks was very spirited.

The first autograph letter in our possession was written by Aldridge to John Cole. He was at the Theatre Royal, Northampton, on 23rd September 1831 doing *Obi* and *Othello*, and writes on the back of the playbill:

DEAR SIR,—According to promise I embrace this favourable opportunity to address you, but am extremely sorry to be the communicator of unwelcome news, but such is the case. Mr. Marshall's child has been for the last ten days afflicted with an inflammation of the chest from which it suffered greatly. It baffled medical aid. Death brought its sufferings to a close yesterday about midday. I therefore need not tell you the affliction they are all plunged in. They are however as well under existing circumstances as can be expected, and desire to be affectionately remembered to you and your family, who I hope are in the enjoyment of that inestimable blessing, Health.

You will perceive by the bill I am announced but for one night. Through the carelessness of the Post Office I did not receive my letter which was written on the 31st of August until the 15th of Septr. the season being just at its close. There was but one night vacant. I however accepted it and had a highly flattering reception and expect to act tomorrow night if permission can be obtained from the proper authorities, their licence having expired. I was very successful at Hull. I act three nights at Leicester and then go to town where you shall hear from me through Messrs. Longman & Co. Until then Adieu, wishing you health and happiness.

That he was "very successful at Hull" is borne out by the fact that he stayed at the Royal Adelphi long enough to play no less than sixteen roles in the following plays: *Othello; The Padlock; The Merchant of Venice; The Brigand, or Alessandro Massaroni; The Slave; Oroonoko; Pizarro; Bertram; Bond of Blood; Obi, or Three-fingered Jack; The African's Vengeance; Paul and Virginia; The Siberian Exile; The Coronation Day of William IV; Valentine and Orson; Rob Roy.*

Six months later, after Dublin and Bath, he is back in Hull, once more trying out new parts, over a period of almost seven weeks, first at the Adelphi, then, on 20th March 1832, moving into the Royal Clarence on Queen Street. He repeats most of the plays previously done, and adds: *The Galley Slaves; Macbeth; The Cannibal King; Father and Son, or The Rock of La Charbonniere; Castle Spectre; Laugh While You Can; Banks of the Hudson, or The Congress Trooper; William Tell; The French Pirate; Frankenstein, or The Man and Monster.*

On 3rd April he offers his services in a benefit for Mr. Jarvis, and on his own benefit night he makes his first appearance as Richard III. This period in Hull is obviously the most intense concentration of try-outs, historically establishing Ira Aldridge as the first Negro to play white roles. It is significant that Aldridge chose Hull as a testing-ground for so many of his new roles, particularly his first white Shakespearean parts. It will be remembered that this was the birthplace and home of Wilberforce, and sympathy would be strong for the young Negro actor, especially in this period when Wilberforce was still leading the fight in the House of Commons for the abolition of slavery in the Colonies. Despite the fact that he found great public support, we have no newspaper reviews of these crowded months of pioneer work. The newspapers of the period covered only the Theatre Royal, and Aldridge played in the Adelphi and Royal Clarence. Later we shall see what an impact his playing of Shylock, Lear, and Macbeth made on his Continental audiences and what Gautier had to say about his transformation into a white man, but at this time we are given no information either about his portrayal of Shylock, Macbeth, and Richard III or his handling of the matter of make-up.

The question of make-up of Negroes in white character parts is a controversial one, particularly in the United States, where the issue presents itself more forcibly than elsewhere. Several plays were produced some years ago in which Negro actors were cast for white parts, and in the preliminary discussion on make-up some were strongly of the opinion that the actor should not whiten his skin, while others believed just as strongly that this procedure would be utterly absurd. But in the few plays where this concept was carried out (and we particularly recall a fine performance in New York by the very gifted Negro actress, Alice Childress, who played the part of a Jewish mother), as soon as the action got under way and the first moment of resistance and strangeness was over, the actor's convincing interpretation of the role soon made the audience forget the colour of skin, and the play proceeded naturally and successfully. From all that can be gathered, it is safe to say that in the matter of make-up Aldridge based himself primarily on the demands of the play and not his own desire to appear as a Negro in these roles.

We can offer little or no information about many of Aldridge's plays. Some were not printed, and the original texts used are no longer available. Others, like *The Coronation Day of William IV*, were strictly topical and probably more of a pageant than a play. Nothing is known of *The Galley Slaves*, *The African's Vengeance*, *Bond of Blood* and *The French Pirate*. They were most likely hack works by the local manager or his resident dramatist, probably pirate versions under different titles of better-known plays. Even the traceable plays were often performed in vastly different versions from those seen originally in London.

About *Rob Roy*, Genest tells us it is a romantic drama in three acts with songs, written by George Sloane and founded on Scott's novel, "but so many changes are made that one is disappointed and consequently disgusted". It was first acted at Drury Lane in 1818. *The Siberian Exile*, a version of *The Exile, or The Deserts of Siberia*, an opera in three acts first acted at Covent Garden in 1808, was written by Frederick Reynolds, with music by Mazzinghi and Bishop. According to Genest, it met with success vastly beyond its deserts. *The Brigand, or Alessandro Massaroni*, a romantic

drama in two acts by J. R. Planche, was first performed at Drury
Lane in November 1829. According to one playbill, "the hero
of the piece is a sort of Italian Robin Hood, Chief of a lawless
band, investing the mountains near Rome. No place was secure
from his emissaries; and so skilful were his disguises that he was
frequently made the confidant of plots laid by his enemies to
entrap him. Such an air of gallantry and chivalry accompanies his
depredations that they were frequently the theme of laudatory
rhymes; and those who paid the dearest for his pranks were often
the first to laugh at his humour." One can just picture Aldridge
in such a role.

Valentine and Orson, a romantic melodrama in two acts, was
written by Thomas John Dibdin, son of Charles Dibdin the Elder.
Both were prolific writers and producers of burlettas and romantic dramas and melodramas of their period. This play was first
produced in Covent Garden in 1804 and acclaimed "one continued scene of unmitigated splendour". It was primarily a spectacle with combats, banquets, and processions, half in dialogue
and half in dumb show. The story is of twins, Valentine and
Orson, who had been lost in a forest by their mother, sister of a
king. One, Valentine, becomes a knight and seeks the hand of a
princess, but forswears her until he can prove that "gentle blood
flows in his veins". To do this he must find his twin brother, and
in elaborate dumb show and spectacle he tracks him down to the
woods, where he finds "a wild man of the woods" cherishing an
old she-bear who had suckled him. It is Orson. They have a
fierce combat (another spectacle), until Orson sees himself reflected
in the polished shield and realizes with whom he is fighting.
Valentine defeats Orson by threatening to kill the poor old bear,
who conveniently dies after Orson has been bound. He is brought
to the court, taught civilized habits, how to shake hands, etc.
When the Princess greets Valentine with an embrace, Orson
wants to do the same, and is much displeased at being repulsed.
This is enough of the plot to indicate the flavour of the play,
which held favour with actors and public over a long period of
time.

Frankenstein, or The Man and the Monster is a version of Mary
Shelley's story by H. M. Milner, first seen at the Coburg in July
1826. *The Banks of the Hudson* was first produced at the Coburg
in December 1829; *Father and Son, or The Rock of La Charbonniere*,

a musical drama by Edward Fitzball, Covent Garden, February 1825; *Laugh While You Can*, a comedy by Frederick Reynolds, first produced at Covent Garden, December 1798. As we have previously pointed out, it is not necessarily in the original versions of these plays that Aldridge performed.

Aldridge had written a farewell address which he distributed to the audiences on his farewell benefit nights. So here too on 2nd April 1832, the night he first plays *William Tell*, by James Sheridan Knowles (Drury Lane, May 1825), the announcements tell us that a poem, *William Tell, the Swiss Patriot*, written by the African Roscius, will be delivered gratuitously to each person on entering the theatre on his benefit at the Royal Clarence Theatre, Hull.

When Aldridge tackles verse he is hardly successful, sinking into the merest doggerel, but it still contains the spirit of the struggle for freedom and must have had its impact on his working-class audience. The following bit is sufficient to show at least his sentiments at the age of twenty-five, in the period when Chartism was gathering power and the fight against slavery in the British Colonies was nearing a successful conclusion:

> My bow! (they give the bow) Tried friend in danger,
> Thou's ever played me true;
> I risk my all upon thy power—
> Life—son—yea, country, too;
> To free my brethren, fetter'd slaves,
> From sinking in inglorious graves. . . .
>
> And should my forc'd and trembling hand
> Destroy my beauteous son,
> Come, vengeance! with thy scatheful brand,
> And make the race be run
> Of that pale tyrant, withering slave
> Who freedom sinks in bloody grave.

Shades of Pyramus and Thisbe!

CHAPTER VII

"*Something So Absurd About It*"

IN December 1831 Aldridge reached one of the high points of his career—Dublin—and the notice and commendation of Edmund Kean. Today Dublin is noted mainly for the writer-geniuses it produced—Wilde, Synge, Shaw, O'Casey, Joyce, Yeats, and its honoured Abbey Theatre, but in those days it was a great provincial capital (second only to London), the key theatre centre of the Irish circuit, and a city of aristocratic life and pomp, with its Lord Lieutenant and his court. The dissolution of the Irish Parliament in 1800 and the Act of Union which made London its capital, had a serious effect on the development of the drama in Ireland. "Between four and five hundred families of rank and opulence which once were residents are no longer to be found in it. . . . Formerly two theatres royal and a circus were supported in Dublin with a proportional exhibition of other spectacles. Now [1818] one solitary playhouse finds encouragement though duly supplied with first-rate performers from London."[1]

In 1822 famine had reduced the population by about one-half; by 1847, the year of the great famine, almost all the nobility and the wealthy had left Dublin, and theatre audiences consisted almost entirely of workers and the lower middle class. Those sophisticated patrons who were still there in the early 1820s began to desert the drama for opera—particularly Italian opera, which first came to Dublin in 1829.

Aldridge arrived in December 1831 to play at the Theatre Royal, Hawkins Street, the only important theatre in Dublin in the nineteenth century. Most of the great foreign actors had appeared on its boards, and though much of the glory and glamour had gone, Dublin was still a magnet for the stars.

In November 1830 John William Calcraft became manager of the Theatre Royal. He had given up an army career to become an actor, and made his first appearance in Edinburgh in 1819 as

Iago to Edmund Kean's Othello, and there he remained playing leading parts until he went to Dublin in 1824. The *Memoir* relates that Aldridge made repeated unsuccessful efforts by letter to get an engagement at Dublin, but could not prevail upon Calcraft to accept the services of a man of colour; there was "something so absurd about it". But Aldridge was not daunted. He made a special trip and had a personal interview with Calcraft, who was sufficiently impressed to engage him.

"Edmund Kean", continues the *Memoir*, "had been previously secured to appear at this theatre and the management endeavoured to dissuade Mr. Aldridge from taking the part of Othello, as the celebrated tragedian was known to complain if his favourite characters were played just previous to his acting them himself. Mr. Aldridge was urged to come forward as Zanga, but he persisted in playing Othello and had his way."

"We live in an age of novelties", said *Saunders's News Letter* on 7th December 1831, "and the one which Calcraft brings before the Dublin audience this evening is not the least singular we have heard of in these days of wonders, an actor of colour *par excellence*. The African Roscius will make his first appearance here in the character of Othello." And Calcraft announces at the same time:

THEATRE ROYAL
Singular Novelty

First Appearance of the celebrated African Roscius (actor of colour). Mr. Calcraft, anxious to gratify the patrons of the theatre has the honour of announcing the most singular novelty in the Theatrical World, viz., an actor of colour, known throughout America by the appellation of The African Roscius. His success induced him to visit England, where he has uniformly there received the most marked applause in all the principal theatres throughout the Kingdom.

The next morning *Saunders's News Letter* confessed that—

we were agreeably surprised at the excellent manner in which he portrayed the jealous Moor. This stranger exhibited as perfect a picture of the workings of the human mind, under the influence of the "green-eyed monster" as we have—we may freely say— for a long time witnessed. His face, truly African, darkened by a tropical sun, in no wise concealed the workings of the passions—

99

a bright and intellectual eye gives an expression to his countenance, which could not fail to produce a marked effect. His voice
harmonious, and capable of the most effective modulation, made
every passage tell, delivered, as they were, with good taste and
precision. We were pleased to see in his acting a complete freedom
from that ranting and "tearing of passions to tatters" which those
who strain too much after upper-gallery applause so constantly
display. After the tragedy concluded Mr. Stanley came forward
to announce the performance of De Begnis and the Italian
Company for this evening, but he could not obtain a hearing
from the loud calls made for the African, who, after some time,
came forward, apparently with considerable diffidence at the
novel situation in which he was placed, and in a very handsome
manner returned thanks for the warm reception he, a stranger,
had met with on his first appearance before a Dublin audience.

Freeman's Journal said that they had seen "few so good im-
personators of this fine character . . . all his points he accurately
conceives and judiciously delivers—sometimes even sublime—
always good—never so low as mediocrity, and had he physical
power equal to his mental capacity there would not, we firmly
believe, be a better Othello on the stage".

"The African Roscius is an actor whose faults can be easily
perceived", said the *Morning Post*, "but whose general good acting
gives a colour to the whole that renders his performance extremely attractive. In the scene where Iago instils the poison into
his mind, the African Roscius discovered much originality. In
the closing scene his acting was peculiarly imposing, and the
applause which attended his exertions throughout the whole of
his performance was enthusiastic and general."

The *Dublin Comet* frankly said that they had screwed their
courage to the sticking point, not believing that any man of
colour could do a Moor of Venice justice, but that after the play
commenced "away flew all our preconceived notions and prejudices. His performance through the whole play was so chaste,
so judicious and so completely Shakespearean that we doubt we
shall ever again look upon the personation of Othello so entirely
fulfilling all that we could imagine of the perfection of acting."

On the 13th he portrayed Zanga, and *Saunders's News Letter*
reports that "after the curtain fell the gods were uproarious for
him to come forward, which he did, but properly bowed them

out of the expected speech—having entered at the left wing, he made his most respectful obeisances as he crossed the stage, and went off at the opposite side without saying a word".

The stock company during this season included the talented Mary Huddart (Mrs. Warner), who later held an important place in the London theatres. It is an interesting sidelight that, years after they played together in Dublin, their sons attended the same school, and in a letter to Dr. Smith in June 1860, Aldridge wrote: ". . . My son, who has just entered his thirteenth year, is at the Collegiate School of Camden Town, and is a great favourite with his masters, who entered a high opinion of his mental capabilities. Out of thirty-seven competitors for two elocutionary prizes, a son of the late Mrs. Warner, aged seventeen, took the first, and Ira Daniel (named after my dear father) took the second."

In this season at the Theatre Royal, Dublin, Edmund Kean immediately followed Aldridge; in fact, their engagements overlapped, Aldridge's last and benefit performance being on 21st December, and Kean's opening being on 19th December. They played with the same actors and in several of the same roles, circumstances which made appraisal of their relative merits easier than if they had each brought their own company.

There is no evidence of any kind that the paths of Ira Aldridge and Edmund Kean crossed before this time—December 1831, in Dublin—though the story has persisted throughout the years that Edmund Kean, while on tour in America, "discovered" Ira Aldridge, engaged him as his valet, took him back with him to England, and gave him his start in the theatrical world. It is, however, not difficult to see how this legend originated.

It is true that Edmund Kean made two American tours, with engagements in New York, and it is also true that Kean was of some professional assistance to Aldridge, as we shall soon see, but the timing of these events precludes any possibility of this romantic tale being correct.

Kean's first visit to New York was in 1820, when Ira was a boy of thirteen. We know that the lad haunted the theatres and managed to obtain some employment which brought him back-stage, but he would never have had an opportunity to impress that great celebrity with his unusual dramatic ability, assuming that he even possessed it at that age. Moreover, he could not have accompanied Kean when he returned to England the next year, because there is ample evidence to show that Aldridge did not leave the States until several years later. Kean's second visit to New York was in September 1825, when Aldridge was already in London. It is safe to say that the possibility of any contact between them in America, other than that of a stage-struck youth gazing upon an idol, may for all time be dismissed, and it is hoped that reputable encyclopaedias, biographical dictionaries, and other sources will not perpetuate this misinformation. It is also frequently stated that Edmund Kean played Iago to Aldridge's Othello. There is no evidence that they ever played together, and this misstatement no doubt arises from the fact that *Charles* Kean, in Belfast in July 1829, appeared as Iago to Aldridge's Othello, and in *Oroonoko* Kean played the title role and Aldridge supported him as Aboan.

In this Dublin season of 1831-2 Edmund Kean appeared in the following roles:

19th December: Richard III
20th December: Shylock
22nd December: Othello
23rd December: Sir Giles Overreach in *A New Way to Pay Old Debts*
24th and 26th December: Lucius Junius Brutus in *Brutus*
27th December: King Lear
28th December: Sir Edward Mortimer in *The Iron Chest*
31st December: Reuben Glenroy in *Town and Country*
2nd January: (benefit) Act IV, *Richard III*
                    Act IV, *Merchant of Venice*
                    Act V, *A New Way to Pay Old Debts*
                    Act II, *Macbeth*
                    Act III, *Othello*
5th January: Hamlet

Aldridge undoubtedly took advantage of this opportunity to see the great tragedian in so many of his best roles. Kean did not play on 21st December, that being Aldridge's benefit night, when he did *The Slave* and *The Padlock*.

An unsigned article in the *Dublin University Magazine* of October 1868 on the History of the Theatre Royal, Dublin, says that "when Edmund Kean saw the African play Othello he sent

for him and complimented him highly. But", the writer hastens
to add, "Kean, when sober, praised everybody. When drunk or
approaching thereto he called all his professional brethren
humbugs." Without comment, we quote the passage in this
article dealing with Aldridge:

On Dec. 7, 1831, the African Roscius, as he was then called,
subsequently known as the Chevalier Ira Aldridge, knight of
several Continental orders never heard of before, was first presented to the public of Dublin. He often visited Ireland after, was
always much applauded, but not particularly attractive. He had a
considerable talent, spoke better English than many who are
"native and to the manner born". Some reports gave him the
adventures and lineage of an Oroonoko. Other accounts reduced
him to a manual origin and said he had been James Wallack's
servant in America. In either case he had received considerable
education. He was not an absolute Negro, but a very dark
mulatto. . . . He appeared the first night as Othello, the second
as Zanga in *The Revenge*, and Alhambra in *Paul and Virginia*. In
the last named part he introduced a nigger melody of the comic
order called "Possum Up a Gum Tree", which elicited more
enthusiastic applause than the lofty declamations of the royal
Moor. His other characters were Mungo and Gambia. His tragic
style was subdued and pathetic rather than fiery or impulsive.
His features were forbidding, in addition to the colour, yet he
found a white woman to marry him. Whether like the gentle
daughter of Brabantio she was won by the story of his life we
cannot say, but she was not a Desdemona either in youth or beauty.
When Edmund Kean saw the African play Othello he sent for him
and complimented him highly. . . .

Not only did Kean compliment him, but, what was more
practical, wrote a letter recommending him to the Manager of
the Theatre Royal, Bath, one of the fashionable theatre centres of
the day. The letter was written from Dublin, 3rd January 1832,
and read:

DEAR BELLAMY,—I beg to introduce to your notice Mr. Aldridge,
the African Roscius, whose performances I have witnessed with
great pleasure. He possesses wondrous versatility, and I am sure,
under your judicious generalship, will prove a card in Bath. I
have not yet recovered from the fatigues of my journey, but hope
to be myself in a day or two. I remain, dear Bellamy, truly yours,
                                                        E. KEAN.

The reference to his "wondrous versatility" suggests that Kean saw him in a variety of roles, including Mungo. Considering that Kean did not possess such versatility, this effort on behalf of the young actor is indeed generous, and the *Memoir* pays due tribute, saying he gave the letter "with the good nature conspicuous in all he did".

S. Durylin, in his very fine essay, appears to have misinterpreted this letter, possibly because of misleading translation. In commenting on the relationship between the Keans, father and son, and Aldridge, he evidently based himself on the *Memoirs of E. F. Yunge* (Mrs. Ekaterina Fyodorovna Tolstoya Yunge, daughter of Count Fyodor Tolstoy). It was at the home of the Tolstoys in St. Petersburg that Aldridge met the Ukrainian poet and artist, Taras Shevchenko, and Mrs. Yunge, then a young girl, acted as their interpreter. Durylin quotes the following passage from Mrs. Yunge's *Memoirs*:

> I remember how they were both very moved one evening when I related to Aldridge the history of Shevchenko and translated to Shevchenko the life of the tragedian from his own words. . . . In order to get into the theatre, Aldridge became a lackey to a certain actor. You can imagine how much suffering he had to go through and how much energy he had to use in order finally to achieve recognition and that, too, not in his own country. Even in England prejudices against the people of a darker race were so powerful that the actor Kean (son or nephew of the famous Kean—I don't remember), learning that Aldridge was engaged to play in the very theatre where he was, angrily refused to play on the same stage with a despised "nigger".[2]

Commenting on this, Durylin says: "It is hard to imagine that the attitude of the elder Kean was much different from that of his son." And referring to the letter to Bellamy, he says: "Kean recommends Aldridge to this theatrical *entrepreneur* for two reasons—one, Aldridge is talented, but he will be a success 'if you assume the task of his tutor', and at the same time he wants him out of Dublin, where he is overshadowing him. Once Aldridge is out the way, Kean will become Kean again after two or three performances."

As we have seen, Charles Kean did play with Aldridge in Belfast in 1829, and nowhere is there any indication of prejudice;

moreover, a glance at the characters of both Keans reveals that their views were, for the most part, at variance rather than in harmony. We also do not share Durylin's opinion that Kean wanted Aldridge out of Dublin because he was being over-shadowed. Both actors were there two weeks, Kean following Aldridge, and it is doubtful whether Aldridge would have wanted to go on again after Kean, even assuming that Calcraft or any other manager would have made such an arrangement. Aldridge would, in normal course, go on to another theatre after finishing in Dublin. Actually, he was already booked for a long season in Hull and the northern circuit, beginning in February, and as a result of Kean's recommendation he received an immediate engagement in Bath, where he appeared on 19th January. This is not to say that Aldridge was not the victim of racial prejudice. The following extract from the aforementioned article in the *Dublin University Magazine* illustrates the kind of attack to which he was subjected even in an enlightened country:

Theatre Royal, Dublin, Season 1833-34. In the course of this season, during the visit of Mme. Celeste, the African Roscius was announced. Celeste's husband, a Mr. Elliott, since dead, at that time accompanied her and superintended all her engage-ments. He was a *Yankee* of the genuine type, shrewd, sharp in worldly matters, overflowing with the inconsistencies of trans-Atlantic liberalism. One morning he came into the manager's [Calcraft] office rather abruptly and under apparent excitement. The following conversation ensued:
"I see you have announced the African?"
"Yes."
"My wife shall not play with him."
"Why not?"
"Because he's a nigger."
"I am not alive to the objection. I am no negrophilist nor do I denounce a man because he happens to be black."
"You are an odd people in this country. In America we don't associate with blacks."
"Neither do we, as a national habit. But he is a good actor and the public like him. His colour is nothing to me, though it were green, blue or red."
"That's all very well for a joke, but my wife shan't play with a nigger."

"I don't think she will be called upon to do so. They are not in the same piece."

"But she shan't be in the same bill, or come into the theatre while he's here."

"That is another view of the case. Am I to understand that you mean to break the engagement?"

"Well, I guess I've not exactly made up my mind to do that; but you oughtn't to have engaged this fellow. He's a thief. He robbed Wallack when he was his servant."

"Who says so?"

"Everybody."

"Everybody is nobody. Did you ever hear Wallack say so?"

"No."

"Nor I either. Can you prove it?"

"No."

"Then you have no right to bring the charge, or repeat what in all probability is mere calumny."

"But you can't go near the fellow. He is abominably offensive. All niggers are."

"Perhaps so. We must keep on the windward side and give him as wide a berth as possible."

The indignant republican, finding the question resolved itself into an absurdity, subsided. But the difficulty passed away. The African's visit was postponed by some accident, and the impending contamination never took place.

The playbill of 21st December, Aldridge's benefit night, carried the following statement:

The African Roscius, having been received by the Dublin audiences on each evening of his performance with enthusiastic applause, will ever feel most grateful for the honour conferred upon him, and construes the approbation of the Irish Public as one of the proudest and most distinguished testimonials which has ever been bestowed upon his professional exertions.

The Irish public had taken the African Roscius to their hearts in the same way as years later did the Russian people under their Tsar. The basic theme of Aldridge's repertoire struck a deeper note in Ireland, approaching the Hungry 'Forties under a foreign King, than in England. Poverty and misery were increasing day by day and it was not hard for an Irish worker or peasant to identify himself with Gambia, the Slave, or with Mungo as he sang,

> Dear Heart, what a terrible life am I led,
> A dog has a better, that's sheltered and fed;
> Night and day 'tis de same, my pain is der game,
> Me wish to de Lord me was dead.

From Dublin, armed with Kean's letter, Aldridge naturally went straight to Bath. During the reign of the Georges, Bath was one of the most fashionable centres of English society and the theatre was much patronized, but by the time Aldridge arrived it was, like Dublin, fast declining. For while Ireland was approaching its Hungry 'Forties, England already had its Chartist 'Thirties upon it. Following the Bill of 1832 which gave the vote to the middle class, the working-class struggle began to surge, and became so widespread that the theatre could not fail to be affected. With the influx of more democratic audiences, society began to stay away, and the period to the middle of the 1860s was one of abandonment of the theatre by the upper classes.

Coming at such a difficult time, Kean's introduction of Aldridge in January 1832 must have been a godsend to Bellamy, who engaged him at once, and within three weeks of seeing Kean, Aldridge was playing on the Bath stage. From 19th to 28th January he appeared in *Oroonoko*, *Paul and Virginia*, *The Slave*, *The Revenge*, *Othello*, and *The Padlock*. He was followed by Macready.

This is what the *Bath Journal* (26th January 1832) had to say of his introduction to its fashionable public:

Othello and *The Padlock*. These two pieces were selected to introduce to the Bath public an actor of colour. So well skilled are the Bath public in judgment that they will be thoroughly convinced that a performance will suffer their patience to the end before they will attempt the sitting out of a long five act tragedy; accordingly we visited the theatre, but little did we think to see the polished Gentleman—the noble bearing which gives outward token of the well-informed mind within. We have seen *Othello* by our best actors, whose points, dwelling vividly in our remembrance, gave little disparagement in their recurrence, while the African Roscius, in some particulars, gave freshness of novelty, and throughout his performance, evinced nothing but the emanations of sterling self-thinking treasures from his own laboratory. In pronunciation, he is exceedingly correct, and in his reading most clear and distinct, in his countenance animated, in expression forcible, in deportment graceful. The whole of the part was exceedingly well executed and our admiration of the actor was felt by all who witnessed him.

After Bath, he again tours the north as far as Aberdeen, and has his second long run in Hull (from February to April).

In December 1832 he is back in Dublin, but this time there is a difference. The stock company is not as good as the previous year, although Miss Huddart is still there and John Vandenhoff is added. This is borne out by *Saunders's News Letter* of 8th December:

> The African Roscius has returned to our city after a twelve-months' absence and appeared last night in a Shakespearean character that may be termed pre-eminently his own, Othello. His impersonation of the heroic Moor was extremely just and pleasing in the majority of the impassioned scenes of this highly-wrought drama, and marked by numberless touches of good taste and refinement. A young lady made her appearance as Desdemona, evidently a novice to a metropolitan theatre, who paid such attention to the manner of her performance that she seemed to consider her share of the dialogue as immaterial in comparison to the appropriateness of her attitudes. Miss Huddart as Emilia was most energetic and affecting and did her best to compensate by the most spirited exertion for the want of support which "poor Othello" had reason to complain of in the cold and quaint mannerism of Mr. Cooke's Iago.

It was one of the practices of the day to permit a person to play the lead in a stock company for one or more nights, depending on the amount of money paid for the privilege. Maybe the Desdemona was one of these. It was not unusual to see such playbills as the one announcing—

THEATRE ROYAL DRURY LANE
Wednesday, November 21, 1832
This evening THE REVENGE
Zanga by a Foreigner of Rank
(his first appearance on the stage)

The "foreigner of rank" is still believed in some quarters to have been Aldridge, but from *The Times* the day after we learn that the anonymous actor was an Italian nobleman named Tarsistro, a friend of Lord Byron.

On the following Friday, 14th December, Aldridge played Zanga and, as all actors have their off-nights, this must have been one of his. The critics have consistently commented on the artificiality of this play and that it contained "little for an actor, be he ever so talented, to hang good acting on". The actor, however, has to put on his motley and play for all he is worth. But there inevitably comes a time when he drops the mask a little and exposes his true feelings about the play. *Saunders's News Letter* of 15th December says:

> The African went through the first three acts as if he was disgusted with the weight of the tawdry phraseology of the dialogue, and wished to sneak the bombast under cover of an unimpassioned tone and manner, but this only served to make the disparity the greater, and the "high and lofty tumbling" of the poetic author more apparent. In the last scene, however, he put forth the full powers of his voice, and singularly energetic demeanour, and convinced us fully that he could, if he pleased, fill the part of Zanga with fire and concentration of feeling requisite to its just personation. However, the lengthy tameness of the preceding scenes formed a penance that outweighs the vivacity of the *finale*, a misfortune which the African might easily avert, for he is decidedly a man of judgment and sterling talent, too. . . .

A week later, 22nd December, one of the most fashionable audiences of the season assembled to see an adaptation of Schiller's *Fiesco*, advertised as being performed "for the first time in this Kingdom". Vandenhoff was Count Fiesco, Miss Huddart was his wife, Calcraft took the part of Verrina, a Genoese nobleman and Senator, and Muley Hassan, a Moor, was, of course, played by the African Roscius. The performance received a full report in *Saunders's News Letter*, and the few extracts which we give clearly bring out the clash between Vandenhoff's and Aldridge's styles of acting:

> The plot of the Tragedy of *Fiesco, or The Conspiracy of Genoa* is already well known and needs no lengthened detail. The dialogue

as prepared for the stage will easily admit of a judicious curtailment, for instance, the Funeral Sermon is tiresome, the boudoir scene between Fiesco and his Countess "drags its slow length" immeasurably long; and when all anxiety is afloat to learn the issue, the audience do not expect a long-drawn speech in favour of republicanism. In saying this, we do not mean to detract from the piece as a literary composition, for it has claims in this regard of the first orders. . . .

The character of Fiesco is suited to the highest range of tragic powers in an actor, but we were rather disappointed with Mr. Vandenhoff's impersonation of the ambitious Count. He was tame and declamatory in the early scene, turgid in the latter part of the piece. Swaying one's arms about as if in a gymnasium is not the way to produce an effect. Another reading may produce in Mr. V. a considerable change for the better. The African Roscius was most excellent as the reckless and ruffian Moor; he was applauded as he deserved. Miss Huddart performed her part with great judgment and feeling. She spoke the epilogue, which was humorous and excellent in very good style. . . . The farce of *The Padlock* concluded the evening's entertainment, in which the African Roscius displayed his versatility of powers as Mungo. Nothing could be more humorous.

Aldridge, although in a smaller part, completely outshines the vaunted "classicist", and only Miss Huddart keeps up with him. The company as a whole must have been below standard, judging by *Saunders's* of 12th January:

On Saturday night the opera of *The Slave* was performed to a fashionable house. The African Roscius of course played Gambia and sustained the part with characteristic simplicity and yet such native grandeur of bearing that the illusion was complete except when his good nature was called on, alas! too frequently to prompt his co-actors who, through negligence or natural want of retention, had become "what my father Shandy figuratively termed 'Leaky vessels'"; we were highly pleased with the truth and beauty of some "new readings" of his own displayed in critical movements and which were duly appreciated by the audience.

This evening the African Roscius takes his benefit—we hope his talent will be appreciated in that sterling manner with which genius has ever been treated by the Dublin public. Their patronage could not be bestowed on a more deserving aspirant for histrionic fame.

Despite having continually to prompt his fellow-actors, Aldridge could still put over to the audience some "new readings". With such a season of poor support, a good benefit night could not be expected, despite his personal appeal. The critics regretted that a better house did not reward his efforts to please in that varied banquet prepared for the public gratification. . . . He gave an excellent performance of Zanga, spoke his farewell address after the interlude, and drew the usual bursts of applause.

Aldridge played in Dublin from 7th December until 16th January, and then went on tour through the south of Ireland. In *Notes and Queries* of 14th September 1872, Maurice Lenihan of Clonmel gives us some first-hand information:

In the spring of 1833 (as well as I remember), I met the African Roscius in Clonmel, where he had been giving one of his theatrical entertainments in the Grand Jury Room of the County Court House. He was of a rather robust make, tall, with all the peculiarities of his Negro race as to his features, except that his colour was a deep brown or bronze rather than black. His manners were bland and polite; he spoke English with a good accent, yet not entirely divested of the peculiarity which is attached by his countrymen to the pronunciation of certain syllables. Being very young at the time, but though young, the conductor of a local journal [*The Clonmel Advertiser*], I wrote and published critiques of Ira Aldridge's performances, which pleased him very much. He wrote in consequence in a fair and clear hand, a short note to me thanking me for my kindness in his regard; and I now send you a copy of the note in question, which I have ever since carefully preserved among my papers, and which may be of interest to the readers of *Notes and Queries*.

He travelled through the south of Ireland at that period, and among other places he visited Limerick, where he was also well received. The reference in the note to the passes or tickets of admission for the printers will be understood by all young and old editors of public journals, who are so frequently solicited by the compositors to obtain free passes for them to the theatre. The following is the note:

Dublin Street (Clonmel)
Monday, 4 p.m.

Dear Sir,—I beg leave to return you my warmest thanks for the flattering notices you have made respecting my humble exertions, much beyond my deserts, but the less my merit the more your bounty. I cannot say much for the variety of this evening's entertainment, but should anything appear worthy of remark, the slightest notice in your widely circulated journal would be of the greatest service to me. I enclose an admission for the printers and one for yourself.

I remain, Sir, Your obliged servant,

IRA F. ALDRIDGE.

Maurice Lenihan, Esq.

He played Othello admirably, and at this distance of time I may state with perfect truth, that I have seldom seen the part acted with greater truthfulness and power than characterised his delineation of the passions of the jealous Moor—love, doubt, hatred, revenge.

MAURICE LENIHAN, M.R.I.A.

Limerick.

From Ireland, Aldridge went to the northern circuit, playing in Aberdeen, Glasgow, and Edinburgh. During this tour he received the following letter from Corbett Ryder, Manager of the Aberdeen Theatre:

MY DEAR SIR,—Your trunk came here since your departure and is forwarded per coach to Glasgow—you left behind a small volume of *Junius's Letters* which, being at a loss how to forward, will keep safe until I have the pleasure of seeing you again in the week.

I forwarded Mr. Knowles a paper which contained honourable notice of your superior talents which we all here hope will make (as it is well entitled to do) a deep and lasting impression in the metropolis. And nothing will give me greater pleasure than to see the African Roscius again in Aberdeen, imprinted with the London stamp.

My dear Sir, yours truly,

C. RYDER.

Mrs. Ryder, Son, and Mr. and Mrs. Catrat unite with mine their best regards to Mr. and Mrs. Aldridge.

PS.—I shall require a new company for Aberdeen next Season towards the end of Autumn. If you can give any good performers the hint to "be early to join" you will oblige me.

C. R.

The "Mr. Knowles" referred to we presume to be James Sheridan Knowles (1784-1862), one of the most successful dramatists of the first half of the nineteenth century, and now that he is associated with Covent Garden, Ryder makes a point of bringing Aldridge to his attention. A few weeks earlier, on Knowles's return to England from a tour of Ireland, he stopped at Liverpool, where a friend asked him, "What success had you in Ireland? A large benefit in Cork, of course?"

"What success?" exclaimed Knowles. "That which an Irishman meets with on his own ungrateful soil. Sir, in Cork, my birthplace, in what they miscall the Athens of Ireland, my benefit amounted to £90, £2 less than a fortnight before they had given to a black man, the Negro actor, the African Roscius. My plays are too liberal for the aristocratic illiberals of Ireland."

Two months later, Sheridan Knowles publicly compliments and embraces Aldridge at his début in Covent Garden!

To return to Ryder's letter, we see that he and his family send their best regards to Mr. and Mrs. Aldridge. In this whole period of continuous touring, with its discomforts and drudgery, Aldridge is usually accompanied by his wife. We learn a little more about her from the *1860 Chronicle*:

In September 1832, while in Liverpool, the writer of this sketch happened to be at the same hotel with the wife of Mr. Aldridge. She was an intelligent lady, the daughter of a late Member of Parliament, and had made a runaway match with the African Roscius. She was a lady of fine accomplishments and great conversational talent. She showed me a bust, in plaster, of her husband, and very anxiously enquired whether he had the true Negro features, seeming especially desirous that he should be perfect in this way. Mr. Aldridge himself was absent on a professional tour, and I did not have the pleasure of meeting him until nearly two years after, in the city of Glasgow, where he fulfilled an engagement at the Royal Theatre, then under the management of the late Mr. Alexander. The engagement was a very successful one, the actor drawing large audiences and winning golden opinions from the Press. The water, however, did not run smoothly behind the scenes. Mr. Alexander, a tall, stalwart, coarse man of great energy and perseverance, had won success in the management by alternately cuddling and scolding his audience in the midst of his own performances, and by bullying his actors behind the curtains. No small portion of the attraction to young gentlemen in the pit arose from his habit of suddenly breaking off in the midst of *Rob Roy* with "Ye gods in the gallery must na licht your pipes at the gas-jets and let your brent papers fall on the gentlemen below"—or as suddenly leaving the boiling cauldron and coming down to the footlights with, "Woman, will you please stop that wean's crying?"

One night, between the acts, Mr. Alexander, in a towering passion at some mishap, turned to vent his rage on Mr. Aldridge; the latter firmly resented; Alexander, uplifted sword in hand, sprang towards Aldridge, the latter, with a similar weapon, quietly disarmed the Manager without stirring a footstep; grasping his sword again, he rushed on, shrieking, "I'll kill him. Don't hold me back"—the latter being addressed to two female supers, who easily led him away.

The good people of Glasgow, at the time we write of, were especially "down upon" two institutions—Popery and the theatre; and a man of repute—which meant a God-fearing, church-going individual—was certain of losing caste if he patronized, or even ventured within the precincts of either. Anti-slavery men, who were for the most part rigid Dissenters, entertained these prejudices in the highest degree. The Secretary of the Glasgow Emancipation Society, the late John Murray, whose distinguished friendship I had the pleasure to enjoy, was so thorough in his anti-Popery and anti-theatre views that it was with some reluctance, on Saturday morning, that I mentioned to him that my old schoolmate, Ira Aldridge, would perform that night at the Royal Theatre. To my surprise and delight, he at once proposed to go, which we did. It was his first and only visit to a theatre. He was "carried away" by the acting of Mr. Aldridge, insisted on an introduction and invited us to breakfast next morning. The reunion was a most pleasant one. When we left, and walked down Sauchiehall Street to the coach (Mr. Aldridge was obliged to leave that morning to fulfil an engagement in Edinburgh), Aldridge grasped my arm, and his large, lamping eyes filled with tears as he exclaimed, "Oh, God, what unexpected treatment to a poor outcast actor!"

The "Mr. Alexander" referred to is John Henry Alexander— "Old Alec"—the Manager of the Theatre Royal, Dunlop Street, Glasgow, and the most eccentric character known to the theatrical profession. He had three almost life-sized statues adorning the exterior of his theatre: Shakespeare in the centre, Garrick on one side, and himself on the other. "There, sir," he would say, "is Shakespeare; there is Garrick; and there is John Henry Alexander—as great a man in his way as any of them."

In Glasgow Aldridge had his usual success, and the *Caledonian Mercury* of 20th March writes of his Othello: "He reminded us of Kean in many of his best passages, and when time may have deprived us of that great master, the African Roscius will not be an unworthy successor. . . . He was loudly applauded in all his points by a crowded and very fashionable house, among whom we perceived many of the most eminent literary and professional characters in the city."

Five days after this was written, Edmund Kean, playing Othello to his son's Iago, collapsed on the Covent Garden stage, whispering, "I am dying. . . ." The world was soon to be deprived of the great master, but the African Roscius was not to be accepted as his successor, however worthy—at least, not in London.

A few years later Aldridge's playbills will proudly list many of these "eminent" characters as his patrons, but already his fame and reputation are such that he is at last invited to perform at the Theatre Royal, Covent Garden. The Glasgow playbill of 21st March announces: "Positively the last appearance but two of the African Roscius, the celebrated trans-Atlantic actor of colour, who has performed through the principal cities of America with the most distinguished applause, also at the Theatres Royal, Edinburgh, Dublin, Liverpool, Birmingham, etc., and who is engaged by Mons. Laporte, Manager of the Theatre Royal, Covent Garden, to appear there in May next."

This time it is true. Following is the text of the original agreement for this epoch-making engagement:

Memorandum that it is understood between Mr. Laporte and Mr. Aldridge, the African Roscius, that he is to appear at this theatre in the character of Othello on Wednesday the 10th April next, being the Wednesday in Easter Week. This Memorandum is drawn up by the permission of Mr. Laporte and signed for him by me.

GEORGE HARTLEY
(*Stage Manager*).

CHAPTER VIII

Covent Garden Theatre

IN the summer of 1832 the management of Covent Garden Theatre was taken over by a Frenchman, Pierre François Laporte, who in April 1833 brought Aldridge to Covent Garden. It was hinted in various circles and in the Press that Aldridge's appearance was responsible not only for the temporary closing which followed, but for the eventual bankruptcy of Covent Garden. Even a cursory review of the situation of the theatre in question and of the English theatre in general shows that this was but another instance of the calumny and denigration to which he was subjected.

Laporte started in July 1832 with a short season of French plays, starring the famous French actress, Mlle. Mars, and the danseuse, Taglioni, followed by a series of "farewell concerts" in August by the great violinist, Paganini. In January 1833 Douglas Jerrold's play, *Nell Gwynne*, was the attraction. In February Charles Kean appeared as Sir Edward Mortimer in *The Iron Chest*. On 20th and 21st March Edmund Kean played Shylock, with Ellen Tree as Portia. The playbills for 25th March announced that "Mr. Kean was last Thursday received in the character of Shylock with acclamation, and in order to meet the generally expressed desire that he should appear with his son, THE TRAGEDY OF OTHELLO will be acted this evening when they will perform together for the first time". It was not, in actual fact, the first time that father and son had played together. They had acted together in Glasgow in October 1828, when Edmund "came down from Bute to play for his son's benefit, taking the part of Brutus in John Howard Payne's tragedy, to Charles's Titus. The house was crowded, as well it might be. In one highly emotional scene, when Brutus fell on Titus's neck and cried, 'Embrace thy wretched father,' loud applause broke forth. 'Charley,' whispered Edmund in the ear of Charles, 'we're doing the trick!' "[1] In April 1829 both Keans were together again in Cork, when the father "collapsed in the middle of *Macbeth* and Charles had to piece out the evening with *Douglas*".

The 25th March performance of Edmund Kean as Othello proved to be a genuine farewell, for the great tragedian was stricken on the stage with his last illness.

To appear on the boards of the Theatre Royal, Covent Garden, in the footsteps of the greatest actor of the period, in the very role which he had made particularly his own, and with the same company, was enough to make many an older and more experienced actor quail, but sixteen days later, with characteristic courage, determination and dignity, Aldridge steps on to the stage of this great theatre, taking up the challenge.

Not only was Aldridge competing with the very vivid memory of the great Kean, inviting comparison with him, but on the very night of his début at Covent Garden Macready appeared at Drury Lane in his best role, Macbeth, and at the Haymarket Sheridan's ever-popular *School for Scandal* was being performed, with Dowton as Sir Peter Teazle and Elizabeth Yates as Lady Teazle. At Covent Garden itself, two days before Aldridge's début, the ever-popular and dashing Irish comedian, Tyrone Power (great-grandfather of the present film star), was making his first appearance that season in *The Invincibles*, with the excellent singer and actress, Madame Vestris (who five years later married the son of Charles Mathews). The following evening this attractive pair were again to be seen at Covent Garden, and the playbill for Wednesday, 10th April, announced that Shakespeare's tragedy of *Othello* would be performed that evening, Othello to be played by "MR. ALDRIDGE (A Native of Senegal), Known by the Appellation of the AFRICAN ROSCIUS, who has been received with great applause at the Theatres Royal, Dublin, Edinburgh, Bath, and most of the principal provincial Theatres. HIS FIRST APPEARANCE ON THIS STAGE." The cast was identical with the one that played with Edmund Kean, with the exception that Mr. Warde replaced Charles Kean as Iago.

On the morning of 11th April, the *Morning Post* said:

On its being understood that he [Aldridge] was about to appear at Covent Garden Theatre in the character of Othello, several publications inserted articles tending to condemn, or rather to annihilate, him unheard, and to question the propriety of his being allowed a trial upon the boards of a principal London Theatre. On the appearance of these articles, Mr. Aldridge, or his friends, distributed printed notices about the town, animadverting upon the injustice of condemning him unheard, and appealing "to the better feeling of a London Public", or something equivalent.

We give the text of the handbill distributed by "Mr. Aldridge or his friends":

THE AFRICAN ROSCIUS
To the Public

Base and unmanly attempts are making in certain quarters to prevent MR. ALDRIDGE, commonly designated the "AFRICAN ROSCIUS", from making his appearance as OTHELLO, on Wednesday next, pursuant to his engagement at the Theatre Royal, Covent Garden, or if he should have the "PRESUMPTION" to appear, he is threatened with DAMNATION!

His heinous offence is that he was born in Africa, and though "descended from a line of Kings" his skin is too DARK to enable him to personate the "DUSKY MOOR", even though he may possess the genius of a Kean, the classic taste of a Kemble, combined with the dramatic appearance of a Garrick!!

To condemn unheard is contrary to the character and known liberality of Englishmen. Talent let it come from what Country it may is deserving of patronage, therefore, fellow countrymen, do not permit a worthy and talented man to be CRUSHED by the slanders and libels of the low and contemptible "catch-penny Press"; the paltry penny critics who have threatened that "he shall be jammed to atoms by the relentless power of their critical (penny rattle? no) "BATTERING RAM", if (what think ye is the modest demand?) his name is not immediately withdrawn from the Bills!!!

As a friend to a meritorious though modest and intelligent foreigner, whose able delineation of many of the principal characters of our most eminent dramatic writers, has been admitted in the numerous criticisms inserted in the Edinburgh, Dublin, Aberdeen, Bath, Brighton, and other provincial papers (from which the article below is extracted) I beg to ask of a London Audience "fair play" on his behalf when he makes his début on Wednesday next.

I am the Public's Humble Servant,

"CRITO".

Garrick Club House,
April 6, 1833

This is the first direct attack of its kind that we know of up to this time. Throughout his many provincial tours and even during his first appearances at the minors in London, there is no record of any such attack. Whatever prejudice did exist was evidently not strong enough nor sufficiently organized to express itself publicly. But London was the capital, and the centre of the pro-slavery "lobby", at this very moment fighting a last rearguard action, for within the year slavery was abolished in the British Colonies. Their attacks on Aldridge grew more virulent as their position grew indefensible, and the appearance of a Negro playing the finest roles in all drama on the boards of Covent Garden was indeed a damning negation, as Aldridge well knew, of their arguments and "theories" about the so-called inferior races. So the challenge was not merely that of actor *versus* actor. It was much more. Aldridge stood upon the stage that night as the lone protagonist of his oppressed and vilified people. With what relish his attackers rubbed it in that he had been a "black servant" while at the same time they idealized Shakespeare, the son of a glover, and Ben Jonson, at one time a bricklayer.

Our study of the contemporary Press brought to light a very interesting fact: that two nights before Aldridge made his début at Covent Garden Theatre, another coloured "actor" appeared at the City Theatre, Cripplegate (where Aldridge is soon to play) —as if to contradict the Garden's claim to "the only man of colour on the stage".

"The City Theatre", said *John Bull*★ the next morning, "produced a black man as Tom Tug in *The Waterman*. An example which Covent Garden followed on Thursday, by exhibiting another Whango Iang in *Othello*, as if, because a man's face is black, he could act that particular part. One of the critics says: 'He failed a little in tragedy, but he is excellent in Mungo.' The City Blackamore got unmercifully hissed—the Covent Garden nigger considerably clapped—this is all a matter of taste."

The Globe deals with this event a little more fully:

An "African Apollo" having been announced to make his first appearance last night at this theatre in the character of Tom Tug

★ A publication founded in 1820 by Theodore Hook, champion of High Toryism, which was known as the paper with the "witty, incisive criticism and pitiless invective which secured for it a large circulation"!

in *The Waterman*, the audience, and especially the gods, who expected to discover in the new pretender all the perfection of their *beau ideal* and the real "impersonation of the sun's bright beams", were not a little surprised at the rising of the curtain, to find his godship in the guise of a strapping, well-whiskered son of Neptune, with a broad, good-humoured face of a complexion about one or two removes only from white, and an accent quite as pure as that of any white Creole of His Majesty's West India colonies. It was evident from the first that the gods, finding their "African Apollo" altogether so much like themselves, had determined to disallow his claim without further investigation, and we have no doubt that the good-natured fellow heartily wished himself again at his more congenial occupation of superintending the stewards' room of an American packet. Having got over his début, however, he will now probably have recovered his voice, and may yet perhaps make good his claim to the high honours of divinityship.

It was a time-honoured trick of the minor theatres to anticipate, if they could, the novelties of the patent theatres. The City Theatre, not to be outdone by Covent Garden, had scoured the East End to find a "man of colour" with histrionic aspirations, and found a ship's steward, a Tom Tug, who was ready to "have a go". They put their "African Apollo" on two days before Aldridge, perhaps hoping that he would last a little longer than he did and run concurrently with Aldridge. Whether the selection of the not very classical character of Tom Tug was an attempt to cast him to type we shall never know, but it is clear that just being a man of colour—a novelty on the stage—however light or dark, was not enough to hold an audience. The attempt of *John Bull* to ridicule the African Roscius together with the African Apollo failed. Aldridge's season at the City Theatre after Covent Garden was highly successful.

We will now see what the London Press had to say about the first performance of the African Roscius at the Theatre Royal, Covent Garden. *The Times*:

An experiment, and not a remarkably successful one, as the emptiness of the house incontestably proved was last night essayed here. The tragedy of *Othello* was performed, the part of the Moor by an individual of Negro origin, as his features sufficiently testify, who calls himself Aldridge, and who has been facetiously nicknamed "The African Roscius". Such an exhibition is well enough at Sadler's Wells, or at Bartholomew Fair, but it certainly is not very creditable to a great national establishment.

We could not perceive any fitness which Mr. Aldridge possessed for the assumption of one of the finest parts that was ever imagined by Shakespeare, except, indeed, that he could play it in his own native hue, without the aid of lampblack or pomatum, just as Stephen Kemble was by nature enabled to present Falstaff without the ordinary stuffing; but Mr. Kemble's Falstaff, notwithstanding his ready-made obesity, was miserably deficient in humour, and Mr. Aldridge's Othello, with all the advantages of *hic niger est*, wanted spirit and feeling. His accent is unpleasantly, and we would say vulgarly foreign; his manner, generally, drawling and unimpressive; and when by chance (for chance it is, and not judgment) he rises to a higher strain, we perceive in the transition the elevation of rant, not the fiery dignity of soul-felt passion. His performance in the third act—that overpowering act —was weak. The *"Vale!"* which is music in itself when delivered by an actor of even ordinary voice and judgment, was miserably feeble. A few plaudits followed it, but "the judicious grieved". Much praise has been given to Shakespeare for the arguments which Iago adduces to prove that nothing but a light, fickle constitution—a hankering after novelty—could ever have induced so fair and gentle a creature as Desdemona to view the Moor with the feelings of love. The performance of last night was a keenly illustrative comment upon that point. Well might Desdemona's father imagine that sorcery, and not nature, had caused his daughter to listen to such a wooer. It is, however, our duty to state that Mr. Aldridge was extremely well received. He "fit audience found, though few". . . .

We were greatly pleased with Miss E. Tree's Desdemona. Her acting was very beautiful in the scene where, in contradiction to the Moor's most rudely-couched accusation, she asseverates her innocence.

The *Morning Post*:

Some curiosity has been excited by the announcement of Mr. Aldridge's performance last night and the circumstances attending it. He is a "gentleman of colour", a native of Senegal, and has for some years past been in the habit of performing in the provinces the parts commonly designated the "black parts" of the drama, such as Othello, Zanga, Gambia, Mungo, etc. The favourable manner in which his efforts have been received in Edinburgh, Dublin, and Bath, and the very flattering terms in which he has been noticed by the critics of those towns, had established for him a degree of fame to which we were anxious to ascertain the validity of his claims. . . . Prejudiced neither in his favour nor against him, but principally with feelings of curiosity, we witnessed his performance of Othello last night. Mr. Aldridge did not present us with so black a face as the representatives of Othello generally assume. His complexion is almost a light brown, and his face altogether not unlike the frontispiece portrait of the *Narrative of a Voyage to Senegal*. It is not capable of very varied expression. His figure is tall and noble, and his manner of walking the stage is dignified, and speaks of long familiarity with the boards. Our opinion of his performance as a whole may be surmised when we say that our impression was, at the conclusion of the play, that any person with sufficient discretion not grossly to overstep the modesty of nature would obtain a certain number of rounds of applause in *Othello*. So admirable is the writing of Shakespeare in this and other of his principal parts, Macbeth, Richard, Hamlet, etc., that that actor must be indeed an arrant pretender who would fail to produce some effect in them. Mr. Aldridge's enunciation is far from correct or pleasing; it is frequently broad and strikingly un-English; but he possesses a fine, full, melodious voice, which might with practice be turned to more advantage. One great and almost unpardonable fault in this actor is his propensity to alter the text of the author. He may be assured that every alteration he ventures on spoils, in the opinion of the judicious, that which he presumptuously imagines he is improving. Examples are at present unnecessary; but we can quote several should we hereafter find occasion. There was nothing sufficiently great or original in the performance to warrant our dwelling further upon it. To sum up its merits, it was doubtless sufficiently good to be considered very curious, but it was not an Othello for Covent Garden Theatre, where we do not, or rather should not, go to witness mere curiosities. At the fall of the curtain Mr. Aldridge very promptly obeyed a call for his reappearance, and delivered a speech, which had evidently been as closely studied as the part he had been acting, thanking the public in very flowing terms for the manner in which he had been received. Though he had not the art to invest the lesson he was repeating with the character of the impromptu effusion it was supposed to be, it was well received, and the announcement of his next performance of Othello met with much applause, unmixed with any opposition. Indeed, there was not any audible expression of disapprobation throughout the whole of the performance.

The *Globe* (evening newspaper):

. . . Nature has been bountiful to Mr. Aldridge in more than the identity of complexion which she has given him for the Moor *et similes*—that is, he possesses a good figure and a speaking, intelligent countenance, not black, but of that oily and expressive mulatto tint which can as easily and skilfully allow the passions to play over its surface as the face of the pale, unripened natives of the North. There were parts of the performance in which the sable aspirant came up to our ideas of Shakespeare's conception fully—these we cannot stop to particularize; and there were also portions of it in which we could have wished him "to Jericho"— we allude to the scene before the Senate, which was nearly all rant, instead of what we conceive to be the true Shakespearean conception—a subdued and artless narrative of facts, combined with a calm and determined tone of self-justification arising from consciousness of integrity. This sin of rant—only an occasional one, however—and some vulgarisms of pronunciation, inseparable, we suppose, from some early passages of Mr. Aldridge's life and occupation—which we allude to rather in his praise than disparagement—are the only faults we have to find with his Othello. But there are beauties throughout his performance which more than compensate for these; and those who go to see the mere novelty of an African Othello will find more than mere curiosity gratified. While there is little to make the judicious grieve, there are parts of his personation of the Moor, particularly after he has indulged in the "green and yellow" sin of jealousy, which are finely conceived, and delivered with all the fire and spirit of a first-rate actor. His reception was very flattering, and at the close of the tragedy he was called for by the unanimous voice of the house, and he delivered an oration of thanks which certainly savoured more of acting than his previous performance. It was, to say the least of it, injudicious—although, as somebody said of one of our most celebrated living poets, it proved "he had a heart, for he got his speeches by it". Mr. Aldridge repeats the character tomorrow.

The *Standard* (evening newspaper):

We made a point of being present, for the last three evenings,* to witness the performance of that singularly gifted actor, the

* This is an error; Aldridge gave only two performances.

African Roscius, who is the first performer of colour that ever appeared on the boards of any theatre in Britain. He had chosen the part of Othello for his first appearance—an undertaking which at present was most hazardous; but notwithstanding the impression which the inimitable Kean has created in this character, and the genius by which he has made it peculiarly his own, the result showed that the African Roscius was fully justified in making the bold attempt. We at once gladly express our unqualified delight with his delineation of this masterpiece of the divine Shakespeare. To attempt a minute description would be as superfluous as difficult; he succeeded in deeply affecting the feelings of his audience, and the representation all through was watched with an intense stillness, almost approaching to awe. At the conclusion, the African Roscius was called for by the unanimous acclamation of the whole house who, upon his appearance, rose *en masse* to receive him with bursts of applause, waving of hats, handkerchiefs, etc., etc. The débutant, evidently deeply affected, expressed his grateful thanks in a very modest and feeling manner, and retired amidst enthusiastic cheering.

The *Spectator* (leading literary weekly):

... His person is tall and well-formed, and his action free, flowing and graceful. His face is not disagreeable, though we have seen better-looking Africans; but it is not susceptible of much variety of expression. His voice is rich and melodious, and sonorous withal; and in passages of tenderness, its tones had great sweetness. It resembles Macready's, but has more volume. Indeed, the acting altogether—though with a due interval—reminded us of that tragedian. His deportment is manly, and occasionally dignified; he moves and speaks with deliberation and self-possession. He evinced a great deal of feeling and nature in his performance; these, indeed, were its redeeming qualities; but they could not reconcile us to its numerous and glaring defects. Its beauties, however, surprised us more than its faults.

An African is no more qualified, by virtue alone of his complexion and the conformation of his face, to personate any Moorish characters—much less such a one as Othello—than a huge fat man would be competent to represent Falstaff on the score of his bulk alone. The property-man can furnish as good a suit of "the shadowed livery of the burnished sun" for stage purposes as Dame Nature herself—perhaps, in his own opinion, a better; and English audiences have a prejudice in favour of

European features, which more than counterbalance the recommendations of a flat nose and thick lips.

In one particular only we might expect a native African to be better qualified by nature to personate a character of his own clime and complexion—that is, in having the fiery temperament of these children of the Sun. But herein Mr. Aldridge possesses no advantage; he is a remarkable exception to the general rule, being on the contrary, tame and *larmoyant*. So that, in fact, he is without even the ordinary natural qualifications which are essential to the verisimilitude of the character.

The swarthy actor is not new to the stage; he has played at several provincial theatres, and at some of the minor houses in London. His declamation is not only ineffective but very faulty; it is marked by numerous instances of false emphasis, incorrect readings, and interpolations of the text even, and by a few vulgarisms of pronunciation. It was, however, free from rant. Othello describes himself as being "unused to the melting mood". Mr. Aldridge's grief is querulous and lachrymous, and his pathos mere whining. In the most violent bursts of passion, he was deficient in energy and power; though in depicting the struggles of mental agony and suppressed emotion, he was vigorous and natural, but he did not in the more calm scenes portray the lofty-minded nobleness of Othello's nature, nor that air of commanding dignity which would be habitual to his station, neither in the impassioned parts did he evince any of that moral grandeur which gives sublimity to the scene as it lives in Shakespeare's page. It is superfluous to enter into any detailed criticisms of such a performance as this. It was upon the whole a failure. The range of characters in which Mr. Aldridge could appear must necessarily be very limited; we therefore expected his acting to be more perfect. He has no genius but is not without talent; and he has two great requisites—a good voice and a good figure. He is said to make a capital Mungo. He was to have appeared in that character and in Zanga on the same night; but the applause bestowed on his performance of Othello induced the Manager to announce its repetition instead, and he is to play them on Tuesday. We think he might perform Gambia.

The *Athenaeum* (weekly journal devoted to literature, science, art, and drama):

On Wednesday, this establishment (one of the two great national theatres which are constantly complaining of the decline of the drama, and constantly kicking themselves behind, for fear they should not go down the hill fast enough), aimed another blow at its respectability, by the production of Mr. Henry Wallack's black servant in the character of Othello—Othello, forsooth!!! Othello, almost the masterwork of the master-mind—a part, the study of which occupied, perhaps, years of the life of the elegant and classical Kemble, a part which the fire and genius of Kean have, of late years, made his exclusive property; a part which it has been considered a sort of theatrical treason for anyone less distinguished than these two variously but highly gifted individuals to attempt; and this is to be presented in an English national theatre by one whose pretenses rest upon two grounds, of his face being of a natural instead of an acquired tint, and of his having lived as a servant to a low-comedy actor. It is truly monstrous; and if (to quote our own remarks of the week before), Miss Ellen Tree's beautiful and touching personation of the gentle Desdemona was enough "to win a nod of approbation from Shakespeare's statue", assuredly this is sufficient to make his indignant bones kick the lid from his coffin.

We have no ridiculous prejudice against any fellow creature because he chances to be of a different colour from ours; and we trust that we have good taste enough to take our hats off to genius, wherever we find it; but we are, on the other hand, altogether above the twaddle of helping the drama to bear an indignity of this nature, merely that foreigners may laugh in their sleeves at us, while we quote this silly exhibition as a proof of England being "the stranger's home".

Mr. Aldridge, formerly calling himself, we believe, Mr. Keene, and now distinguished by the appellation of "The African Roscius", is really an extraordinary person; for it is extraordinary that under all the circumstances, a natural quickness and aptitude for imitation, should enable him to get through such a part as Othello with so little of positive offence as he does. But there it ends. Looking to his birth, parentage, and education, nothing short of inspiration could possibly make him a fit delineator of Shakespeare's Othello; and this is an extent to which it is not very likely that Providence would choose to go, to produce such a result. That Providence has not done so in this instance will be amply evident to those who do not permit their judgment to be run away with by that which we have admitted to be extraordinary; who do not let their hands get the start of their heads, or suffer a false feeling of compassion for the individual to supply the place of sound and unbiased opinion.

It is impossible that Mr. Aldridge should fully comprehend the meaning and force or even the words he utters, and, accordingly, the perpetual recurrence of false emphasis, whenever his memory as to his original fails him, shows distinctly that he does not. In the name of common sense we enter our protest against a repetition of this outrage. In the name of propriety and decency we protest against an interesting actress and decent girl like Miss Ellen Tree being subjected by the manager of a theatre to the indignity of being pawed about by Mr. Henry Wallack's black servant; and, finally, in the name of consistency, if this exhibition is to be continued, we protest against acting being any longer dignified by the name of art.

Theatrical Observer, 11th April:

. . . This gentleman, it is said, has been highly successful in the provinces, and judging from the applause he met with last night, he might be said to have passed the ordeal of a London audience with like success. We cannot, however, think him calculated to fill the place of Mr. Kean, whose inimitable performance has spoiled us for seeing anyone else in the character, while the remembrance of his excellence remains so vividly impressed on our minds.

Mr. Aldridge looked the part well, and his acting was more than respectable, though it fell short of excellence; he has certainly the merit of not over-acting his part, but then he does not express the individual bursts of feeling, nor the deep and accumulating tide of passion which hurries on the noble and generous Moor to deeds of blood and death; he also whines occasionally in a manner inconsistent with the lofty nature of the character and has a disagreeable habit of pumping up his breath. He was a good deal applauded, and called for after the play, when he delivered a short speech expressive of his thanks, which, if it were an impromptu, was highly creditable to him; he said he should be wanting in gratitude and thankfulness if he did not respond to the flattering applause he received, he felt this was the stranger's home, where the germ of talent was fostered till it bloomed, and that his heart must be cold ere he forgot the kindness he had met with, etc.

Theatrical Observer, 13th April:

The African Roscius, as he is called, repeated the character of Othello last night and was again most favourably received. This gentleman who now calls himself Aldridge played some time ago at the Coburg Theatre under the cognomen of Keene and was, at no very distant period engaged in a menial capacity—we do not mention this with any unkind feeling, as we think it highly to his credit that he has by his talents raised himself to a station so much above that which nature seemed to have intended for him. Dodsley who as an actor, bookseller and author enjoyed some celebrity was originally a footman, and Broome who so successfully made it a matter of honest boast that though he had been a servant he had by dint of natural talent and industry triumphed over all the many disadvantages under which he had originally laboured.

Theatrical Observer, 19th April:

A punster remarked in a conversation relative to the merits of the African Roscius that his performance was a very *fair* one for a *black*. As love and the effect of jealousy form the ground work of the Tragedy he was well adapted for a-mour, and that no part could be more soot-able! Mr. Aldridge had even improved upon Shakespeare as there was death-less than usual in it from his not being obliged to dye himself!

So Ira Aldridge's memorable appearance at Covent Garden is over, and the Press notices are before us. We have given them so fully in order that their basic attitudes, their contradictions and agreements, may be revealed.

Aldridge was by no means the only victim of the type of "criticism" contained in the *Athenaeum*. Supposedly a reputable journal devoted to the arts and sciences, instead of giving its readers the benefit of legitimate criticism, it indulged in the most slanderous, low-level diatribes from which nobody was immune. A brief passage from *The Athenaeum Exposed*, published anonymously in London in 1863, shows the type of grievance that members of the scientific, literary and art world consistently had against this journal: "Such 'criticisms' have but to be read to be at once condemned as the most offensive and unjustifiable by every person of common sense, ordinary taste, good feeling, and gentlemanly spirit. The wonders are that the profession have endured them patiently so long. . . . The writers of such notices seem not to be aware that artists have feelings that may be wounded—often very sensitive feelings—and property and interests that may be injured; . . . that calling names, insult, ridicule and abuse are not criticism at all. . . . How such evils are to be corrected is a very difficult question indeed. The Press has a fearful power and it abuses that power to injure and insult, to a degree that is becoming intolerable."

★   ★   ★

This, then, is Ira Aldridge at the age of twenty-six, with only eight years' professional experience behind him. All things considered, it is true that he still had a great deal to learn, but did his performance deserve the damning criticism and insults, the devastating remarks and the ridicule heaped upon him by the Press? Here he was, competing with Edmund Kean who, when he appeared on the same stage two weeks before, was forty-six years old and had been a professional actor since childhood. Kean, too, had faced a poorly attended house at his début. It is interesting and significant that, although he was engaged to play Othello for one night only, with such celebrities as Madame Vestris and Tyrone Power to follow on the next night, it was announced that Othello would be repeated on Friday, the 12th, and that Zanga and Mungo, scheduled for that night, would be given the following Tuesday, the 16th. The playbill of Thursday, the 11th (the day following Aldridge's début), announced: "The Public is respectfully informed that in consequence of the enthusiastic reception of Mr. Aldridge (a Native of Senegal) and by the unanimous desire of the audience, he will have the honour of repeating the character of Othello tomorrow evening, and on Tuesday next (the 16th) he will perform in Zanga (*The Revenge*) and Mungo (*The Padlock*)."

He gave his second performance of Othello, as scheduled, and prepared for Zanga and Mungo the following Tuesday. On Saturday, the 13th, and Monday, the 15th, Tyrone Power and Madame Vestris appeared in *The Invincibles* and *The £100 Note*, followed by *The Elfin Sprite*. And then a strange thing happened. On Tuesday, the 16th, *The Times* announced in its theatre column: "Covent Garden: The public is respectfully informed that in consequence of the indisposition of several of the principal performers there will be no performance this evening."

Thus was Aldridge's third appearance cancelled. He was not seen as Zanga or as Mungo.

Now, Covent Garden had a stock company from which were drawn the various actors playing with Aldridge and with Power and Vestris, some taking part in all these productions. In such a large establishment there would be no problem of substituting for any player taken ill. It is noteworthy also that the performances of Tyrone Power and Madame Vestris are not affected at all, for they appear on Wednesday and Thursday following the cancellation "in consequence of indisposition of several of the principal performers" in the cast with Aldridge. On Friday, the 19th, again we have an announcement: "The Public is respectfully informed that in consequence of the prevailing illness there will be no performance this evening. Mr. Sheridan Knowles's new play, to be called *The Wife, A Tale of Mantua*, is unavoidably deferred for a few days. Mr. and Mrs. Wood have entered into an engagement for a limited number of nights at this theatre, being positively the last of their performances in London. Madame Vestris will shortly resume her part of Apollo in *Midas*."

On Saturday, the 20th, the public "is respectfully informed that this theatre will reopen on Wednesday next, when will be produced Mr. Sheridan Knowles's new play, to be called *The Wife, or Tale of Mantua*, with other entertainments in which Madame Vestris will appear."

So we see that the theatre was actually closed for five days. Whether any members of Aldridge's cast were really affected by the "prevailing illness" or whether this was a diplomatic way of cancelling the performance we shall never know, but we do know that there was no further mention of the promised appearance of Aldridge as Zanga and Mungo, whereas all the other stars continued, as billed.

The reasons for this withdrawal are very significant in the light of Aldridge's later attempts to return to the patent theatres of London. The *1849 Memoir* makes the following explanation:

> Certain of the public Press—and a few individuals—were inimical to the histrionic pretensions of the African. There was but little opportunity for assailing him directly and seriously, for in this country men must give something like a reason for what they say in earnest. Ridicule, however, is within the reach of the most unscrupulous and unthinking. Miss Ellen Tree was the Desdemona of Mr. Aldridge's Othello, and certain admirers of that lady (who was then unmarried and, as now, a special favourite)

were envious of the Moor's familiarity with her fair face, and ridiculed his privilege. Burnt cork and grease, an imitative and dirty dye, upon a tallowy skin were, in their fastidious and jaundiced eye, unobjectionable as compared with a veritable and natural hue of our Creator's own painting. Men who have since grown older and, if we may judge from their literary pursuits, wiser, took a pleasure in scoffing at "the idea" of "a Negro" filling an intellectual character, and surpassing themselves among others in his delineation of poetry, pathos, and passion. It was "the idea" alone which warped their better taste and judgment, for in reality there was nothing to mock. Had Laporte persisted in his undertaking, Mr. Aldridge would soon have been established as a generally known, popular, extraordinary actor; but he did nothing of the kind. Prejudices, too, will come even across the great Atlantic.

> *Coelum non animum*
> *Qui trans mare currunt.*

And of this fact Mr. Aldridge has been repeatedly reminded upon coming in contact with actors from the United States. . . . He is perfectly conscious of his own moral and physical power as compared with those of men who would avail themselves of the mere force of prejudice to "put him down"; and the quiet dignity of manners, gentlemanly address, and deportment of the African seldom failed to check conduct the very reverse.

It is possible that Aldridge was given his opportunity to appear at Covent Garden in the first place because Laporte, the new lessee, was a Frenchman, with the Revolution not too far behind, and with a liberal attitude toward colour. Coupled with this was, no doubt, the practical consideration of presenting a "novelty" and drawing the crowds. Nevertheless, be the experiment ever so successful, Laporte had to be cautious. We do not know what influential forces prevailed upon him to curtail Aldridge's engagement. He could not afford to ignore the threats already referred to and the hostility of influential sections of the Press, and had to yield to the pressure. There was backstage pressure as well, for the *Memoir* goes on to say:

American actors, and some actors who have been in America, to this very day scoff at the African "because that he is black", while they themselves are but little admired for all their whiteness. We can very easily understand the latent animosity and open hostility that one performer feels for and shows to another, according to the circumstances which call forth such sentiments, but we have more difficulty in accounting for the unprovoked, uncharitable, unreasonable and unjustifiable attacks made upon an individual by educated men whose interests can never clash with his, whose profession teaches liberality, and whose principal boast is strict impartiality. But there are many mysteries as to theatrical criticism that puzzle the uninitiated. Be that as it may, the respectable portion of the Press, with one consent, extolled the African Roscius during his exceedingly brief engagement at Covent Garden.

It would be futile at this time to attempt to identify the "American actors and some actors who have been in America". We know of no American actors in the Covent Garden company at that time, though Tyrone Power, a native of Ireland, had been to the United States, and Joseph Wood and his wife, Mary Paton, were about to leave for that country. Madame Vestris was known to be reactionary in her outlook, and possibly voiced objection to the presence of Aldridge in the theatre in which she was performing. Another of the principal performers, Miss Ellen Tree (who later married Charles Kean), quite conceivably may have been under pressure by her friends and admirers not to allow herself to be "pawed about by Mr. Henry Wallack's black servant". It was not, however, until years later, after she and her husband toured the United States, that she expressed such opinions as that the people in England who were sympathetic to the struggle of the Negro people in the United States had been duped by Harriet Beecher Stowe, who had done "a cruel injustice to the southern people and had absurdly ennobled the negro [*sic*] into an angel without wings".[2] Then, of course, there was the hostile Press. All this undoubtedly had its effect, but the fact is that Aldridge came to Covent Garden at a bad time; the long-continued financial crisis of that great theatre was the subject of much editorial comment in the contemporary Press. The *Spectator* of 4th May 1833 carried a long and interesting article on the breaking up of the theatrical monopoly and the plight of the "two huge overgrown houses which have long been tottering to their fall".

We give the text of two letters (to our knowledge the only ones extant of that period), which Aldridge received after his appearance at Covent Garden:

SIR,—Although an entire stranger to you, I cannot refrain from offering you my warmest congratulations upon your successful début of last night. Having had the pleasure of seeing you both at Southampton and Bath, I have from that time cherished a deep interest for your further success, and on seeing by the bills of Covent Garden that you were engaged at that House afforded me more than ordinary pleasure, and with much anxiety for your success did I witness your performance and a more flattering reception could not have been expected even by the most sanguine. With respect to the Press, fear them not—you have the best friend Man can have, viz. the Public! ! !

The hand-bills alluded to, and the evident party feelings expressed by the Press will only stimulate the Public in favour of your highly deserving merit. I conjure you, do not let them act upon your mind, keep up your spirits, for you have many powerful enemies, as Talent is invariably followed by envy and detraction.

I fear I shall not be enabled to witness your second appearance, but I will endeavour as nothing will afford me more pleasure than being one of the number to establish your fame, although I am in full confidence of your victorious, nay Glorious, success.

Believe me to remain,

Your sincere well-wisher,

N. GEARY.

While Mr. Geary enjoined him not to fear the Press because the public were his best friend, a vociferous minority of powerful people, organized, proved to be a more potent force than a majority who remained only "well-wishers", and this minority, combined with the economic situation of the major theatres, played their part, and Aldridge never again appeared at Covent Garden. He did, however, return to London to play at the Lyceum in 1858 after a successful Continental tour, and again in 1865, with all his medals, orders, and decorations, at the Haymarket with Madge Robertson as his Desdemona.

The second letter is of a more personal nature:

DEAR ALDRIDGE,—I have just this morning seen the *Globe* of Thursday last. I need scarcely say the pleasure it gives me to hear of your success, and as I also find by it that you repeat the character on Thursday, I hope the repetition will make, if possible, a greater impression than the first. However, I rest satisfied as I feel certain from the remarks, your rising celebrity cannot in any way be

checked by your ill-wishers as I think you have now advanced a
step beyond their power. I would feel very happy in receiving a
paper from you as it is a very difficult thing to see in this part of
the country.

I remain here until Saturday next as I will have to wait for my
Benefit a week longer than I expected, owing to the conduct of
the blaguard [*sic*] I have to deal with, Burrows. I suppose I need
say no more on the subject as I understand you have reason to
know the gentleman. I hope Mrs. Aldridge is quite recovered in
her health and I also hope you take every care of her. Believe me,
my dear friend, one who studies the interest of her *companion* as
much as she does yours, deserves that in return which I will not
now deem to dictate to your feelings, at the same time I trust you
will not consider what I say *presumption*, but had I not your
success and happiness so much to heart as I have I should not have
thus *offended*. I am about writing a letter to my mother and as you
may feel assured she would be happy to hear of your success.
I shall inform her as far as I know. I joined Copeland at White-
haven, but he did not answer my letter as I expected, but delayed
doing so until the day before the elections began, consequently I
made nothing of it.

Lancaster is a *damd* bad Theatrical town. We have been very
well received. Great applause and all that sort of thing, but very
little money.

I have written to Alexander, Glasgow, last night and today I
send a letter to Leeds and another to Wakefield, to W. Burroughs,
so you see, I as yet don't know to what place I go from here, but
should you direct a paper or a letter to me here, it will reach me
as I will be here until 20th at all events. Charlotte joins me with
kind remembrances to yourself and Mrs. Aldridge, and believe
me, dear Aldridge, your humble but sincere friend,

H. H. BENET.

PS.—I stop at Mrs. Barton's where you lodged. I find her a
very nice woman; she requests of me to offer you her compliments. Direct for me at Mrs. Barton's, Highgate, Kendal.

H. H. Benet obviously is a brother actor who probably played
with Aldridge in some provincial company, and he too is aware
of the opposition. Burrows must be the local manager of the
Kendal Theatre, with whom he is having his troubles. Alexander
is the eccentric "Old Alec" whom we have already met. Benet's
inquiry about Mrs. Aldridge's health, and the gentle reproof that

follows give one of the few clues we have of the relationship between Aldridge and his wife. The rest of the letter touches on the normal problems of the touring player who knows not which theatre, if any, will receive him next. He is staying in the same digs in Kendal at which Aldridge stopped.

*   *   *

Those two days, 10th and 12th April 1833, will for ever be red-letter days in the history of world theatre and human progress, for in those days a lone Negro from an enslaved people challenged the great white actors in the very heart of their Empire, in their own Theatre Royal, Covent Garden, in one of the greatest roles conceived by Shakespeare. Some thirty years later, following the example of Aldridge, another Negro actor, Morgan Smith, appeared in one of London's minor theatres, the Olympic, as well as in the provinces, in many roles—Othello, Shylock, Macbeth, etc.—with some measure of success, and then disappeared from the scene. It was almost a hundred years later that Paul Robeson appeared at the Theatre Royal, Drury Lane, in *Show Boat* and at the Savoy in *Othello*, with Peggy Ashcroft as Desdemona and Sybil Thorndike as Emilia, and in 1943 he played a record-breaking *Othello* for the first time in New York, on Broadway, only a short distance from the site of the little African Theatre where the African Roscius got his start.

CHAPTER IX

The Surrey Theatre and After

COVENT GARDEN is over, and immediately comes an offer from the Surrey, one of the more important of London's minor theatres. Davidge, who had engaged Aldridge at the Coburg in 1825, was its Manager and, knowing what a drawing card he was, made haste to engage him.

"Mr. Aldridge, a native of Senegal", announced the Surrey on 17th April, 1833, "and known by the appellation of the AFRICAN ROSCIUS, is engaged at this Theatre for Two Nights; and will have the honor of making his first appearance on Monday next, 22nd April, in Shakespeare's play of *Othello*." And at the bottom of the playbill: "N.B. The circumstances of a MAN OF COLOUR performing Othello on the British Stage is indeed an epoch in the history of Theatricals; and the honor conferred upon him in being called for LAST WEEK AT COVENT GARDEN THEATRE by the unanimous voice of the Audience to receive their tribute of applause is as highly creditable to the native talent of the sunny climes of Africa as to the universal liberality of a British Public."

The same playbill shows Henry Wallack appearing in two of that evening's offerings, *The Smuggler's Fate!* and *The Shadowless Man*. So he too may have been instrumental in bringing Aldridge to the Surrey after the Covent Garden close-down. This appears to have been a difficult period for Wallack, who, three months earlier, was in the Insolvent Debtors' Court, where he attributed his plight to the failure of his trip to America and the heavy expenses to which "professional gentlemen" were subjected. He is now playing leads at the Surrey, but, as the playbill shows, Aldridge gets top star billing, while Mr. H. Wallack is listed in the same small type as the rest of the cast. Thus did the protégé overtake his patron! Wallack also played in the "after pieces" following Aldridge.

Originally he was announced for two nights only, but as far

Playbill for the Theatre
[Roy]al, Wolverhampton, 1846,
[with] woodcuts of Aldridge in
[som]e of his parts.

9. Ira Aldridge as Aaron in *Titus Andronicus*, Britannia Theatre, Hoxton, 1852. Engraving of a daguerreotype, in the Raymond Mander and Joe Mitchenson Theatre Collection.

10. Ira Aldridge as Mungo in *The Padlock*, c. 1840. From an oil painting by an unknown artist in the Enthoven Collection, Victoria and Albert Museum.

as can be ascertained from existing playbills, he made eleven appearances spread over a month. Nothing new was added to his repertoire during this engagement. *Sambo's Courtship*, given on 7th May after *Paul and Virginia*, is but another name for *Laugh While You Can*, with Aldridge in the title role of Sambo.

Thus far no proper reviews of these performances have come to light. It seems that the Press, having exhausted themselves, for and against, on the Covent Garden engagement, let it go at that, but not so the low-level scribes. We give the text of three unidentified newspaper items which would ordinarily be beneath notice, did they not serve to show the attempts made to inflame the public against the Negro actor, and the kind of attack and ridicule which would under no circumstances be directed at a white actor, however incompetent:

Our friend the Roscius took a benefit on Monday at the Surrey, and government having gained intimation of the contemplated proceeding, a large body of police was marched early into the neighbourhood, for as it was supposed the nigger's personal friends would muster in great numbers, it was natural to expect that the assembly would consist of all the blackguards of the metropolis. Happily, we have not heard of any fatal result. The Old Commodore* from the crossing in Tottenham Court Road occupied a private box and every specie of black, whether the nigger darkened by nature or the sweep dyed by his professional pursuits, was in attendance to do honour to this respectable associate. We fainted at that part of *The Padlock* where Mungo spills the beer, for the Roscius sucked it off the stage with a frightful relish for the filthy deed! and on coming to, we found ourselves in the laboratory of a highly respectable chemist adjacent to the establishment.

On May 10th it was announced that the African Roscius would play a white part, whereupon appears the following:

At the Surrey the unhappy Nigger has been facetiously advertised for a *white* part, and as his black face has brought nothing to the treasury, they have been trying the experiment of having him stuccoed and whitewashed as a dramatic novelty. Chalk and plaster of paris have, however, failed as much as his native soot,

* Billy Waters, the one-legged Negro crossing-sweeper, immortalized in Pierce Egan's *Tom and Jerry*.

for not all the whitening in the kingdom will transmogrify the unseemly nigger into the shadow of a genius. The man seems to rely solely on colour for his inspiration, and imagines that though nature has made him an Othello, he has only to resort to the paint-pot to become a Romeo. Talent is, however, not to be thrown in, in distemper colours, and not twenty coats of paint would make an actor of the black whom we have so wholesomely flagellated. Instead of hearing that a play is in rehearsal, we shall be told that the *die is cast*, and that instead of such an actor being about to study a certain part, the African Roscius will shortly be painted for a new character.

★   ★   ★

We had promised not to mention the nigger's name again, but we have received a letter from a person signing herself, "A Sufferer", who complains that the Roscius used the most indecent language in the avenues to the theatre. We are sorry we cannot interfere in this, for our control does not extend to the nigger's private peculiarities; that he should not have the manners of a gentleman cannot surprise us, seeing that he was once a slave, then a footman, afterward a Roscius and now, thanks to us and to *The Times*, a quack detected.

We do not know how Aldridge reacted to these scurrilous scribblings, but it is doubtful that he could have shrugged them off without some anger and bitterness. Certain it is, however, that theatre managers in London were not indifferent to them.

During his long engagement at the Surrey, Aldridge took two nights off, 17th and 18th May, to appear at the Pavilion Theatre, Whitechapel, in *Othello*, and a week after leaving the Surrey he returns to the Pavilion on 27th May in *Alonzo of Castille, or The Treacherous Moor* (Zanga, in *The Revenge*). The playbill, perhaps in an effort to counteract the attacks just mentioned, announced:

TO THE PUBLIC

This is the first person of Colour (*a black man*, vulgarly called) that ever appeared in England as an aspirant to the Histrionic Art; and it cannot fail to prove interesting at this period, when Negro emancipation is about to be accomplished,★ to behold one of that ill-used and degraded race portraying the finest passions of the human mind, with a knowledge of his author so correct, and

★ Slavery was abolished in the British Colonies that year (1833).

a demeanour so appropriate, as to stamp him at once the "Gentleman and Scholar".

Through the month of June he has a run at the City Theatre, Milton Street, Cripplegate (not to be confused with the City of London Theatre, Norton Folgate, near Bishopsgate Station, where he plays several years later). It was the City that tried to steal some of Covent Garden's thunder by presenting the African Apollo, and now they have the African Roscius! His engagement began on 11th June under John Webster's management and, as *John Bull* put it, he was "considerably clapped".

In the midst of his London engagement he finds time to dash to Bath for a single appearance in *Karfa* for the benefit of Mr. Mulleny, a colleague, which means that he played gratis. Following this, he began an extended tour of the provinces, not returning to London until fifteen years later, when he has another long run at the Surrey.

By the time Queen Victoria came to the throne, Aldridge's reputation was firmly established throughout the British Isles, but though he had won the hearts of the people of England, he had failed to capture the fancy of London society.

After starting his fresh tour of the provinces, we hear of him first in Swansea, Wales, on 1st August in *Pizarro* and *The Padlock*, and on his benefit night, 3rd August, he does Oroonoko and Shylock. The following extract from the local Press is typical of the notices he received:

> On Monday evening Mr. Aldridge sustained the part of Othello; and though we have a strong recollection of the powers of Kean and Macready in the character, yet the chaste style and correct judgment of Mr. Aldridge left us very little, if anything, to regret in the comparison. He was warmly applauded throughout. His Mungo in *The Padlock* displayed the versatility of his talent, and astonished and delighted the audience. Vociferously encored . . . rapturous applause. . . .[1]

A week later the same publication said: "We were highly gratified with his personation of Oroonoko; but his Shylock was to us sustained with an ability far exceeding our conception of his capabilities and he was warmly applauded throughout."

But while Aldridge was delighting the provincial audiences and critics, his enemies were still at work, and the following item went the round of the sensational Press:

DEATH OF THE AFRICAN ROSCIUS. A melancholy and fatal accident occurred to Mr. Aldridge, the African Roscius, last week. Mr. Aldridge was returning in his carriage from the seat of Colonel Powell when, within half a mile of Llandillo, one of the horses took fright at the blaze of light from the iron works with which the county is studded; this occurred at the brink of a precipice, over which the carriage swerved with its inmate, dragging the horses and postillion. The footman had a most providential escape. He was in the act of alighting to seize the horses' heads as the carriage was precipitated over the cliff. It is needless to add that Mr. Aldridge, the postillion and the horses were killed on the spot—the carriage being dashed to atoms. The place where this frightful accident occurred is 120 feet from the summit to the bottom. . . .

Llandillo is not far from Swansea, where he had just finished playing.

The *Memoir* comments on this report:

The success of a hoax of the above kind depends more upon its apparent seriousness than evident probability, and the particulars of the "melancholy and fatal accident" were so carefully and minutely set forth that nobody doubted them. The author knew well how to lie, but we do not envy him his merit, nor the satisfaction he derived from his vicious invention. In all probability he was a Yankee who forged the falsehood, for such hoaxes have come from that country until the cry of "Wolf" would not be believed in this, were it ever so well founded. Mr. Aldridge, however, was not injured by the groundless report in question. On the contrary, it made his name the more known, increased the interest which those who knew him took in his welfare, and served as a strong advertisement in widely circulating his fame. In time it became generally known that the African Roscius was alive and still prospering.

On 19th August Aldridge writes from Aberystwyth, Wales, to a Mr. J. Tierney of 74 Drury Lane, obviously a brother actor:

DEAR SIR,—I have this day received your favour and in return beg leave to say my arrangements will not permit me to be in

London at the time you mention the benefit takes place, or I
should be most happy to tender my services on the occasion. . . .
I have been very successful, indeed, Thank God. . . .

In November he is back in Hull, where he plays all his stock
characters for about two weeks and introduces a new one, Tomba,
an Esquimaux Chief, in *Captain Ross*, probably a version of *Captain Ross, or The Hero of the Arctic Regions*, by an unrecorded
author, which had been produced at the Pavilion Theatre, Whitechapel, in the previous October. The Hull play was obviously
revised to give it particular local interest.

CAPTAIN ROSS'S VOYAGE OF DISCOVERIES!
Benefit
of the
African Roscius

and positively his last appearance here, on which occasion an
original Drama will be produced, founded on the unparalleled
adventures of Capt. Ross . . . the Patriotic and indefatigable
Circumnavigator.

PROGRAMME OF THE SCENERY

Residence of Capt. Ross in London. Deck of the Discovery Ship.
Preparations for Sailing. BOOTHIA'S ISLAND. Manners and Customs
of the Attempt to explore THE NORTH WEST PASSAGE. ICEBERGS.
Extensive view of the Arctic Regions. Interview of Commander
Ross with the Yacks. Etc., etc.

Spectacle again, and on the same bill, extracts from *Othello*,
Bertram, *The Merchant of Venice*, and *The Padlock*, as well as
comic dances, duets and a sailors' hornpipe by members of the
company in between! So Aldridge adds yet another nationality to
the characters he portrays, but clearly there was little for him to
do in this role; he was almost part of the scenery.

One extract from the *Hull Mercury* at this time is worth noting:

. . . In mentioning the African Roscius on a previous occasion,
we stated that the mind displayed in this performance was of a
character completely to put to shame those calumniators who
have stated that the intellect of the Negro race is inferior to that
of his brothers; and we find that the critics, wherever he has
appeared, perfectly coincide with us. His performance of Othello
was such as can be equalled by very few actors of the present day.

He has very much improved since first we saw him. From his evident industry, and the enthusiasm he evinces for his profession, it is to be presumed that he will not remain stationary, but will rise further in eminence.

He then goes on to Dublin, where he again plays with Miss Huddart. *Saunders's News Letter* of 18th December comments on the very poor attendance at one of his performances, "but notwithstanding the house rang with continued bursts of applause called forth by the touching and energetic but chaste acting of the Moor. Miss Huddart was also much applauded and indeed deservedly. At the conclusion of the play there was a general call for 'Roscius' and Mr. Barry, who had come to announce the entertainments for this evening, was forced to retire. In a few moments he reappeared, followed by Mr. Aldridge. Loud and enthusiastic applause hailed him."

On 23rd December we again see an announcement of "his last appearance in Dublin previous to his departure for his native country". It may be that after Covent Garden he felt the time was propitious for him to try his own country, particularly as many other English stars were making successful American tours. He does not go, however, and on the playbill of the Cork Theatre for 23rd April 1834 we see that he is "performing prior to his departure from this Kingdom"; but on 15th August of that year, Aldridge himself writes a letter to Mr. Maxfield, Manager of the Southampton Theatre:

DEAR SIR,—Having to revisit Swansea and Cheltenham, which Engagements do not commence until the beginning of the ensuing month Septr., and being on the eve of returning to my native country, from the success I met with on my first appearance in Southampton, I should be most happy to act a few nights with you previous to my departure immediately, or at the termination of my Cheltenham and Swansea engagements, if your arrangements will permit.

I have an entire new cast of Characters besides three original pieces written expressly for me, one entitled *Hassan the Moor* which was played ten successive nights in Dublin and fourteen in Cork the last season, besides after-pieces which will enable me to be in both each night. The cost in getting the pieces up before named would be comparatively nothing and the principal parts come in the hands of few. I finish here on Monday night and shall wait the favour of your reply, which I most earnestly solicit by return of post. *I will come for fourths and a half benefit.*

Hoping you are in the enjoyment of that inestimable blessing, health, I subscribe myself, Sir,

Your Most Obdt Svt.

IRA F. ALDRIDGE.

The African Roscius.

What American negotiations, if any, were being carried on at that time we do not know. Perhaps Henry Wallack, who now had close connexions with the New York theatre, proposed such a visit, as we know for a fact that he did years later, in 1858. However, Aldridge did not return to his native country.

In 1835 evidence of the quality of Aldridge's acting comes from two unimpeachable sources—from professionals of the very highest calibre, both foremost artists in their own spheres, Miss O'Neill and Madame Malibran.

Eliza O'Neill (1791-1872), later Lady Elizabeth Wrixon Becher, was one of Ireland's greatest actresses. She was considered the successor to Mrs. Siddons on the English stage and was celebrated for her Shakespearean acting, particularly her portrayal of Juliet. She heralded the advent of realism on the English stage, as did Edmund Kean, and they were both criticized for it by the aristocrats of the time. She could therefore appreciate what Aldridge was doing, and as a great actress herself her judgment of her contemporaries is worthy of the deepest respect. In a letter to a Dr. Galway of Mallow, Ireland, she wrote:

. . . I have seen him [Aldridge] in Cheltenham and Cork and during my professional as well as private life, I never saw so correct a portraiture of Othello amidst the principal luminaries of my age. It is true, Kean reserved himself for particular passages, which were made to deliver with startling effect; but as a whole, his performance was not superior to the Roscius, whose acting throughout is transcendently uniform.

According to our records, Aldridge's first appearance at Cheltenham was in August 1833, and at Cork in April 1834, and it must have been at these performances that Miss O'Neill saw him. Her criticism gets down to the basic quality of an actor's art—of any work of art—the unity of the whole. Kean's illuminating of Shakespeare by "flashes of lightning" is too well known to stress, but after such flashes, the darkness would tend to be darker. Aldridge, too, had his passionate and dynamic passages, as did Miss O'Neill herself, but he never lost sight of the whole, and was "transcendently uniform". One could ask for no higher praise from one professional to another, and thus, according to one of the great tragic actresses of the time, Aldridge ranks with the great Edmund Kean.

Madame Maria Malibran (1808-36) was the famous operatic singer, who made her début at Covent Garden in the same year that Aldridge made his first major appearance at the Coburg. Her gifts as an actress equalled a soprano voice of unusual beauty and phenomenal compass, and she was proclaimed in England as the greatest singer-actress known. In the course of her short life she had travelled extensively throughout England, Europe, and the United States, and was in a position to compare Aldridge with the great actors of those countries, and this is what she wrote to him from Manchester on 18th April 1835:

> Mme. Malibran presents her grateful respects and compliments to the African Roscius for the high treat afforded her last night in his intellectual personation of Othello. Mme. Malibran never witnessed in the course of her professional career in both hemispheres, a more interesting and powerful performance, marked throughout by that strict adherence to nature which should be the characteristic of every dramatic portraiture. In returning the volume so kindly lent by Mr. Aldridge, she begs to tender her best thanks and sincere wishes for his continued success.

But Aldridge receives not only high praise—he also receives the kind of treatment which produces an occasional letter like the one he wrote on 3rd August 1835 from Kanturk, Ireland, to a Mr. McDonald of the City Mart, Patrick Street, Cork:

> SIR,—In answer to a letter from me bearing date February, you requested me to address you in the course of 10 days, when you will inform me what your arrangements were with respect to myself. I did so nearly a fortnight since from Charleville, but to my surprise received no reply whatever. Not being aware of having merited such neglect, I have thus again addressed you.
> I have the honour to be,
>   Yours Resp'y,
>   I. ALDRIDGE.

CHAPTER X

Patrons

IN the nineteen years between his Covent Garden appearance and the beginning of his Continental tour, Aldridge wandered and worked throughout the provinces of England, in the second stage of preparation for his triumph and recognition in Europe and Russia. In these lean years he made many friends in Ireland and Scotland, where sympathies leaned more toward the representative of an oppressed coloured people than toward Englishmen of their own colour. Ever the realist, he took steps to establish his *bona fides* as a gentleman, a man of culture and good manners. To this end he obtained many written testimonials and introductions from important public figures, ending up with a list of "patrons" that would have graced any royal society. Following are samples of the type of letters written in his behalf:*

From the Honourable Mrs. Lyons to Mrs. Bond of Derricor Castle:

> *Lediston.*
> *July 20, 1837.*
>
> DEAR MRS. BOND,—Will you excuse my writing to solicit your influence and interest in favour of the African Roscius? Mr. Aldridge is deservedly esteemed, both in public and private life. His rehearsals from Shakespeare are beautiful; also his Zanga, and many other parts suitable for his colour. He dined with us three days, meeting Lady Chapman, and her party, my own family, and Hon. Mrs. Dease, etc., as he fortunately happened to be in this country when we, who are rarely so gay, had a long run of company; and in the evenings he was most good-naturedly generous of his talents, and delighted us with a sweet voice to the guitar, and his amusing comic songs. He was popular, to a great degree, to those who knew him here.
>
> Yours, etc.,
>
> E. M. LYONS.

* Source: The Harvard Theatre Collection.

From Mr. Evander McIvor, Banker of Dingwall, to Mr.
George Murray, the Honourable the Provost of Tain, 2nd
May 1840:

I take the liberty of introducing to your friendly notice Mr.
Aldridge, whom you saw perform here on Thursday evening with
so much success. I need only say that, as Provost of Tain, your
patronage will be of consequence to him, and that you will find
him not only excelling very eminently in his profession, but a
gentleman, both in manners and education.

Testimonial from His Grace the Archbishop of Tuam, John
McHale, 11th November 1837:

The character for excellence in dramatic performance which
the African Roscius has attained throughout the country he has
amply sustained by his exhibitions in this town—as I am informed
by persons very competent to form a correct opinion.

He has enhanced his professional character by rendering it sub-
servient to the interests of religion; and we have to acknowledge
with gratitude that, on more than one occasion, he has devoted
his talents to the forwarding of the Cathedral of this diocese.

From 1835 to 1839 he played mostly in Ireland. "In his uphill
struggle after eminence," says Dr. Smith—

Mr. Aldridge met warmest encouragements from the Irish
people. Some of his best friends are among the middle and higher
classes in Dublin and Belfast, who urged him constantly to
aim at the highest excellence; and among the common people
he has friends and supporters who cheer him on as only Irishmen
can cheer. When we look today at the sentiments of Mitchell,
Meagher, and O'Connor, on the one hand, and at the chronic
hate with which the Irish masses in America act out such sentiments towards the coloured man in America, we are led to alter
the celebrated line, "Those who cross the ocean change their skies
but not their minds", and exclaim

> *Qui trans mare currunt*
> *Coelum et animum mutant.* *

(Those who cross the seas change both their skies and their
minds.)

* The original reads:

> *Coelum non animum*
> *Qui trans mare currunt.*

An Irish newspaper of this period carried an article entitled "Tipperary Theatricals—the African Roscius and Amateurs":

> This highly gifted individual, Mr. Aldridge, the celebrated African Roscius, has been sojourning in Tipperary for the last week, and has received from the inhabitants of the town generally, as well as of the surrounding country, a tribute of respect seldom tendered to any of the Thespian fraternity. . . . On the boards, as the personator of the avaricious Shylock, the jealous Othello, or the vengeful Zanga in Dr. Young's *Revenge*, he has no competitor, and we may justly say, in Shakespeare's words, "We ne'er shall look upon his like again".

"In private life", observed the *Memoir*, "the pleasing and happy manner, the gentle and unassuming deportment, the suavity and grace with which Mr. Aldridge is endowed have won for him many friends whose esteem will, we trust, be as permanent as his theatrical fame will be pre-eminently lasting." Our study of Ira Aldridge shows how very short, in reality, was his theatrical fame, though it glowed very brightly in his lifetime. Once his story comes out of its undeserved obscurity, his fame will inevitably become "pre-eminently lasting".

Aldridge did everything possible to make his profession a "respectable" one. Indeed, certain critics chided him for bowdlerizing Shakespeare which, in fact, he did, for in this way he believed he could bring "respectable" audiences into the theatre. Better a bowdlerized Shakespeare than none. We will examine later, for example, how he turned *Titus Andronicus* inside out.

During these years Aldridge, battling against the economic depression and the Puritan attitude towards the theatre, drew audiences where others failed. In the spring of 1838 he writes and performs "A Grand Classic and Dramatic Entertainment", which was billed as follows:

THE AFRICAN ROSCIUS
(*Of the Theatre Royal, Drury Lane,*★ *and Covent Garden*)

BEGS leave to announce to the Nobility, Gentry, and Public in general, of Belfast and its Vicinity that, during the process of a highly successful professional tour over this country, he will, in the ensuing week, have the honour of giving his Entertainment, consisting of Dramatic Readings, Illustrations, Extracts, and

★ Here the writer of the bill matter stretched the truth a little.

Impersonations, embodying his principal characters, as portrayed by him throughout the principal Cities and Towns in the United Kingdoms. A brief introductory LECTURE on the DRAMA, containing the favourable opinions on the Stage of most of the ancient distinguished Divine Writers—A Memoir of the African (written by himself and delivered by him on his recent engagement in the Theatre Royal, Dublin)—His Scene in ROLLA, the CORA of his opening night, and amusing Anecdotes of Mathews's well-known Trip to America, &c., &c.

The following selection, from the most Popular Plays of the present day, comprises the chief illustrations which shall be produced in succession, forming an entire series of Dramatic and Classic Readings, at once novel and interesting, divested of all objectionable matter such as has, for some time, actuated prejudicially against the moral tendencies of the historic profession, and got up with a fastidious respect to the reformation of the present Stage, being suited to the expectations of all classes and persuasions of society—the moral character of which has met the approbation and support of the several respective Clergymen throughout this Kingdom, generally:

OTHELLO, REVENGE, BERTRAM, CASTLE SPECTRE, BLACK BRIGAND OF JAMAICA, MERCHANT OF VENICE, OROONOKO, THE SLAVE, THE PADLOCK (consisting of all the original music), together with JIM CROW! and other Comic Extracts, which shall duly be announced.

For further Particulars—Nights of Performance—Prices of Admission, &c., &c.—see Handbills.[1]

This announcement gives some idea of the nature of the "Classic Entertainment" which so pleased his Irish audiences, and shows that he made a conscious effort to make his material acceptable to "all classes and persuasions of society". Here he includes a brief lecture on the drama, of which we have only the extract contained in the *Memoir*, but it is sufficient to show that it is basically directed against the Puritans, who were still attacking the theatre as they did in Shakespeare's day:

LECTURE IN DEFENCE OF THE DRAMA

Bigotry and fanaticism have excited themselves in all possible shapes to annoy the professors of the dramatic art; but, fortunately, for the honour of the stage and dignity of human nature, it has found patrons and friends in the persons of the greatest and most learned men in the most enlightened periods of the world's history. Nothing can more strongly prove the importance of dramatic amusements than the diametrically opposite opinions that have been entertained upon the subject—opinions that have uniformly run like parallel lines for centuries—unbending, and without the smallest inclination to converge. From a reflecting mind, this view of it alone must claim the most serious investigation. Sculpture, painting, and music are still cherished, and have also been appreciated and esteemed commendable by all, with the miserable exception of the most ignorant; and the Drama, when viewed in its proper light will stand as high as the loftiest of the arts and sciences.

Like every other art and science, however, profession or trade, it has its opponents and its enemies. Among these are many who argue for their opinions on fair, reasonable and honourable terms. There is also another class, twenty times more numerous, more inimical, but less injurious, to the cause of the Drama than the first, and this last class founded their animosity on a basis of folly, ignorance and bigotry, combine in crying it down with the utmost avidity and bitterness. It has also, along with its truly great and eloquent supporters, many unthinking, ill-judging, and ill-advised friends, such as are common in every state, station, business and degree of life, whose ill-digested arguments in its favour are more destructive to its success than otherwise and, consequently, are of that description which, as Hamlet says, "would be much more honoured in the breach than in the observance".

Luther, upon most subjects, would be attended to with respect, if not conviction, and one would imagine that his view of the Stage alone would induce the serious part of the community to attend to the directions of the Stage, not to its destruction. He says, in comedies, particularly those of the Roman writers, the duties of the various situations of life are held out to view, and as it were, reflected from a mirror. The office of parents and the proper conduct of children are faithfully delineated and, what to young men may be advantageous, the vices and characters of profligate women are exhibited in their true colours; excellent lessons given to them how they should conduct themselves toward virtuous women in courtship; strong exhortations to matrimony are brought forward, without which no state, no government can subsist.

After delivering this, he would continue with dramatizations of sections of the Memoir which he had written and which later was the basis of the *1849 Memoir* from which we have been quoting. This procedure is a direct parallel with Mathews's entertainments, *A Trip to America*, where he mimics the Yankees, contemporary life, the African Theatre, and Aldridge. The difference is that Aldridge looked at the United States through the eyes of an American Negro. From a playbill of the Theatre Royal, Belfast, 22nd April 1846, we see included in his "Entertainment" such topics as "A brief glance at the American Character, or the Modern Republican versus the Ancient Roman", and "Liberty and Equality, or the American Slave Market". There is no record of how he actually dealt with these subjects. Perhaps he compared the Ancient Romans and their slaves with the modern republicans and theirs. After all, the Roman Roscius was not only allowed to practise his art, but was honoured by the Emperor himself, whereas the modern republican crushed even the first signs of an African Theatre run by Negroes who were not slaves, but freemen!

Another item in the "Classic Entertainment" was "England, or the Negro Emancipation. The Slave's gratitude." Here Aldridge could pay tribute to the land that gave him freedom to perform on the stage equally with the white, and to the great mass movement against slavery and its actual abolition in Aldridge's lifetime. And he could quote one of his roles, Gambia, in *The Slave*—"No sooner a slave touches English soil than he is free!" Then would follow some Negro songs, "West India Courtship", "Lubly Rosa, Sambo Come", in which he would accompany himself on the Spanish guitar, at which he had become proficient. Then came "Schoolboy Reminiscences—First Impression", "Passages from Early Life"—his portrayal of Rolla (*Pizarro*), the Cora of his opening night. Here Aldridge takes a leaf out of Mathews's *A Trip to America* and parodies Mathews's parody of himself and his black comrades at the African Theatre, perhaps giving a scene from *Richard III* as it was played by them. Then there would be more Negro songs, "Miss Lucy Long", "The Negro's Address to His Mistress, or The Midnight Serenade", ending the programme with the song which he later made famous all over Europe, "The Negro Hunt, or Opossum Up a Gum Tree". In later presentations of this "Classic Entertainment", Aldridge sang "his celebrated Song of Jim Crow, with many whimsicalities and local allusions to Hull . . .". This famous song was introduced to

England by T. D. Rice, who, after making a success in the States, appeared at the Surrey Theatre in London in 1836. Many versions of the song "Jump, Jim Crow" exist, and Aldridge made such amendments and additions as he thought would add to the local interest. So we see Aldridge taking over Mathews's "Opossum" and Rice's "Jim Crow", and in his own inimitable style greatly pleasing his audiences; but there is this difference: Mathews and Rice were white men impersonating the Negro, whereas Aldridge was the genuine character, and he brought out aspects of these songs which the others could never comprehend. As one writer said of him after "nigger minstrelsy" had been introduced to the English public by the Ethiopian Serenaders in 1846: "No mock 'Ethiopian Serenader' could come near this 'veritable nigger', whose good nature, humour and even wit are so commonly ridiculed."[2]

The "Classic Entertainment" would end with excerpts from the plays listed on the bill, inevitably including his most successful and everlasting comic role of Mungo.

The first record of this type of composite entertainment we find in May 1838 in Belfast, and the last in April 1846, also in Belfast. It appears to have been most successful in Ireland. The first bill included extracts from about ten plays in his repertoire, but in the last it is sandwiched between two complete plays, *The Royal Slave* and *Paul and Virginia*. The desire for full-length plays rather than extracts seems to be typical of theatre audiences generally, but one may consider this run over eight years as highly successful, for it was not only "A Grand Classic and Dramatic Entertainment", but an educational one as well, and certainly Aldridge succeeded in educating "all classes and persuasions of society" to come to his shows, as may be seen by the Hull playbill announcing this very entertainment and listing a most impressive array of patrons, including such distinguished personages as His Majesty Leopold, King of Belgium (Queen Victoria's maternal uncle), the Duke of Wellington, Sir Walter Scott, Sir E. Bulwer Lytton, Lord Brougham, one of the great dandies and leader of fashion of the period, Prince Esterhazy, Austrian Ambassador to the British Court, to name just a few. The Army and the clergy were also liberally represented in this impressive list of supporters. It may have been the patronage of King Leopold which prompted Aldridge to choose Belgium for his first Continental appearance, as we shall see, but there is no specific record on this point. A further step in his efforts to achieve approbation and "respectability", and consequently further support, was to become a Freemason. On 26th March 1838 he is made a Brother Mason of the Grand Lodge of Ireland, and in January 1839 an Excellent Brother of the Grand Royal Arch Chapter of Ireland in Dublin— a tribute to the liberal attitude of the Irish to a black man. He was not backward about using this affiliation, sending out special letters to "Brothers" over the signature "Ira Aldridge, M.G.R.A.C.", soliciting their support of his performances. Nor were his brethren shy in calling upon him, as witness a letter from Clonmel in January 1839:

MY DEAR ALDRIDGE,—I received your favour and do assure you that I would not for one moment differ as to terms if I could afford it, *but I tell you on my Solemn word as a Brother* that in consequence of the heavy expenses of building the Cork Theatre which I am satisfied you will say is one of the handsomest and most comfortable you have seen, that I am at this moment *struggling* and I may so say, *you must assist the Brother*, and I will pay you punctually and honestly.

On my soul I am delighted you are getting on so well and I pray you will *have a bumper on Friday evening*. I ask you as a favour to take the terms for the Cork Theatre, as my expenses there will be extremely heavy and on my obligation, and I will if in my power at some future time return the compliment—I will give you the Third for hire—and if you wish Mrs. Conner engaged tell her husband to let me know in a word his lowest terms for their joint services, as of course she would not come without him.

I send this to my friend Murray, one of the agents of the Sackville Street Coach office, who will send it to you free; now I again entreat you will not ask me more than the *Five Pounds a Night*, as I really under present circumstances *could not afford to pay it*—your Benefit in Cork I know will be an immense house and pay you well besides stopping here for a few nights will break the journey. I will expect your reply at your earliest convenience, and am, with most respectful compliments to Mrs. Aldridge,

Yours faithfully,

FRANK SEYMOUR.

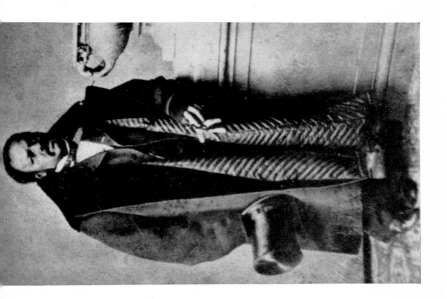

1850s.

12. *Right:* Ira Aldridge as Othello, Constantinople, 1866. From a photograph in the Raymond Mander and Joe Mitchenson Theatre Collection.

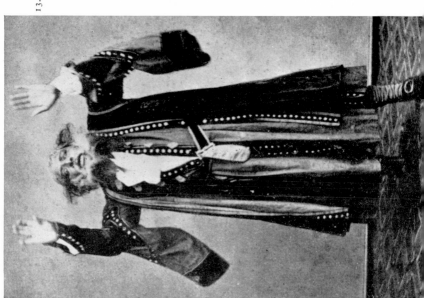

13. *Left:* Ira Aldridge as
Shylock.

14. *Right:* Ira Aldridge as
King Lear. From a photo-
graph in the Bakhrushin

We see here that Mrs. Aldridge receives a mention. For the most part she remains in the background and, were it not for an occasional reference such as the above, her existence would go unnoticed. But she accompanies her husband on many of his tours, and in the conditions of travelling in those days he must have relied on her a good deal to make life tolerable. She was proud of him and did all she could to further his career, especially in the early years. "She made him work", we were told by Miss Amanda Aldridge, and she kept an eye on the workings of the box-office, as we shall see.

In September 1840 his father died in New York at the age of sixty-eight. While we have no direct expression of his feelings on this occasion, it must have been a sad time for Aldridge, for there are indications that he was greatly attached to his family, despite the long separation from them. As late as 1860, we find him inquiring of Dr. Smith about the welfare of his stepmother, his brother Joshua, and other members of his family. In making plans at various times to visit the United States professionally, he was probably motivated in part by a wish to see his relations. Daniel Aldridge must have been proud before the end to know of his son's amazing success, and he would have been prouder still, and not a little bewildered, had he seen the Hull playbill less than a year later showing that his son had reached that height of respectability and honour to which any actor, especially a black one in a white society, could aspire.

It is understandable that at this point in his career Aldridge should be contemplating a tour of the United States. We know that he had been considering it since 1834. His virtual exile from London, the parlous state of the theatre in the provinces, and his own insecure economic position, despite his popularity, prompted him to consider such a step. The *Theatrical Journal* may write, "Mr. Aldridge, the African Roscius, whom our correspondent mentioned last week as having been very successful in the North, keeps a corps dramatique of his own and he drives them about from town to town in an elegant and capacious turnout, the produce of his receipts",[3] and the *Roscommon Journal* may write, "He has succeeded, though yet a young man, in realizing a handsome fortune",[4] but this is only the publicity side of the medal. John Coleman wrote a first-hand account of the conditions under which Aldridge worked as late as 1845:

When I returned to Derby, Martin met me on the Elvaston Road, with a note from the Duchess ordering me to come to tea (teas were substantial meals in those days), and inviting me to spend my last night at the play with her, alleging that she had already secured the seats. A new Shakespearean hero was announced for the Christmas holidays, the famous African Roscius. Mr. Ira Aldridge—so this gentleman called himself—stated that he was the son of an African Prince of illustrious descent. His family had been sold to slavery, but he had escaped from bondage, and found shelter in "the land whose foot the slave no sooner touches than he becomes free" (*vide The Slave*). To be sure, the sceptical (the late Doctor Joy* among others), alleged that the so-called prince had been James Wallack's dresser in New York, that he had caught stage fever from *Handsome Jim* and, knowing that there was no possibility of his being permitted to put foot on the stage in the States, he had made tracks for London, where he played his cards so well that he actually made his début at Covent Garden as Othello.

As I reached the market-place I saw the prince driving down the High Street in his carriage, and a very princely affair it was. The coachman on the box, the flunkeys behind, and the distinguished-looking coloured gentleman inside attracted crowds as it leisurely rolled along.

Poor Prince! When I came to know him two or three years later, he told me that on this identical occasion the gorgeous equipage had been in pawn at the railway station, and it was only through the kindness of the officials he was permitted to borrow it to parade through the town, for the purpose of attracting an audience. He, or the carriage, or both, drew a crowded house, of which the Duchess and I were units. The play was *Othello*, and the farce *The Virginian Mummy*—from tragedy to comedy with a vengeance!

The performance appeared rather peculiar, inasmuch as Desdemona and Emilia were conspicuous by their absence, and even *The Virginian Mummy* was acted without the aid of a lady! Desdemona, being indispensable in the last scene, spoke from behind the bed-curtains, which were artfully draped so as to conceal her from the audience. At first I thought that, from a sense of propriety, the fair-haired daughter of the isles declined to be seen in a nightdress; but when a partial derangement of the drapery afforded a glimpse of an elderly matron, with a large

* Stage Manager for Calcraft at the Dublin Theatre Royal and later general factotum to Charles Kean.

pair of blue spectacles and a larger Roman nose, reading the part from a book, I was somewhat disillusioned. *The Virginian Mummy*, however, restored good temper to the audience, for Mr. Aldridge was a genuine comedian, and the vagaries of Ginger Blue kept the audience in roars of laughter and sent everybody away satisfied.

That was a fateful night for me. It sent me away dreaming. I had never seen *Othello* before. Despite its being mangled and mutilated thus barbarously, it stood out a heartrending tale of human love and human woe, the one perfect play of all the ages. It held me spellbound, and has held me ever since. If this effect could be produced by a Negro and a handful of barn-stormers without even a Desdemona or an Emilia, what might not be achieved with proper treatment? A Moor, too, a noble Moor, a son of the princely Abeuceranges, tinged only slightly with "the burnished livery of the sun", instead of an elderly, obese, woolly-headed Ethiopian, attired like a cymbal-player, and blacker than a Christy minstrel. Heavens! What a chance for distinction![5]

At the time referred to, Aldridge was thirty-eight years old, he was more copper-coloured than black, and, though getting a bit stocky, he was not obese!

★   ★   ★

The objective of playing once again in a major London theatre was ever uppermost in Aldridge's mind, and his continued successes in the provinces were beginning to bear fruit in this connection. By 1846 we find frequent comment in the Press in various parts of the country on London's boycott of Aldridge. The *Edinburgh Weekly Express* said: "We are sorry that our London managers have not as yet secured his services, for it cannot be doubted that his success would be immense. It is true he had had offers made him, but has very properly refused them, being from establishments the frequenters to which are not likely to appreciate his talent or add to his respectability as a gentleman and an actor."[6]

★   ★   ★

The date of Aldridge's first appearance as Fabian in *The Black Doctor* is uncertain. The text of this play, as published in London in the 1870s in Dicks' Standard Play series, says on the outside cover, "*The Black Doctor*—By Ira Aldridge", but on the flyleaf we get a little nearer the truth with "*The Black Doctor*—A Romantic

155

Drama in Four Acts—Adapted to the English Stage by Ira Aldridge", and we are further told that it was "First Produced at the City of London Theatre, July 1841". But this is an error; the Dicks series are notorious for wrong casts and data. The play is an adaptation from *Le Docteur Noir*, written by Auguste Anicet-Bourgeois and Pinel Dumanoir, produced at the Theatre Port-Saint-Martin in July 1846 with Frederic Lemaitre, the great French actor, with whom Aldridge was favourably compared, as Fabian, in which role he was *"poetique et terrible"*. Our first trace of it in London is at the City of London Theatre on 9th November 1846, but the adaptation was by Thomas Archer, and Fabian was played by a Mr. Lyon. A second version by John V. Bridgeman followed four days later at the Victoria. Our first record of Aldridge in the role is in Bath and Dublin in February 1847, and it remained an important part of his repertoire for many years, though he does not appear to have played it outside of England. He may, of course, have made a version of the play for himself from one of the already existing translations.

The play deals with the love of a young and beautiful French noblewoman for the mulatto doctor who saved her life. The playbill of the Theatre Royal of Dundee for 29th May 1848 announces the last night but two of Aldridge's engagement and the "First Night of a New Spectacle entitled the *Lovers of Bourbon*" (the dual name of *The Black Doctor*), and gives the following précis:

The hero is Fabian, the Creole, who has acquired the name of the "Black Doctor". The first act is supposed to pass in the island of Bourbon, and Fabian, having displayed his skill in the family of the Marchioness de la Reynerie, is made free. He has dared in secret to love Pauline, the daughter of the noble, and believing that her affections are devoted to the Chevalier de St. Luce, he takes advantage of the accident which enables him to be her guide in a distant part of the island, to bring her to a spot where the rising tide will destroy both. There he discloses his hidden passion, and at the moment when death is at their feet, Pauline declares that she has ever felt a kindred emotion for the Creole. The waves swell round the rock on which they stand, and the curtain falls at this moment. The scene then changes to Paris. Fabian and Pauline have been saved—they are wedded in secret, and he is attached to the household of the Marchioness as domestic physician. The Count de St. Luce, encouraged by the mother, presses his suit, insults the Creole, of whom he entertains a latent jealousy, and driven to despair, the daughter of the Marchioness reveals the fact of her marriage, when Fabian is consigned to the Bastille. The third act discloses some of the history of that celebrated fortress, St. Luce being confined in a state apartment for some trivial political offence, while his rival, immured in the dungeon near the moat, loses his reason, tortured by the imagined death of Pauline. The Bastille is attacked and destroyed by the people, and Fabian is again free, but no longer conscious. Accident brings him to the château, of his wife, who has fled from the violence of the mob, being one of the noblesses, and this the crowd having assailed, her husband, to whom a transient memory of the past awakens, is killed by a shot not designed for him, and the curtain falls.

The importance of *The Black Doctor* for Aldridge lay in the fact that Fabian, a Creole, loves and marries the daughter of an aristocratic white family. On the one hand he achieves his freedom through his skill as a doctor—he is equal to the white man there; and then he, an ex-slave, is honoured with the love and hand of a white woman of the noblest stock—again the races are equalized. The subject of "mixed" marriages is one that is rarely touched upon today; in fact, it is forbidden in films by the censor's code in England and the United States, but in Aldridge's day it was a legitimate plot for the stage. The only modern play of note dealing with the marriage of a Negro man and a white woman is O'Neill's *All God's Chillun Got Wings*, in which the black man's struggle for love becomes a struggle of hate, and the dark-skinned man who in the last century became a skilled doctor, in this century cannot even pass an examination. Though a melodrama, *The Black Doctor*, as adapted by Aldridge, was an attempt at a tragedy of nobility; O'Neill's play makes of mixed marriage a tragedy of sordid despair.

*   *   *

In May 1847 a son was born to Ira Aldridge whom he christened Ira Daniel. At this time Mrs. Aldridge was forty-nine years old and had been in ill health for many years. Obviously, the child is not hers. Amanda Aldridge, with whom we talked in the year before she died, could shed no light on this child beyond saying,

"He was a mistake." Thus far our efforts to trace the boy's mother have proved unavailing, but there is every reason to believe that she was a white woman. Mrs. Yunge tells us a little about him: "In January 1859 Aldridge left. After that I met the African tragedian once again in 1862, in London, where I visited his house, and became acquainted with his little son, who, although he had the rather large features of his father, was completely white, with ginger hair." From the Census Report of 1861, we learned that he was born in St. Pancras, London, but there was no birth registered there in the Aldridge name. Not knowing the mother's name, it was impossible to trace a birth certificate, assuming that the birth was registered at all.

For the year 1846-7 there is, for the first time, a year's consecutive report of his appearances in the first volume of a new periodical, the *Theatrical Times*. A few typical items therefrom will suffice to show the impact he was making on audience and box-office:

Wolverhampton, September 5. Before the curtain rose, the house was crowded in every part and numbers were unable to obtain admission. . . . Mr. Aldridge was received on each occasion with the greatest possible enthusiasm, and being called before the curtain at the close the audience simultaneously rose and a waving of hats, handkerchiefs and cheering ensued, which continued until he retired. The attendance during the week has been excellent.

Brighton, September 26. African Roscius enthusiastically applauded. . . . Proposals have been made to Mr. Aldridge from the Surrey Theatre to appear there at the termination of Mr. Macready's engagement.

Dublin Theatre Royal, March 6, 1847. The Lord Lieutenant and the Irish Court were present to see him. . . . His Excellency applauded Mr. Aldridge frequently during the evening.

Reporting from Bath, the *Era* of 22nd March 1846 said:

Mrs. Macready has formed an engagement for a few nights with the African Roscius. His Othello on Tuesday evening introduced him to an audience universally acknowledged to be endowed with critical acumen and he passed the ordeal in a blaze of triumph. Like Garrick with his Richard and Jerry Sneak, this really wonderful import from Senegal, who ought to have been chargeable with a heavy protective duty on behoof [*sic*] of British industry, played Mungo in *The Padlock*. Roars of laughter for the slave were the Irish echo to the tears for the jealous Moor.

In August of the next year the same periodical reported from Peterborough that "The season here has been unusually unproductive. A considerable improvement has been made in the business by the engagement of Mr. Aldridge, the African Roscius, who during the week has played to excellent houses." And from Ulverston: "Mr. Aldridge is one that contributes much to the treasuries of his provincial employers. The house was crowded to excess."

In January 1848 he fufils a second engagement at the Theatre Royal, Chichester, acting one night under the patronage of the Duke of Richmond, and a few nights later he plays Othello and Mungo at the Town Hall, Arundel, for the Duke of Norfolk and the guests at Arundel Castle. He now has a bit of trouble with Mr. Holmes, the Theatre Manager, claiming that he was not paid his proper fee, and Holmes accusing Aldridge of behaving in "a most ruffianly manner" and walking out of the theatre during the performance!

So Aldridge is packing them in at the very time that the *Theatrical Journal* (10th July 1847) carries an editorial deploring the state of the drama in the provinces:

Never has the drama been in so depressed a state in the provinces as at the present moment, half the theatres in the country are either closed or about being so, and some of them without any immediate prospect of being reopened. In Liverpool the Theatre Royal, the Adelphi and the Liver are shut up; in Glasgow both the theatres are closed; in Birmingham, Bath, Bristol, Plymouth, Wolverhampton, Brighton, Norwich, Newcastle-upon-Tyne, and Nottingham, the theatres are also shut and the companies dispersed. At Manchester, opera is being performed at the Theatre Royal and they are struggling to keep the Queen's Theatre open with a dramatic company. The Theatre Royal, Dublin, is closed and the Irish theatres, almost without exception, are similarly circumstanced.

The *Memoir* makes the following remarks about the continuing boycott of Aldridge by the London theatres:

159

Mr. Aldridge never abandoned the desire of making himself generally known and popular in London. To that end he had studied deeply and laboured long in his profession. The lapse of some years had wiped him from the memories of the comparatively few who had seen him act in the Metropolis, and curiosity concerning him was very often expressed. Not unconscious of his own natural disadvantage—that of his colour—he awaited, with characteristic modesty, the invitation to appear again, to which his provincial reputation entitled him; but the legitimate drama had been long at a discount. One or two managers lacked, to say the least of it, the moral courage to engage him, when opportunity occurred. The success of Mr. Brooke, however, at the Olympic,* a gentleman with whom Mr. Aldridge had often acted in the country, drew him near London, and the management of the Surrey Theatre having offered him tempting terms, he accepted them and his name again figured "on the Surrey side".

Together with the deepening crisis in the country and its effect on the theatre, there were also problems developing within Aldridge's own orbit—that of his repertoire and of the calibre of actor with whom he had to play. It had become increasingly clear as the years went by that his repertoire was getting out of date—except for Shakespeare. The melodramas acceptable in the 1820s and 1830s were becoming less acceptable in the '40s and '50s. Critical comment began to appear, such as: "The part of Rolla [*Pizarro*] with the African Roscius is not, in our opinion, a character by any means as well suited to that gentleman's power of acting as others, to which during his present engagement we have had occasion to refer [i.e., Othello, etc.]. . . . We are sorry for his sake that the character is not one better qualified to develop his talents."[7] And: "The character of Bertram is a terrific exemplification of human passion and it is only in the hands of such a person as Mr. Aldridge that it could be at all tolerated by a discriminating audience—because the dialogues do not possess the power of exciting either sympathy or regret; and the author appears to gloat solely on the dark and malignant side of the human character. But the African Roscius, as well as the immortal Kean, has made the piece somewhat acceptable, by the true representation he has given of the revengeful and despairing Bertram."[8]

* January 1848.

Despite this reaction on the part of the discriminating section of the audience, Aldridge and the local managers were forced, by box-office considerations, to put on the same melodramas rather than Shakespeare. The masses wanted violent action, spectacle, and "penny-plain, tuppence-coloured" passions.

Then there was the eternal problem of the quality of his supporting cast. Everywhere he had to accept the existing stock company, and to perform with few or no real rehearsals. Sometimes he found himself playing with important actors like Vandenhoff, Phelps, Stuart, and G. V. Brooke, and actresses like Ellen Tree and Mary Huddart, but more often he had to put up with inexperienced or incompetent professionals. The Press was aware of his problem and sympathized. One critic said of his Othello: "Indeed, we cannot characterize his action in this last scene by any other epithet than that of terribly magnificent. For our own sakes, as well as his, we could have wished to see him better supported."[9] Not only was this true throughout the provinces, but in London as well.

In February 1848 we see a little item in the Press: "We are enabled to state on authority that Mr. Aldridge, the African Roscius, has refused offers made to him by the management of the Surrey Theatre." The following week, "Mr. James Wallack makes his appearance at the Surrey immediately as Hamlet", and the week after that, "We understand that Mr. Aldridge, the celebrated African Roscius, has accepted a very liberal offer from Mrs. Davidge of the Surrey Theatre", and soon thereafter we are given the specific information that "Mr. Aldridge is to have £60 for five performances a week at the Surrey".[10] Wallack may have been instrumental in clinching this deal. Mrs. Davidge is none other than the widow of the Manager who engaged him at the Coburg in 1825, and who had died in 1842.

It will be seen that he is receiving £12 a night, about double the amount he receives in the provinces, but he has obviously been holding out for a special fee. At this period there was a good deal of complaint in the Press and elsewhere at the exaggerated increase in actors' salaries and fees. One journal informs us that Mr. and Mrs. Charles Kean will not appear at Bath or Birmingham that season because they demanded a half-share in the total receipts, which the managers would not give; that fifty years before, Mrs. Siddons, John Kemble, and George Frederick Cooke received £10 a night and half clear benefit and were satisfied; in 1822 Macready had £20 a week, in 1832 £30 a week, but in 1839 £25 per *night*![11] In 1832 Tyrone Power was earning £20 per week, and in 1840 £120 a week. Ellen Tree had been earning £15 a week, went to America for two seasons, and on her return received £25 per *night*.

Now Aldridge is earning £12 a night, but when he goes to Russia in 1858 he will be paid "for each representation 400 silver roubles" (£60 sterling), with free quarters at the Government's expense and an equipage at his disposal during his stay in St. Petersburg.

So once again, after fifteen years, Aldridge is at the Surrey, in a very successful run though the *Theatrical Times* makes the very significant remark: "Houses would be better if the management had advertised him properly." This time there is complete Press coverage. The *Morning Post* of 21st March 1848, commenting on Aldridge's portrayal of Zanga in *The Revenge*, said: ". . . It was interesting to witness the acting of Mr. Ira Aldridge, a native of Africa, giving utterance to the wrongs of his race in his assumed character, and standing in an attitude of triumph over the body of one of his oppressors. Mr. Aldridge is an intelligent actor, and his elocutionary powers are admirable. Compared with the people by whom he was last night surrounded, he might with strict justice be considered a strict Roscius."

The *Morning Advertiser*, 21st March:

. . . His acting was excellent throughout. Without attempting to institute a comparative criticism between the performance and merits of this gentleman with any of those who might be considered to be his competitors, we may venture to say that he stands, without question, in the first class.

The *Douglas Jerrold Newspaper*, 25th March:

On Monday, Mr. Aldridge, a Negro, performed the part of Zanga, and though the selection of such an individual looked like the parading a piece of reality, by having a real black man to represent the ideal character, and further, seemed to be a piece of vulgarity, yet we thought it our duty to witness it. We were agreeably disappointed. Mr. Aldridge is an undoubted Negro, but is gifted with an intelligence of perception, dignity of action, and force of expression that not only do honour to his particular race, but to humanity. He reads with much feeling and appreciation of the author, and there is a force and vigour in his passionate enunciation that is stirring, and perfectly free from imitation or rant. He especially possesses a freedom of gait and natural dignity of movement, derivable probably from the unconfined nature of his early life. He has nothing of the savage, but his freedom from the petty manners of conventional training. He made as much of Zanga as it is possible to do of so wordy, blustering and clumsy an Iago. He has a slight foreign accent, and his voice, like most of his countrymen, is thin in the upper tones. He immediately afterwards performed Mungo in *The Padlock*, and with so much humour, and with such characteristic songs that it gave universal satisfaction and it is doubtful whether his forte be not rather comedy than tragedy. It is certain he is a man of no mean amount of talent, and his range is considerable, as is proved by his clever delineation alike of Zanga and Mungo. He was enthusiastically received by a very excellent house and we are quite sure his complexion will be no impediment to his receiving the applause due to his merit.

The Times, 26th March:

. . . His delineation of the proud, revengeful Moor was finely conceived and executed with great dramatic effect. In the soliloquies and those passages in which the reflective powers of the mind are at work, while the material action is suspended, he possesses the rare faculty of completely abstracting and separating himself from all external objects, or of only receiving impressions from those that harmonize with the state of his mind. Zanga's opening soliloquy in the first act, during the storm, expresses his mental condition very forcibly. In sense of emotion, Mr. Aldridge is exceedingly natural; his grief and joy seem to spring directly from his heart, and have a contagious influence upon his audience. Nothing could have been more admirably portrayed than the exultation of Zanga when he finds that his schemes for the destruction of Alonzo are ripening to success. There is a mad intoxication in his joy—an intensity in his savage delight that is scarcely less terrible than his rage. Of the better feelings of our nature we have but few indications in the character of the Moor, brooding for his long-cherished vengeance; occasionally, however, we have touches of humanity gleaming athwart the dark picture, which was elicited with great effect by Mr. Aldridge. The remembrance of his father's death and his country's wrongs, and his own degradation, which had burned into his heart, is obliterated when he beholds his enemy at his feet, and the late remorse of a noble heart was expressed with deep feeling and pathos, when he exclaims:

> "And art thou dead? So is my enmity—
> I war not with the dust."

As regards his general delineation of the Moor's character, it was marked by careful study and judicious consideration. Mr. Aldridge played the part of the Negro servant with extraordinary humour and natural drollery. The childlike simplicity of the Negro character—easily excited to mirth or sorrow—with its love of fun and mischief, were admirably portrayed by him.

The *Telegraph*, 29th March:

A native-born African appearing on the stage is somewhat of a curiosity in histrionic annals; and it afforded us a pleasing proof of the wearing away of that prejudice against men of a colour different from our own, which has long lurked in the hearts of nearly all of us, that Mr. Aldridge, the African Roscius who, on Monday night performed the part of Othello at this theatre was, by a numerous and respectable audience, most favourably received. Mr. Aldridge's impersonation of the brave man who loved "not wisely but too well" is a treat of high order.

The *Era*, 26th March:

This was not Mr. Aldridge's first bow to a London audience. Some years ago he performed two nights running as Othello at Covent Garden and afterward went through several parts at the Surrey. He was at that time very young, and has since, by continual practice, improved himself in every respect as an actor. He was, however, highly successful when he last appeared in London. The papers spoke of his performance in terms of unequivocal commendation; but nevertheless the novelty of a man of colour representing Shakespeare's intellectual heroes so as to meet the most serious approval of critics, and the extraordinary circumstance of Mr. Aldridge (although a black) taking his stand in the profession as a gentleman and a scholar, capable of receiving the poet's creations, and portraying his thoughts in a display of

histrionic art—notwithstanding the general approval he met
with and the encouragement he ought to have received, he made
but little way as an actor of great pretensions, and soon disappeared from the London boards. Ridicule had something to do
with this. The disadvantage of colour, which excluded him from
all chances of success in America, was not entirely overcome
in England among a prejudiced, wanton and unthinking few, who
could not let an opportunity pass for sneering at and ridiculing
the "presumptuous nigger". One publication in particular, now
out of print, was particularly unmerciful, and its lampoons were
sadly discouraging to the tenacious young Roscius, for ridicule
does not always blunt the feeling of those against whom it is
directed but, on the contrary, often makes them more susceptible.
Mr. Aldridge however is, in our opinion, likely to outlive such
petty attacks as he was then subjected to. His appearance at the
Surrey has been promising in the extreme and we think his
London engagements this time will be both gratifying and
profitable to him. He is a very excellent actor. Like all of his
race, and his country itself, he is one of extremes. The earnestness
of seriousness is equal to the heartiness of his mirth. As Zanga he
is exceedingly fine, looking the character of the Moor to perfection and acting it with great power and correctness. . . . It was
interesting to mark the subdued tone and superior acting of the
African as compared with the wild and unmeaning rant of those
who "supported" him. In his passionate deliveries he received
much applause, and upon those occasions his voice rises to ringing,
clear, and distinct accents, while at others he speaks in a measured
and grave style almost too sober to be in keeping with the fiery
nature of the Moor.

We look upon him as an extraordinary personage, and quite
a curiosity to those who take an interest in the physiology of
man. In farce he is exceedingly funny. You see the veritable
nigger, whose good nature, humour, and even wit, are so commonly ridiculed. As Mungo he is very amusing, giving way to his
absurdity with all the zest of one of his colour. Mr. Aldridge
sings, too, and his "Opossum Up a Gum Tree" is one of the
funniest things that can be imagined. No mock "Ethiopian
Serenader" could come near it. It is novel to see one who has
been obtaining much applause in portraying passion in its most
poetic shape, descend to the broad farce of mock drunkenness, and
cramming into his capacious mouth a lighted candle, which he
mistakes for the neck of a bottle in the other hand; and it is only a
man of natural genius who can do both so as to be commended

for the faithfulness of his mimicry. . . . We advise the anti-slavery people who visit Exeter Hall upon great occasions, to see Mr. Aldridge at the Surrey Theatre. His appearance there is a "great moral lesson" in favour of anti-slavery.

The *Era*, 2nd April:

Mr. Aldridge is something more than an African; he is a scholar and a gentleman; at least, he acts like one. In *Othello* . . . the workings of his mind, the sensations of his heart, were conspicuous in his swarthy visage, and depicted in every gesture. At the close, and after the death of Desdemona, when he awoke to the consciousness of the deception that had been practised upon him, in the frenzy of his remorse he lifted the lifeless body of his murdered and wronged wife from the bed as though she had been an infant. There was something terribly touching in this display of physical strength, brought forth by mental agony. He was loudly called for at the fall of the curtain.

The *Theatrical Times*, 1st April:

. . . His enaction of the jealous Moor exceeded all the expectations we had formed of his talents as a Tragedian. From the most pathetic exhibition to the lowest depth of passion, his impersonation left upon our minds a feeling of the deepest admiration. . . . But it was in the third act, and before the hoarseness which was painfully apparent towards the conclusion, had seized the actor, that the triumph of genius was manifested. . . . The concluding scenes called forth the powers of the actor to their fullest extent and rendered his performance one of the finest pieces of acting that we have seen for some time. . . . We now have a word or two to say as to the male portion of the dramatis personae *who were supposed* to support the actor that night. First as to Iago, Mr. Elphinstone, never again attempt the enaction of a Shakespearean character—for mercy's sake spare us this degradation of the Avonian bard, and confine yourself to the extreme barbarism of an ultro-melodramatic part. . . . Messrs. Vining and Butler as Cassio and Roderigo utterly and entirely mistook their characters; two greater exhibitions of low buffoonery we never witnessed. . . .

Commenting at this juncture in Aldridge's career, the *Memoir* says:

The African, notwithstanding all that has been said of him, has yet to be brought fairly and completely before the London public, by whom he is, comparatively speaking, unknown. His engagement at the Surrey Theatre has just terminated with offers to renew it; but it is on the Middlesex side of the water that he must take his stand and be thoroughly tested. Punch, seeing a joke and availing himself of it, said lately, "*Ira est furor brevis.* The theatrical critics are loud in praise of a real Ethiopian traged-ian, Mr. Aldridge, with the unusual name of Ira, which is, no doubt, symbolical of its owner being 'the rage' wherever he goes." Mr. Aldridge will, no doubt, soon come forward more con-spicuously than he has hitherto done, and justify the above remark.

But it was not until seventeen years later, after his triumphant tours of western and eastern Europe and Russia, that "on the Middlesex side of the water [at the Theatre Royal, Haymarket] he took his stand and was thoroughly tested".

Following the Surrey, Aldridge made a brief appearance at the Standard, a minor theatre in Shoreditch, London's East End; then resumed his provincial tours with his usual unqualified success and acclamation. He proves himself to be more than just a great actor and a godsend to the box-office. Besides being a "gentle-man and a scholar", as the Press took such pains to point out, he was a warm and sympathetic individual who engendered respect and affection in his audiences and colleagues. Three months after the Surrey, in Dundee, Scotland, he was presented with a brooch set with costly stones, inscribed: "Presented to Ira Aldridge, Esq., the African Tragedian, by a few friends in admiration of his great and varied talents as an actor and of his character as a gentle-man." Foremost among these few friends was J. W. Anson, Director of the Dundee, Perth, Arbroath Circuit, to whom Aldridge brought rich box-office returns. Anson was a man of some initiative, and his stock company, in which he and his wife played leading roles, was of a higher than usual standard. Later, when Aldridge was on tour in Europe, Anson became his agent in London.

Aldridge's performance of Othello at Dundee was hailed by the *Arbroath Guide* as "a perfect performance such as we venture to say could not be surpassed. We have had the pleasure of seeing Kean the Elder, Young, Macready, and other tragedians of celebrity in this part, but great as these were, as a whole we prefer Mr. Aldridge's impersonation of the Moor to that of any actor we ever saw. Shakespeare speaks of 'a jewel in an Ethiop's ear'; when listening to Mr. Aldridge, the Ethiop becomes the jewel and both ears and eyes of the spectators seem as if bewitched by the grandeur of the conception, deep pathos, and the energy and vigour of his playing. Mrs. Anson was the Desdemona; this lady was as fascinating as ever, and made all that could possibly be made of the part." He was so successful in Dundee that he was re-engaged, and the *Theatrical Times's* correspondent, after commenting on the beautiful appearance of the newly painted scenery, said crossly: "On Mr. Aldridge's benefit we were unable to obtain a seat at 8 o'clock, the house was so crowded, and we hear complaints of the house being overfilled. Mr. Anson should have sufficient respect for his patrons to obviate this."

John Coleman, who at fourteen had seen Aldridge act under the most difficult circumstances, and as we have seen, dreamed of the day when he would play with the great actors, by 1850 found himself playing Iago to Aldridge's Othello at the Theatre Royal, Bristol. We have Coleman's own account of his first appearance in *Oroonoko*, when he played Aboan to Aldridge's Oroonoko:

The Woolgars were followed by the African Roscius, who enacted Othello, Zanga in *The Revenge*, Oroonoko, and the Slave to crowded houses. During this engagement I had one or two opportunities for distinction, and made most of them. My grand coups were made in Aboan in *Oroonoko*, and Alonzo in *The Revenge*. . . . Oroonoko is a Prince; so is Aboan, both gentlemen of colour. The Roscius, who was dark as ebony, toned his sable hue down to a copper tint; on the other hand, I was black as burnt cork and Indian ink could make me. Our tragedian, Mr. Benson, lent me his Othello wig; the ladies lent me half a dozen coral necklaces and bracelets, and a heap of glittering geegaws and gimcracks. Being the colliers' pay night, they trooped in from Bilston and the adjacent neighbourhood, crowding the pit, the gallery and the upper circle to overflowing. I had to precede and pave the way for the reception of the Roscius, and when I strutted on in all my finery, to my astonishment the pit "rose at me", and the gallery followed suit. It was the first really great reception I ever had. I placed my hand on my heart and bobbed and bowed. The more I bobbed, the more the audience applauded.

Amidst the uproar, on strode Oroonoko. A dead silence ensued; for a moment a pin might have been heard drop. Then an Olympian exclaimed to his "butty", "Say, Dick, I'm gawmed if the fat 'un ain't the real blackamoor!" To which Dick responded, "Naa, lad, that canna' be, for t'other chap's a d——d sight blacker!"

There were no young men in the company, so I "chummed" with a little, melancholy low comedian yclept "Miserable Dicky". This doleful droll had been a protégé of the renowned Robert William Elliston, under whose banner he had served at Leamington, Coventry, the Olympic, Drury Lane, and the Surrey. . . . Whenever I acted a part of importance, my old friend never left the wings, and every Sunday after dinner he held a post-mortem examination on the week's work. I thought I had distinguished myself in *The Revenge*, and told him so.

"Distinguished be d——!" he burst out. "You spoke the words right enough—you've a voice to thank God for, if you only knew how to use it! You can fence, you can dance, but you don't know how to use your legs or your arms, don't know how to come on the stage or how to go off—you don't know how to walk or even to stand! Why, even that hideous old buck-nigger looked like a man beside you, with your legs tied up in knots. Atop of all this, you're giving way to Mac's worst mannerisms;* you mug and you growl like a bear with a sore head! Cut it—Cut it! Stamp it out, or it'll stamp you out, and you'll be a thirty-bob-a-week Hamlet as long as you live! That's what you'll be!" That was the most useful object lesson I ever had in my life. Every word Dicky said was true, though I didn't know it till he opened my eyes. Knowing it, I resolutely set to work to cure myself, and never rested morning, noon and night till I succeeded in doing so.[12]

These remarks of the low comedian, "Miserable Dicky", indicate the attitude of some of the small-part characters with whom Aldridge had to work, and "hideous old buck-nigger" is probably one of the milder epithets employed behind his back.

The inadequacy of Aldridge's melodramatic repertoire, and its unsuitability to his dramatic powers, were by now apparent, but this consideration alone cannot force a change. Always the decisive factor is the box-office. So, when the audience began to

* The reference is to Macready.

show weariness of the old melodramas, a change became imperative. Murray of the Theatre Royal, Edinburgh, wrote to Aldridge briefly and frankly in July 1850: "I think Othello would be your best part, and the second night *Obi* and *The Padlock*. *The Black Doctor* produced no effects when we last did it, and I should doubt its doing so now." There was general agreement that the time was ripe for something new, but what?

Aldridge tried adaptations of Scott's novels, *Guy Mannering* and *Rob Roy*, but they did not remain long in his repertoire. At times plays—or, rather, pageants and spectacles—of topical interest were put on, like *Captain Ross* (Hull, 1833), or patriotic spectacles like *The Coronation of William IV* (Hull, 1831), and *The Afghanistan War* (Plymouth, January 1852), but they did not meet with the sympathies of the audience and were withdrawn after a few presentations, to be followed by the more reliable and acceptable *Othello*. So we find Aldridge searching desperately for roles appropriate to his complexion and his stature as an actor. He finally decides to tackle a play seemingly almost impossible to stage—Shakespeare's *Titus Andronicus*.

Titus Andronicus is a play of unmitigated horror which has seldom been produced. It could not be used by Aldridge in its original form, because that would have been contrary to his avowed policy of offering to the "respectable world" only such productions as were suitable for all the family and without offence even to the most sensitive religious feelings. It is not suitable for any squeamish audience even today unexpurgated! In his prologue on the original playbill he declares that its original form and plot render it "repugnant to good taste and modern refinements". He therefore proceeds not only to adapt it, but to alter it completely! He collaborated on it with one C. A. Somerset,* who, on his own, attempted original plays and made adaptations of others which he hoped would be accepted by Aldridge. At the time they were working on a revised *Titus*, Somerset submitted a play called *The Robbers*,† saying, "You might play Charles Moor well, especially as the small brigand's beard, whiskers and moustache would conceal a great portion of the face; besides, there is something in the name of *Moor* which,

---

* Author of *Shakespeare's Early Days*, *A Day at the Fair*, *Sylvana*, and other one- and two-act farces.

† Probably an adaptation of Schiller's *Die Rauber*.

to the million, would make the complexion by no means inconsistent"!! Knowing that Aldridge excelled also in comic pieces, he wrote him: "I have long projected one of the very peculiar character entitled *The Forest Inn, or A Night in the Back Woods*, in which the Negro servant, waiter or help, will impersonate three, four or more characters and give specimens of the various types of Negroes, as the Dandy Negro, the free Negro, the Slave, the laughing nigger and a very old and deaf Negro with white hair. The plot of this one-act piece is highly affected, novel and ludicrous, and we would concoct it together (after *Titus*) in a day or two." There is no record of Aldridge having accepted either of these two worthy offerings.

J. J. Sheahan said many years later: "The version of *Titus Andronicus* in which he acted was very much curtailed and altered from the original of Shakespeare. I remember at least that one great scene from a play called *Zaraffa, The Slave King* (written in Dublin for Mr. Aldridge) was imported into it."[13] We are not certain of the exact date of Aldridge's first performance in *Titus*, but our first traces of it are in Paisley in November 1849, in Belfast on 13th May 1850, and on 24th July of that year in Edinburgh, where, according to one writer, the adaptation was ineffectual and did not succeed, but the representation of Aaron was good.[14] Aldridge may have been encouraged to attempt it first in Paisley, where the Manager was J. W. Anson. *Titus* was especially revived for a season at that classic home of melodrama, the Britannia, Hoxton, in March 1852, and in April 1857 it had its last run there.

What, fundamentally, did Aldridge do to *Titus*? He says that his adaptation differs from all the other adaptations of Shakespeare on one important point: that horrors only are expunged and the poetic gems retained. This is true, but not the whole truth. The one really important point of departure was that the play was adapted from the point of view of the Negro, the Moor, for Aldridge turned the central villain of the play, Aaron the Moor, into a hero! The *Era* of 26th April 1857 summarizes Aldridge's treatment of *Titus*:

During the past week Mr. Aldridge has appeared as Aaron in *Titus Andronicus*, a part which he has made completely and emphatically his own. *Titus Andronicus* is not a favourite play and

171

we do not know that we ever saw it produced before on any stage. Indeed, as published in the best editions of Shakespeare's works, it would be utterly unfit for presentation, for a more dreadful catalogue of horrors and atrocities than it consists of would be impossible to conceive. . . . In fact, there are numerous internal evidences that the play is not written by Shakespeare, and we are strangely inclined to agree with Malone, Johnson, and others that it is spurious. The *Titus Andronicus* produced under Mr. Aldridge's direction is a wholly different affair; the deflowerment of Lavinia, cutting out her tongue, chopping off her hands, and the numerous decapitations and gross language which occur in the original are totally omitted and a play not only presentable but actually attractive is the result.

Aaron is elevated into a noble and lofty character. Tamora, the Queen of Scythia, is a chaste though decidedly strong-minded female, and her connection with the Moor appears to be of a legitimate description; her sons Chiron and Demetrius are dutiful children, obeying the behests of their mother and—what shall we call him?—their "father-in-law". Old Titus himself is a model of virtue and the only person whose sanguinary character is not toned down much is Saturninus the Emperor, who retains the impurity of the original throughout. Thus altered, Mr. Aldridge's conception of the part of Aaron is excellent—gentle and impassioned by turns; now burning with jealousy as he doubts the honour of the Queen; anon, fierce with rage as he reflects upon the wrongs which have been done him—the murder of Alarbus and the abduction of his son; and then all tenderness and emotion in the gentle passages with his infant. All these phases of the character Mr. Aldridge delineated with judgment and great force of expression. He thoroughly appreciates the recondite beauties of the author, whenever they exist, and every syllable is uttered with meaning. He rants less than almost any tragedian we know—he makes no vulgar appeal to the gallery, although, at such a house as this, the appeal is a tempting one—he is thoroughly natural, easy and sensible, albeit he has abundance of physique at his command when the exercise of it is required. In a word, he obviously knows what he is at, and there is as little of the "fustian" about him as there is in anybody on the stage. We are gratified to find that his judicious impersonations appeared to be fully appreciated by the immense audience, whose orderly demeanour and wrapt attention during the more thrilling parts of the tragedy were quite remarkable. Mr. Aldridge was ably supported by the rest of the excellent company. . . . The appointments appeared to be all tolerably correct; there was the Roman lictors with their fasces, the popular banners with the well-known S.P.Q.R. and so on; and as the processions were all arranged and the details generally carefully carried out, the representation was eminently successful.

The first revival of *Titus* not only afforded Aldridge an opportunity to show his versatility in a version of the tragedy prepared by himself, but it also created theatrical history, for it had not been produced for 128 years, though his playbills claimed it was 200 years since its last production. James Quin played Aaron in the revivals at Drury Lane on 13th August 1717 and 28th July 1719 and at Lincoln's Inn Fields on 21st December 1720. It was produced again at Drury Lane on 27th June 1721, with Thomas Walker as Aaron. To our knowledge it was not done again until the Old Vic production of the 1923-4 season (the tercentenary celebration of the publishing of the First Folio), with Wilfred Walter as Titus and George Hayes as Aaron. Then there was the very fine production by Peter Brook at the Shakespeare Memorial Theatre, Stratford-upon-Avon, in August 1955, when Titus was played by Sir Laurence Olivier, Lavinia by Vivien Leigh, and Aaron by Anthony Quayle, and at the Stoll Theatre, London, in 1957 with almost the same cast, after a Continental tour.

At this period Aldridge is busily occupied in all phases of his productions, particularly in a search for new plays. He is in active correspondence, collaborating with one William H. Hillyard, who is working on a play with a leading role for Aldridge as a Mogul prince. Aldridge arranges to buy the licence so that he may have exclusive rights and control; he makes financial arrangements with Hillyard, discussing details of production, number of acts, costumes and so on. A letter from Hillyard goes into some interesting details: ". . . A plumed turban is the ordinary insignia of Mohammedan state. The scimitar, though not a usual accompaniment, may be worn for one scene without any great violation of costume. . . . Djalma will, of course, be a Mohammedan as all the native princes, the Hindoos, the Rajahs are insignificant and petty in power compared with their Tartar conquerors. The period about 1740 so as to allow of a little less formal costume for the Europeans. These could be managed by a tale of the present times. . . . I am glad to hear that *Andronicus* had succeeded so well and that the people of Paisley have acquired the mind to appreciate it. They have certainly wonderfully improved. . . ."

In addition to his many problems and worries, he often has to concern himself with seeking financial backing to supplement his own investments in his productions. In April 1850 he received a letter from Mr. F. Caple, Manager of the Theatre Royal, Chester, in which he says: ". . . I don't see the way clear and therefore cannot say that I should like to join in the speculation. Will it not be necessary to obtain permission of the Government? I think it would be better if the Proprietors of the Theatre would share; we should then secure their interest! I need not say that this would make them work for the concern!" Mr. Caple must have changed his mind, for on 19th October 1851 the *Era* carries a brief item: "Mr. Aldridge, the African Roscius, commenced his engagements for six nights on Monday last, October 13. . . . We are sorry to say that the house had not been so well filled as the spirited manager, Mr. Caple, deserves."

During this period, while there is ample information about his theatrical activities, there continues to be little said about his personal life, but the following letter from J. A. Coates, evidently an Irish farmer with whom Aldridge and his wife stayed while on tour, gives some indication of his warm and intimate relations with people. The letter was written in the summer of 1851, when the Aldridges were in Scotland:

MY DEAR ALDRIDGE,—We were all very much shocked and grieved to hear of the terrible accident Mrs. Aldridge has met with; we trust she is very much better by this time. We have frequently heard of such mishaps, but never until now has anyone for whom we were much interested been concerned. May we hope to hear soon from you letting us know how she is getting on. The Smithers leave tomorrow and appear much pleased with Ireland. We were at Butts of Purdy's brow and the Giants' Ring yesterday; Mr. and Mrs. Levy were of the party. A most delightful day we had. Has your Edinburgh trip proved remunerative? Will Mrs. Aldridge be sufficiently recovered to leave? I think it is fortunate she bled, as I am in hopes it will save her from fever attendant upon the shock; what a terrible affair it must have been. Tell her how much we sympathize with her and let us know how she is getting on. Mrs. Flood has got the book you mention. Poor Terror has not "tasted blood" but he has tasted and torn the middle out of a favourite quilt, and but for the interest Mrs. A. took in him my mother and Mrs. Flood declare he should never taste anything else. Have you heard anything of your guitar yet. I am sure we are much obliged with the trouble you have taken with the one you returned for Eleanor. We have got a long chain for Terror and we have put him on it. Renown lies in the open door where the swallows build opposite the stable and coach-house. My mother is getting better, as also Mrs. Flood; the rest are in their usual health. Peggy has turned out a great cheat, she does not give more than 8 or 9 quarts in the day. Nancy's time will be up the 4th of next month and she gives 3 quarts a day yet, we cannot put her dry. Miss Peg's temper is such that we cannot fatten her, we are afraid we have the Hay nearly all saved. It blows and threatens rain today, we fear for a good deal of it not yet made up with.

With best love to Mrs. A. and you, believe me,

Most sincerely yours,

J. A. COATES.

Early the next year he is back in England, touring Plymouth, Leicester, Bury, Leeds. In February we read that he is exceedingly ill and confined to bed as the result of an accident, and his performances of *Othello* and *The Padlock* scheduled for Bury are cancelled. Of these two accidents we have no information. Some of the smaller provincial towns had no newspapers of their own in those years, and their important news was covered by the county Press, which was often only a weekly and could not give adequate coverage. A further search may yet uncover the facts about these mishaps.

*　　　*　　　*

By this time, the inescapable fact was that Aldridge had reached an impasse in his career, and he began to look for a way out of the endless round of provincial tours, with its heartaches, hardships, and frustrations. True, he had won fame and glory and, to a degree, fortune, but there was as little prospect now as twenty years before of his being accepted at the principal Metropolitan theatres. He had made a single appearance as Othello at the Royal Shakespeare Theatre in Stratford-upon-Avon on 28th April

1851, but his appearance in Shakespeare's birthplace did not have any effect on the Metropolis. In 1851 Macready finally retired. He had played farewell seasons at the Haymarket, but took his final farewell at Drury Lane in February 1851. Though this was the year of the Great Exhibition, the classic drama was unfortunately not to the taste of the visitors. James Anderson attempted a season at Drury Lane, but lost heavily. The Haymarket, with its more popular dramas and comedies was successful. Covent Garden had been used entirely as an opera house since 1847, and any public for the Shakespearean drama was catered for by the lavish productions of Charles Kean, then at the beginning of his management at the Princess's Theatre, where he established a new standard of scenic production. With such a situation prevailing, Aldridge had to do something drastic and decisive. As we have seen, he did from time to time throughout the years announce his intention of making a professional visit to the United States. How many of these announcements were theatre gossip and how many were based on actual negotiations we cannot say, nor can we say why these plans did not materialize.

If not the United States, then the Continent was the only other practical alternative. True, there would be the language problem, but by now Aldridge was confident that he could reach any audience, no matter what their language, by the sheer force of his acting, particularly in his two well-rehearsed roles of Othello and Mungo. So the decision in favour of the Continent is finally made.

Before he sets out, he makes one final try on London by appearing at the Britannia in *Othello*, *The Padlock*, *The Slave*, *Bertram*, and *Titus Andronicus*. His success is such that he appears at the theatre nightly from 17th March until 17th April 1852, and is hailed in the Press as "a star of the first magnitude". But still there is no invitation to the West End of London, and in July of that year he leaves England for even greater successes abroad.

CHAPTER XI

First Continental Tour

ON 14th July 1852 Ira Aldridge left the shores of England for the Continent. The *Ipswich Journal* of 8th May romantically told its readers that he was "taking his farewell of English audiences previous to rejoining his tribe in some distant part of the world", but the fact is that he left "with a carefully selected troupe of comedians for Brussels, in which city he made his first Continental appearance at the Theatre Royal St. Hubert as Othello; he afterwards travelled to Aix-la-Chapelle, Elberfeld, Cologne, Bonn, Baden, Basle, etc." This we learn from a letter in *Notes and Queries* of 9th November 1872, by C. H. Stephenson, who was in a position to offer this detailed information because he was a member of this first company. From the playbill of the Stadt-Theater, Leipzig, of 23rd November 1852, announcing Aldridge's first appearance as Othello, we see that Mr. Stephenson plays the Doge of Venice, Mr. Stanton, Iago, Mr. Perfit, Cassio, Mr. Rose, Brabantio, and Mrs. Stanton, Desdemona. Stephenson must have been a competent actor, for we find him in the role of Edgar when Aldridge made his first English appearance as King Lear in Hull in June 1859. They may have been a carefully selected company, as he says, but the fact is that after six months Aldridge is playing without them, speaking his roles in English, with the local companies playing in German. It is of significance that his first stop is in Belgium, whose King, Leopold I, is one of Aldridge's patrons. He is Leopold of Saxe-Coburg, a cultured man who encouraged art, science, and education and who, with his wife, Princess Charlotte, sponsored the building of the Royal Coburg in London. He was "elected" King of the newly-formed kingdom of Belgium in 1831.

Just as the times were in Aldridge's favour when he arrived in England, so were they in his favour when he came to the Continent so soon after the 1848 revolutions and hardly two years after the establishment of the Confederation of German States, the first attempt at the national unity of that country. Despite the unification, the various states that made up the nation—Saxony, Prussia, Hanover, Westphalia, Bavaria, etc.—still retained their feudal autonomy, and their highly developed system of royal patronage of theatres continued to prevail, so that good theatres were to be found, not only in the capital, but throughout the union, a healthy situation for the theatre which still exists in Germany to this day.

The first notice we have of Aldridge's tour is from Cologne, where L. Schuking writes:

> A Negro actor is so far removed from the tradition of the English theatre and the rules of English declamation that he must be considered a completely original phenomenon. Effects previously studied, such as those of Rachel, are completely unknown to him. Nevertheless, he expresses like a master gusts of passion, cries of sorrow, soft tones of tenderness and good-naturedness. He is of handsome build, wide-shouldered and tall. His acting and mimicry in shattering scenes are incredible, and certainly no one has understood Othello as well as he. Once in Cologne, when, during the course of the play he grasps Iago by the throat one of the spectators shouted out, "Kill the villain! Strangle him!" Brought to himself by the general laughter of the audience, he rushed out of the theatre saying, "Well, you just can't listen calmly to that actor!"[1]

In September he is in Frankfurt-on-Main, where he has a lithograph drawn and printed for distribution as a souvenir, and where he receives his first Continental recognition by fellow artists, who present him with a laurel wreath and the following address:

> Sir, we have learned with unfeigned regret that already you are on the eve of your departure. We cannot let pass by this occasion without giving vent to the feelings of our sympathy and our respect for your person, without expressing to you the high admiration of your superior histrionic talents. Sir, you have exhibited your powerful dramatic conceptions on boards on which there have shone not only the first stars of our German nation—France, Italy, even England herself, have sent us occasionally their highest interpreters of our art. Still there has been but

one voice as to the excellence of your performances. And how could it be otherwise? For have we not seen you follow up the great principle of all dramatic art laid down by the world's greatest poet, by your own immortal Shakespeare, when he says that the sole end of all playing was and is the holding up the mirror to nature.

My brother artistes have charged me with presenting you with this simple token of their respect and admiration. Please to accept it and to take it with you to your far-off country, and let it tell your friends and your countrymen that *real worth*, from what quarter it comes and in what shape it appears finds ever ready acknowledgment in this, our great German country, and that the hearts of your German brother artistes of this free town of Frankfurt are with you, wishing you all that happiness which you as a man and as an artiste so richly deserve.

He made his first appearance in Basle on 3rd October in *Othello*. That his wife is with him we learn from the following letter to an unknown addressee:

RESPECTED SIR,—I hope to arrive by the first steamer on Wednesday from Mannheim, and I will feel much obliged if you would direct some of your people to procure for me a *private lodging*, likewise for my troupe. My Lady being in delicate health, we prefer a private apartment to a hotel, two or three rooms will be sufficient, and I will feel further obliged by some person awaiting my arrival at the Steam boat. A Vaudeville* will be required to be acted previous to the representation of *Othello*, according to the copy enclosed. Hoping you will excuse the trouble I have taken the liberty of giving you, I remain, Sir,
                              Your obliged Svt.,
                                        IRA F. ALDRIDGE,
                                        African Tragedian.

He played *Othello*, *The Padlock*, and *Macbeth* in Leipzig, "nearly two weeks to crowded houses. He has been presented to the Royal Family and starts in a few days' time for Vienna. The present proprietor of Drury Lane has offered him an engagement but it is impossible he can accept it for the next six months."[2] At Saxe-Coburg he was presented in the Royal box to the Duchess of Saxe-Coburg-Gotha. On 12th December he is in Dessau and

* Aldridge uses the French designation of a light or comic opera when referring to pieces like *The Padlock*.

writes the following letter to H. Marr, Theatre Director of Weimar, where he is soon to perform in the theatre that Goethe and Schiller made famous:

> Sir,—I have the honour to be in receipt of your letter to Messrs. Stunn & Koppe, and in conformity with it I beg to say that I will give my first representation on Wednesday next, 15th inst. and the second on Friday 17th. I enclose copy of the bill for the first representation and I will feel obliged by your giving my proposed visit every possible publicity. I will also thank you to recommend me to a Hotel moderate in charge and near the Theatre. I expect to arrive in Weimar on Tuesday afternoon. I have the honour to be, Sir,
>
> Your Obd. Svt.
> Ira Aldridge,
> *African Tragedian.*
>
> PS.—A short Vaudeville will be necessary to be given previous to Othello according to the enclosed bill. I.A.

On 3rd January 1853 Aldridge and his company, much reduced in number, appeared in the Italian Opera House, Berlin. On the 16th they gave a command performance at the Court Theatre at Potsdam. His success there was phenomenal and his share of the proceeds of the first four presentations amounted to the equivalent of £520. At his first appearance in Berlin the orchestra stalls and pit were filled to overflowing by a very distinguished audience, according to the Press, but the rest of the house was sparsely occupied. This is not surprising, since here was an English company playing to a German audience, and French, rather than English, was the preferred foreign language of most Germans. Aldridge must soon have come to the conclusion that it was better for the plays to be given in the mother tongue of the audience, with the single exception of his own role. Events were to prove him right in this most daring innovation, never before or since attempted by an actor in so many different countries.

The *Preussische Zeitung* throughout January carried not only laudatory notices, but long and detailed reviews and essays on his performances. Here for the first time we find serious critical analyses of his work. In one article they declared that, although a Negro—

Mr. Aldridge is a pupil of the English theatre whose greatest tragedians like to bring out the sharpness of their Shakespeare, as is well known. The German actors only grope, and sometimes too anxiously, after the motives; the English mimes know no other bridge across the street of feeling than a bold jump and quickly change the moods of the compatriots they are portraying, as the scenes of Shakespeare change. This is glaringly illustrated to good purpose in *Othello*, and from this national point of view the wild, multi-coloured, sparkling truth of nature which Mr. Aldridge gives to the Moor, inflamed with jealousy, deserves the highest recognition. The acting and miming are clear interpreters of the artist, who speaks in a foreign language. His face is the fiery mirror of his soul. The spectator forgets that he is in a theatre, and without realizing it becomes deeply affected and transformed and is torn by the conflicting turmoil of passion which flows from the eye of the artist, rushes with such naturalness in the tone of his voice, and is seen in the nervous play of his hands. . . . What I never thought possible, to see before me a Shakespearean figure in the fullness of its power and passion and fantasy—here it was realized with the most exhaustive expressiveness. After this Othello it would be an anticlimax to have to see an ordinary Othello again. What abandonment, passion, beauty, greatness, and sense—the elements without which the heroic Othello would not be Shakespeare's Othello, and which no other actor has ever given me in the least. . . . A Negro from Africa's Western Coast had to come to show me the real Othello, the great, one and only, the most beautiful male artist that one can imagine. . . . In the highest point of his role, Act III, Scene 3, a scene which has no equal even in Shakespeare, he shows the most astonishing artistry and his judgment and understanding reach their highest point. . . . If Shakespeare were to present this play himself, as he had written it, he could not have presented it better even to the tiniest detail. . . . If he were Hamlet as he is Othello, then the Negro Ira Aldridge would, in my eyes, be not only the African Roscius, but the greatest of all actors.

After seeing his next role, the critic goes on to say:

His Macbeth shows generally the mighty stamp of his understanding and expression. . . . I expected his Macbeth to be not as good as his Othello. . . . I did not think he would understand Shakespeare's intentions in *Macbeth* because of its metaphysical development, whereas *Othello* is more familiar and within his scope. I was afraid that this hot-blooded son of the tropics could not cope with the galvanic, the metaphysical, fantastic and ghostlike in the first two acts of *Macbeth*, which was so Nordic; that he would not understand this most peculiar mood, nor would have the strength necessary for this, but with every scene I felt growing in me, to my surprise, the conviction that this original genius is equal to everything . . . the greatness of his acting and the indescribable kingly nobility which is in every feature, in words of majesty, in a style so far above the ordinary theatre contours, that we can only express our feeling when we say we have never seen anything more magnificent since the ancient figures of the Athenian stage.

Another critic starts his piece by quoting Plato:

"A great tragedian must at the same time be a great comedian if the actor is to be like the poet." This Mr. Aldridge has shown on the same evening by his very comic performance of the Negro Mungo in *The Padlock*. Comic burlesque through the most natural humour is lifted to the highest comic effects. When Mungo at last understands, a whole forest full of animals could not make more noise than Mungo is making. Even the old chandeliers shake with laughter, and the gas flames shake with laughter. It is hard to describe his antics, how, with the funniest gestures of his limbs, he dances about and sings, so that even the dignified Pyramids would themselves shake with laughter if they could see how comical he was.

He was greeted at curtain fall with unanimous salvos of applause and flowers, and a laurel wreath was thrown to him. The King of Prussia, H.M. Frederick IV, his Queen, the Prince and Princess, and the whole Court were there. As a climax, he received the following letter from Baron von Mulsen, the General Intendant of the Spectacles Royal, Berlin, dated 25th January 1853:

It affords me a very great pleasure that His Majesty the King has charged me to make you acquainted how very satisfied and highly interested he found himself in your performance. As a proof of his approbation, His Majesty has given you the Golden Medal for Art and Sciences, which I was ordered to remit to you. With how great a pleasure I followed this order in just acknowledgment for your excellent productions you will have seen and felt yourself.

This was followed in a few days by another communication from von Mulsen saying: "His Majesty the King will speak to you and has commanded me to present you to him tomorrow morning. I am waiting on you tomorrow morning [1st February] at 10 o'clock in the Chamber of the General Intendant, 55 Charlottenstr. in a White Cravat and Gilet. With great consideration . . ."

The medal was the Prussian Gold Medal of the First Class for Art and Science, which had previously been awarded only to Baron von Humboldt (1769-1859), the great German naturalist and explorer, to Gasparo Spontini (1774-1851), the Italian composer, and to Franz Liszt. Among Aldridge's papers was found an autograph of Liszt, which suggests that the two artists met. Baron von Humboldt assisted at the presentation and offered his congratulations. The German Press, in reporting this event, said: "May this success contribute to convince humanity that the human spirit everywhere is equal." This medal, as well as his other decorations, unfortunately are no longer in existence.

At his final appearance in Berlin he took leave of the public with an epilogue which he wrote and had translated into German, and delivered on 13th January after a performance at the Berliner Hofbuhne. In this epilogue, which differs from the poetic epilogue he used in England, he says, "A child of the sun, black my countenance, yet I stand before you in the light of my soul," and offers his gratitude to the happy lands in which he roamed and where he found hospitality; "and when one day I shall return homeward to the South, your graciousness will burn like an altar in my heart . . .". But, as we know, Aldridge did not return "homeward to the South", where "roamed untamed, as yet unawakened, a lonely race of humans".

After Berlin came other cities in the German Federation— Bremen, Breslau (now Wroclaw), Stettin (Szczecin), Dresden, Karlsbad (Karlovy Vary), Hamburg, Posen (Poznan); then on to Austria-Hungary, stopping in Prague, Brunn (Brno), and Budapest.

In Dresden he meets the world-famous Jenny Lind (the Swedish Nightingale), and her husband, Otto Goldschmidt, the pianist and composer. An engraving of Jenny Lind was presented by her husband to Aldridge on her behalf, after one of his performances which she decided not to attend because she was expecting a baby and was afraid she would be too emotionally affected by his acting! It was discovered years later that Aldridge's second wife and Jenny Lind had studied voice with Herr Berg at the Royal Theatre School in Stockholm. In 1883, when Miss Lind was teaching singing at the Royal College of Music in London (a post she accepted at the express wish of the Prince of Wales, later Edward VII), Aldridge's younger daughter, Amanda, a promising young musician of seventeen, won a scholarship to the College, and soon became the protégée of that illustrious teacher. "You must never drop your father's name, Amanda," Jenny Lind told her. "You must always call yourself 'Ira'. Your father was the greatest Othello of them all. I am proud to have been his friend." Amanda had been christened "Amanda Christina Elizabeth", but thereafter called herself "Amanda Ira Aldridge".

Some time in February Aldridge is in Prague. With the crushing of the 1848 revolution and the re-establishment of the autocratic Austrian Empire, the national aspirations of the Czechs, Slovaks, Hungarians, Serbs, and Croats were ruthlessly suppressed. They were to be Germanized in language and institutions. Prague had been for centuries a centre of learning and culture, but nationalist drama was frowned upon, and the theatres produced mostly German drama and Italian opera. The Stavovski Divadlo (Estate Theatre) was opened in 1783 with a Lessing drama, and the *première* of Mozart's *Don Giovanni* took place there with great success. Only occasional performances in Czech were tolerated until in 1862 a national theatre of their own was built with funds contributed by the Czech people. But when Aldridge first came, in 1853, the theatre was still playing in German. The patriotic Czechs did not attend—at least, not until Aldridge came. We reproduce a cartoon in *Rubezake*, showing the Czech Theatre in Prague before Aldridge's arrival, inhabited by rats, and after his arrival, with long queues waiting at the box-office!

March finds Aldridge in Vienna, famous for its Hofburgtheater, modelled on the lines of the Comédie Française. The director of that lovely theatre was Heinrich Laube (1806-84), who contributed a great deal to raising the standards of the training and acting of the company and enlarging the theatre's repertoire. A Viennese critic, quoted in the French edition of the *Memoir*, said: "Ira Aldridge is without doubt the greatest actor that has ever been seen in Europe. . . . It may well be doubted whether Shakespeare himself had ever dreamed for his masterpiece, *Othello*, an interpretation so masterly, so truly perfect." It was here that the Emperor of Austria, Franz Joseph, then a young man, presented him with the Medal of Ferdinand.

In April he arrived in Budapest. From the opening of the first Hungarian National Theatre in Budapest in 1837, the State theatres have played the leading role in Hungarian theatrical activity. Despite the oppressive policy of Austria, when Aldridge arrived Budapest had Hungarian as well as German theatrical companies. He acted with both alternately. After his début, banquets were given in his honour by the Hungarian magnates and by the German and Hungarian theatrical companies, at which he was presented with many gifts and tributes in prose and poetry.

At a special meeting of the Hungarian Dramatic Conservatoire he was made an honorary member and delivered a speech in English on the drama of Shakespeare, Schiller, and Goethe.

On this tour, as in all others, he made many personal conquests, and on returning home received a spate of letters and poems expressing a wide range of sentiments. Anna C. of Budapest is full of sisterly love when she sends him birthday greetings in July 1853:

> Accept the myrtle wreath,
> 'Tis all I can offer thee;
> As verdant through life till death
> Shall my heart's fidelity be.
>
> Let it speak of a sister's love
> That can never know decay,
> Let it praise the power above
> To prosper thy natal day.

If it is the same Anna who writes the following letter* to him in London two years later, her sisterly feelings have undergone a change:

* Translated from German.

My Dearest Ira,—The news of your severe illness makes me wretched. I am beside myself with pain and heartrending. My foreboding has not vanished; you are ill, my dear Ira, and must suffer so much and I cannot be with you. While here I am twiddling my thumbs day and night and not able to do anything for you except to pray for you with my whole soul. When I read your last lines to me, my heart almost breaks with sorrow and anguish, because I cannot be by your side to help you; it makes one most unhappy. Who will take care of you, since your wife is also ill. God alone can help you, my true friend. He will not forsake you, He will hear my prayers and restore your health. We will count upon His aid.

Do not worry on my account, my Ira, though I am far away, my heart and thoughts are ever with you. My love grows daily deeper and more tender, the longer I do not see you the more clearly I see that you are everything to me, and that my love will only end with my death. I have never believed what those who despised you have said. I do not ask what the world says; if you love me, nothing else matters, and you are my world.

Your son's letter gave me great pleasure; when I know that you are better I will write to him as well, but not yet, for I am too sad. Greet him and kiss him for me many times. My mother also sends you her kindest regards and hopes for well-beloved Ira. Could I only be with you, my true care would soon bring you back to health. When you are better write to me if you have the time to spare, if only a couple of words. I do not ask any more.

My dearest friend, I am so miserable and sad that I could die with crying. I shall not be happy until I have news of you. May God bless you, heal your pains, strengthen you, soothe your sufferings, and send you support. He can uphold you. Nothing else can.

Farewell, my dearest Ira. My love will always await you.

Your true,
Anna.

PS.—I received your letter yesterday 6th April.

Friend A. sends him a coronated letter from Budapest written "Friday in the afternoon at 4 o'clock":

My Dearest Friend!—The newspaper which you send caused me very great pleasures. I would have written you already a very long time ago, but I did not know where you are. I thought you do not remember me any more. I shall never forget of the happy and pleasant days which you have spent in our house. I am convinced that my English letter will also cause you a little pleasure and to surprise you.

I learn only since five months and I must say that I have not been always diligent. I never doubted of your gentle inclination to me and it is my sacred and greatest wish. And I make a request of you, as to my true friend, if you can send me any useful English books, only be so kind, little poesies. I wish to translate them into the Hungarian language; please you will send them as soon as possible.

I remain with respect your faithful and truely,

FRIEND A.

Matilda of Budapest went so far as to advertise in the London *Times* for a position as governess, so that "I could see you, my grand Aldridge".

He left Budapest with honours and recognition, but we find no record of his ever having returned.

In January he is in Danzig, where he receives the highest of eulogies. One critic writes: "Ira Aldridge is the greatest dramatic artist we have ever had. He has caught all the sympathies of the public. The critics of Berlin have completely exhausted themselves in praising this lion of the day. His Othello, Macbeth and Shylock leave him without a rival in the annals of the theatre."

All of 1854 is spent on the Continent, touring mostly Germany and Switzerland, although he also briefly visits Lithuania and Holland. We have a few pages of his diary covering 28th February to 26th July 1854, which we give in full, interspersing it wherever we have additional or explanatory information.

28th February—Memel. My dear Ira very very ill.

(Ira Daniel is not quite seven years old and, with Mrs. Aldridge, whom he calls "Mamma", is travelling with his father. The illness could not have been very serious, because he soon recovers.)

4th March—Marienweder. Leave March 2 and arrive at Marienweder two days later.

187

5th April—Rostock (Prussia). Commence at Rostock. *Othello.* Great house—middling returns.

11th April. My last night of engagement. *Othello.* An excellent house, bad returns.

12th April. Another performance, Rostock. For the benefit of the Recipient, Herr Schellhorn. I acted gratis. A very good house.

19th April—Mecklinburg-Schwerin. Commenced in Mecklinburg-Schwerin. An excellent house, *Othello.* The Grand Dowager Duchess present, but obliged to leave for Ludwigslust, her daughter expecting to be confined.

21st April—Mecklinburg-Schwerin. Excellent house, gross [*sic*] applause, the Intendant very complimentary.

On 6th May the director of the Heidelberg Theatre writes to him:

DEAR SIR,—Being aware of your approaching arrival at Frankfurt, there to delight the public by your excellent representations, I take the liberty of inviting you to see us here for the same purpose. I am persuaded, dear Sir, you will find nowhere a more honourable reception than in Heidelberg, one of the first universities, the seat of science with inhabitants manifesting always the fine taste and taking a lively part in the dramatical art, versed in your language by constant intercourse with English and Americans. Heidelberg is the residence of a great many strangers, being attracted by its beautiful scenery as well as by its famous professors.

I have witnessed myself your most surprising performances at Frankfurt two years ago, where I was Manager of the German Drama, and where I was so very happy in participating of the homages done to your eminent talent by the members of the stage. It would afford me a high pleasure to renew the personal acquaintance with you, dear Sir! And to gain the thanks of a great public fond of arts.

I beg to honour me with your kind answer and to let me know your conditions. I remain, dear Sir,

Your most obedient Servant,

AUGUST HAAKE.

27th May—Heidelberg. Arrived here, rehearsal in the afternoon, fine looking girls; Desdy and Emilia, Frauleins Wilhelmina and Mathilde.

(Haake, who also played with him in Frankfurt, here plays Iago to Aldridge's Othello.)

29th May—Heidelberg. Othello. Great applause. Emil Devrient came from Karlsruhe and sent his compliments; very full house; Herr Zimmern, Banquier, called upon me.

(Emil, Eduard, and Otto Devrient, members of the famous German family of actors, were at that time running the Hoftheater at Karlsruhe.)

6th June—place not specified. Second performance, *Kaufmann** and *Padlock*. Herr Schrumer and Fraulein Franke from Darmstadt, the latter for Fraulein Grueman very ill, who was to have played Portia.

9th June. Visited a Knipe or a Society of German Students (The Vaudations), met also a young Scotchman, Hall, from Glasgow, a nice set of fellows, songs by them more noisy than harmonious, feats in beer-drinking, invited for morning to see Duels between the opposite Corps. Mr. Bilhardts, an American, accompanied me, a very liberal and educated young man.

10th June. Visited the Hinchgasse on the opposite side of the Neckar, a large place set apart for the meeting of the different Corps of Students for the express purpose of Duelling with the Rapier. These duels are frequently fought to the mutilation of each other (the weapons being extremely sharp) without any feelings of animosity previously existing, and when there is, it is of the most trivial character, yet made a pretext for these sanguinary and bloody conflicts. I saw sufficient in a very short time to satisfy me and left. Acted *Macbeth* in the evening. Wreaths, etc.

19th June—Solothurn (Switzerland). Opened last night (Sunday) in *Othello*—very full house indeed, great applause and wreaths. Lodged with Herr Walker, bookseller, the bugs at first troublesome, but Mrs. A. would not rest until they were exterminated. Had a visit from the Sister of the Bishop, who was much beloved and who had lately died.

20th June. Beautiful view of the Jura Mountains. A pretty little chapel outside the town with two skeleton relics of Martyrs, tricked out in trinkets—a most repulsive effect. Conducted over the Arsenal by a Lieut.-Colonel with a very bad breath, but very obliging. A variety of implements of early Swiss

* Note the German *Kaufmann* for *Merchant*.

warfare, a group of William Tell and his son. Splendid church.

21st June. Gave a night at Berne, the inhabitants principally speak French, a pretty little theatre. The Directress fastened my cloak. Mrs. A. did not come over. The house middling, very rainy, with thunder and lightning. Got to Solothurn about five in the morning.

22nd June. Enacted Macbeth, a very good house, the Artists very shy indeed.

26th June. Last night (Sunday) played Shylock and Mungo.

28th June—Berne. Opened here in *Othello*, a very full house, swindling at the doors to an unlimited extent. Met Mr. Fay, the American Secretary of Legation, whom I had previously met in Berlin. The Hon. E. Murray, the British Minister, was very complimentary. Mr. Christie, his Sec., gave a party and invited me to entertain them and sent me a couple of books by way of remuneration. Met the Sardinian Minister, his Son and Sister. View of the Alps, the Jungfrau appearing to advantage.

29th June. Berne reminds me of Chester in respect to walking under cover in rainy weather. On entering the town the effect is most pleasing from the number of red pillows in the windows of the houses for persons to rest their arms on in leaning out of window. The Town Clock is a great curiosity as a piece of mechanism. Heard it strike twelve.

30th June. Heard the rehearsal of a Concert to be given that Spohr attended, in the Church. Introduced to a Professor Domme and family—very interesting group and all enthusiastic and very talented. Saw an Apollo Belvedere from one of the sons Herman. Mrs. A. ill from the fresh paint and dislike to the landlady who is a widow and anxious to take in travellers, having formerly kept a hotel at Thun.

1st July. Visited the Studio of Herr Scheller, an eminent artist, to whom I sat for a Portrait for the French Exhibition (the last scene of *Othello*).*

3rd July. Last night repeated *Othello* and tonight *Macbeth*. Dined with Dr. Domme and family (his Lady and four sons).

4th July. This was the day of the rehearsal of the Oratorio, not the one I have previously set down. Supped afterwards with Dr. Domme.

5th July. Left this morning by Diligence for Baden, where we arrived about four, passing through Aarau, dined and tendered

* Thus far we have been unable to locate this painting.

a bad five-franc piece in payment. Baden a miserable place, the most so of any place I have yet seen in Switzerland. Their prey is the visitors to the baths, which as usual they tell you cure all diseases. Mrs. A. made worse by taking them. Business indifferent.

10th July—Zürich. Last night played Othello to a capital house, great applause, but a very bad return of cash, the cashier a notorious rascal let with the theatre. Lodged at the Hotel Bauer, a most comfortable house and very moderate in charges. The son speaks English very well. The Directress settled with me.

(Times had evidently not changed since the Elizabethan dramatist, Thomas Dekker, in dedicating one of his plays to his "friends and fellows, The Queen's Servants", wished them a full audience and one honest doorkeeper.)

11th July. Mrs. A. remained at Baden, to which place I returned and my dear Ira was waiting for me at the station.

13th July. Repeated *Othello*, a very full house, villainous return.

(The correspondence between Richard Wagner and Mathilde Wesendonck contains, in the section "Zürich, 1853-8", a note from Wagner: "For your attention: Wednesday, *Othello*, with Ira Aldridge. Tickets should be secured well in advance.")

17th July. Last night *Macbeth*, very full house, the returns getting worse. Mrs. A. determined on going to the doors. The next Vorstellung brought Ira some clothes here of Parisian fabric. Zürich is beautiful beyond description, its historic connections, its magnificent scenery, its beautiful bay or Sea, render it one of the most interesting places in Switzerland. I sang "By the Margin of Fair Zürich's Waters" while sailing on them, so pellucid, so clean.

18th July. Enacted Shylock and Mungo, a very full house but not quite so good as the previous night, but one third more returned. The rogues one and all caught in their own net by the dexterity and determination of Mrs. A. I refused to go to St. Gallen, but at last, through the entreaties of the Directress, left in the afternoon by Diligence, passing through Winterthur, where a Musical Festival had just been celebrated. Arrived at nine.

19th July—St. Gallen. This morning at St. Gallen, lodged at

Madame Wild, poor Tigre very affectionate friend. Met here with Dr. Mullen who prescribed successfully for Mrs. A. Herr Hausen a regular diner out, bought here some of the Swiss manufactures. Magnificent church. Sent here to Herr Convel's for my bill.

21st July. Opened in *Othello*, a very good house.

22nd July. Visited the Felsen Keller [Rock Cellar] on a high rock situated, being very cool air beautiful (*schöne Madehar*). Also went to a still higher prominence where we lunched and had a fine view of the Appenzell view of the Lake of Laustane [*sic*] or Boden See.

24th July. My birthday, celebrated by the Troupe, serenaded in the morning with Dr. DuNegal a barrel of beer enveloped in grape-vine.

26th July. Played Macbeth, and afterwards celebrated the Directress's birthday.

These few items of his diary give us some interesting details of the role played by Mrs. Aldridge while on tour. She shows herself capable of dealing in a businesslike way with his affairs, handling rascally cashiers, looking after Ira Daniel, and in general, being kind and helpful, despite her poor health. Here too we have glimpses of the African Roscius sailing and singing on the pellucid waters of Lake Zürich, a magnificent picture it must have been, the black singer with the wonderful voice, against a background of blue waters, green slopes, and snow-covered mountains. And then his birthday celebrated with a barrel of beer enveloped in grape-vine!

On 26th July, the Professor to whom he was introduced on 30th June writes the following letter to him from Berne:

DEAR SIR,—Not long ago returned from an excursion to our mountains I found your kind letter in my house, and now in all haste I write these few lines, very anxious indeed that you perhaps have already left St. Gallen. Before all I beg you to accept for yourself and for your lady the most affectionate greetings of every part of my family, and the most hearty thanks for your faithful remembrance of ours. Your souvenir, good Sir, will be ever lasting in our hearts. The intelligence of your success at Zürich—although a mere necessity in my eyes—made us the purest joy, as if a member of our family had earned the applause. Your Tell-poem did not be received in the "Bund" because he has no "feuilleton" but we hope it will be published in the

Eid Genossische Zeitung at Basle; and my son Herman is performing the necessary steps. Mr. Sheller proceeds in his great Othello-Picture.

Your purpose to go to Munich opens us the view to meet you again in a few weeks, and to salute once more as man and as artist. Concerning Mr. Dingelstadt, who is as much I know a very accessible obliging and honest man, I do not be acquainted with him—*perhaps* I get a letter that would introduce you to him; but certainly nobody in the world could give you a better recommendation than you possess already in the renowned name "Ira Aldridge".

Will you be so kind to send me for further communication your ulterior address? In the hope of *Wiedersehen* I remain with high respect,

Y.O.S.,

DR. HERMANN DOMME.

On 24th August while in Munich, he starts negotiating for a tour of France. As we see from the following translation of a letter in French, he is, as usual, his own manager and Press agent:

SIR,—For three years I have toured the principal cities of Germany, Austria, Hungary, etc., where my representations have been crowned with the greatest success. It is unheard of that a person of African nationality should have attempted to play dramatic roles. The success I have had in the greatest theatres of Germany, that is to say, at Berlin, Vienna, Wurtemburg, Frankfurt-on-Main, has increased my desire to make an attempt in the French capital.

His Majesty, the King of Prussia, has condescended to honour me with the Large Gold Medal for Art and Sciences, the Emperor of Austria with the Medal of Ferdinand, and Switzerland with the White Cross. I have also received letters of recommendation from the courts of Prussia, Austria, and Saxe-Coburg to the court of France.

My intention is to come to France with a troupe of English players to give the following representations: *Othello*, *Macbeth*, *King Lear*, *Richard III*, *The Merchant of Venice*, and *Bertram*.

My conditions are as follows: I ask for a guarantee to cover the expenses I will have to bring my troupe to Paris, and the engagement must be for twelve nights. For each performance I ask for half the net receipts or a fixed salary.

193

I take the liberty of offering my services, and waiting for the favour of your prompt reply, Poste Restante, Frankfurt-on-Main.

I beg to sign, Sir,

Your obedient servant,

IRA ALDRIDGE,
African Tragedian.

PS.—If you need other information, please get in touch with Baron von Mulsen, Intendant-General of the Theatre Royal, Berlin, or Mr. Seguin, dramatic agent, St. James's Theatre, London.

IRA ALDRIDGE.

The plan does not materialize because of disagreement over terms; also because of ill health, and he does not get to Paris until twelve years later.

A letter written from Neisse on 28th October to an addressee unknown (probably the Editor of the *Tagesblatt*) reveals some of the difficulties he encounters with fellow-actors, although on the whole his relationships were good:

> MY DEAR SIR AND FRIEND,—I regretted that the intelligence of the serious indisposition of my Son prevented me remaining for a few hours in Prag in passing but I hope ere I leave Deutschland to shake you by the hand and say how thankful I am for your kindness during my sojourn. I hope yourself and family are in the enjoyment of that inestimable blessing health. I have had a great deal to contend with since I last saw you, arising from the petty jealousy of various Schauspielers,* but of that hereafter. I am in expectation of returning soon to England, and go from there to Paris with an English troupe. Recommend me to your young friend Mr. Epstein, kiss your little Son for me, and if you can spare space in the *Tagesblatt* for the enclosed Acrostic you will further oblige your sincere and grateful friend
>
> IRA ALDRIDGE.

The next day he writes from Leipzig ordering "200 copies of my portrait of Othello struck off and forward same to York House correspondent in Braunschweig", and asking if they would give place in their pages to a portrait of himself in the character of Shylock and King Lear. The envelopes in which many of his letters were sent have not been preserved, so it is

* Actors.

sometimes only by inference and clues obtained from other material that we can guess to whom they were addressed. This last letter we judge to have been written to the Editor and publisher of the German theatre journal, *Theatre Chronik*, Dr. Victor Koelbel of Leipzig, who later became Aldridge's representative in Europe, arranging and publicizing his tours, as seen from subsequent letters. We have not been able to locate a copy of the acrostic which he enclosed in the above two letters. The use to which these portraits were put is seen by the announcement in *Czasu* (Times) of his first appearance in Crakow, Poland:

> The Theatre in Cracow under the direction of Carl Gaudelius. Tuesday, 7th November 1854. Free lists suspended, with higher prices. First guest appearance of Herr Ira Aldridge, First Tragedian of the Drury Lane Theatre, London, in *Othello* (Schlegel's German translation). Herr Ira Aldridge's role in the English language. The well-executed portrait of the Negro artist as Othello is available for 1 florin, as well as the Negro songs from *The Padlock*, the German Biography of Ira Aldridge for 30 kronen. The printed role of Othello in German—all can be had from the Box Office in the evening.

Aldridge arrived in Crakow with his wife and son on the night of 2nd November, and stayed at the Dresden Hotel. He made his first appearance in *Othello*, followed by *The Merchant of Venice* and *The Padlock*. The local Press said that he had little success with the theatre-going public, as he played in English with the German theatre company, not the Polish. English was practically unknown in Crakow, although those who saw him apparently understood him well, thanks to his mimicry and expressiveness. But the fact that he played with the German company did not make a good impression on the Poles, as famous as the Irish for their stubborn, proud nationalism. Aldridge had been playing with German companies for the past three years and had not yet attempted to play in English with a Polish company. That was yet to come.

The period in which Aldridge visited Poland, between 1854 and his last visit in 1867, was a very difficult time for the Polish theatre because of the struggles for liberation and revolt against the Russian Tsars as well as the Austrian and Prussian governments, amongst whom Poland was divided. Sharp censorship did not permit the showing of many plays from the world's dramatic treasury, among them many of the plays of Shakespeare. The actor was therefore limited in his choice of repertory, *King Lear* and *Macbeth* especially being strictly forbidden by the Tsarist censor for reasons not hard to fathom. Conditions in Crakow, however, were better than in Warsaw, as the Austrian censorship was not as strict as the Russian.

Despite his initial lack of success, he was given favourable and serious reviews in the Press. One critic said:

The write-ups of incidents in the life of the "Black Artist", his portraits, brochures and life sketches, the unanimous praise rather than criticism, provoked such a mistrust in us, that at times we even accused the serious journals of falling in with the general trend of popular opinion, which it is sometimes difficult for even the strongest to combat. We must admit, however, that by the third act we gave our soul to the genuinely talented artist. We were no longer amazed at the audacity of Shakespeare in making the proud daughter of a Venetian Senator fall in love with "a black devil", as Emilia calls him elsewhere, when newly awakened jealousy stirred his African blood and roused even that noble lion to anger.

Shakespeare's Othello is not just a black Nubian or native of Senegal; he is but a Mauritanian in the service of the Republic of Venice, and only in disdain or comparison did the author use the expression "black" to show his blackness. Terrifying was Othello's lament, "Farewell . . . Othello's occupation's gone. . . ." Then he was possessed with revenge in the form of a cold-blooded, calculated crime. And in the fifth act we see Aldridge slowly arrive at the conviction that he is fulfilling the duty of an honest judgment. On the other hand, how full of emotion was the short scene in the second act! But let us not talk any more of his performance, for in a short review we have no intention of drawing water from the sea with a spoon. . . .

His ugly features, according to the European standard of beauty, became richly beautiful, the sonorous organ of his voice became gentle to a murmur, and his strong eye melted with tenderness. And with that, what confidence and meaningful gestures! At moments the most terrifying elevated fury of a wild beast, but not a scuffle, a howl, but not a shriek in his voice. So must have been Othello as the poet's genius created him.[3]

The same paper two days later says:

In the role of Shylock, Ira Aldridge showed himself a great artist, with great resources and strength, one who has in his power every means of producing great effects. In a word, he is an all-out artist used to covering a wide range of scenes. If in *Othello* he was so outstanding amongst the general players, it was the very power of his role which gave him the opportunity to interpret this single character in whom the whole tragedy is concentrated. On the other hand, in *The Merchant of Venice*, Shylock does not represent anything in himself; he is only a necessary cog in the general layout, the same as Antonio, Bassanio, Portia, etc. Yet every exit of Shylock was an event. He did not enter into the general pattern and he could not on his own make a whole of the part, as in *Othello*. He gave the impression of its being only a study. The rest of the performances as a whole were beneath criticism. If one wishes to play any role of Shakespeare, one must know by heart the whole of Shakespeare. One must absorb it not only with the body, but also with the soul, not only with expressions, but also with the mind. If one wishes to learn Shakespeare, one needs to know many things before that. There are strong foods which require strong digestive systems, and they would be harmful for weak ones. Episodic roles like Lancelot, Pistol, etc., can be played in isolation, not necessarily closely linked with the whole action. And Mr. Hassly was a good Lancelot.

In *The Padlock*, Ira Aldridge wanted to give us a picture of the life of a Negro slave in the West Indies, though changed a little and more real than the sentimental book of Beecher Stowe, and this was also a new side to his talents.

There have been various published references throughout the years to Aldridge's financial contributions to the Abolitionist movement, but very little specific information could be found on this point. Frederick Douglass, William Wells Brown, William and Ellen Craft, and others visited England in the Abolitionist cause in Aldridge's time, and there were various organizations through which he could have forwarded money. In an article in the *Amsterdam News* (New York Negro daily newspaper) on 20th November 1943 we are told that "he sent back thousands of dollars to help his enslaved people and said many times that he could never be happy as long as one of his race was in chains". And Carter Woodson informs us that Aldridge was among the prominent Negroes who contributed through the Negro State Conventions operating from 1830 to 1861.⁴ The Press of Saratov wrote: "Since the commencement of the struggle for the liberation of the blacks, the famous tragedian has donated half of his takings, i.e., of the money received from his performances, into the funds of an organization for the work of freeing the slaves. Such a regular, voluntary deprival of half his own means of livelihood fully characterizes his moral and civil development as a man and an artist."⁵ It is interesting that our first specific information in this matter should come from a Polish newspaper:

> Though Ira Aldridge performs at present on the stage in Crakow, it is not from the things written about him as an actor that he will be remembered, but as a human being. The artistic triumphs which Ira Aldridge has gained in a few years throughout Europe are known to all; it would be unnecessary therefore to reiterate them. Less known, however, is how he uses in a noble and disinterested manner the material gains from his triumphs. This artist has taken upon himself the task of showing Europe that his race is capable of educating itself, and not only by showing himself on the stage does he speak for the emancipation of the Negro, but also his actions are in the same spirit. Not long ago the Press brought news of a beautiful trend in his character which carries his name from mouth to mouth, and we are impelled to repeat it. A Negro family called Wilson, a father, mother, son, and two daughters, fled from slavery in Baltimore and reached New York during the night. Nevertheless, through the Fugitive Slave Act of 1850, they were captured and arrested for the crime of demanding freedom; and it costs a lot to buy them out in the country of freedom. They were then put up for sale individually, the mother and father to be sent to the plantations of Georgia; both daughters were destined to a sad and degrading fate, which often befell fugitive slaves. The Society for the Manumission of Slaves in New York at the time had no funds to buy out the family, and Ira Aldridge, playing at that time in Austria, had learned from the English Press of this incident, and at once sent to New York the money needed to buy the freedom of this family. In this way does Ira Aldridge use his earnings.⁶

That his charity did not confine itself to the Abolitionist movement is evidenced by a letter written to him later in the year by the President of the Institution for Women and Girls at Stavropol, thanking him for his performance at a special benefit for the Institution and informing him that the net proceeds were 457 roubles 90 kopecks.

Such was the impact professionally and personally that Ira Aldridge made on Poland in 1854. He did not go back until 1862, returning in 1866, and again, finally, in 1867.

CHAPTER XII

Chevalier Ira Aldridge, K.S.

IN the spring of 1855 the family is back in London, where we find Aldridge still negotiating for a Parisian appearance and making efforts on behalf of a German company. The following two letters were obviously written to the same person, probably someone in Germany. The first is written from 22 Judd Place, London, on 20th April:

MY DEAR SIR, Your favour of the 17th came to hand last evening. Enclosed I beg to acknowledge one also from dear Fraulein Schneider. I would have written immediately in answer to your last but I could not speak decisively on one point or the other. On Wednesday next it will be definitely settled as to Paris and on the same day I will be informed if a German troupe will be brought over. Herr Carl Formes is at the Royal Italian Opera and not with the German Opera as last season. The German Opera is at Drury Lane together with an Italian Opera and it is not yet decided whether they bring a Deutsch Gesellschaft to co-operate.

In making my very best and kindest regards to my dear Desdemona, tell her that her interests are ever uppermost in my thoughts, and that if a troupe is decided on every effort shall be made on my part to obtain for her a Contract. It is not Mr. Mitchell of the St. James who speculates in the matter or I could speak positively in the matter. Directly I ascertain I will write, most probably on Wednesday next.

I am very thankful to you and Fraulein Schneider for the kind enquiries respecting the health of myself, Mrs. A., and my dear Ira. Mrs. A. is still very weak indeed, Ira quite well, and I am still indisposed, being under the daily care of a Physician and not leaving the house only on urgent business, and then in a closed carriage, so I have not partook of the gaieties of this week from the visit of the Emperor and Empress* who, to use a theatrical phrase, have been received with great applause.

* Napoleon III of France, and Eugénie.

The weather is beautiful. Will you tell Mr. Magfuhrt that I will have antwort for him which will be enclosed in my next brief to you. I will also trouble you with two or three commissions. I have not yet been well enough to go a-book-hunting but hope to have the Bilds and books in ordering and left at your friends by the latter part of next week.

My best respects to yourself, your family individually and all friends. I will thank you to tell me if Mad. Toussaint would accept of my bild. I do not remember but I think I gave one to dear Madame Belifante to whom and the family remember me kindly. Write me if you can in reply, *do not pay postage.* I will write to Mad. Toussaint. I hope Herr Von Biene is perfectly recovered, and until I again hear from you

I remain truly yours,

IRA ALDRIDGE.

"Ich bin sehr Krank"

Aldridge makes use of his knowledge of German, probably newly acquired, by interspersing his letters with German words and phrases. The postscript, "I am very sick", is indeed ominous. The second letter is headed merely "London, Thursday morning", and it is likely that both letters were written to Dr. Victor Koelbel of Leipzig:

MY DEAR SIR,—Late yesterday evening it was decided that under circumstances the idea of bringing a German troupe to London this season should be abandoned; Mr. Mitchell has declined embarking in the speculation as all the gentry are expected to visit Paris during the summer, and coupled with the war* he does not think a proportionate return could be depended upon; even the German Opera is postponed until the next year. A troupe from the Theatre de la Gaite are acting here at present, but notwithstanding the *entente cordiale*, they have failed to create a sensation.

Make my sincere respects to dear Fraulein Schneider; and express my regrets that I have not been enabled to accomplish what I so ardently hoped for, but hope that the next season I may be more fortunate in her behalf, tell her also to rest assured that I will not lose sight of it, and will through you always know her locale. Pray give my best respects to Herr Magfuhrt and tell him the foregoing and when a Deutsch troupe is determined on, I will

* The Crimean War, which France and England had entered on the side of the Turks against the Russians.

use what little influence I have in the endeavour to serve him.

Now with respect to myself, I do not go to Paris at present. I could not agree as to terms; besides, my health is unsatisfactory, and I am recommended quiet. Under these circumstances I decline having the biography published at present. I will therefore thank you to give it me in French, together with the *Zeitung's* notices P.P., also the letters of introduction you promised for Paris, and on their receipt I will acknowledge them, in the mean time I will endeavour to procure the work respecting Cambridge. Send all to your friend in the Minories* through whom I will also make my communications.

I hope all your family are in the enjoyment of that inestimable blessing health, remember me most kindly to them, in which feeling Mrs. A. and Ira join. They are both better in health than I am.

With sincere respects, I remain
Very truly yours,
IRA ALDRIDGE.

During his negotiations for a German tour he receives the following letter, presumably from a theatre manager:

DEAR ALDRIDGE,—As soon as you fix the form of letter to German managers, we can translate it and send letters off. Think over the towns where success is probable.

It is *rus in urbe*—"country in town"—the other saying is *urbs in rure*—"town in country", and either will apply to your villa being so near the great cosmopolitan resort. The preposition "in" in this case governs the ablative, consequently *urbs in rure*, and *rus in urbe*. You will now understand the matter thoroughly and you can say to a friend:

my rus in urbe, or
my urbs in rure

for I think I may take it both ways, seeing how near your villa is to town and above all, the world's resort, the Crystal Palace. Perhaps it will be well to drop me a line before you call respecting German letters so that I may not be out.

Thanks for your enquiries respecting my young one; he is getting on well.

Yours very truly,
J. H. KEENE.

* A banking district in the City of London.

He must have spent the next few months resting, in accordance with medical advice, because his next appearance was not until 13th August, when he plays Othello, Macbeth, Shylock and once more *Obi, The Slave*, etc., at the Theatre Royal, Plymouth. The playbill announced "His first appearance after an absence of three years from England, during which period he had the distinguished honour of appearing before Frederick William, King of Prussia". He tours the usual eastern and southern circuits, Yarmouth and Norwich, and at Christmas he is at Worthing.

"The presence of Aldridge made business distinctly better", writes Mary Theresa Odell quite correctly in *The Old Theatre, Worthing* (published in 1938), but continues with some quite incorrect statements about his early life and schooling in the East End of London, and his career as an actor, finishing up with: "Occasionally he was absent from this country for long periods, and when he came back he was covered with orders, diplomas, etc., that had been bestowed upon him by foreign potentates; he displayed these with great ostentation; whether they were genuine or not is open to question. . . . There are two other Negro tragedians at the same period, Keene and Morgan." Keene is, of course, Aldridge, and Morgan must be a reference to the Negro actor, Morgan Smith.

In 1856 he continues in the provinces in the same repertoire, but, if we are to accept certain uncorroborated statements, with one notable addition—on 13th May 1856 he appears as Hamlet in the Adelphi Theatre, Sheffield. There is some controversy as to whether he ever played this role. We have Aldridge's own statement at a public dinner (specific date unknown, but probably in the early 1830s), when he commented on Mathews's burlesque of the African Theatre, that he never played Hamlet, i.e. up to that date. In 1872 J. J. Sheahan, who claimed a thirty-year friendship with Aldridge, stated categorically in *Notes and Queries*: "Mr. Aldridge never played Hamlet." We have, however, at least one account of a contemporary who stated specifically that he saw Aldridge in *Hamlet*, though he is not specific as to the date. This is William Wells Brown, a fugitive slave, who came to Europe in 1849 to represent the American Peace Society at the Peace Congress in Paris, and stayed in England and on the Continent for several years. Mr. Brown said that on looking over the columns of *The Times* one morning—

I saw it announced that Ira Aldridge, the African Roscius, was to appear in the character of Othello, and having long wished to see my sable countryman, I resolved at once to attend. . . . The house was well filled, and among the audience I recognized the faces of several distinguished persons of the nobility, the most noted of whom was Sir Edward Bulwer Lytton, the renowned novelist—his figure neat, trim, hair done up in the latest fashion— looking as if he had just come out of a band-box.

He describes the performance and the audience's reaction, and then goes on to say:

The following evening I went to witness his Hamlet, and was surprised to find him as perfect in that as he had been in *Othello*; for I had been led to believe that the latter was his greatest character. The whole court of Denmark was before us; but not till the words, " 'Tis not alone my inky cloak, good mother," fell from the lips of Mr. Aldridge, was the general ear charmed, or the general tongue arrested. The voice was so low, and sad, and sweet, the modulation so tender, the dignity so natural, the grace so consummate, that all yielded themselves silently to the delicious enchantment. When Horatio told him that he had come to see his father's funeral, the deep melancholy that took possession of his face showed the great dramatic power of Mr. Aldridge. "I pray thee do not mock me, fellow-student," seemed to come from his inmost soul. The animation with which his countenance was lighted up during Horatio's recital of the visits that the ghost had paid him and his companions was beyond description. "Angels and ministers of grace defend us," as the ghost appeared in the fourth scene, sent a thrill through the whole assembly. His rendering of the "Soliloquy on Death", which Edmund Kean, Charles Kemble, and William C. Macready have reaped such unfading laurels from, was one of his best efforts. He read it infinitely better than Charles Kean, whom I had heard at the Princess but a few nights previous. The vigorous starts of thought, which in the midst of his personal sorrows rise with such beautiful and striking suddenness from the ever-wakeful mind of the humanitarian philosopher, are delivered with that varying emphasis that characterizes the truthful delineator, when he exclaims, "Frailty, thy name is woman!" In the second scene of the second act, when revealing to Guildenstern the melancholy which preys upon his mind, the beautiful and powerful words in which Hamlet explains his feelings are made very effective in

Mr. Aldridge's rendering: "This most excellent canopy, the air, look you, this brave o'erhanging firmament, this majestical roof fretted with golden fire. . . . What a piece of work is a man! How noble in reason? how infinite in faculty! in form and moving how expressive and admirable! in action how like an angel! in apprehension how like a god!" In the last scene of the second act, when Hamlet's imagination, influenced by the interview with the actors, suggests to his rich mind so many eloquent reflections, Mr. Aldridge enters fully into the spirit of the scene, warms up, and when he exclaims, "He would drown the stage with tears, and cleave the general ear with horrid speech, make mad the guilty and appall the free," he is very effective; and when this warmth mounts into a paroxysm of rage, and he calls the King "Bloody, bawdy villain! Remorseless, treacherous, lecherous, kindless villain!" he sweeps the audience with him, and brings down deserved applause. The fervent soul and restless imagination, which are ever stirring at the bottom of the fountain, and sending bright bubbles to the top, find a glowing reflection on the animated surface of Mr. Aldridge's coloured face. I thought Hamlet one of his best characters, though I saw him afterwards in several others.[1]

Andrews, in his unpublished notes, quotes extracts from the above, but attributes the review to the newspapers of the time. As for the alleged performance in Sheffield, we have not been able to find a playbill of 13th May. The *Sheffield Daily Telegraph* of 15th May 1856 reported that the audiences at the Adelphi Theatre "have been very large during this week. The African Roscius is evidently the right man in the right place." On 16th May, his benefit night, he played Macbeth, Ginger Blue, and Obi: on 17th May, his last night, he played Richard III. This daily newspaper and the weekly *Era*, which had an exhaustive coverage of the provincial theatres, have been perused very carefully for this period, but nothing could be found to substantiate his playing of Hamlet in Sheffield.

Archibald Haddon, an English journalist, appears to offer another piece of evidence. After a radio broadcast in London on Aldridge in the early 1930s, he received a letter from an English actor saying that he had played First Grave-digger to Aldridge's Hamlet.[2] We are, however, sceptical about this, as the actor would have been a centenarian by then. The greater likelihood is that he played with Morgan Smith, the Negro actor who played

Hamlet and other Shakespearean roles in England in the late 1860s and for about two decades thereafter, but not as successfully as Aldridge.

We reproduce the playbill of the Theatre Royal, Wolverhampton, 9th October 1846, which depicts in woodcuts all of Aldridge's major roles. The first woodcut on the left shows Othello and Iago, and the second appears to represent Hamlet meeting the ghost on the battlements of Elsinore. Playbills of that period need not be accepted as conclusive evidence of anything, but a study of the other woodcuts on this one shows them all to represent roles that Aldridge definitely played. It may be concluded that Aldridge had not played Hamlet at the time he made his public statement, that he did possibly attempt it in England before 1846 (*vide* playbill woodcut) and possibly in 1856 at Sheffield, but that he did not retain it in his repertoire for his own good reasons. If he gave only a few performances of it, Sheahan, being in Hull, might not have known of it.

He continued his usual provincial rounds until 13th April 1857, when he once more played in London, still not at a West End theatre, but for his good friends, the Lanes, of the Britannia Theatre, Hoxton, where he does *Othello* and *Pizarro* and revives *Titus Andronicus*. Here the woodcut is different from the Wolverhampton bill. It is a copy of a daguerreotype of Payne of Islington (not far from Hoxton). This daguerreotype was taken at the time he first played the part at the Britannia, and was engraved for Tallis's *Drawing Room Table Book* in 1851. This issue of the magazine also includes an engraving of Aldridge (from a daguerreotype) as Mungo, and a two-page biography, repeating the usual legends. Later the engraving as Aaron was used in the same publisher's edition of the complete works of Shakespeare. It is the most well-known picture of Aldridge in England.

In March 1857 he receives another letter from J. H. Keene, which opens up new horizons for him:

DEAR MR. ALDRIDGE,—I have just received a letter from Major Pringle, Stockholm, enclosing one from the Director of the Theatre Royal. The letter offers £25 a night for Othello—the only character he requires—number of representations not to be limited beforehand. The best time between the middle and end of May. The Consul thinks you would be able to do something at

Copenhagen on your way to Stockholm and afterwards at St. Petersburg.

In great haste, yours,
J. H. KEENE.

The best day at the theatre is Sunday. The Consul wants to know if you would object.

Major Pringle is obviously the British Consul in Stockholm, and the fact that he personally arranges to bring a Negro actor to Stockholm indicates Aldridge's prestige on the Continent. A full description of his journey and interesting personal details are contained in a long letter written to his wife from Stockholm:

MY DEAR MARGARET,—You will be glad to hear, dearest, that I have safely arrived here. I left Stettin on Tuesday between 12 and 1 and got here by 12 yesterday—an exceedingly fine passage, Thank God, and no sea sickness, the Baltic Sea being comparatively as smooth as a looking glass. We stopped at two places on the way, Swinemunde in Prussia and Kalmar in Sweden, the latter place half way which we reached about half-past twelve on Wednesday. They stayed about an hour and a half to discharge cargo, and I with some gentlemen sauntered into the town, and going to a Confectioners to get some coffee—in all the Swedish papers I was announced—it spread over the town like wildfire that I was there and such a crowd assembled at the steamer, their curiosity excited in the highest pitch but no rudeness. The Officers of the Regiment stationed there requested to be introduced to me —which accordingly they were by the Captain of the steamer who is an officer in the Prussian service and resided in England for some time. It was telegraphed from Kalmar to Stockholm that I was coming by the steamer and on my arrival Major Pringle was waiting to receive me—a carriage also with attendants awaited me and accompanied by the Major drove to my lodgings.

A word of the Major. He is the most perfect gentleman mingled with the soldier you ever saw. He has shown me all the attention possible. I dined with his family yesterday and in the evening they gave a party to meet and introduce me consisting of a great many English and the members of the different legations, among them an Attaché of the Austrian Legation, the Consul for the Cape of Good Hope and his lady and a great many other persons, including the English Chaplain. Mrs. Prieste is a member of the Dunmore family, her uncle being the present Earl of Dunmore and her cousin is the Hon. Mr. Murray who was resident Diplomatic Minister at Berne when we were there and who is now the Ambassador to Persia. Mrs. Pringle spoke most indignantly of the book her cousin wrote in favour of the slave-holders, you remember—and said that the Queen acted nobly in declining her services as Maid-of-Honour. The summer or warm weather did not commence here until the day before yesterday, and there is not a leaf or scarcely any green to be seen, all is rock with trees growing out of them but the most beautiful I ever saw, from five o'clock yesterday morning until we arrived here 'twas like a beautiful panorama.

Major Pringle would have had me to stop in his house had there been room, but he is moving it, being so confined that he is obliged to send his son out to sleep. I am very glad, for had I been there I should have been under restraint. I have lodgings very clean and airy taken for me by the Director, but I do not know what the arrangement is as he was absent in the country yesterday and I expect him this morning. He left a letter for me with the Major in which he placed his Box at my disposal, but the Major advised me not to gratify curiosity as they are all anxious to see me.

Now for yourself, my darling, and my very dear Ira, both of you may God protect, such is my daily prayer. I am anxiously awaiting a letter from home and I beg of dear Mr. Groom to give me a long one. I am between nine and ten hundred miles from you, and letters arrive here but twice a week. I wish to know how you are, and how your cough is, better I hope. I trust that my dear Ira is well. I had a most unpleasant dream last night respecting him and awoke crying. Tell him he is not to drink strong tea as Mrs. Pringle says nothing can be worse, she having lost an interesting little daughter from that cause. I hope that he is attentive to you and I am sure that he is a good boy. Kisses for you and him and God Bless you both.

Since writing the foregoing the Director has called, having returned from the country. I am to attend a rehearsal tomorrow and fix the first appearance. They have been at work with *Othello* ever since they have received it and have not yet perfected themselves. The King who is ill has expressed a wish to see my first representation, all the Royal Family will be present also. You would be very much puzzled with the language here, it is different to anything else we have heard, a great many words are like English, but all unlike German.

Major Pringle has just called and has politely offered to enclose

my letter which will reach you through the Foreign Office. I
hope to see you in a month or five weeks, please God. The
theatre here closes at the latter part of June.

Have you been out yet, have you been to the Zoological
Gardens? Get out as much as possible. I am so anxious to hear
from home. How is Bob, Hec, and Dash? I will send a newspaper occasionally. They are very anxious to see me in Deutschland, Sachse wished me to act if but for one night which I would
have been happy to have done but could not. Give my best and
kindest regard to Mr. and Mrs. Groom. I hope Mrs. Groom is
getting better of that coldness in her feet.

As usual the leading man is grumbling about the disadvantage
he says he will be at not understanding English. He forgets that I
am at a greater disadvantage, his language is understood by the
entire audience while I am but partially so. However, that is
easily got over. I had forgot to tell you that there is no real night
here, and a little farther off at Bothnia the sun never sets at this
season of the year, just going below the horizon for about eight or
ten minutes. The entire night you can read.

This letter shows his affection and close relationship to his wife,
who is now almost sixty years old and ailing. "My dear Ira" is
now ten. There is no dearth of information about Aldridge's stage
career, but this letter to his wife is one of the few pieces of original
source material that sheds some light on him as a man, a husband,
a father, and a friend. He dreams that his son is ill and wakes up
crying. He is preparing to play before the King, but he has time
to worry about his wife's cough and to ask about the dogs and
about Mrs. Groom's "coldness in her feet". The important
matter about the grumbling leading man and the whole knotty
problem of a bilingual performance he shrugs off as "easily got
over".

His success was great both with the Court and the general
public, and on leaving Stockholm he was accompanied to the
boat by many hundreds of admirers.

In October 1857 he is back in London playing at another minor
theatre, the City of London, presenting all his old melodramas.
What a let-down it must have been to return from a European
capital, patronized by Royalty and the whole Court in the King's
own theatre, where he presented Shakespeare's greatest plays, to
his own capital to play in a minor theatre in the East End, where
he has to revive his old melodramas to please the groundlings.

But all the time he is negotiating to return to the Continent. In January he is once again in Saxe-Meiningen, and the *Illustrated London News* of 3rd July 1858 reports:

At Saxe-Meiningen, last January, after his performance of Shylock, Baron von Tillich, the General-Intendant, by command of the reigning Sovereign, presented Mr. Aldridge with the Royal Saxon House Order with the medal in gold; and the month following he was introduced, kissed hands, and received his diploma from the Royal Highness. What enhances this great distinction is that Mr. Aldridge is the only actor, native or foreign, so decorated. It is, moreover, expressly stated in his diploma that he is permitted to wear the medal next in order to the members of the Royal House of Saxony, and it is accompanied by a beautiful decoration in the shape of a Maltese Cross in gold. The best proof, therefore, that can be given of the appreciation of his merits as an actor and a gentleman by those foreign Potentates is to be found in the fact that he has been presented with these costly medals and the authentic credentials by which they are accompanied.

Here is the translation of the letter which accompanied the decorations:

His Highness the Duke, acknowledging Mr. Ira Aldridge's eminent merits as a dramatic performer, has graciously condescended to bestow on him the Golden Order of Service, affiliated to the Order of the House of Ernest, with the permission to wear it on the neck with the ribbon of the said Order. In warrant of this,

HARBON,
for the Ministries of Sachsen Meiningen.
Meining, 31st January 1858

The reigning Duke was Bernhard, brother of Queen Adelaide of England (consort of King William IV). Bernhard's son, George II (1826-1914), who succeeded him, was a talented artist and lover of the theatre and played an important part in the annals of the European theatre. He began by designing scenery and costumes for the Court Company, but this he did only after exhaustive study and research, reproducing historical periods with absolute accuracy. He designed not only the setting, but also the composition of stage movement and crowd movement, and insisted on continuous rehearsal of the supers in costume, giving everyone some action, some by-play, making a crowd or an army a living organism. He concentrated on developing an harmonious relationship between actor and setting and on greater use of a three-dimensional stage. In 1878 the Meiningen company, which had already become famous, came to London and earned great acclaim, then to Moscow, where it influenced the young Stanislavsky, and so the ripples of reform spread—the initiation of some of which may be attributed to the Chevalier Ira Aldridge, Knight of Saxony, as he ever afterwards proudly called himself.

Further evidence of Aldridge's direct influence on the European theatre is given by Dr. Michel Kovatchévitch in an essay, *Shakespeare in Serbia,*★ in which he says that Aldridge came to Serbia in 1858 and performed *Richard III, Othello,* and *Macbeth,* the first time a Shakespearean play had been performed in that little country! The town in which he played was Novi Sad, in the Voivodina, then under Austrian and Hungarian domination. It was and is still known as the "Serbian Athens", and was the cultural and intellectual centre for all Serbs. Here began the Serbo-Croat National Theatre, but "Shakespeare was not included in the repertory", says Dr. Kovatchévitch, "because the technique of acting Shakespearean plays was unknown until Aldridge showed them how! A young Serbian romantic poet, Lazar Kostitch, became a keen admirer of Aldridge, and through him, of Shakespeare. A year later, in 1859, Kostitch published a translation of part of *Romeo and Juliet.* In 1860 a fine building was erected in Novi Sad called the Serbian National Theatre. . . . The first actor to play Richard III in Novi Sad was Lazar Teletchki, who had studied the role under Kostitch, and learned from him to play it on the lines of Ira Aldridge. In 1866 the Serbian review, *Matitza,* published a complete translation by Kostitch of *Romeo and Juliet,* which was acted in the National Theatre. This was the first time that a play of Shakespeare was acted in its entirety in the Serbian language. The translation was a great literary achievement. . . . Encouraged by his first success, Kostitch went on to translate *Richard III* and *Hamlet.* The National Theatre in Belgrade, erected by Prince Michael Obrenovitch, was inaugurated after his death on 30th October 1869. The company consisted of actors from Belgrade itself and from Novi Sad." Thus we again

★ Given as a lecture at the *Institut Française* in London, 10th June 1943.

see the initial impetus which Aldridge gave to the young national theatre movement, and the gratitude of the Serbs and Croats is expressed by a plaque which today adorns the National Theatre in Belgrade, dedicated to the African Roscius, the first actor ever to perform Shakespeare in Serbo-Croatia, which today is Yugoslavia.

*   *   *

He returns home, his prestige so greatly enhanced by his successful Continental tour that he is offered an engagement at the Lyceum Theatre, London. While there was no longer any legal distinction between "legitimate" and "illegitimate" theatres, the Lyceum enjoyed a certain importance, having been one of the original "licensed" burletta theatres, and being situated in the West End. It was first built as a hall in 1772 and as a theatre in 1794. It had housed the burnt-out Drury Lane company in 1809, thus achieving a patent status while the company was within its walls, but a licence as an opera house was a reward to its manager for his hospitality. When Aldridge came to it in 1858, it was under the management of George A. Webster.

The playbill announced "The First Appearance of the Celebrated and Only African Tragedian, Ira Aldridge, Member of the Prussian Academy of Arts and Sciences, etc., etc. . . . previous to his departure on his third tour through Germany". The Press reactions are worth quoting extensively:

The *Illustrated London News*, 31st July 1858:

The Lyceum: Mr. Ira Aldridge, with whom our readers have recently been made acquainted by means of his published portrait and memoir in our columns, was enabled on Saturday to obtain his long-sought appearance before a West End audience. The triumph thus achieved over the usual prejudice against colour is highly to the credit of the manager who, whatever may have been his other mistakes, has, in freely recognizing the claims of his sable brother, done reasonably and well. The part selected for this interesting début was that of Othello—a part, of course, peculiarly fitted for the experiment. The veritable Moor, so to speak, stood before the spectator, and appealed in his living and natural lineaments to human sympathy.

And the *Athenaeum* devotes as much space to this performance as to his Covent Garden appearance twenty-five years before, but now in a different tone:

We had occasion last week to remark that provincial managements, like that of Mr. George Webster in relation to the Lyceum, were accompanied at least with one good—they gave opportunity and opening for neglected talent. On Saturday this observation was corroborated in a manner not likely to be soon forgotten. Most of our readers have, no doubt, heard of Mr. Ira Aldridge, "the African Roscius", and seen placards so headed in the public streets and advertisements in the public Press. For something like a quarter of a century, indeed, has this gentleman occasionally repaired to the metropolis, on visits to the East-End theatres and saloons, where he has regularly commanded a high rate of remuneration; and in the provinces he might have been frequently found recorded as achieving a success equal with the best. More recently, we have read of him as acting in Germany, and being the admired of princes, who have garnished his person with honours and medals, not in general accorded to the professors of his craft. The prejudices which the courtly and the polished have thus set at naught, have hitherto prevailed in England, so far at least as to dissuade West End managers from the belief that the sable African could possibly be an actor sufficiently good to command the suffrages of a fashionable audience. The provisional manager of the Lyceum has been daring enough to arrive at a different conclusion; and on Saturday evening Mr. Ira Aldridge appeared on these boards, in the character of Othello.

Of the fitness of the part to the actor there cannot be two opinions; yet, perchance, though we read in the text of Shakespeare of "the thick-lipped" Othello, even before his appearance, we have some repugnance to subdue when he really appears on the stage with the labial peculiarity of which we had been forewarned. And not without reason: for we rightly expect Art to imitate rather than copy Nature; and have long been accustomed in this instance to substitute a very distant imitation for a close copy. This feeling, however, gradually subsides, when we find that not only does the sable artist pronounce our language distinctly and correctly, but with elocutional emphasis and propriety, and that his general action is marked with elegance and ease. One small peculiarity, too, soon subtly indicates itself with remarkable significance. We have before us an Othello, with his hands ungloved, and the finger-nails expressively apparent.

We begin to perceive the play and action of the hand, and the remarkable assistance which its variety of gestures may give to the meaning; and then to recollect with some surprise that this is an advantage of which Othellos have been in general deprived.

Slight as this may seem, to the critical observer it is wonderful what additional animation this unwonted sign of life gives to the entire man. Another advantage Mr. Aldridge has is the sweetness and softness of his voice which, in the level tones particularly, is both pleasing and effective. These concentrate a degree of pathos that penetrates the seat of feeling. His higher tones are, however, thin and exaggerated; and where they begin a sentence are too artificial to be thoroughly true to the nature and passion which they are designed to suggest. The trick, which we here unreservedly condemn, has doubtless been found effective with less refined audiences, but with one more cultivated, must be used as sparingly as possible. We have noticed the same fault with some American actors, who constantly resort to it as an elocutionary expedient, which from its frequency becomes so far from effective that it strikes an unsophisticated ear as perilous and absurd.

Rightly or wrongly, Mr. Aldridge has formed a conception of Othello peculiarly his own, and interprets many portions of the text in an original manner. He softens some points which other actors make specially prominent, and brings others into relief that they are accustomed to suppress. We have therefore much to reconcile ourselves to during the course of the performance; and experience an amount of uneasiness in the number of questions raised, and which require after-reflection to settle. Evident it is, however, that Mr. Aldridge has thought on the matter from his own point of view and may, in many instances, have good and valid reasons for his preference. Certain words or phrases, too, in the text appear to offend his sense of delicacy, and he frequently changes them for substitutes less bold or more polite. This is a weakness of which he should at once rid himself. The greatest actor will depend most on his poet, and let him be responsible for his own words. We permit no man to stand between us and Shakespeare. . . . So far as our acquaintance with Mr. Aldridge extends, we have formed a favourable opinion of his talents. The audience testified theirs, by calling him before the curtain at the end of the third and fifth acts. He is manifestly an intelligent man; has studied his art with earnestness, and gained facility in its exercise.

214

Despite this and similar criticism, he continued to make such revisions in Shakespeare's text as he saw fit, and a letter that he wrote from Brighton on 2nd October 1860 (to an unknown addressee), shows that he did so consciously and deliberately:

SIR,—The circumstances under which I address you will plead somewhat in excuse for the liberty I have taken in doing so. Being from my Colour limited in my Repertoire and regardless of Schiller's warning, *"Lass doch niemand Hand an Shakespeare's Werke um etwas wesentlich daran zu andern; es bestraft sich immer selbst"*,★ I have attempted the adaptation of *Titus Andronicus*, and should your time permit I shall be highly gratified by your presence on Wednesday evening.

I am, Sir, Your obliged Svt.,

IRA ALDRIDGE, K.S.

Aldridge was mistaken in attributing this "warning" to Schiller. It was August William Schlegel who said this in one of his lectures in Vienna, in relation to a German poet who had transformed the witches in *Macbeth* into beings entirely different from those Shakespeare had in mind.[3]

And finally, we have *The Times*'s lengthy review:

On Saturday evening the Lyceum Theatre so far advanced beyond the dull insignificance of its reopening in the previous week that it appealed to the curiosity of the public. Mr. Ira Aldridge, the "African Tragedian", was announced in the character of Othello, and Mr. Ira Aldridge is just one of those persons of whose name everybody has heard but whom nobody in the western part of London has seen. It is true that he appeared in the same character at Covent Garden Theatre in April 1833, when M. Laporte was manager, but since April 1833 more than a quarter of a century has elapsed, nor do we believe that he made on that occasion an impression sufficiently strong to defy the encroachments of time upon memory. Nevertheless, his visits to the theatrical establishments on the other side of the water and in the eastern suburbs have been sufficiently numerous to guard him against oblivion, and a man who is remembered, if only by name, for five and twenty years may be said to have earned a sort of celebrity, especially if it

★ "Let no man lay hand on Shakespeare's works to change anything essential in them; he will be sure to punish himself."

is accompanied by some exclusive characteristic, like that which pertains to Mr. Ira Aldridge, as the "only actor of colour on the stage".

In Germany, whither he proceeded with an English company some six years ago, the admiration earned by his talents was of a far more decided kind than in this country. From the King of Prussia he received the large Golden Medal of Art and Science; in Austria he was rewarded by the Order of Leopold; in Switzerland he was endowed with the Medal of Merit. As for the list of his Imperial and Royal patrons, one might almost take it for an index to the Gotha Almanac, and a very imposing figure does it make, printed in large type, and set up near the entrance to the Lyceum Theatre. On the authority of a little pamphlet which is entitled *A Brief Memoir and (sic) Theatrical Career of Ira Aldridge, the Tragedian*, and to which we are under great obligation for the knowledge we now display, we are enabled to affirm that the admiration of the German Sovereigns was reflected in the German Press. A Berlin paper declared that "it was truly wonderful to see an African treading the boards of a theatre in the part of Othello, in which Mr. Aldridge was not to be surpassed". A Danzig critic went further, and exclaimed with enthusiasm, "Mr. Ira Aldridge is most decidedly the greatest dramatic artist we have ever seen". Even this was not enough, as the proposition might be true as well through the limited experience of the eulogist, as through the unlimited genius of the actor. Therefore, to avoid all possibility of equivocation, a Viennese panegyrist beats the Danzig gentleman all hollow by the bold declaration, "Mr. Ira Aldridge, is, without exception, the greatest European stage actor that ever lived". The particular journals in which these high eulogies occur we are not in a position to indicate. The expressions of opinion are to be found on the last page of the little pamphlet, with no further heading than the name of the city to which they belong.

Heralded by such unmeasured and inconsiderate laudations, it might naturally be imagined that Mr. Ira Aldridge was a much worse actor than he really proves to be. Although his dress, which is after the short tunic fashion of Mr. Edmund Kean, is so highly adorned and with such glittering material as to remind one of those little tinselled figures that appear on the toy stages of children, there is nothing like offensive assumption to be found in his manner. When he is in his quieter moments he gives the notion of a conscientious man, unspoilt by flattery and honestly endeavouring to do his best. His articulation is extremely distinct, and his delivery and gestures are marked by the greatest care, though they do not appear to be regulated by any very distinct conception of the part, and would not stand the test of a minute analysis. His speech to the Senate, for instance, is that of an elocutionist, who is aware that a variety of emphasis and action is necessary to give general effect to the oration, but is not so clear as to the connection between the particular oration and the circumstances under which it is spoken. The passages in which Mr. Aldridge appears most to sympathize with the part he undertakes, and to be most inclined to exchange the declaimer for the impersonator, are those in which the softer elements of Othello's nature are exhibited. There is now and then a touch of genuine pathos in his tones, and if his acting throughout had been up to the level of the utter despondency with which he exclaimed, "Fool, fool, fool", in the last scene, there would have been little to desire as far as one side of the character is concerned. On the other hand, the scenes of stormy passion are those in which he is least effective. He can be loud enough on occasion, but he never for a moment awakens the notion that any real feeling lies beneath the external violence. Nor is he even able to sustain a strong emotion. He lets a passion drop when it ought to be still mounting, and picks it up again with an altered pitch of voice that has a very odd effect, and thus we have alternations of tempest and calm that are the more perplexing because we never can discover any law, however eccentric, to which they are subject.

The circumstance that Othello is a black, and that Mr. Aldridge is a "coloured gentleman" naturally causes the Moor to hold the first place in the actor's repertory, and there is no doubt that many people would go to see Othello played by a Negro, on the same principle that induced a past generation to patronize the Falstaff of Mr. Stephen Kemble because the necessity for stuffing was obviated by the portliness of the artist. But we wish, for the sake of Mr. Aldridge, that a milder, or at any rate a quieter man of colour than the maddened Moor of Shakespeare could be found within the precincts of actable drama. Is *The Revenge* too far bygone to render a revival impossible? Or could we not imagine, without too great violence, that Cato became a little tanned by his sojourn in Utica? There is no doubt that Mr. Aldridge would be far more at home in declamation or in the delineation of the gentler emotions than in that atmosphere of passion in which no one can breathe freely without something akin to inspiration, and if there was a doubt on the subject at the fall of the curtain on Saturday, it was completely dispelled by the speech which Mr. Aldridge made when the applause of the audience had brought him to the footlights, and which was, in both matter and manner, a model of good sense, good taste, and good feeling.

As, however, Mr. Ira Aldridge, for reasons at which we have hinted, will still, no doubt, cleave to Othello as his principal part, we would advise him so far to comply with modern usage as to soften the circumstances of Desdemona's murder. It is now the usual practice to drop the draperies in front of the alcove, and thus render the horrible deed as indistinct as possible. But on Saturday night Desdemona was so plainly smothered before our eyes, and altogether so roughly handled, that when Miss Ness, who played the part, showed by the words spoken to Emilia that she was not dead in reality, it was a great relief. Let us also suggest that in the laudable endeavour so to modify the text that a minimum of offence may be given to ears polite, some slight attention be paid to the structure of the verse. For instance, when Othello says in the amended version, "She turn'd to folly, and she was—false,"* he gets rid of a very ugly word, but he speaks in an acatalectic metre that closely approaches no metre at all.

In the general acting of the play there was nothing remarkable. Mr. Stuart was full of intention as Iago, but the elaboration of his design seemed to delay execution. Miss Annie Ness, the Desdemona of the evening, at first seemed strongly disposed to walk through the part, but ultimately gave signs of feeling and intelligence.

It is at this time that Aldridge once again thinks of returning to his native country. What more could he achieve to impress his countrymen? Honours from royalty, membership in high and learned academies, patronage from the most varied audiences, from kings to commoners, performances in most of the royal theatres of Europe, acclaim as an actor of outstanding merit, and now—received in the West End of London.

* The original reads: "She turn'd to folly, and she was—a whore."

CHAPTER XIII

St. Petersburg

ON 19th August 1858 the *New York Herald* carried the following two advertisements, one under the other:

DRAMATIC—IRA ALDRIDGE. This great tragedian will visit this country in November next. Any lady competent to support him in his celebrated roles will address Agent, *Herald* office, stating when and where they may be seen. None but those of the first order of talent need answer.

IRA ALDRIDGE, THE AFRICAN ROSCIUS, WILL probably appear at the Academy of Music, in his transcendently great characters of Alexander the Great, Zanga, Gambia, &c., about the middle of November.

A month later, on 29th September, the *Journal* of Prague announced his appearance in that city and noted that "he is engaged to appear on the New York Stage in November".

Obviously, Aldridge was planning to go to the United States, and this is further attested to by his letter of 4th June 1860 to Dr. James McCune Smith of New York, in which he mentions Henry Wallack's suggestion of a visit to America in 1858, "but my dear wife would not entertain the idea, her prejudice is so rooted against the Americans for their treatment of our oppressed race generally". Whether Mrs. Aldridge's sentiment was decisive we do not know, but on 2nd November, instead of being in New York or at least *en route*, he was on his way to St. Petersburg, as we see from the following letter he wrote to the Editor of the *Athenaeum* from Reval:*

SIR,—The encouraging manner in which you were pleased to notice my late efforts in London enables me to take the liberty of acquainting you with my progress in Russia.

* Now Tallinn, capital of Esthonia.

After leaving Bohemia I came direct to Riga, from thence to Mitten and am now on my way to St. Petersburg where I am engaged to give 12 representations in the Imperial Theatre, receiving for each representation 400 Silver Roubles, £60, with free quarters at the Governmental expense and an Equipage at my disposal during my sojourn in the Imperial City. At the termination of my engagement in Riga, His Excellency the General, Governor of the East Provinces of Russia, Prince Suvoroff,* made me a magnificent present in silver, the produce of the Ural mountains, which I hope to have the pleasure of showing you on my return to England.

A slight notice of the foregoing, if space will permit, will materially serve and much oblige, Sir,

Your obedient servant,

IRA ALDRIDGE,

(African Tragedian).

So we see that even before he reaches the capital he is being fêted and given magnificent gifts. Now he has an equipage at his disposal and will not have to resort to the pawnshop. The terms offered by the Imperial Theatre are indeed unusual. A provincial actor in those days would earn about 25 roubles a month, and a city actor as much as 100 roubles. Aldridge gets 400 roubles for a single performance, and the greatly increased prices of admission, as we shall see, meet with no resistance by the public. He arrived in St. Petersburg a few days after writing the above letter, and gave his first performance on 10th November. In the course of his Continental tours he had entered the Russian Empire, but this was the first time that he penetrated Russia proper.

In the United States the struggle between the North and South was gathering momentum, and this was not without its influence on Russia, which at that time incorporated what is now Latvia, Lithuania, Esthonia, part of Poland, and Bessarabia. It was overwhelmingly agricultural, and of a population of about 70 million the vast majority lived in a condition of serfdom, either as Crown peasants or as virtual slaves of individual landowners. The power of the landlord was absolute, similar to that of the slave-owner in the United States. He could order a marriage to take place and he could dissolve it; he could separate the serf from his family and sell him either with a parcel of land or without it. After the

* Son of General Suvoroff, who defeated Napoleon in 1812.

American and French revolutions and the wave of revolts in
Europe in 1848, the serfs and the intelligentsia of Russia began to
intensify their demands for reform. The latter, though in a
much better position than the serfs, were hamstrung by police
censorship and the general oppressiveness of the régime. This
class saw the contrast between backward Russia and advanced
Europe, and by the time Ira Aldridge arrived they were only too
eager to support a figure who was to them a symbol of liberation
from slavery and backwardness. After Russia's devastating defeat
in the Crimean War in 1856, Alexander II saw that the time had
come for the abolition of serfdom. In the first months of his
régime he had already undertaken to relieve his people of some of
their most oppressive burdens. Now he spoke of the need for
laws equally just for all, equally protecting all, and in a speech to
the Moscow nobility he made the startling declaration: "It is
better to abolish serfdom from above than wait until the serfs begin to liberate themselves from below." His draft for liberation
was published in December 1857. Aldridge arrived in Russia in
November 1858, and the emancipation statute was finally promul-
gated in March 1861. More than 10 million male peasants with
their families were granted their personal freedom. But the Tsar,
despite his reforms, met with strong opposition from various
classes. The gentry wanted more political power in return for the
loss of their economic privileges; others demanded a constitution
on democratic lines; while the intelligentsia advocated not only
radical political change, but a social revolution. This last group
could not openly attack the régime because of the ruthless repres-
sion of freedom of thought, but they did it indirectly, through
their literature, newspapers, and literary and artistic criticism,
making analogies that were understood by their readers, if
not by the police. Thus, in writing about Aldridge's arrival,
K. Zvantsev said:

> In our contemporary history there is an event which creates a
> whole sphere of life and thought, i.e. the liberation of the Negro
> in the United States; this becomes something *internal*, not only for
> the enslaved people, but for all of us. That is why for us, at this
> particular time, the role of Othello performed by this artist of
> genius, with all its subtleties of tribal and climatic character,
> has a universal mighty significance. . . . From Othello is torn the
> deep cry, "Oh misery, misery, misery!" and in that misery of the

African artist is heard the far-off groans of his own people, oppressed by unbelievable slavery and more than that—the groans of the whole of suffering mankind.[1]

Harriet Beecher Stowe's *Uncle Tom's Cabin* was published in 1852, and immediately crystallized anti-slavery sentiment. It was translated into thirty-seven languages, and was particularly successful in Russia, where the progressives of the day were on the side of the Negro slaves. Nikolay Chernyshevsky, socialist writer and critic, in his propagandist novel, *A Vital Question; or What is to be Done*, declared: "I am for the illiterate blacks against their civilized slave-owners in the United States."

The leadership of the radical movement when Aldridge arrived was in the hands of some of the most brilliant men Russia ever produced, including Chernyshevsky, who, together with the poet Nekrassov, was Editor of the foremost periodical of the time, *Sovremennik* (Contemporary), which devoted much space to Aldridge.

At this moment in history, 1857-8, when the Tsar was promising emancipation to the serfs and other basic reforms, the anti-monarchists, socialists, revolutionaries, and their Press supported him, but when the great wave of reaction set in once more, Chernyshevsky was arrested and spent more than twenty years in exile; in 1866 *Sovremennik* was suppressed, and the revolutionary movement took more violent forms. These are some of the factors which explain why Ira Aldridge, on his arrival, was received with honour by both aristocrat and radical, and yet by 1862 two of his productions, *Macbeth* and *King Lear*, were banned, more adverse criticism is found in the Press, and he received less co-operation in the theatres, and by 1864 he was no longer permitted to perform in St. Petersburg.

When Nicholas I was Tsar of Russia, he personally controlled and censored the theatre, even to the supervision of the repertory and the assignment of roles to the actors! There were two imperial theatres in St. Petersburg, the Bolshoy (big), used mainly for opera and ballet, and the Maly (small), which produced drama. The Maly was later rebuilt and became the Alexandrinsky, which still exists. There were also the Youth Theatre and the Circus Theatre, in which Aldridge made his first appearance, under the auspices of the Imperial Theatre Company. The Bolshoy catered mainly for the Court circles and the Maly for the bourgeoisie.

The three great actors of the period were Vasilly A. Karatygin (1802-53), who represented the official Court outlook of romantic pseudo-classicism, Pavel S. Mochalov (1800-48), an emotional, romantic actor of the rising bourgeois circles, and Mikhail S. Shchepkin (1788-1863), who more directly represented the rebellious circles of the intelligentsia. Shchepkin was the first militant, realistic actor who, according to the critic Belinsky, combined the passion of Mochalov with the technical perfection of Karatygin. He created the role of the Inspector-General in Gogol's masterpiece, and was a friend of Pushkin and Griboyedov, the founders of Russian drama. He had been a serf whose talent so impressed liberal circles that his freedom was bought in order that he might join the troupe of the Imperial Maly Theatre in Moscow. His realism, expressed in the satirical plays of Gogol and Griboyedov, had its roots in his own serf past, and it is therefore natural that he should feel a deep kinship with Aldridge.

An actor devoting himself primarily to Shakespeare had been unknown in Russia up to that time, and Durylin remarks: "The appearance of Aldridge was extraordinarily timely; the Russian actors awaited such a one in order to learn from him how to master their art, and the Russian spectators in order to delve into the mighty feelings and thoughts of Shakespeare." They knew only a bowdlerized adaptation of *Hamlet*, though it was performed by Mochalov. Of the other plays, they had only a slight acquaintance with *Othello*, *King Lear*, and *The Merchant of Venice*, while *Macbeth* and *Richard III* they had never seen at all!

When Aldridge arrived, he found no one of distinction playing Shakespearean roles, Karatygin and Mochalov being now dead, and Shchepkin in retirement. There was, in fact, a complete absence of Shakespeare, even at the Moscow Maly Theatre, which at one time had been the centre of Shakespearean production.

All in all, the time was propitious for Aldridge, and he came on to the stage of Russia to stagger his audiences as Kean had staggered London, shattering the artificial school of external poses and decorative declamation with such realism that some found his "naturalness was even unpleasant", as we shall see. He played for thirty-one nights in the Imperial Theatre of St. Petersburg, twenty-one of which were devoted to *Othello*.

Of his first appearance, *Sovremennik* wrote:

Ira Aldridge! This name is known only to a very few, and when posters appeared announcing that the African tragedian from the Royal Covent Garden Theatre and the Lyceum Theatre, London, would be presenting his début in the role of Othello, with a German troupe in the Circus Theatre, the greater part of the inhabitants of Petersburg were amazed, and asked: "What is this?" Curiosity was rife. A black tragedian! That's certainly original! Although we don't understand a word of English, certainly we can't miss seeing a *black tragedian*. Added to which, the English Othello will have a German Desdemona—that indeed is strange and fascinating. And for the first performance of Aldridge, the theatre was packed from floor to ceiling, so that already in the morning of the *première*, it was impossible to get even a *loge* or a stall. . . . When Othello appeared on the stage, after some welcoming applause, there came a deathly hush, that uninterrupted silence which follows from intense curiosity, mixed with involuntary respect for talent, which already promised something unusual . . . it seemed as if the thousand-odd people in the theatre for these minutes held their breath. All binoculars were focused on the débutant.[2]

Mrs. Yunge describes her reactions to Aldridge's first performance:

Although I never saw Karatygin, the representative of the school of classic declamation, nevertheless, the reality of Aldridge's acting made a deep impression on me; after the first performance I wrote in my diary: "When he enters the stage his simplicity almost *unpleasantly* astounds one." Gradually I began to value this simplicity and was so attracted by the acting of Aldridge that I compared him to that which I saw as the grandest thing in nature —with the Imatra waterfalls.*

Some frankly said that they did not know what to make of it, as did one writer whom Durylin quotes:

As to the acting of the African tragedian, well, we find ourselves completely baffled by it, because in it we find so many unusual, savage and uncontrolled elements, entirely unknown to us until now, and if we consider this acting from the point of view of our theatrical art, then it appears quite strange and often, even, not altogether skilled, but the talent of the artist is so tremendous

* Falls and rapids on the River Vuoxen in south-east Finland.

224

that it completely dispels these routine impressions and carries us into another world, unknown to us, into the world of uncontrolled and savage passions, whose depicter was Shakespeare and Shakespeare alone. In the role of Othello Mr. Aldridge was extraordinary—he is a genuine tiger, and one is terrified for the artists who play Desdemona and Iago, for it seems that actually they will come to harm, and after the fall of the curtain one wants to call for them, if for nothing else but to make sure they are alive.[3]

This is the beginning of a rumour that spread over the next few years; that his passion was so uncontrolled that he actually injured the actors playing Desdemona and Iago.

But to return to his style of acting. Four years later, in Moscow, the leading critic, Almazov, wrote:

Aldridge has nothing in common with those theatrical personalities from the West who visited us in recent times. His qualities consist not in picturesque poses and gestures, not in a melodic singing diction, not in an artificially (pseudo-majestic) tragic gait. No. He does not think of picturesque poses; he does not think about gestures, which come from him of themselves, as an involuntary effect of this or the other feeling which inspires him; he performs no coquetry with his voice, which is very pleasant, but which one doesn't think about, following his acting; for he concentrates all your attention only on the inner meaning of his speech. He does not bother either about the majestic stride, but moves about completely naturally, not like a tragedian, but like a human being. No externality, no ballet-like grace and agility of movement, but a highly truthful understanding of art, a deep knowledge of the human heart, and an ability to feel the subtlest spiritual movements indicated by Shakespeare and to bring them to life before the public—that is what constitutes the essence of his acting.[4]

The St. Petersburg correspondent of the French paper, *Le Nord*, wrote an interesting article on Aldridge which appeared on 23rd November 1858. In those days French was the language of diplomacy and of the upper classes, and at one time aristocratic Russia disdained its native tongue and spoke only French, except to their servants and serfs. The Napoleonic invasion saw the beginning of the end of French influence, and with the upsurge of nationalism after victory, the Russian language once again came into its own. It was Pushkin (descendant of an Ethiopian general brought to Russia by Peter the Great) who played the greatest part in bringing the "vulgar" Russian tongue into literature and drama. French theatre troupes had been the fashion in St. Petersburg from the time of Catherine the Great, but by the time Aldridge arrived, they had been replaced by poorer German companies. So the critics searched among the French actors to find one with whom Aldridge could be compared, and Rachel, the greatest tragedian of them all, was chosen for tragic acting, and Leblanche for mimicry and pantomime. Following is the *Le Nord* article:

Perfidious Albion, jealous of the success of the French artists of St. Petersburg, has sent us out her Mr. Ira Aldridge, an African by birth, but there are few white men like him to interpret the beauties of Shakespeare. She doubtless wished to show us that, though occupied in fabricating knives and hosiery, she has found means to cultivate the *beaux arts* in her foggy London. We must own that the specimen which she sends proves that the dramatic art is far from extinct in the country of Garrick and Kean.

The name of Aldridge was completely unknown to the greater part of our public. The journals that we are in the habit of reading make a great deal of the least vaudeville played at Paris; but they leave us in complete ignorance as to all that regards other European theatres. Paris prides herself on possessing the monopoly of artistic reputation as well as that of revolutions. The public, however, always runs to meet with open arms a good tragedian; and they were curious to see an Othello who needs neither crêpe nor pomatum to black his face. Some expected a success to excite laughter more than tears, knowing that Iago and Desdemona would play in German.

I forgot to tell you that the want of an English troupe has forced Aldridge to play with German actors. Well! They who speculated upon laughing were strangely mistaken. From his first step on the stage the African artist captivated the entire audience by his harmonious and sonorous voice, by his simple, natural, and dignified declamation. We have now seen for the first time a hero of tragedy speaking and walking like a common mortal, void of exaggeration either in posture and exclamation. We soon forgot that we were at the theatre, and we began to follow the action of the drama as if it were real history.

The scene in the third act when the sentiment of jealousy is excited in the savage Moor, is the triumph of Aldridge; from the first moment of the cunning accusation against Desdemona, you see his eyes flash, you feel the tears in his voice when he questions Iago, followed by stifled sobs that almost choke him, and when at last he is convinced that his misfortune is beyond doubt, a cry of anger or rather the roaring of a wild beast escapes him, coming from the very bottom of his heart. That shriek still seems to sound in my ears; it sent a thrill of horror through all the spectators. Real tears roll down his cheek, he foams at the mouth, his eyes flash fire; never have I seen an artist so completely identify himself with the person he represents. An actor told me that he saw the great tragedian sob for several minutes after he came behind the scenes.

The public did not fail to be deeply touched, all wept, both men and women. Boileau* was right when he said to the actors, "Cry if you wish to make others cry." Rachel in the fourth act of *Horatio*† is the only artist that ever produced such an effect. I have no room to allow myself to analyse the piece, scene by scene; suffice it to say that the execution of the fifth act was not less perfect. At the first representation poor Desdemona was seized with such a fright on seeing the terrible expression on the face of the Moor that she jumped out of bed and ran away screaming with real terror, and it was with great difficulty that she could be brought back.

Notwithstanding his fierce nature, Aldridge knows how to contain himself in scenes that require calm and concentrating passion. These opposite qualities could not fail to be appreciated in the part of Shylock, the Jew in *The Merchant of Venice*, a part still more difficult, and much more ungrateful than that of Othello. You should see him tremble with speechless indignation and horror before the tribunal that would force him to be converted to Christianity; such impressions can never be forgotten. The several critics can find only one fault in him—namely, the bad habit he has of turning his back upon the public when speaking to the actors at the further end of the stage. Holland, the Director, having made some observations with regard to this at one of the rehearsals, an altercation took place which might have terminated tragically, but which fortunately did not.

* Nicolas Boileau Despreaux (1636-1711), French critic who exercised great influence on French literature and drama.

† *Les Horaces*, tragedy by Corneille, in which Rachel made her début at the Comédie Française in 1838.

In the same publication, on 15th December, another article appeared:

Aldridge arrived at St. Petersburg preceded by an almost fantastic reputation. Is the artist really an African? Is the African a great artist? I remember the favour of the floating sticks [*batons flottants*], and could not but apprehend that the pompous commendations which the foreign journals bestowed upon this lion on the stage would require to be considerably lessened. . . . No sooner did the Moor make his appearance than I felt myself, I confess it, instantly subjugated, not by the terrible and menacing look of the hero, but by the naturalness, calm dignity, and by the stamp of power and force that he manifested. . . . At the last words he pronounced, I forgot actors, the theatre, and even Shakespeare . . . (may his majestic shadow forgive me!)—all my faculties were strained in admiration. . . . What above all characterizes Aldridge is that he produces his effects more by the expression of his face than by the words he utters, or his gesture. They say he is not handsome; I find it impossible to give an answer to this question. I only saw on his brow the sublimity of genius. I repeat it, that I had not the actor before my eyes, but Othello himself; lightning flashed out of his eyes, and every line in his face served to reflect the passions of his African soul; joy, tenderness, grief were depicted with admirable truth. Hearing him utter those ravishing and fascinating words of love, to which his organ gives an indefinable charm, one easily conceived how Desdemona, the daughter of Venice, the patrician damsel, allowed herself to be captivated by the Moor: "This to hear would Desdemona seriously incline."
. . . What rank is to be assigned to him among artists? He is neither Ligier, nor Bocage, nor Frederic Lemâitre. I have not seen either Talma or Kean, and cannot state whether they acquire the same great ability; but at all events I can venture to affirm that they did not excel it.

The United States also had a chance to learn about Ira Aldridge through the Russian correspondent of the *New York Herald*, who wrote:

An American Negro named Ira Aldridge has been performing at the Imperial Theatre in several of Shakespeare's pieces and has met with great applause. His principal character, of course, is Othello, and he portrays the jealous African with such truth and energy that even those amateurs who recollect our great Russian tragedian, Karatygin, acknowledged the superiority of the sable successor. In Shylock, too, he shows unusual dramatic power; and, painted and tricked out for the stage, he passes very well by lamplight for "the Jew that Shakespeare drew". The worst is that Mr. Aldridge is accompanied by a German troupe who perform the parts assigned to them in their vernacular, and the effect produced by their German answers to his English speeches is the most comical imaginable and puts all illusion out of the question. Only think of Othello calling for his handkerchief and Shylock claiming his pound of flesh in English, and Desdemona excusing herself or Portia expounding the law in Hoch Deutsch. Fortunately, the majority of our Petersburg audiences, both English and German, are "heathen Greek", so that the incongruity of the performance is not felt by them so strongly as by the comparatively small portion of the spectators who are acquainted with the two languages.[5]

And now comes the *pièce de résistance*—an essay by one of the greatest critics and novelists of France, Theophile Gautier (1811-73), who was on an extensive tour of Russia and happened to be in St. Petersburg at the very moment of Aldridge's appearance. This essay is contained in Chapter XII of the first volume of his *Voyage en Russie*, and we quote it in full, not only because of its importance as a piece of dramatic criticism, but also because it is the only omission in the American translation of Gautier's complete works, as brought out in our Chapter I:

Our stay in the city of the Tzars coincided with the visit of Ira Aldridge, the celebrated Negro American actor; he played at the Circus Theatre, which stands near the Grand Theatre. He was the lion of St. Petersburg, and it was necessary to book several days in advance in order to obtain a good seat at one of his evening performances. His first part was Othello, and, thanks to his origin, Ira Aldridge was able to dispense with all the colouring aids of liquorice juice or coffee grounds; he had no need to hide his arms under a chocolate-coloured woollen covering. He had the natural skin for the part, and it was no effort for him to assume the role. His first entry was magnificent, he was Othello himself, as created by Shakespeare, his eyes half closed as though dazzled by an Afric sun, his manner orientally carefree, with that Negroid grace of movement which no European can imitate. As there was no English company in St. Petersburg, but only a German troupe, Ira Aldridge spoke the text from Shakespeare, and Iago, Cassio, and Desdemona replied in Schlegel's translation. The two languages, both Saxon in origin, did not contrast too much, especially for us, who, speaking neither English nor German, concentrated mainly upon the play of the features, the actions, and the emotional phases of the drama. This mixture, however, must have been strange to those who knew both languages.

We had been anticipating a vigorous style, somewhat uncontrolledly energetic, a little wild and fierce, after the manner of Kean; but the coloured tragedian, doubtless in order to appear no less cultured than the white man, acts wisely and restrainedly, in a majestically classical style much resembling that of Macready. In the last scene his passions remain within bounds; he smothers Desdemona in a most gentlemanly way, and he roars most decorously. In one word, as far as one can judge an actor under such circumstances, he appeared to us to have more talent than fire, more skill than inspiration. Nevertheless, let us hasten to state that he produced a great performance which drew forth endless applause. A more lurid and fiercer Othello might perhaps have succeeded less well. After all, Othello had lived for a long time among Christians, and the lion of St. Mark must have tamed the lion of the desert.

The repertoire of a coloured actor would appear to have to confine itself to coloured plays; but when one considers it, if a white comedian daubs himself with sepia to act a black part, why should not a black comedian powder his face with whitening in order to play a white part? This is just what happened. Ira Aldridge acted the part of King Lear the following week in such a way as to produce an entirely successful illusion. A flesh-coloured headpiece of papier mâché, from which hung some silvery locks of hair, covered his woolly thatch and came down almost to his eyebrows like a helmet; an addition of wax filled in the curves of his flat nose. A thick coat of grease paint covered his black cheeks, and a great white beard enveloped the rest of his face and came down over his chest. The transformation was complete; Cordelia would never have suspected that her father was a Negro—never has the art of make-up been more effectively used. That Aldridge had not whitened his hands was a caprice which is easily comprehensible, and they showed below the sleeves of his tunic, brown as a monkey's paws. We considered him better in the part of the old King, pestered by his spiteful daughters, than he was in the Moor of Venice. In the former he acted; in Othello he was just himself. At times, his outbursts of indignation and anger were superb, but at the same time there was a feebleness, and senile trembling, and a sort of somnolent drivelling such as one would expect from an old man on the verge of his eighties who is being changed from an idiot to a madman by the weight of intolerable misfortunes. One surprising fact which showed just how much he had himself under control; although robust and in the prime of his life, Ira Aldridge, during the whole evening, did not make one youthful action; his voice, step, and gestures were all those of an octogenarian.

The success of the black tragedian stimulated the rivalry of Samoilov, the great Russian comedian, who also acted Othello and Lear at the Alexander Theatre with a spirit and power which were altogether Shakespearean. Samoilov is an actor of genius after the style of Frederic;* he is changeable, temperamental, often sublime, full of flashes of inspiration. He is at times ludicrously bad; and while he portrays the hero admirably, he can play the part of a drunkard equally well. He is, moreover, a man of the world with excellent manners. An artist to the fingertips, he designs his costumes himself, and pencils caricatures as witty in their execution as in their conception. His impersonations were popular, but not as popular as those of Ira Aldridge—to be frank, Samoilov could not make himself into a Negro.[6]

We do not believe it was "caprice" or "coquetry", as some translators call it, that prompted Aldridge to play with unwhitened hands. It would seem rather that he was trying to say to the audience, "Let me remind you, I am still a Negro!" As far as we know, this is the only occasion on which he did this. In the photographs we have of him as Lear and Shylock his hands appear to be whitened.

Such was the first impact Aldridge made on his Russian audiences, the critics, journalists and foreign correspondents. There were also, of course, the antagonistic and the prejudiced. For instance, A. F. Pisemsky, writing on 24th November 1858, said: "The African tragedian is playing Shakespearean roles here, and Petersburg is in ecstasy; personally, I cannot judge, as I know not a jot of English, but from all accounts it seems to me that this gentleman tragedian is passionate, but stupid."[7]

Another expression of the general view is found in a letter from the critic, V. V. Stassov, to Balakirev, composer of the music for *King Lear*: "Tomorrow I will tell you what *talent* we saw yesterday in the role of Othello. He is a Negro, he has, of

* Frederic Lemâitre (1800-76).

course, many shortcomings, but his talent is tremendous, and certainly in my time I shall never see a better Othello. I advise you not to miss him, in order to understand about Shakespeare."[8]

But it was not only his Othello which made such an impression. Of his Shylock, the critic of the *Northern Bee* said: "Last Wednesday we saw Mr. Ira Aldridge in his second role, that of Shylock. And in this case too he was exceptionally fine, and called forth from many knowledgeable people the sincerest acclamations that such an actor they had never seen in their lives. This testimony was also given by the Germans, who knew well the famous Ludwig Devrient in this role."[9]

Later on a Moscow critic, Bazhenov, wrote of his Othello, Lear, Shylock, and Macbeth: "The evenings of these productions were undoubtedly the best that I have ever spent in the theatre; it was a festival of genuinely artistic representations of the finest creations of Shakespeare; before me passed, one after the other, four beautifully interpreted, completely living characters, which will certainly never be wiped from memory."[10]

That the social and political atmosphere of the period played a part in strengthening the impact of Aldridge on the Russian people is borne out by various expressions in the Press, such as Zvantsev's:

> I am firmly convinced that after Aldridge it is impossible to see Othello performed by a white actor, be it Garrick himself. A present-day white European, as compared to the African, with his leonine and at the same time childlike nature, is more like Iago, a tamer of wild animals! . . . Seeing before one the tamed Othello in the net of the tamer, seeing the wild lion in the power of the educated European (the Iago of contemporary history), one involuntarily thinks of the many generations of black people suffering under the whip of American slave-traders, and one remembers that daring and good woman who decided, once and for all, to stamp their brows with the mark of Cain.* . . All this has been represented by Shakespeare so truthfully, so powerfully, that, without the slightest exaggeration—one risks hating all his white heroes, or at least, the Venetians that surround Othello, not excluding, possibly, even Desdemona herself. It is a pity that even she is not black![11]

* The reference is, of course, to Harriet Beecher Stowe.

(a)

(a)

(b)

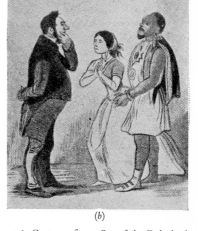

(b)

5. Cartoons from the Czech newspaper *Rubezahe*, wing (a) the theatre before the arrival of Ira ridge, and (b) after the announcement of his per- nances.

16. Cartoons from *Son of the Fatherland*, Russia, 1858. (a) Aldridge as Othello, shaking his Iago. (b) Before a judge with Desdemona.

DESDEMONA: Save me! This savage one day will really suffocate me!

JUDGE: You must be more careful, Mr. Othello. If you do actually suffocate her, what will happen then?

OTHELLO: *Nichevo*. Just you give me another Desdemona better than this one.

17. Mikhail Shchepkin (1780–1863). From a drawing by Shevchenko.

18. Ira Aldridge and Shevchenko. From a drawing by Pasternak.

As we know, he almost invariably followed Othello with the role of Mungo. It was, from the theatrical point of view, a *tour de force* that set the seal on his versatility. In one evening and on one stage he showed that the noble African general and the humble African slave were fundamentally one. It is true that the audiences were convulsed with laughter at the antics of Mungo, yet some of them recalled that "it produced a heavy, sad impression because it reminded them vividly of some of the saddest scenes in *Uncle Tom's Cabin*".

The Russian historian, M. P. Pogodin, had a similar impression which he expressed more emotionally:

General opinion places Negroes as the very lowest link between human species; many forced them to give way to the superiority, mental and moral, of their white relations, apparently of a more noble breed; but just look at Aldridge: there he is, an African, with round face, dark skin, curly hair, wide nostrils, throaty sounds. He doesn't attract your attention with any of the elegant forms you are used to; external beauty does not help him to give you a favourable first impression . . . further, he expresses himself in a foreign language; but such is the power of his spirit, such is the might of his art, that you surrender to him from the very first minute, you understand what he says, you apprehend all that he feels, you listen, it seems, to every beat of his heart. You pass with this magician through every stage of human passion . . . [all] are expressed by this Negro with equal incredible power . . . and deep in the heart of every ecstatic spectator, sacred conscience is heard; no, under the dark skin the same flaming blood is excited, the poor heart beats with the same common human feelings, from the strained breast bursts the same heavy sighs as ours, a black body quivers from pain the same as the white. . . . What a wonderful spectacle for the friend of goodness to see, when a whole people, black or white, awaken to human life! These are the thoughts that were awakened in me by the acting of the African Negro in— what do you think—in the farce, *The Padlock*; when the cruel master raised his stick above the beaten Negro, I saw one thing only—such a quivering movement of his spine, his shoulders, that my very own body was shaking; in my imagination I saw the history of a whole people.[12]

Incidentally, the page proofs of this section on Aldridge were blue-pencilled by the Tsar's Censor, according to Durylin, who had access to the original in the archives of the State Censor.

As if to point the parallel further, in his later performances of *The Padlock* Aldridge interpolated Russian folk songs, which he sang in the original language, in particular *"Vo Piru, Vo Besye-dushki"* (While Feasting, While Gossiping), and the audiences did not see any incongruity here, because they were songs of slaves, black or white.

Mrs. Yunge gives a vivid description of Aldridge's first appearance in Russia:

> He arrived in St. Petersburg in the winter of 1858. We took several boxes side by side, and our whole company went to see him in *Othello* and came into such an indescribable state of ecstasy that after the performance we rode to the hotel where he was staying and waited for him to return. My God, what happened there! Starov kissed his hands, "his noble, black hands!" I was quivering from excitement and confusion, unable to translate everything which was spoken and shouted by those around him; at one and the same time was heard Russian, French, English, and German. Altogether it was rather foolish, but fine, and we were all very moved.

After *Othello* and *The Padlock*, Aldridge played Shylock and King Lear.

> . . . Other artistes we have seen gave Shylock the character of a soul-less merchant, ridiculous in his demands and his insatiable anger and impudence, presenting him as a caricature. Mr. Aldridge understood this personality otherwise. He presented to us Shylock as tight-fisted and greedy, but at the same time proud and firm in his convictions, filled with revenge, hatred and anger towards the Christians, enemies of his people and race. Ira Aldridge is a mulatto born in America and feels deeply the insults levelled at people of another colour by people of a white colour in the New World. In Shylock he does not see particularly a Jew, but a human being in general, oppressed by the age-old hatred shown towards people like him, and expressing this feeling with wonderful power and truth. In his acting are most wonderful effects, both loud and soft; with the first he astounds the listeners, with the last he makes an even greater impression. And his very silences speak. The last scene before the Court he plays almost without a word, but with intriguing eloquence. One may say he reads Shakespeare between

the lines. There is no need to stress the effect which this rare artist made on all his spectators. This effect would have been even more powerful if he had played with an English company. We notice that sometimes, unnecessarily, he uses odd sentences in German. Either all or nothing. Unfortunately, other performers gave him very weak support. Portia and Desdemona were played by actresses of talent, but already no longer young, and made for Kotzebue, for Iffland,* very much for Gutzkow,† but not for Shakespeare. Portia did not look to advantage in the masculine costume of an advocate. We remember in this role Madam Berendorf, beautiful, stately, noble, very handsome in black velvet and in the long mantle of an advocate. Mr. Landfogt is a handsome enough man, but in his multi-coloured, ugly costume, looked ridiculous amidst the black Venetian mantles. But all these things were wiped out by the brilliant acting of our incomparable guest![13]

As to the "odd sentences in German", it must be remembered that Aldridge was playing with a German company and that they used German texts. After a long soliloquy, it may be that he spoke the last sentence in German as a cue to the next actor. This is, of course, only conjecture, but, whatever his reason, it is doubtful that he did it "unnecessarily". Whatever he did on the stage was always carefully planned, however spontaneous it may have seemed.

Zvantzev comments that Aldridge's interpretation reminded him more of the Wandering Jew than the Jew Shylock, and while this is perhaps intended as a criticism, it only emphasizes Aldridge's great artistry, for he depicts Shylock not merely as one individual—a moneylender of Venice named Shylock—but a representative of all the wandering and oppressed Jews of history. Similarly, in *Othello* he portrayed not just a specific Moor with a specific fate, but the suffering of the whole Negro people at the hands of the white. And who will deny that Aldridge's development of the character of Shylock is consistent with the conception of the great author who, at the time that Marlowe and others were still depicting the Jew as a monster and buffoon, dared to

* August Wilhelm Iffland (1759-1814), German actor and playwright, whose plays at one time were more popular in Europe than Schiller's, but which are now forgotten.

† Karl Ferdinand Gutzkow (1811-78), German writer, author of the great Jewish play, *Uriel Acosta*.

show for the first time in a work of art that a Jew is a man like other men; and Aldridge's very existence challenged those who would not accept the fact that a Negro could be as great an artist as other men.

Aldridge's success as Othello and Shylock, apart from his talent, is due to the fact that he had been playing these roles for over a quarter of a century. They were part of his whole being. He instinctively knew each move, each gesture, each nuance, and all the stage business was at his fingertips. This, particularly, impressed his fellow-actors and audiences, who were accustomed to a haphazard style of theatre production and lack of precision in stage business.

* * *

It was in St. Petersburg that Aldridge attempted for the first time in his career the character of Lear, which even this capital had seldom seen. The play itself is considered the most difficult of all Shakespeare's plays and, according to Lamb, the part of Lear, if not the whole play, is unactable. Goethe thought the whole tragedy was not sufficiently substantiated. Leo Tolstoy denied the naturalness of its climactic development. Most critics find the opening scene not sufficiently motivated for the future development of the tragedy.

Lear was not well known to the Russian theatre-going public, and there had been no worthwhile production within living memory with which Aldridge could be compared. At this point Samoilov undertook to challenge Aldridge in this very role in this very city. A few lines from a special essay in the *Northern Bee* shows how Aldridge emerged from this challenge:

> Samoilov presented *himself*, but did not represent Lear. From the very beginning to the end of the play he presented a man who acts according to whims, and in his despair goes mad. But he did not express the stormy passions and force of character of this senile man who is driven to lunacy from spiritual anger, from the tortures of a father's heart. . . . It seemed to us that [Samoilov's] Lear did not fully feel what he said and did. . . . After a few days we saw Ira Aldridge in the same role. . . . Aldridge is a real Lear and in the most powerful Shakespearean scenes he is most wonderful. Here is Lear, the real Lear as we imagined him to be![14]

The writer goes on to point out the disadvantages Aldridge had to contend with as compared with Samoilov: a bad supporting company, playing in a foreign tongue, a hacked-about text. Nevertheless, "that did not prevent Mr. Aldridge from holding our attention, from bringing us to pity, to terror, to tears. Mr. Aldridge is a great actor!" Of Samoilov, Bazhenov said: "We saw that the actor had studied and knew his role, but he did not feel it and did not live it." Pogodin summed up the difference between the two actors by saying: "Aldridge was extraordinary in Othello, Lear, Shylock. No, they were not studied roles, they were very Othello, Lear, Shylock themselves. You see how feelings come to birth in his heart, how the words are sought for in his mind."[15]

Such was the impact of Aldridge's interpretation on St. Petersburg society that a revival of *Lear* some five years later was forbidden by the Tsar's Censor. His performance must have been too much for the Court, particularly as this and other characterizations were used by the anti-Tsarist forces as ammunition against the whole autocratic régime.

Macbeth was at first banned by the Censor, but so high was the praise of his performance in the reviews from Germany, which were copiously cited in *Sovremennik*, that he and his supporters never ceased struggling for the relaxation of censorship. Though never allowed in St. Petersburg, it was permitted in Moscow in 1862 and later in the provinces, where it was at first played without permission by the simple device of not announcing the name of the play! The means of communication being what they were, by the time the Censor learned of it, Aldridge was far away.

His success, as the contemporary critic, Panayev, pointed out, "was not because of 'his African appearance', as these gentlemen suggest; it was not his savage physiognomy, not his voice, rising to the howl of a jackal, and not the green-whites of his eyes (we are using their expressions), not his rages, which won over the audience to Aldridge's side, but that inner flame which reveal in him a first-class tragedian".[16]

*   *   *

Now we come to another aspect of his Russian tour—his successful relations with other actors. Durylin tells us that actors came to his productions as if to a class in theatrical art, and Mrs.

Yunge says: "In 1858 the influence of Aldridge on our actors was tremendous. Martinov, Maximov, Sosnitsky, Karatygin,* Grigoryev, Bourdin, Leonidov were all in ecstasies over him and gave him an ovation to which he warmly responded, fully conscious that they wanted to learn from him; certainly the acting of many of them afterwards became simpler, livelier, and more thought-out. . . . Aldridge had an even better influence on Martinov. Our greatest comedian then felt what his genuine calling was and unexpectedly blazed in drama as a star of the first magnitude. Here was one who had a truly creative genius, one who could shake the souls of people to their very depths. How sorry we were afterwards that Aldridge never saw him in his dramatic roles."

Martinov died two years after Aldridge's arrival, but apparently, according to the critics, in this short time he did indeed play like a star. Under the influence of Aldridge, the comedian almost overnight became a dramatic actor and created an unforgettable Tikhon in Ostrovsky's *The Storm*, in which drama, it was said, Martinov reached the same heights of truth as Aldridge in the tragedies of Shakespeare.

The oldest and most honoured artist of the St. Petersburg stage, I. I. Sosnitsky, who among other roles had created the Mayor in Gogol's *Inspector-General*, wrote to an actress friend: "In all my life I have never seen such talent and never imagined to what heights a talent of genius could reach."[17] This may be attributed to Russian exuberance, but it recalls the words of the Irish critic of the *Comet* twenty-seven years before: "We doubt we shall ever again look upon the personation of Othello so entirely fulfilling all that we could imagine of the perfection of acting."

The entire acting troupe of the Imperial Theatre of St. Petersburg united to honour Aldridge. They had a group photograph taken with him, but Samoilov, who felt that Aldridge was encroaching on his repertoire of Shakespearean roles, was not there. The left- and right-wing Press took sides in this controversy, the right wing maintaining that Samoilov was superior to Aldridge in all but the *black* roles; that Shylock and Lear demanded too great a make-up which, despite all his artistry, failed to deceive the eye.[18] Mrs. Yunge said: "V. V. Samoilov alone was supercilious and snobbish to Aldridge—from jealousy, everybody

* Not to be confused with Vasilly Karatygin (1802-53).

said. However, despite this and the fact that he loudly attacks the African, he, maybe more than anyone else, copies him, and in many places of his Lear imitates him!" The Press in general considered Aldridge the better actor.

Before he leaves St. Petersburg, "the whole theatre company of the Imperial Alexandrinsky Theatre of the Capital of All the Russias" give him a benefit night, which Zvantzev described as one of the most brilliant theatrical presentations ever to have taken place in St. Petersburg. His account of this event in the *Theatrical and Musical News* is unique in the annals of the theatre:

. . . The appearance on the stage of the recipient of the Benefit was greeted with a triple explosion of delight, in which it was impossible to distinguish applause from shouts, stamping of feet or knocking of chairs; such a deafening hurricane I have not heard since the time of Viardo's last visit to us. Mr. Aldridge in *Othello* surpassed himself, despite the fact that every one of his roles he performed always and everywhere with equal artistry; but one can only guide inspiration to a certain degree, because inspiration itself guides the true artist, according to the time and circumstances; the true artist, more than at any other time, is under the power of inspiration in the decisive minute of his triumph, those minutes in which are defined exact expression of the love and respect of the public to him. Our public fully expressed these feelings to Mr. Ira Aldridge during the course of and at the conclusion of the performance. But if anyone has a greater right to be proud of their cultured, unpretentious, truly brotherly feelings to his mighty talent, it is the actors and actresses of the Russian dramatic troupe, who devoutly attend nearly all his performances of the plays of Shakespeare and who on this occasion were to be seen scattered amongst the stalls and boxes. All the three daughters of the Russian King Lear, with their suite, decorated three loges in a row, between them sat the veteran of the Russian stage, Mr. Sosnitsky, who, at the end of *Othello*, went into the orchestra pit and from there presented Mr. Aldridge with a mass-ive gold bracelet in the name of all the Russian dramatic troupes. On it was inscribed, "To Ira Aldridge, the great interpreter of the immortal Shakespeare, from the Russian Artistes, St. Petersburg, 1858", and with it a beautiful hand-illuminated scroll at the top of which was a verse by P. I. Gregoryev:

By means of your mind, talent and labour,
    You revealed to Russians mighty Shakespeare!

And now or for ever we'll never forget
Your Othello and Shylock and Lear.

This scroll, made of parchment, had inscribed on it in Russian and English: "To Ira Aldridge from the Russian Dramatical Artistes, 1858." The inscription was surrounded by aquarelle decorations with allegorical figures painted in gold and silver, some in a golden halo, some in clouds, some in laurels and flowers; at the very top the three muses; on the left side an inscription in Gothic—King Lear during the storm; on the right side, Othello with his dagger; underneath the inscription Shylock sharpens his knife. Under each illustration is an appropriate quotation from Shakespeare, whose bust occupies the centre of the scroll. At the bottom are actual signatures in the following order: N. V. Samoilova, Orlova, Snyetkova, Snyetkova,* Levkeyeva, Fedorova, Zhuleva, Vladimirova, Saburova, Schubert, Linskaya, Podobedova, Sosnitsky, Grigoryev, Karatygin, Leonidov, Markovetsky, M. Maximov, Stepanov, Goltz, Maximov, Martinov, Bourdin, Zubrov, Alekseyev, Malyshev, Gorbunov, Yablochkin (from Moscow), Samarin, and Poltavtsev.

If the bracelet and the illuminated address had been presented to Mr. Ira Aldridge in the name of the whole public, then for him, as also for us, it would not have had a hundredth of its importance and significance. Where the audience numbers thousands it would not have been difficult to find thirty sincere and passionate lovers of art in general, and of this great talent in particular; but where thirty dramatic artists, belonging to one and the same troupe, unanimously and clearly express unquenchable feelings of sympathy and admiration both of the art and the personal character of a foreign visiting artist—then here is a mighty tribute to art, here is a rich foundation for Shakespeare! For such actors and actresses it is a joy to translate his creations into their mother tongue, their labour is conscientious and unstinted. Such evidence of respect on the part of the troupe of the Alexandrinsky Theatre balances the attempted production of King Lear.†

Together with the bracelet and illuminated address on the stage were many wreaths, bouquets, and poems of different sizes and qualities. Having the opportunity of carefully inspecting the wreaths, verses, and bouquets which Mr. Ira Aldridge kept in a particularly large trunk, I have picked out from the various verses in different languages the following anonymous one, written on a big, beautifully decorated scroll:

* There were two actresses with this name.   † With Samoilov as Lear.

Come, brothers of the whole world wide,
A Russian thanks extend in pride
To him who gave us Shakespeare whole
With all his nature, mind and soul.
Othello, passionately tender,
A jealous tiger fear engenders.
Dread creditor Shylock starts,
Whets his knife and cuts our hearts,
Capricious and pedantic Lear,
A king from head to foot appears.
So thus we bless his way with peace,
Presenting him these laurel wreaths.
Such guests are rarely to be found.
Aldridge! To thee our brows touch ground,
And so bid all families in posterity
With Jews and Moors and Kings to be.[19]

The scroll in the possession of the authors to whom it was presented by Aldridge's daughter shortly before her death has now been presented, with other souvenirs and portraits, to the Enthoven Theatre Collection of the Victoria and Albert Museum, London, where it is hoped they will form the nucleus of a section devoted to Ira Aldridge. It is here reproduced.

A few days after the benefit, Count Tolstoy presented his portrait to Aldridge with the following inscription written in English:

May this portrait remind Mr. Ira Aldridge of a man who has been much struck by his high genial and scenic talent*—his intellectual and cultivated mind—also his pure and elevated soul! The writer esteems himself particularly fortunate in having had the happiness of making the acquaintance of so distinguished an artist.

The Count Theodor Tolstoy
Vice-President of the Imperial Academy of Arts, St. Petersburg

It was at the home of Count and Countess Tolstoy that Aldridge met the Ukrainian poet and revolutionary, Taras Shevchenko. He came to Russia in the same year that Shevchenko arrived

* Tolstoy probably had in mind the Russian word *genialnye*, the adjective of "genius", for which there is no equivalent in English. "Scenic" he no doubt intended as a translation of *tsenitcheski*, meaning "dramatic" or "histrionic".

241

in St. Petersburg after nine years' penal military service in the Orenburg fortress. He was born a serf in Morintzi, Kiev, in 1814, and in his youth worked as shepherd for one Engelhard. His artistic talents came to the attention of the artistic circle, by whom sufficient money was raised to buy his freedom so that he might study at the Imperial Arts Academy, from which serfs were barred, and in April 1838 he became a free man. In 1840 his first collection of verse, *Kobzar,*★ was published. The spirit of all his work was grief and anxiety for his enslaved people and for the oppressed Jewish people. His work, like that of Aldridge, was an expression of protest, and he finally fell foul of officialdom by writing several satirical verses about them, just as Pushkin had done. In fact, when Pushkin lay in his coffin after the fatal duel instigated by a provocateur, Shevchenko sat in a corner of the room and drew a portrait of the greatest of Russian poets. In 1847 he was sentenced to lifelong military service and, to make his misery complete, he was deprived of drawing and writing materials. From exile he wrote to Count Tolstoy, "A terrible punishment! All my life had been dedicated to divine art . . . but how to deprive myself of thoughts, of feelings, from that unquenchable love for beautiful art? Oh, save me, for one more year will kill me."[20] The Count was instrumental in obtaining his release, and it was in his house that Shevchenko and Aldridge met.

On 30th December Shevchenko received the following note from the Countess: "Please, Taras Grigorievitch, come tomorrow between 7 and 10 p.m. Ira Aldridge is going to recite from Shakespeare."[21] To Mrs. Yunge, then a girl of fifteen, we are indebted for another of the few intimate accounts we have:

Aldridge began to visit us almost every day. He was very fond of us, and we could not help but be fond of him. He was a sincere, good, careless, trusting, and loving child. His character was very similar to that of Shevchenko, with whom he became very close. It would happen that Aldridge would come in with his quick, energetic step and at once ask, "And the artist?" That is what he called Shevchenko, for every attempt of his to pronounce that name ended up with his shaking with laughter over his hopeless attempts, repeating, "Oh, those Russian names!" We sent for Taras Grigorievitch and "the artist" appeared.

★ A wandering minstrel in the old Ukraine who sang folk songs, accompanying himself on a kind of zither.

I remember how they were both very moved one evening when I related to Aldridge the history of Shevchenko and translated to Shevchenko the life of the tragedian from his own words. . . . For lengthy conversations they needed me as a translator, but in brief conversations they understood each other very well; they were both artists, and that meant that they were observant, and both had very expressive faces and Aldridge, by gestures and mimicry, could represent everything that he wished to say.

Particularly memorable is the session in the studio of Shevchenko when he drew the portrait of the tragedian.* Without my sister and me, they really could not get very far, first because, however expressive their mimicry, still explanation in words became necessary, and secondly, and most important, because it was difficult to get rid of us even if they wanted to. My sister and I squatted on a Turkish divan, Aldridge on a chair opposite Shevchenko, and the session began. For a minute only the scratching of the pencil on paper could be heard—but could Aldridge stay long in one place? He began to squirm, we cried out to him that he had to sit at attention, he made faces and we could not keep from laughing. Shevchenko angrily stopped his work, Aldridge made a frightened face and once again sat for a while quietly without moving, then suddenly he said, "May I sing?" "Oh, you. . . . All right, sing!" Then began a touching, sad Negro melody, which gradually passed into a more lively tempo and ended with a mad jig by Aldridge around the studio. Following that, he would act a whole comic scene (he was an excellent comedian). Taras Grigorievitch was caught up by his merriment and sang Ukrainian songs, then became engrossed in conversation about the typical features of different peoples, about the similarity of people, folk lore, etc., etc. Despite the fact that these merry and interesting pastimes, to the pleasure of both me and my sister, dragged out the sessions, the portrait was finished and turned out to be a lifelike and good resemblance.†

My memories of Aldridge, as of a great artist, continually mix with various minor happenings, depicting him as a good and simple man, one with whom we so pleasantly passed the time that one cannot but want to relate some of these frivolous happenings.

Once we went with him to the Hermitage Gallery. As he had

* Now in the Tretiakov Gallery, Moscow.

† In 1913 the Russian painter, L. O. Pasternak (father of the Soviet poet, Boris Pasternak, one of the best translators of Shakespeare), reconstructed this scene in an interesting painting.

very little time, and the museum was open only on certain days, this visit was very difficult to arrange. However, we arrived, and suddenly they won't let us in because Aldridge is not in evening dress! The mobile physiognomy of the artist stretched into a sad grimace; he so wanted to enjoy the paintings with us. Suddenly his face again took on a merry expression and with a mischievous wink he beckons my sister and me to one side, saying, "Pin up my jacket with a safety-pin." No sooner said than done! Aldridge, in an improvised "tail jacket", proudly passed through the galleries. . . . He often sang German songs, and with his English accent the effect was often very original, so the time passed in the serious enjoyment of art and in frivolous fun, which was yet dear to us in its sincerity and the time passed so quickly that we didn't notice how soon the time for parting came.

Regrettably, we have found only one or two allusions to Aldridge in Shevchenko's writings, and his *Journal* ends only a few months before they meet, but he is known to have remarked in a letter to Shchepkin of the Moscow Maly Theatre: "The African actor is here now; he does wonders on the stage. He shows us the living Shakespeare. I don't know whether he will be coming your way. But there is nothing else new whatsoever." The German company with which Aldridge played did not come up to standard, and Shevchenko particularly disliked Desdemona. "Why didn't you strangle her in the first act?" he demanded. Aldridge's playing of King Lear, his complete transformation into a senile white octogenarian, brought Shevchenko to an emotional frenzy. He rushed into Aldridge's dressing-room and embraced him, kissing his face and hands, the tears streaming down his face.

When Aldridge left St. Petersburg, the entire theatrical world, Shevchenko, and many others accompanied him to the station. On his way home, Aldridge sent a letter to the Russian actors in which he said: "In my person you have shown your sympathy and love for my oppressed people."

CHAPTER XIV

Back in England

THE summer of 1859 finds Aldridge back in the provinces of England. In Hull on 17th June he presents, according to the play-bill, "*King Lear* (as performed by him on the Continent with the most unbounded applause), being his first representation of that character in England". It will be recalled that just a quarter of a century before it was in Hull that he first attempted Shylock, Macbeth, and Richard III. He must have had some special encouragement there, probably from Sheahan. James Joseph Sheahan was a well-known historian and author of several authoritative works on Hull. Although he had a long and close friendship with Aldridge, he makes no mention of him in his *History of the Town and Port of Kingston-upon-Hull*, published in 1866, in which he devotes a chapter to the Hull theatres. Regrettably, he does not deal with the actors, dramatists, and productions of the period, but confines himself to the ownership of the theatres, when they were built, when they burned down (as most of them did), and similar factual information. Mr. Sheahan died on 23rd December 1893 aged seventy-nine at 55 Blake Street Hull, and his son, also named James J. Sheahan, lived at the same address. Efforts, thus far fruitless, have been made to trace the descendants of this family in the hope that there may still be in existence diaries, letters, or other documents which may shed some additional light on Ira Aldridge, the man and the friend.

It is also interesting to note that in another book devoted entirely to the Hull theatres, *Evolution of the Drama in Hull and District*, by Thomas Sheppard, published in 1927, there is also no mention of the name of Ira Aldridge.

The industrial city of Hull played an important part in his theatrical career. Yet, though pioneering events unique in the history of the theatre took place there, no records have come down to us of the impressions of the critics and audiences. The only reference to his Lear which we could find was a brief statement some months later by the critic of the *Cambridge Independent Press*, who wrote, *inter alia*: "Last night was performed *King Lear*, the character of Lear by Mr. Aldridge, Mrs. Mayland enacting Cordelia. It was a theatrical treat." That is all, and only a few months before, when performed in Russia, it had stimulated pages of enthusiastic and brilliant critical analysis! This may be explained at least partially by the fact that Shakespeare was relatively new to Russian and some European audiences, but, of course, was not a novelty in England. English audiences were better able to judge his delivery of the lines than foreign audiences, as we see from the review of the *Brighton Gazette* of 29th September 1859: "We saw him on Monday in *Othello* and were much pleased. It might have been but fancy, but certainly he appeared to have thrown off much of that fearful straining of the text and emphasizing of every syllable which we last year condemned. At any rate, we were much better pleased with his performance than we have previously been. He is without doubt a great tragedian, an actor, and an artist. His tread of the stage is firm and dignified, his carriage majestic, his glance truly thrilling. Would that he could still more divest himself of the fault to which we alluded. . . . He also appeared in low comedy and was great both in *The Mummy* and *The Padlock*, convulsing the house with laughter." The "fault" which the critic had condemned the previous year was "an immense weight being thrown into many single words, and a repetition of them over and over again, not to the gratification but to the wearying of his audience. As a facetious friend remarked to us while Mr. Aldridge was repeating the word 'Free', he was giving it to us with 'Free times Free'."[1]

The Cambridge critic who dismissed his Lear so casually made up for it by his praise of other performances, as did the audience, for there was a full house. It was ten years since his previous appearance in Cambridge, and the local critic writes: "He appeared in *Othello* and enacted the Moor with consummate ability. In fact, it was really a wonderful performance, and he received unbounded applause; his conception of the character is singularly correct." Then came his Shylock: "Mr. Aldridge was really great as Shylock. It was a magnificent performance", and the critic particularly singles out the original piece of mime Aldridge added to the end of the trial scene which so impressed his European audiences, adding: "He certainly has a versatile genius, for he excels in tragedy; he is likewise excellent in comedy."

Though the Press was laudatory, the university town of Cambridge did not appreciate Aldridge as much as later on did the university town of Kazan, for we find such announcements as "Wednesday evening being cold and wet, there was not that good attendance that the performance [of Shylock] deserved", and "On Thursday the play of *Othello* was repeated to a poor house". Aldridge did not draw full houses all the time, a thing one tends to forget in retrospect, as, for example, a letter written by a friend from Brighton indicates: "I don't think you must be well satisfied with the reception you had in Brighton that Saturday night; the theatre had hardly any good company in it, and the commoners in the gallery overhead made such a terrible noise all the time."

This is practically his last performance in England before "retiring" to Russia! In November he is performing at Cardiff, where he is billed to "make his first appearance since his return from Russia".

Excellent criticisms can be quoted for practically every performance. A few weeks later in Leicester, "He stands unequalled . . . a consummate artist . . . justly entitled to the proud position he now holds . . .". And, indeed, his playbills now enumerate the many orders he has collected in his European tour (not one, however, from England), such as the one of the Theatre Royal, Birmingham, 23rd May 1859:

Great Night of the Season
for the benefit of Mr. W. Roberts Tindell, when he has great pleasure in announcing the engagement of the celebrated African Roscius, Mr. Ira Aldridge (on his return from Russia).

Knight of the Royal Saxon Ernestinischen House Order, and Recipient of the Verdienst Medal of the Order, in Gold, presented on the 31st of January, 1858, by His Highness Duke Bernhard, Reigning Sovereign of Saxe-Meiningen, and Brother of the late Queen Adelaide of England.

Member of the Prussian Academy of Arts and Sciences, and holder of the Society's Large Gold Medal (First Class) presented by His Majesty Frederick William IV, at Berlin, 25th January, 1853.

Member of the Imperial and Archducal Institution of "Our Lady of the Manger", Pesth, 1856.

Corresponding Member of the Royal Bohemian Conservatoire of Prague, September, 1858.

Recipient of the White Cross of Switzerland, "*Pour la Merité*," Berne, 1854.

Member of the National Dramatic Conservatoire of Hungary, Pesth, 2nd of March, 1858.

Member of the Russian Hofversamlung of Riga, 14th October, 1859.

Honorary Member of the Imperial Academy of Beaux Arts, St. Petersburg, and holder of the Imperial Jubilee de Tolstoy Medal, St. Petersburg, 19th December, 1858.

To this may be added, for the record: The Grand Cross of the Order of Leopold, presented by the Emperor of Austria, *c.* 1854; Member of the Associate Order of Nobles, Highest State Honour, Bessarabia; and his very first State recognition: Honorary Commission of Captain in the Republican Army of Haiti, 17th Regiment of Grenadiers and Aide-de-Camp to the President of Haiti, 2nd December 1827.

Despite all this, Aldridge's performances are not always mentioned in the local Press, not necessarily the fault of the local journalists. For them he is always good copy, but racial prejudice, lack of space or often interest in the theatre may account for some of the silence. There is a hint of some such element in the following letter which Aldridge received from Jersey:

Moreland House,
Aug. 30, 1860.

DEAR SIR,—Be good enough to let me know what pieces will be performed tomorrow night (Friday) that I may write a local for tomorrow morning's paper, calling attention to your benefit. I regret exceedingly that owing to circumstances which I will explain if I happen to see you, it has been impossible to do you justice in the *Independent*. I much regret this, for you have my warmest regard and good wishes. Perhaps we shall be more fortunately situated when you again visit Jersey. Please say when you intend to leave the island. Is Friday really your last appearance? Please send an answer by bearer, or forward in the course of the afternoon.

Yours faithfully,
G. JULIAN HARVEY.

19. The Countess Olga Tolstoy.

20. Théophile Gautier.

21. Annette Langenbaum.

22. Helena Fabminskaya, Maria Mirska and P. Neketan, Odessa, 1861.

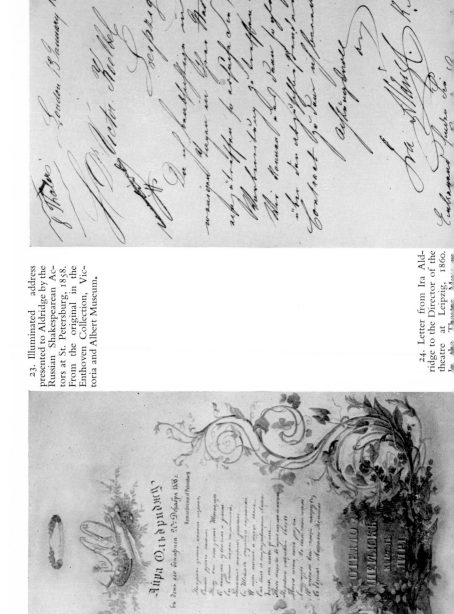

23. Illuminated address presented to Aldridge by the Russian Shakespearean Actors at St. Petersburg, 1858. From the original in the Enthoven Collection, Victoria and Albert Museum.

24. Letter from Ira Aldridge to the Director of the theatre at Leipzig, 1860. In the Theatre Museum

Apparently the *Independent* blue-pencilled this writer's contribution, and the writer is evidently trying to get a mention in another newspaper.

In the summer of 1860 Aldridge writes the letter to Dr. Smith to which we have previously referred, and which is one of the most revealing documents of this story. We now quote it in full:

> *Wellington Lodge,*
> *Wellington Road,*
> *Kentish Town, London.*
> *June 4, 1860.*

Jas McCune Smith, M.D.

MY DEAR FRIEND AND SCHOOL-FELLOW,—I received the *Anglo-African* containing a memoir of myself, and I readily detected the author. It is unnecessary to tell you the conflicting feelings, the pleasing reminiscences, it awakened. I was a boy again; the thoughts and incidents of other days came rushing thick and fast upon me, the retrospect causing both pain and pleasure.

I have great pleasure, my dear friend, in congratulating you on the progress you have made in your profession—or I should have said progress and popularity, both of which are well known in this country.

My dear wife, I am sorry to say, has been suffering from ill health, and has not left her room for a considerable period. She desires her kindest regards and remembrances, and hopes with me to see and welcome you at our residence, where you will be sure of a hearty welcome.

My son, who has just entered his thirteenth year, is at the Collegiate School of Camden Town,* and is a great favourite with his masters, who entered a high opinion of his mental capabilities. Out of thirty-seven competitors for two elocutionary prizes, a son of the late Mrs. Warner, aged 17, took the first, and Ira Daniel (named after my dear father) took the second.

You will be glad to hear that I met with an unparalleled success in Russia. I gave seventy-one representations in the Imperial Theatre of St. Petersburg, and received extraordinary honours, pecuniary and otherwise. I send you enclosed a list of the principal orders, decorations, and medals which I have received, together with the dates of my warrants, and diplomas which, with a portrait executed in St. Petersburg, with a few notices, may perhaps interest you.

If it will not be too great a trespass on your time, I would feel

* North London Collegiate School, located in Camden Town.

greatly obliged if you would see my dear brother Joshua, and say I should be glad to hear from him, giving him my address. His son David visited me some three years since, and promised on leaving to write; but he neglected to do so. I would be glad to know if my stepmother is living, and what her circumstances are.

Mr. Henry Wallack suggested a visit to America in 1858, but my dear wife would not entertain the idea; her prejudice is so rooted against the Americans for their treatment of our oppressed race generally.

I purpose becoming a subscriber to the *Anglo-African*, and if I cannot obtain it through a London publisher, I will order it direct from Mr. Thos. Hamilton himself, to whose care I take the liberty of sending this, in the hope that it will reach you safe.

Yours, among the numerous memoirs that have been published of me, is the only correct one. I saw in the *American Cyclopaedia* what purported to be a biography, but it was most incorrect. I never was in Baltimore, or learned German in America. Besides, they confuse me with poor Jim Hewlett.

All things must have an end, and so must my letter, and in the hope of receiving a few lines from you at your earliest convenience, I remain, my dear friend,

Truly yours,
IRA ALDRIDGE, K.S.

Dr. Smith's reply is not extant, to our knowledge, and we therefore learn nothing about the stepmother. Joshua has numerous descendants in various parts of the United States, among them being Mr. Ira Lewis Aldridge of New York, from whom we learned that the David referred to (his grandfather), was a seaman, which explains the circumstances of his visit to his famous uncle in London about 1857.

*   *   *

Now comes Aldridge's geniuenly final appearance in the provinces of England. In October 1860 he is in Brighton and Southampton, and November finds him in Glasgow, presenting the usual programme of *Othello*, *The Padlock*, *The Slave*, *The Black Doctor*, *Macbeth*, *Obi*, *Bertram*, *Titus Andronicus*, and *Robinson Crusoe, or The Bold Buccaneer* (a play by Pocock, acted for the first time in Covent Garden in 1817), in which Aldridge played Man Friday, the Carib slave of Robinson Crusoe.

The *Brighton Gazette* of 4th October 1859, reviewing *Titus*

Andronicus, gave Aldridge full credit for "having expunged the horrors and purified the language, even to the extent of a thorough perversion of the author's meaning". The *Brighton Herald* of 6th October said:

> Mr. Ira Aldridge tells us that being a man of colour limited in his repertoire he was ambitious of adding Aaron the Moor to his list of characters and therefore "adapted" *Titus Andronicus* for modern representation.
>
> This adaptation we witnessed on Wednesday evening [3 October], and we must say that the question as to Shakespearean tragedy did not arise. Mr. Aldridge has not attempted to grapple with the difficulties presented to the modern adapter; he has not wasted time in puzzling over the Gordian knot. He has cut it. Beyond the title, a few incidents, and some scraps of language, his *Titus* has nothing in common with Shakespeare's. In point of fact, Mr. Aldridge has constructed a melodrama "of intense interest" of which Aaron is the hero. The character is a strong one, and not unsuited to his powers, as was shown by his being called twice before the curtain during the piece. . . . Mrs. Calvert's impersonation of Lavinia . . . she succeeded in rendering extremely interesting.

In reviewing *The Tempest*, which was given on the 15th, the *Brighton Gazette* said: "When we first saw *The Tempest* underlined, we expected it was for the purpose of introducing Mr. Ira Aldridge as Caliban. Why does he not attempt it? In his hands it would, we are convinced, be a wonderful conception." Indeed, it would have been, and it would be interesting to know why he did not tackle it,* particularly as he was still making the point that his colour limited his repertoire—which point was losing its validity, since he was now performing some of the greatest white roles in world drama! Also, he may have felt that the portrayal of a primitive creature would not fit in with the theme underlying most of his work—the equality of black and white. Or perhaps he was not interested in it because it was not the star role.

Aldridge had sufficient support and encouragement from Russia to warrant his decision to leave the British stage. A letter from Countess Catherine Tolstoy written from Wiberg on 5th July 1859 indicates how much they would welcome him back:

* The Negro actor Canada Lee played Caliban in Margaret Webster's production of *The Tempest* in New York in 1945.

DEAR MR. ALDRIDGE,—Excuse me that I did not write to you before; do not think that it is because you did not answer us the last time we wrote to you. We know very well that you are occupied and have no time to spare. Therefore allow me to write to you without waiting for your letter, but if you could spare a moment to write to us and tell us how is your health and that of your wife, it would not be a time lost, for you know what a pleasure it is to receive your letters. I have so much to tell you that I do not know with what to begin.

My papa is no more Vice-President of the Academy of Arts; he is made the assistant of the Grand Duchess Mary, and the Emperor gave him two thousand a year for the lodging.

We are all glad of that change, because papa will be quite exempt of business, and will rest after his long service. Now that he is free, we hope to go abroad next year. Only one thing troubles me—that is, that we must leave the Academy. You cannot think how I am sorry to leave it. I am born there, and am so used to it.

The same day that we received these news, we were celebrating papa's jubilee, it was on the 16th May, the day of your son's birthday. How I pitied that you were not here, all hearts were in one, and that one was full of love for papa.

Now we are already six weeks in the country. How I wish you were with us! Every time that we go in a boat on a beautiful light night in June, when every leaf is reflected in the calm water, when nothing disturbs the quiet of the night but the noise of some distant bell or of our own oars, I think, why are you not here. I know that you would also be charmed by this beautiful nature. If you could but come to Petersburg in the month of August, and then come to us, it is only seven hours' journey, we would be so glad.

Papa is now here with us. He and mamma make you their compliments. I remain,

Yours truly,
CATHERINE TOLSTOI.

On 26th December 1859 he writes a letter to Dr. Victor Koelbel, publisher of *Theater-Chronik*, Leipzig, dealing with negotiations for a "farewell tour of Deutschland", which indicates that he was now considering giving up his tours of western Europe to concentrate on Russia:

76 Euston Road, London.

MY DEAR DOCTOR,—I received your last wekommen [*sic*] brief und ich antwort folgende. I told Herr Roeder that I intended making a Farewell tour in Deutschland that I should have no objection, but would rather like to commence in Berlin, and authorized him to make arrangements for me at the Frederick Wilhelmstadt Theatre. I did not authorize him to state that he had the exclusive right of making arrangements for me. Herr Roeder is in error if he states otherwise. I receive the *Chronik* regular and will thank you ab ihre beguemlichkeit to schicken meine recknung. With respect to Pesth, I should have no objection to visit that City, but at present it would be highly impolitic to do so. If it could be made worth while I should visit Deutschland this season, if not I will defer it to the next. Please to place the following in your Gastspiele Chronik, Manchester, in Jany., Liverpool ditto, Bath and Bristol im letze halbe Jany., Edinburgh Feb.

Ich wunsche sie glucklich weinachts zeit (Merry Christmas), and I remain

Truly yours,

IRA ALDRIDGE, K.S.

We have little to go on as to his problems, but they must have been the same as confront others in the profession—promises, protracted negotiations, and negative results, for six months later, on 6th June 1860, he is again writing to Dr. Koelbel, notifying him that he has changed his address to Wellington Lodge, Wellington Road, Kentish Town, and that he proposed to visit Germany in the autumn. The family does not remain in Kentish Town for very long, because soon after his second successful Russian tour he is able to buy a house in Hamlet Road, Upper Norwood, which he named Luranah Villa, after his mother and daughter. Later he bought a number of other houses in the same road. The last letter from Wellington Road is one written by Ira Daniel on 7th November 1860 to his father, who is in Glasgow giving his last performances before leaving for Russia:

MY DEAR PAPA,—I will send your hamper tomorrow. We have got to be received by Lord Lieutenant Enfield this evening at 7 o'clock and I am going. Mamma is not very well today. Dr. Popham was here on Monday last to see Mamma. Anne is better, the Doctor has not got his money yet. We are very dull without you.

Mamma and I send our best love and kisses, and I remain your affectionate son,

IRA DANIEL ALDRIDGE.

I send kisses for you, Papa. Send us some, don't forget.

By the end of 1860 Aldridge appears to have made all preparations to leave for Russia, and he settles his final bill for the various necessary things that have to be done backstage:

Masquerade and Theatrical Repository,
35 Bow Street, Covent Garden,
London

Ira Aldridge Esq.   *December 28, 1860*

To SAMUEL MAY,

THEATRICAL PROPERTIES OF EVERY DESCRIPTION

Actors and Amateurs supplied with
every requisite at the lowest
possible charges

	£	s	d
To Balance of Account	£3	14	0
To suit of brown silk tights 3 cord double warp Brown wool trunks and body . . .	2	0	0
To hire of dresses, King Lear, etc. (Richmond) .		10	0
To repairing and re-trimming armour, Black Doctor—Othello, new black velvet breeches, jewelled bracelet, etc., 1859 & 1860 . .	3	0	0
To re-trimming Othello short robe, hat Black Doctor, Shylock buttons and lining, Macbeth robe shirt, fly, cloth of gold robe, armour dress, armour legs, pair of buckles, jewelled arms and legs	6	10	0
Suit of brown wool fleshings		16	0
To hire of dresses and carriage, Brighton . .	2	10	0
	£19	0	0

So, with his armour and costumes repaired and re-trimmed for Othello, Shylock, and Macbeth, Ira Aldridge sets out once more for a long and extensive tour in Russia, for his day and even for today one of the most ambitious any actor has ever undertaken. There he remains for the rest of his life, except for one last appearance—at the Theatre Royal, Haymarket, in 1865.

CHAPTER XV

Moscow

IT was 1862 before Aldridge came to this great city. Between 13th September and 19th October he gave fourteen performances, his repertoire now including *Macbeth*. The censors must have considered the burghers of the "big village" less sensitive to this chronicle of kingly crimes than the aristocrats of the capital, for they finally relaxed and removed their ban. The Tsar not being resident in Moscow may also have been a consideration.

Journal Iskusstvo (Journal of Art) of November 1862 gives a picture of what the city had gone through before Aldridge arrived, some fifty years after Napoleon had found it a blazing city and retreated ignominiously:

The annals of our dramatic history for the last sixty years present some most striking features, fluctuating naturally with the political circumstances of the period. Three magnificent temples dedicated to dramatic art have been destroyed by fire and, phoenix-like, others more splendid have risen from their ashes. Our land has been devastated by the invader, the plough-share transformed into a weapon of warfare, the progress of art and science checked, yet amid this turmoil our drama has retained its place, now drooping and rearing its head, taking the proud and pre-eminent position of national constructor and conservator of public morals. In this time some of our best dramatists have flourished—Gogol, Pushkin, Ostrovsky, and others of less note. Among artistes, Michaelov, Maximov, Martynov, Karatygin, etc. . . . Latterly we were visited by the great Rachel, and after by the no less celebrated Ristori; in these we had perfect illustrations of the French and Italian schools of tragic art. It was indeed high art, but, as we remarked at the time, there was not a sufficient co-mingling of Nature with that high art to make us sympathize with the sufferings so forcibly portrayed by these great artistes and that feeling seems to have been shared by our public, as was evidenced by the second visit of the latter talented lady, the theatre being literally deserted. It now becomes our duty to chronicle the visit of indeed a most singular guest. In the years of 1858 and 1859 the curiosity of our public was excited by the accounts in the various journals of St. Petersburg of the appearance there of a black actor; persons visiting the new metropolis, having seen him, returned with enthusiastic praises of his wondrous talent. We confess we were somewhat incredulous and sceptical, deeming that the singularity, unprecedented as we believe it is in dramatic history, of a Negro assuming the sock and buskin, together with the proneness of the multitude to praise any novelty, however extravagant, that it chooses to set up for worship, we made no comment. Contrary to expectation, we were not favoured with a visit, as is usual on the occasion of celebrated artistes visiting St. Petersburg, and which caused great disappointment at the time. At the commencement of the present year it was rumoured that Aldridge would positively visit this ancient city of the Tsars during the present season. His sojourn at Nizhni-Novgorod in our locality seemed to strengthen this report, which was confirmed by the appearance of an *abonnement*** for ten representations, which, although at considerably advanced prices, was soon bought up. Subsequently his first appearance was announced for Thursday, 13th, in the role of Othello.

In St. Petersburg he had played with a German company under the auspices of the Imperial Alexandrinski Theatre. Here in Moscow he performs with the Maly Theatre company, who play, of course, in Russian.

The Maly Theatre, the oldest in Moscow, was built in 1804, and despite Napoleon and Hitler, the original building stands to this day, its unbroken tradition a source of pride to Moscow. There was a saying that "in Moscow one went to college, but studied at the Maly". It became the home of Ostrovsky, "the Balzac of the Muscovite merchants", whose statue adorns the portals of this theatre as Molière's adorns the Comèdie Française. Although it was an official Court theatre, it represented the more liberal sections of society and in its productions and interpretations expressed progressive ideas. These found expression not only in the plays of Gogol and Griboyedov, whose *Inspector-General* and *Wit Works Woe* (respectively) were first produced here, but

* Season ticket.

in the introduction of a more realistic style of acting, principally through Shchepkin, who trained the whole Maly company in that direction. At the insistence of Pushkin, Shchepkin wrote his autobiographical notebooks,* which give valuable insight into the mind and methods of a great actor. In 1838 the great Prov Sadovsky (1818–72) joined the theatre, and created the comic roles in Ostrovsky's plays, as Shchepkin had done in Gogol's.

When Aldridge arrived in Moscow he had the field to himself; there was no other actor playing Shakespeare. In St. Petersburg he was challenged at least by Samoilov. The great interest in Aldridge and his success can be judged by the fact that, after opening at the Maly, most of his performances were given in the Bolshoy, which was about three times bigger, and that vast theatre was always sold out. There is no record of any other dramatic production being transferred to the Bolshoy, which was intended only for the performances of ballet and opera. The following item is typical of many that appeared in the Moscow journals after his first performance:

At an early hour the theatre was filled by an anxious audience. The first scene passed off with comparative indifference, and at its change an almost painful silence ensued Othello's address to the Senate. Without going into a particular review of M. Aldridge's acting, we may boldly assert that Shakespeare himself could not have desired a more able exponent of his great genius. In person, M. Aldridge is rather above the middle height, copper-colour complexioned, of commanding figure, unrestrained and unstudied action; with such a soldier we can readily understand the confidence reposed in him by the Venetian Republic. He appeared to us a being born to command and to be obeyed. In himself honest as a child, in his actions, particularly with Desdemona, tender and delicate as a young maiden; but Othello, maddened with jealousy, an enraged tiger, yet beautifully observant of Hamlet's advice to the actors. Our audience, usually so apathetic, knew no limits to its applause and calls during the progress of the play and at its close were incessant. What we have hitherto read of M. Aldridge was not exaggerated; he is certainly a very great artist, and everyone who wishes to see Shakespeare represented to the life must go and see Ira Aldridge, who develops and explains all the grandeur of the great Poet.[1]

* *Zapeski Aktiora Shchepkina* (Memoirs of the Actor Shchepkin), Academia. Moscow, 1933.

The Moscow Press was filled with articles on his acting. Not only reviews, but essays and dissertations were written, and to these Russian critics, as before, we are indebted for a more thorough analysis of Aldridge's acting than is to be found in any other country. Censorship being strict, particularly on political and social themes, writers took advantage of artistic and cultural events to expound their social ideas, and in the African Roscius and in Shakespeare they had a unique opportunity.

Shchepkin, of course, came to see Aldridge's Othello. Aldridge, anxious to know how this old master liked his performance, asked Ketcher, the Russian translator of Shakespeare, to take him to Shchepkin. An eyewitness of this memorable meeting gives the following account of it:

I happened to be a witness of a very original scene with Shchepkin. . . . I saw him from the "gods" of the Maly Theatre in the role of Othello. Later I was able to see two other famous tragedians in the scene where Iago arouses Othello's suspicions against Desdemona. Both of them—Salvini and Pakkoni—in my view stand higher than Aldridge, but nevertheless, in the scene of despair, when his ruinous deception is revealed to him, then Aldridge was incomparable. To this very day, despite the passing of sixty years, I see him before me, as if alive, tempestuous and permeated with the one thought; the necessity of immediate revenge on his wife for her betrayal. He cannot stand on his feet; he sways to and fro; he sits heavily on a small table at the bedside of his wife and does not know how to await the end of his cross-examination; he does not know where to put his hands, which are itching to suffocate Desdemona; he bangs them on his knees and feverishly presses them to his side—terrible and inevitable, like a bursting tempest, it seems to me that to this day I hear his cry, "Desdemona, Desdemona!" filled with such inexpressible despair, for which there are no words in the human language.

And then it happened that while I was sitting with Shchepkin, just as he had declaimed to me, with tears in his eyes, "Houstku", a poem of Shevchenko, in the anteroom was heard a ripple of laughter, and immediately following entered Ketcher, with a shock of grey hair on his head. He it was who had translated Shakespeare into his own native tongue. He had brought Aldridge to be introduced to the famous Russian artist, and so was an interpreter between them. After mutual greetings, Aldridge was interested to know whether this stout little old man with the good-natured eyes and clever smile had seen his acting.

"Tell him," replied Shchepkin to Ketcher, "that I have seen him and was highly satisfied—here is a man with tremendous talent!" On hearing this, Aldridge bowed low, but asked Ketcher to convey to Shchepkin that what he wanted was criticism, and on this he insisted, despite Shchepkin's mock-modest protestation that he had no right to criticize so great an artist.

"Well, all right. Then tell him," he said in a swift flow of words, "that I am not satisfied with him in the second act, and I do not like the whole of his scene of Desdemona's arrival. When the galley which has brought her reaches the shore and she steps on to dry land, Aldridge calmly and majestically goes to meet her, gives her his hand and leads her to front stage. How can that be possible? He forgets that Othello is a Moor, that in him flows and boils hot southern blood, that for some considerable time he has not seen his wife, whom not only does he love, but who is passionately in love with him . . . and there she is before him, an object of worship and . . . why, all his blood should pound in his heart, he should throw himself like a wild animal, forgetting everything around him, take hold of her, crush her in his embrace, bring her to the front stage, and only then remember that he is a military commander, and that inquisitive eyes are watching him. Then he must do that which Aldridge has been doing from the very beginning. And tell him"—and Shchepkin jumped off his chair in a burst of artistic passion—"that he must cover her with kisses. Kiss her hands and her feet; yes, and tell him that"—and then he made an energetic gesture not suitable to be repeated in print. Aldridge, listening to Ketcher's translating, smiled and bowed his head in agreement.[2]

Lentovsky, who lived in Shchepkin's house, added that Aldridge "then sat with Shchepkin for about an hour, explaining either by pantomime or through the interpreter. In *Othello*, Mikhail Semyonovitch (Shchepkin) considered him unbeatable, unattainable. . . . Seated at the table, the two famous ones laughed a lot together, sang the Russian song '*Vo Piru, Vo Besyedushki*', which Alridge performed in *The Padlock* when he played the unforgettable role of Mungo."[3]

In the Bakhrushin Museum in Moscow is preserved a photograph of Aldridge in the role of Othello, which he presented to Shchepkin on that historic day, on the back of which is inscribed:

"To the Father of the Russian Stage, Monr. Shchepkin, with the lasting respect of Ira Aldridge, K.S., Moscow, 2nd Dec. 1862." Only one year later the great Russian actor was dead.

Aldridge also made the acquaintance of another great actor of the Maly Theatre, P. M. Sadovsky. Alekseyev writes about this in his *Memoirs of an Actor*:

> Aldridge frequented the Russian theatre and praised the artistic acting of Sadovsky. In his turn, too, Prov Mikhailovitch [Sadovsky] looked on the English tragedian with approval. They became acquainted in the artistic circle. Sadovsky ordered wine to be brought. An interpreter was about to join them, but Prov Mikhailovitch waved him away. "You, German, scram," he said to him. "Without you we shall understand each other far better."
>
> And they did! Sadovsky didn't know a word of English, nor Aldridge Russian. However, they sat together for a considerable time and remained highly satisfied with each other, although during the course of this period not a sound was uttered. They looked piercingly at each other. Sadovsky would take a deep breath and shake his head, as if pleading with his talented co-drinker; the same Aldridge would do. Then Aldridge would grasp the hand of Sadovsky and press it firmly. Sadovsky would then reply the same way. If one smiled, so did the other. Then again a deep sigh, handshakes and smiles. So passed the whole time in these external signs of respect for each other. The demand for wine to support this eloquent discussion was made in turn and also by mimicry. Pointing out the empty bottle to the waiter, Sadovsky or Aldridge would make a significant gesture, and a fresh bottle would replace it. Their contemplative period having come to an end, they rose, embraced each other three times and parted.
>
> On the way out, one of Sadovsky's friends stopped him and asked, "Well, how do you like Aldridge? What was the long discussion all about?"
>
> "He's a fine fellow, good-natured, and above all, he's no gossip. That's what I like."
>
> Such a scene characterizes better than anything else artists by nature and not by calling.[4]

One of the many examples of Aldridge's influence on the Russian actors is the instance of L. L. Leonidov (1821–89) who on 25th November 1859 played the lead in *Othello*, based on a new translation by P. I. Weinberg. He was considered a follower of

Karatygin, but after seeing Aldridge's Othello he surprised the critics by rejecting much of the characteristics of the pseudo-classic school and in many respects successfully followed the example of Aldridge.

A most powerful impression was made by Aldridge on a young student, V. V. Charsky, who gave up his academic studies to become an actor, and dedicated his life to the re-creation of the characters of Shakespeare. His judgment of Aldridge was recorded in 1907 by G. N. Durylin, brother of S. Durylin, whose interest in Aldridge dates from that moment:

> The acting of Aldridge made a terrifying impression. Actresses were frightened to play with him; so terrifying was he, he even caused actors to forget they were on the stage acting a scene—it became naked, shattering reality. And he himself was as cold as the nose of a dog. And after that shattering scene he laughed in the wings like a baby. The scene of smothering Desdemona he so led up to, that actresses were afraid of it, as if it were reality. Aldridge was extraordinarily simple in his choice of costume. People were astonished at his playing Othello in a simple, blue-striped costume. I have never seen nor ever shall see another such Othello.

P. A. Strepetova (1850-1903) gives her first impression of Aldridge: "I was eleven years of age when Aldridge came to Nizhni-Novgorod. I saw this tragedian-genius in *Othello*, *Macbeth*, *Merchant of Venice*, and carried away an unforgettable impression of his acting. Above all, he astonished me (and not me only) in *Othello*. I will not attempt to dissect these impressions, because I do not wish to profane by weak description that which I carry in my heart like a saint."

Strepetova, an abandoned child, had been adopted by a theatrical make-up man, and lived her entire child life behind the scenes. There Aldridge showed her the affection which he had for all children. "He loved children very much," she wrote, "but my happiness did not last long. Having finished his performances in Nizhni, the English tragedian went to Kazan. With his departure the box-office takings fell, the theatre itself became like an orphan. My God, how miserable, petty and low appeared to me now the local Nizhni celebrities! 'When shall I see, if but once again, genuine and fine actors and actresses',

I thought to myself as I heard the ugly whining of the Trusovy couple or saw the clownish farce of Madame Sakharova."[5]

Thus did Aldridge kindle in the hearts of future actors the flame of an ideal of how genuine and fine acting could be, in the midst of the backwardness and sordidness of the old provincial theatre of Russia.

Another actress whom Aldridge profoundly impressed was a leading member of the Maly Theatre, Glikeria Mikolayevna Fedotova (1846-1925). She was a pupil of Shchepkin and Samarina and made a successful début at sixteen, just before Aldridge came to Moscow:

> Feelings completely new and never-experienced came over me when I saw Aldridge. Black, not handsome, voice somewhat throaty, he played in English, while our actors replied to his cues in Russian, which, of course, disturbed the wholeness of the impression, yet, despite this unpleasant mix-up of languages, he caused us to forget it all and so enchanted us with his brilliant acting; he was so charming, good, naïve, and touching in his tender scenes, and so terrible and merciless in his anger. Yet at the same time pity for his pure nature, this good soul, brought us to tears; all Othellos are pitiful, but in all the others one presumes or feels and sees more human wisdom and cunning, but this simple child of nature forced us to suffer with pain in our hearts, and the sorrow of the audience was inconsolable, because before them was the suffering of a helpless child. And there cannot be a sorrow more torturing than to watch the sufferings of the help-less spirit of a child. He was a superb tragedian.[6]

Two years later, a then unknown actor, Davydov, played with Aldridge in Tambov. (Davydov became one of Russia's greatest actors and, indeed, founded a whole new school of acting.) He felt the same way about Aldridge as did Fedotova and the others:

> Aldridge made a tremendous impression on me. His arrival turned my head completely, and my participation in one of his productions gave me so much preparation and hard work, al-though in my role I had not a word to say! . . . He played in English, but the local group, of course, in Russian, and it was amusing to watch him and our actors when they tried to express themselves in mimic and gesture, although Aldridge pronounced a certain number of Russian phrases quite distinctly.

He was good-natured in private life, but on the stage he was demanding and insistent and his stage business (*mise en scène*), his plan of acting, he carried out with exceptional thoroughness, according to a well-prepared and thoroughly worked-out scheme, taking into consideration, of course, the acting of local artistes, the production, and the conditions of the stage and theatre.

I particularly well remember him in the role of Othello, and although several decades have passed, yet I remember quite clearly the role he created, individual moments of his performance, and neither Rossini nor Salvini, whose acting I was later able to enjoy, could efface from my memory Othello-Aldridge. His mimicry, gestures, were so expressive that knowledge of the English language for the understanding of his acting was not needed at all. I shall never forget the scene of the mockery of Desdemona and the scene of spiritual enlightenment that follows it. To this very moment I remember his wonderful mimicry when Othello approaches the couch of Desdemona, pulls back the curtain and, holding the dagger in his hand, illuminates the countenance of the sleeping Desdemona. In one moment his face expressed feelings of tenderest love and heavy doubts, despairing sorrow, and hate and anger.

Imbued with deep artistic inspiration and that excitement which grips an artist when he feels that the role which he has thought out and is creating reaches the public, all these external signs of genuine inspiration deeply moved the audience and left an ineradicable impression. The last scene was the apotheosis of his original treatment and understanding. One must point out that this artist played the tragedies of Shakespeare with certain changes, which he brought with the plays. He drank in with his ears the dying whisper of Desdemona, with tremendous suffering he looked at her waxlike face, and afterwards, giving stormy vent to his feelings of despair, threw himself at the foot of the bed, on which now was lying the dead Desdemona and, crying without restraint, as if lost to the world, took her in his embrace and tenderly, on one note, repeated the name of the unfortunate one. The voice of the artist here sounded like a 'cello, and depicted such a clear picture of profound despair that there was not one spectator in the theatre who did not weep and pity Othello, as for a child stumbling, lost in a welter of emotions.[7]

Writing in 1903, I. N. Zakharin (Yakunin) said: "His acting made such a deep impression on me that for several days I was completely under the spell of this tragedian-genius. . . ." He sought a meeting with Aldridge, and finally managed to see him in the English Church in Moscow. "I had the opportunity of seeing the face of the tragedian quite close, and I was particularly struck with his eyes—black, large, shining. . . . Many, many years afterwards I saw the no less famous Salvini in *Othello* and afterwards in *Hamlet*, but his acting did not make the impression on me that I experienced in 1863 in Moscow."[8]

Another facet of his influence is the interest he aroused in Shakespeare. In those days only a few Shakespearean plays were performed, and then only infrequently. Proper translations did not exist, and only those few who were especially interested or concerned made any effort to check the originals. It was Mochalov, for example, who first insisted that *Hamlet* be translated directly from the English original instead of from the French, as hitherto!* And the version of *Lear* in German, as it was first performed in Russia, was from the Tate and Garrick bowdlerized version. Aldridge, it appears, was the first to present *Lear* in its original, though truncated, form, without the happy ending!

Yanzhul, a young student at the Gymnasium in Riazan (who later became a distinguished academician), on learning that Aldridge was to play in that town in three or four months, began an intensive study of English, and "to my satisfaction I achieved my aim and in three months, with a miniature edition of Shakespeare in my hand, word by word I almost understood all that Aldridge was speaking".[9]

But there is another side to the medal, and, in fact, it was the very attacks of certain sections of the Press which acted as the main stimulus for further articles in defence or in explanation of Aldridge and his work. Bazhenov, in a long analysis in the newspaper, *Moskovski Vedemosti* (Moscow News), said, "Above all, what forces me to express myself somewhat over the performances of Aldridge are the extreme opinions about him which have appeared in the Press. I shall not attempt to bring to notice the complete revulsion aroused by the acting of this artist in some people (or, more correctly, in one person) who must have looked at him through very dark-coloured glasses, and the complete delight of others, seeing him through rose-coloured glasses."[10]

The "one person" refers to N. S. Sokhanskaya, who, under the

* That by Ducis—a bowdlerized version.

pseudonym, N. Kokhanovskaya, wrote short stories in the 1850s in the best journals of the time, alongside those of Turgenev and Goncharov. The newspaper, *Dyen* (The Day), was published by I. S. Aksakov, a protagonist of the pro-Slav school of thought. The Slavophiles, as they were called, wanted "Russia for the Russians" and a return to the ancient culture of orthodox Slavic Russia. No imitation of Europe, with its rationalism and individualism, but Russian faith and peasant communal life with direct access to the Sovereign without a parliament—those were its aims. After seeing Aldridge in *Othello*, Kokhanovskaya wrote a letter to the Editor of *Dyen*:

A full-blooded Negro, incarnating the profoundest creations of Shakespearean art, giving *flesh and blood* for the aesthetic judgment of educated European society and our Russians as well—the Venetian Moor is not only in the role, but in a black skin. . . . How much nearer can one get to truth, to the very source of the highest aesthetic satisfaction? But *what is truth*—at the least, that which we call artistic, i.e. the highest enjoyment and expression of the human spirit? As the spirit is not the body, so the truth of art is not this profoundly raw flesh which we can take hold of, and call by name and, if you please, feel, pinch with our unbelieving, all-feeling hand . . . and lo, from beyond the sea they take, transport to us, and handing over, let us look and see, so to speak, the apotheosis of Shakespearean creation; not an imaginary, but a genuine savage, black, natural-born Othello. And we saw . . . what did we see? Savage, wild flesh in earrings and shining armour, shaming the spirit of contemporary art. And that genuine shame is ours, the shame of our aesthetic feeling which thinks, from the skin-surface blackness of Aldridge, to make a deeper and fuller penetration into the spirit of Shakespearean poetry—which thinks that thick blue lips, because they *are* thick and blue, express more truthfully the cry of the human spirit, the cry of a spirit expressing the world spirit of the poet! And what emerged? Emerged that which must necessarily have emerged from the immutable action of flesh, impinging on spirit. The cries emerged terribly, naturally savage; the howls and moans of a beast, feeling that he is wounded like a man, were genuine, leonine, animal cries. . . . Not the Moscow Maly Theatre, but the African jungle should have been filled and resounded with voices at the cries of this black, powerful, howling flesh. But by the very fact that that flesh is so powerful—that it is genuinely black, so naturally *un-white* does it howl—that savage flesh did its fleshly work. It murdered and crushed the spirit. Our aesthetic feelings made a mistake in its expectations. They forgot that *spirit is the true life-giver, flesh profits nothing*. And every noble, simple, sincere nature in which is preserved the holy sensitiveness of *that* spirit, such a one cannot . . . one's spirit cannot accept it— and in place of the highest enjoyment, this blatant flesh introduced into art, this *natural* black Othello, pardon me, causes only . . . revulsion.[11]

The Editor of this important newspaper gave his approval of these sentiments, though attempting at the same time to endow his racial theories with a high artistic tone, even quoting Schiller and Hegel to this end: "The reality of the artistic impression of Mme. Kokhanovsky", he wrote, "finds complete justification in the following verse of Schiller:

> *"Die Kunst soll nie die Wirklichkeit erreichen,*
> *Und siegt Natur, so muss die Kunst entweichen.*

That is, art must never pass over into reality and, where Nature is overpowering, then art must retreat. This thought of Schiller was adopted and developed by Hegel in his *Æsthetics*. Our personal opinion is very close to Mme. Kokhanovsky, in particular, about which we shall still have occasion to speak."

The journal *Razvlecheniye* (Entertainment), in its issue of 11th October 1862, published a brilliant satire on Kokhanovskaya by Vladimir Monumentov, entitled "Aldridge in Moscow—a Lyrical Scene". The scene shows an editor seated at a table in his office reading *On Ancient and Modern Syllables*, by Shishkov. Suddenly a female colleague rushes in. She is pale, her clothes are awry:

COLLEAGUE:

> I tore in rage my ginger hair,
> The mantle of mourning I donned.
> "It's all inside!" I cried aloud
> On seeing Aldridge in *Othello*!
>
> Reared in spiritual lassitude
> On the mysteries of the Russian folk,
> Better it were if I had stayed at home
> 'Neath the skies of my native Ukraine!

In sweet peace I should never have grown,
Nurtured on meat-pies and dumplings,
If I had known how *raw flesh*★ grows
And swears at spirit so fleshily.

I solemnly swear to that black race,
The tribe that gave birth to Aldridge! ...
But I grow faint. .... Cider, give me cider!
With whisky wet my brow! ...

She falls into a faint. The EDITOR *brings her to. She rises and
once more begins to declaim.*

With Byzantine brush strokes
Quickly I sketch for you
This spectacle disgraceful:
Just behold—that body is black,
And on that body earrings and armour!
On the face is seen no reddish hue,
Only *lips that are thick and blue,*
As thick as a fist, and a big one at that!
Where am I—midst the Maly Theatre
Or in the deserts of Africa?
I hear only wild-animal cries. ...
I tremble in fear (a maiden am I),
I understood that wail so miserable:
That is flesh howling so obstinately!

She makes a step forward. Her eyes gleam with a mad light.

Black body! Black skin!
This raw flesh made manifest in earrings!
Spirit is the life-giver,
Flesh is the nothingness!
With cider wet my brow! ... Ahh! ...

Once again she faints. The EDITOR *holds her up.*

As we attempted to point out in the chapter on St. Petersburg,
despite the liberation of the serfs and the few reforms that went
with it, the basic structure of the society, with its many evils,
remained the same, with the result that the social and political

★ Monumentov's footnote: "All expressions printed in italics have been
taken by us from the wonderful article by Mme. Kokhanovskaya printed in
Dyen, No. 39."

climate grew progressively worse. The revolutionary movement became more vocal, students rioted in St. Petersburg and Moscow, and in May 1862, in the face of the strictest censorship and police terror, a leaflet was circulated making some amazing (for that time) demands—for elective national and provincial assemblies, elective judges, abolition of monasteries and of the institution of marriage! The leaflet warned that the ruling class would, of course, resist, and that the people must strike down their enemies pitilessly wherever they might find them. Needless to say, the ruling class struck first, and in July 1862 many radical leaders were arrested and exiled, among them Chernyshevsky, Editor of *Sovremennik*, which had so strongly supported Aldridge. So we see that by the time Aldridge came to Moscow, reaction was in full swing again.

In contrast to the cordiality and friendly co-operation of the actors of St. Petersburg, Aldridge now found hostility, even in the theatre. Bazhenov, an authority on the Maly Theatre, said: "Aldridge played here in conditions most disadvantageous for him. All the four tragedies of Shakespeare were mercilessly cut; practically all our best actors (may they be shamed for this sin) refused to participate in his productions; as a result of which roles were distributed without selection and given to whomever befell."

As we have already seen, Aldridge was the standard-bearer of realism, both in interpretation of theme and in style of production and acting. Understandably, the success of these innovations would lead to professional jealousy, as in the case of Samoilov, but when the fears and disturbances on the social and political planes were added, hostility became more widespread, more organized, and more vociferous. Rumours spread that it was dangerous to play with him, particularly for actresses, because his savage nature endangered not only their nerves, but their very lives! Already in 1858 the reactionary paper, *Sin Otyechestva* (Son of the Fatherland), had started these reports, and caricatures appeared stressing this aspect of their "criticism". The woodcut, here reproduced, has the caption: "The unenviable position of Iago, when Othello, in a fit of jealousy, lightly shakes him by the lapels."[12] Several issues later appeared another caricature, even more pointed, entitled "The Trial". Desdemona and Othello are standing before the Judge:

DESDEMONA: Save me! This savage one day will really suffocate
me!

JUDGE: You must be more careful, Mr. Othello. If you do
actually suffocate her, what will happen then?

OTHELLO: *Nichevo.* Just you give me another Desdemona better
than this one.[13]

He had crippled Iagos and suffocated Desdemonas, so the
rumours went, and the tragedy was that otherwise intelligent
people believed them! A theatrical backer, A. A. Stakhovitch,
relates in his *Memoirs* that once, while conversing with Aldridge
at Voronezh, he asked how *Othello* went in the Moscow
Maly Theatre, where Desdemona was played by the well-known
actress, Nikulin-Kositzkaya. Aldridge replied that the Moscow
Desdemona was upset by the rumour that in the heat of his
acting he suffocated several Desdemonas, and she was frightened
to play with him. "This is all exaggerated," Aldridge continued.
"I have played that role more than three hundred times in my life
and in all these times I have suffocated possibly two, maximum
three, Desdemonas; and stabbed, I think, one Iago. You must
agree that out of three hundred times that is not a high percentage,
certainly not enough to upset your Moscow Desdemona."[14]*
This statement, apparently, shook Stakhovitch who, in his own
words, "did not ask the excitable tragedian any more questions".
It may be that our Russian theatrical backer did not appreciate
Aldridge's ironic humour, and Durylin believes that he took it
literally and for that reason discontinued his questions. Durylin
goes on to say that this "stupid and shameful rumour was started
in America by ill-wishers envious of Aldridge, and, passing
through Europe, forced its way into Russia. The enemies of
Aldridge, American and English actors, attempted through such
rumours to terrorize the white partners of the black tragedian."
This may be so, but we have found no substantiating evidence. To
begin with, hardly anyone in America was aware of Aldridge's
existence, still less would they have known what was happening
to him in the provinces of England or the depths of Russia.
Durylin is thinking in terms of modern journalism, not of nineteenth-century means of communication. We have evidence of

* This is a translation of a verbatim report, but obviously he must have
played Othello many more times in thirty-seven years.

only one previous instance of a direct protest about appearing with Aldridge, and that was in Dublin in 1833-4, when the Yankee husband of Mme. Celeste told Mr. Calcraft, the Manager, that he would not permit his wife to appear at the same theatre with Aldridge. This was an out-and-out case of colour prejudice, having nothing to do with fear of Aldridge's roughness. In the *1849 Memoir* reference is made to certain American actors in England who adopted a superior attitude toward him, despite his being the star and they the walk-ons, but there was no refusal to play with him. There were other rumours, such as the hoax of his accidental death in Wales in the 1830s, but it would appear that the tales of his being a menace to the life and limb of his fellow-actors originated in Russia, where the realism of his acting contrasted so much more startlingly to the existing style than in England or the United States.

Before his arrival in Saratov, for example, the local Press was already at it: "Long before the day of the performance many were concerned with the question: Who should play Desdemona— Mme. Medvedina* or Mme. Roslavskaya? Some chose the former, calculating that her solidity and strength of bones would enable her happily to withstand the forthcoming attack on the part of Othello during her smothering; others spoke for Roslavskaya because of her superior talent."

The following episode should be sufficient to settle once and for all the matter of his roughness. It is related by the Russian actress, M. I. Belizary, and concerns her aunt, A. P. Novitsky-Kapustina (1818-1908), who played with Aldridge in Kharkov and Kiev:

Aldridge possessed a raging temperament. In the fifth act Othello suffocates Desdemona. Aldridge's eyes went bloodshot and he foamed at the mouth. My aunt was terrified to death. The part went right out of her head, and for a moment she stopped—and the scene was being played at a terrific tempo. Suddenly in her ear she heard Aldridge whispering in Russian, "*Nichevo, Nichevo*" (It's all right. It's all right). And then he continued in English— in a burst of rage. His hands gripped her by the throat. He is smothering her with the pillow. Before her that terrible face, and in a flash that whisper, "*Nichevo; nye boysya*" (It's all right; don't be frightened). Neither the public nor even the actors standing in

* Russian for female bear.

the wings, overcome by the acting of the tragedian, noticed anything. At the end of the act, a storm of applause. And still trembling from the terror she had experienced, poor Desdemona came out hand in hand with the black monster, who was now calmly smiling at her.[15]

Not only was Aldridge overshadowing the best actors of Russia, not only was he interpreting Shakespeare from a new, liberal point of view, but he was a Negro to boot! In certain circles this was adding insult to injury with a vengeance. Furthermore, the radical Press supported him unequivocally, his very existence serving as a weapon in their struggle against Tsarism and autocracy. These critics unerringly put their finger on the reasons for the attacks and rumours. One critic, A. Ivanov (pseudonym of A. I. Urusov, a left-wing lawyer), wrote in 1862:

A certain section of the public received Aldridge coldly and antagonistically. Naturally! Just imagine to yourself that suddenly appears a gentleman—of "black blood", as is the "happy expression" of Mme. Kokhanovskaya—appears and puts very many respectable people in danger of being heavily compromised. Suddenly in that very Maly Theatre, where the worth of Mme. Kolosova and the short-comings of Mr. Kolosov give occasion for our Aristarks to reveal their most unusual subtle taste and pointed Attic wit, with which nature has so plentifully endowed them—suddenly on these boards appears Aldridge, preceded by a tremendous reputation, Aldridge the interpreter of Shakespeare, and with inexplicable impudence puts Aristarkov in a most unpleasant position. To bring judgment on him for his general performance is rather awkward, and alas, his general performance somehow gives no occasion for it. Keep silent? That would, of course, have been best, but not at such a time. As it is, there are enough people infected with scepticism, nihilism, and other moral defects, and at the same time the authority of Aristark would be undermined. Praise him? Difficult. One must find some justifiable way out, but where? Consequently, the best thing is to slander. And so they began to slander. They accuse Aldridge of too much naturalness, others of too much artificiality, a third—and the most numerous—with both one and the other. That's best of all, because Aldridge can't get out of that. One of these accusations must hit their mark. Pity it is that the shortcomings are incompatible and in these accusations there is no sense whatsoever.[16]

Soon after this was written, Urusov was exiled for his association with the Nechayev group.★ His analysis was correct, as a
study of the Press attacks on Aldridge shows. Almazov made the
following comments in *Russki Vestnik* (Russian Herald) in 1862:

> Many consider that Aldridge is cold, that his acting is not warmed
> by true feelings. Maybe it seems so to them because Aldridge
> never exceeds the bounds of true art, and in the most impassioned
> places of his role he remembers the advice of Hamlet to the actors:
> "And in the very whirlwind of passion to beget a coolness." . . .
> Others say the opposite, that Aldridge roars and shouts so loudly
> that a more suitable place for him would be the African jungle
> rather than the stage of the Maly Theatre. The people who say this
> about him no doubt are seeing the tragedy for the first time, and
> have never heard such cries and shouts from ordinary tragedians.
> If only they had heard Karatygin! In general, the reviews of our
> theatrical dilettantes about Aldridge are a little hurried and
> superficial.

The rebuffs that Kokhanovskaya received from the Press were
such as to cause both her and her Editor to desist from publishing
any further attacks, but she remained unrepentant, though her
Editor appeared a little more open-minded, judging by the
following letter he wrote to her:

> Well, you certainly "got it in the neck" for Aldridge! Both in
> verse and prose, and in Moscow and Petersburg papers. I am very
> angry with myself that I allowed you to print that letter. Better it
> had been someone else, and not you, who took upon themselves
> to debunk the false delight of the public; you, as an artist, should
> stand aside from polemics, from the pushing and shoving on
> literary squares. As it happened, I did not see Aldridge in *Othello*,
> but I saw him in *Macbeth*, where I didn't like him, and in *Lear*
> where, on the other hand, I liked him very much. That is under-
> standable. In *Lear* he must play the white-headed (grey) old man
> and not give any free play to his Negro nature, doing everything
> to hold it in check, hide it; in other words, in this role he appeared
> not as his natural self, but as an actor, and the result was very good
> because as an actor he is wonderful and clever. The more opposed
> the role is to his nature, the better he can make up and use every

★ Named after Sergei Nechayev, a schoolteacher of St. Petersburg, who was
the first to attempt an organization of revolutionary conspirators. He was the
model for the younger Verkhovenski in Dostoyevsky's *The Possessed*.

method—grease paint, false hair, etc., to hide his African type, so much the better.

This is indeed an admission from a Slavophile, though it was not published at that time. To this, Mme. Kokhanovskaya, replied:

You say that I got it in the neck for Aldridge, and regret that you printed my letter—and why did you allow me, an artist, into the literary hurly-burly? A vain regret! Just because I am an artist (if, finally, I am so called), I had to raise my voice of outraged, artistic feelings, insulted by this black flesh in the sphere of the colourless spirit. I do not repent! For me, my artistic feeling is a completely second conscience, and the revulsion which I received from Aldridge was so great that I, as from a heavy sin, could only be relieved of it by a public confession—no way else.

I shall not, of course, enter the hurly-burly of the literary squares, i.e. interfere with a wounded self-esteem, and I do not think of replying to these verses and proses if only for the simple reason that I have not read them.[17]

One of the rebuffs that Aksakov and Kokhanovskaya received came from Almazov:

There are people to be found who attribute certain shortcomings to Aldridge because of his Negro descent. They consider that he plays with unnecessary naturalness, breaking and insulting the laws of fine art; that he is like an animal and that his acting is a matter of flesh and not spirit. But these gentlemen, it seems, do not take into consideration that Aldridge is not a savage Negro, captured only yesterday, but a Negro who has received in Europe an aesthetic education. Truly, in parts of the play, where it is necessary, he very vividly represents the movements of a man in whom is suddenly awakened the feelings of a savage, but he does this deliberately and these are not his personal feelings, but the result of his observations of the nature of Negroes, which he has had the opportunity of studying most closely.

Moscow journalists have not come out in favour of Aldridge. One very respectable and highly esteemed newspaper even said that Aldridge gave it almost feelings of revulsion. This impression it justifies by citing Schiller and basing itself on the philosophy of Hegel—I quote here a verse of Schiller not in criticism, but in honour of Aldridge:

> *Es Liebt die Welt das Strahlende zu schwarzen*
> *Und das erhab'ne in den Straub zu zieh'n:*
> *Doch furchte nicht! Es gibt noch schone Herzen,*
> *Die fur das Hohe, Herrliche ergluh'n.*
> *Den lauten Markt mag Momus unterhalten:*
> *Ein edler Sinn liebt edlere Gestalten.*

(Of which a rough translation is:

> How the world loves to blacken all that is bright,
> And bring the highest down to the dusty low;
> But have no fear! There are lovely hearts alight
> That for the high and wonderful still glow.
> The noisy market Mammon may amuse,
> The noble mind loves noble forms to choose.)[18]

Urusov expressed his concern over the attacks on Aldridge by the following note in his *Memoirs*: "*Dyen* and *Nasha Vremya* (Our Time) have taken up such a savage attitude to Aldridge that a translation of these articles into a foreign language, even if only English, would have given a most sorry impression of our level of culture."

In spite of everything, however, Old Russia comes out with great credit, on the whole, in her treatment of Ira Aldridge, the African Roscius, and the following incident related by Mrs. Yunge may serve as an epilogue to the racial outlook of Kokhanovskaya and her ilk:

In 1864, when Ira Aldridge was for a short time in St. Petersburg (but did not perform on the stage), he visited me nearly every day. My eldest son was then about one year old and, on taking him for the first time to see Aldridge, I was terribly worried that the child would be frightened by his appearance, and that my black friend, who so passionately loved children, would nevertheless be grieved. No doubt he also thought something similar—but the child soon dissipated our fears. He at once stretched out to Aldridge and settled into his arms. Aldridge's face lit up, he began to dance with the little fellow around the room and never let him go from his arms the whole day, even during dinner.

CHAPTER XVI

The Provinces of Russia

THANKS to Durylin, the local Russian Press, and the sketchy diaries and scattered papers of Aldridge, we are able to reconstruct at least a partial account of his tours of the Russian provinces.

From 1861 to 1866 he made several long tours, one of them lasting eight months, from June 1864 to January 1865, through the Volga and Central Russian provinces. He also visited southern Russia, the Ukraine, and the Western Region. He is known to have played in Rybinsk, Novgorod, Kaluga, Samara, Saratov, Astrakhan, Kharkov, Rostov-on-Don, Kiev, Odessa, Zhitomir, Kishinev, Zhiradovo, Simferopol, Tver, Stravropol. He undoubtedly played in many other places of which direct information has not yet come to light.

No foreign actor, before or since Aldridge, has ever touched this territory and, for that matter, neither did the important Russian actors, not even Shchepkin or Mochalov, play in such a large number of Russian towns. Some of these places had never seen a professional company or a Shakespearean play. Even such a large and important city as Odessa had never seen anyone with a Shakespearean repertoire until Aldridge came.[1] It remained for Ira Aldridge, an American Negro, to be the first to bring not only Shakespeare, but theatre proper, to the distant Russian provinces, and to bring, furthermore, a modern, realistic style of production, acting, and interpretation that was to leave an indelible mark on the theatre history of Russia.

A critic of Odessa wrote in 1866: "It is already some years that Aldridge, in the role of a strolling missionary of art, has enlightened the Russian public with the light of the immortal creations of Shakespeare; at the present moment there is not one provincial city, it seems to me, not one well-known fair in Russia, where the light of Shakespeare's genius has not penetrated, thanks to this travelling tragedian."[2] Durylin sums it up by saying that the sojourn of Aldridge in Russia for those seven or eight yearly tours "was a whole epoch in the cultural life of each town".

Travelling through an undeveloped country in those days was a very difficult and trying experience. The roads were little more than cart tracks, which turned to thick mud in the rain. Aldridge called them "such desperate roads". It might be pleasant enough when he could chug down the wide Mother Volga, like on the Mississippi, but long journeys in winter in a stagecoach or horse-sleigh could be agonizing. One photograph shows him wearing a long fur coat and cap with turned-down brim and ear-flaps, but even this garb would be inadequate protection from the bitter cold on a protracted journey.

In the first of the following three letters to Amanda, the young Swedish woman whom he later marries, he talks of going to Astrakhan. This would be for the purpose of catching one of the paddle-steamers. But first we give the text of a letter written to him by the captain of such a steamer, and, as the original is not available, we offer it in the literal translation in which it was found:

DEAR SIR,—It has for a long time troubled my mind not keeping my promise to you before now, but many things have come into the way, the photograph and a visit to my brother at Vladimir where we spent one month, the happiest for a long time.

I am now commanding a large steamer of 100 horsepowers, just the same construction as my second brother has and my way is now from Nizhni to Astrakhan.* How happy would not I be to have you once more as passenger on my boat. Russia is as it was as you left it.

My wife sends to you her photograph and her best respect.
    Believe me to remain,
     Your humble servant,
      GUSTAVE VON SCHULTZE.

PS.—It should make me very happy if your time would allow you to send me a few lines from old dear England.

The letters to Amanda reveal not only the hardships of travel, but also show that despite his amazing successes he had financial

---

* Aldridge was in Nizhni in September-October 1862.

problems. The first letter was written from Kybrusk, Russia, on 30th May 1864, a few weeks after the death of his first wife and before his legal marriage a year later to Amanda:

MY DEAR AMANDA,—I gave my first performance last night (*Othello*) to a good but not a great audience. Things are very bad in Russland at present and I intend, please God, to finish, as it will not be worth while returning, particularly as I am not allowed in St. Petersburg.

The weather is still warm, but I have caught a bad cough. I have played six times and now am going straight to Astrakhan, so that I can make the return journey before the cold weather sets in. I am most impatiently waiting for a letter from you, my dearest Amanda. The post goes for home from here three times a week. I am very miserable and quite alone all the time. Business was bad on Thursday. Has Angelina visited you? My greetings to Madame Molte and her son.

Kiss my Luranah and Fritz for me. I hope the two of them are well and you also. I have seen a nice little dog who is very intelligent. If I had known things were so bad in Russia I would have stayed at home. I hope, however, to do good business in Astrakhan, but even so you must economize, and I must do the same. I am very anxious to sell my equipage if it is possible.

Enclose your next letter in this envelope, so that it will not have to delay by first of all going to Moscow. Write me a long letter when you are able. Have you any news of Mr. Stirling, wife and friends. I have had no communications from one or the other; the Prince of Light is forgotten perhaps. I am anxious to hear from Luranah Villa.

With love and kisses to yourself and the children and hoping that you may all continue in health and happiness until it pleases God that I again see you at no very distant period, I remain,

Now and ever your affectionate,

IRA ALDRIDGE.

The next was written on 1st December 1865 from Semperkoff, on the road to Odessa:

MY DEAR AMANDA,—I received your last letters and I am glad to hear that you and the children are in health. I hope you received the money. I am in middling health. The travelling at present is dreadful, such desperate roads and so cold and cheerless.

The English engineer and his wife, a German, who are leaving this country promised to call upon you and say they had seen me. When they do so ask them to lunch and show them any politeness you can.

I will write when I get to my journey's end. I suppose the little stranger may be soon expected. God bless it. Keep a merry Christmas. Kiss Fred and Luranah for me. Best respects to Mademoiselle. I am glad that Simpson is to be with you, it will be less expensive and more comfortable.

Things are very indifferent in this country. The cattle plague has been very bad and trade generally. Everything is dear in the extreme. I received a letter from Ira and expected one from Mr. Grist.

God bless you all, I remain,
Affectionately yours,
IRA.

Since the death of Margaret, young Ira has been at boarding school, and Mr. Grist is the Headmaster. Later on the boy comes to live with the new family in Luranah Villa.

The third letter is a short and sad one written on 2nd January 1866, while still on the way to Odessa:

MY DEAR AMANDA,—I have been for the last fifteen days unable to leave my room. I took cold and was very ill on the journey and on my arrival here was prostrate. I am now scarcely able to sit up but hope ere this reaches you to be enabled to resume my journey to Odessa. I do not know what the direction will do in the matter, I am so much behind my time.

I send you twenty pounds through Mr. Ray. I expect to find letters from you in Odessa. I hope all are well with you. Kiss the children and I wish you all a happy New Year.

My best respects to Madlle. who I hope is in health. God bless you all and I remain,
Affectionately yours,
IRA ALDRIDGE.

Amongst other trying conditions, Aldridge had to contend with the jealousy of the local "stars", to whom he must have been a most formidable competitor. Not only would he now receive the benefit receipts, but the originality of his performances and his innovations in production were causing them to suffer by comparison. The usual rumours about his rough treatment of his fellow-actors were followed by actual attempts to sabotage his performances and even those of actresses who dared to play his Desdemona. One young actress, A. N. Mochalova, who played Desdemona with Aldridge in Odessa at his request, in later life related:

Now came the scene of the murder. After saying my prayers, I laid in the bed. Othello enters. Suddenly I feel that the boards of the bed under me are shaking; I feel my legs are hanging through the boards. In a flash I understood. They've sawn the boards so as to ruin the scene . . . if I fall through there will be a scandal. But already Othello is over me. My heart sank. Instinctively I stretched myself right out, pushing my feet and back against the bottom of the bed. Suddenly the boards gave way. I looked at Othello in terror and whispered, "Gently, gently." He understood. "A, racaglie," he ejaculated in a suppressed undertone and, continuing to act, he quickly let down the curtain over the alcove. In a second, swaying, he appeared on the steps of the platform. He did not forget to pull to the curtains, and the public never noticed anything. But, they say, his face was terrible to behold. His eyes blazed like a wolf. And, it seemed to me, that if any of my dear comrades who had arranged this intrigue had fallen into his hands, he no doubt would have strangled them. But the public sat still in terror, seeing only the face of such a tiger. His ovations continued without end.[3]

Durylin states that Aldridge had to teach a large number of his provincial actors the art of the theatre, and *en passant* he gave them lessons in actors' ethics. At the first rehearsal he politely assembled the actors, calling them by the parts they were to play, getting acquainted with them, and on parting said, "I hope to see you in the best of health." Such manners were unknown in the theatre of that time.

Dalmatov tells us that "at first the behaviour of Aldridge on the stage disappointed everyone to some degree. He muttered to himself, sometimes not even looking at his partner and not hearing him, but he acted and received his cues as if understanding exactly what those around him were saying and pointed out to everyone their positions in the most businesslike way, clearly, sympathetically, most politely, so that towards the end of the rehearsal everyone felt at ease and cheerful. Soon they were all enchanted by him, except the local tragedian, who was dissatisfied with Aldridge's acting; he did not roar, howl, nor whine.

And when Aldridge was on the stage, the tragedian, who had got drunk, brooded in the wings and cried, 'I'm here, you ugly mug. Come on out!' He was completely disgusted with the acting of the visiting artist; he broke all the traditions of the loud-voiced Karatygins."

Aldridge was good-natured and amiable in private life, but stern and determined as a producer, demanding from his actors a thorough knowledge of their lines, carefully thought-out acting, a strict observance of the business and *mise en scène*, and consideration for the ensemble. At the same time he was kind, understanding and helpful to the actors, carefully explaining to them the significance and content of their part and its relation to the play as a whole, going through it with them as often as necessary. Russian actors learned for the first time what a producer was; they followed his instructions and gained a new respect for their art. Aldridge's productions were the best, particularly in their ensemble, that the Russian provinces had in the 1860s.

Mrs. Yunge relates that "a very educated actress" who played with Aldridge in Odessa told her that Aldridge arranged everything down to the minutest detail of the production, and explained everything himself. Fearing that their lack of knowledge of English would handicap the Russian artists, he would point out to them a certain gesture which he would make to indicate their cues. "But that was not necessary", said the actress. "We so respected him, placed him on such a plane, tried so hard, that we all knew our roles, and everything went smoothly. Once it happened that Aldridge forgot the prompt book and there was no time to send for it; we persuaded him not to worry, and played without a prompter."

With Aldridge playing in a language foreign to the rest of the cast, there was always a danger of actors missing cues, however well-rehearsed or conscientious they might be, and things did not always run as smoothly as in Odessa, when the actors paid Aldridge the compliment of playing without a prompt book. Shortly before Aldridge's visit to Saratov to play with Medvedyev's local company, considered to be one of the best in the provinces, the following note appeared in the local Press:

The company have a big task ahead of them. . . . We sincerely beg the actors to learn their parts well and, if but for this one

25. Ira Aldridge, c. 1865.

26. Margaret, his first wife.

27. Amanda Paulina, his second wife.

28. Ira Aldridge with his elder son, Ira Daniel.

29. His elder daughter, Luranah.

30. His younger son, Ira Frederick.

31. His younger daughter, Amanda.

production, to rely less on the prompter. . . . The most difficult task confronts Alexandrova, who will have to play Cordelia, Lady Macbeth, Desdemona.

The actors did not respond to this appeal, for the next day, commenting on Aldridge's *première*, the same newspaper said that it was "unsatisfactory because of the hurried way in which the parts were studied, which impeded Aldridge's playing".[4]

Luckily, we have some precise details of how Aldridge managed with his cueing in these bilingual productions. Nadimov-Shamshensko, in his unpublished memoirs, says:

In 1861 Aldridge played in Odessa, in English, *Othello*, *The Merchant of Venice*, *King Lear*, and *The Padlock*, the whole of his repertoire, for which he received one-third of the box-office takings. Prompting did not turn out to be as difficult as anticipated. It was only necessary to make certain notes during the performance; should he make a gesture of the right hand upwards or the left, or take certain steps to the right or left or proceed up-stage or down-stage, if he did it once, then you could be sure at the tenth time he would do exactly the same gestures or movements, and after that the prompter could safely give the cue to the next actor; there would be no pause and no interruption of his soliloquy. He played ten performances, and at not one of them was there a mistake or misunderstanding.[5]

Sometimes there were two prompters! One did the actual prompting and the other saw to it that the players responded in time to Aldridge's cues.

Despite his patience and politeness to his fellow-actors, Aldridge was sometimes driven to desperation. Davydov gives one instance:

It was difficult for our actors to play with him. But patiently he issued his instructions through a translator, gave advice and, when everything was going well, rejoiced like a child, slapping himself on the sides and good-naturedly crying, in broken Russian, "*Ochen khorosho! Ochen spasibo!*" (Very good! Very much thanks!). I remember one episode that didn't escape my attention. Desdemona was played by a somewhat talentless local artiste, who was under the protection of the local Governor of the province. In the scene when a volcano of revenge is burning in the breast of Othello, she, also wanting to act, no doubt, began to stroke her crumpled clothes with paralysing calmness and indifference. Such an attitude to her business so hurt him that, running up to her, he deliberately grasped her arm so sharply that the face of Desdemona at once reflected deep spiritual suffering and physical pain. . . . Suddenly breaking off his speech, the tragedian smiled, looked into the face of the actress and added caressingly, *"Ochen khorosho! Ochen spasibo!"* and then continued the broken-off scene.[6]

The contrast between Aldridge's professional style of acting and production, learned from the English school, and the local provincial standards of old Russia was often dealt with by the contemporary critics. Commenting on Aldridge's visit to Saratov, a critic said:

> The appearance of Aldridge on the provincial stage must not end without leaving a trace. In so far as their strength and possibilities allow, the provincial dramatic actor must learn from Aldridge that the work of the dramatic actor is not in shouts, not in bass-like notes, and not in a bull's bellowing, but . . . simply in passion of acting. Whether the tragedian is silent, whether he speaks to himself, makes a movement, gesture or sound—everywhere there is passion in its thousand tones. . . . No doubt this is a tall order, but the tragedian must needs study, and not limit himself to an occasional swoon or bizarre shout. . . . There are to be found some gentlemen who quite sincerely say that a certain dramatic actor, Bobrov, who lived once upon a time in Saratov, surpassed Aldridge . . . and certainly he had a bass like a church cantor and a paw like a shovel, and a height like a regimental sergeant-major. . . . "From the sublime to the ridiculous is but one step", we thought as we watched the actors performing with Aldridge. Aldridge had to have great patience and artistic ecstasy in order to forget the ensemble around him. It was a consolation that those playing with Aldridge at least knew their lines, but of those in Astrakhan even that could not be said. . . .[7]

It is to the credit of the local actors that they were willing and had the courage to risk comparison with this certain box-office draw. Aldridge would go, but they would remain.

Benefit nights, as we know, were a vital source of income for the impecunious actor, and we find Aldridge ever ready to participate in the benefit of a rival. We have an interesting account of his generosity to an actor outside his own company. A. A. Alekseyev happened to meet Aldridge in Kiev, where they were both acting at the same theatre:

We played alternative performances, and it was understandable that his participation brought big box-office takings, while mine attracted only a small public. Realizing my uselessness to the *entrepreneur*, I soon gave up further performances on the condition that I should have a benefit night to recoup some of my expenses. The Manager agreed and permitted me to put on what I liked and with whom I liked. Having such permission, I naturally approached Aldridge with a request to participate in my benefit.

"Very good," he replied through the interpreter, "I'll play for you and even sing. I have with me a Russian vaudeville in which I play the role of a Negro lackey. I already performed this vaudeville in St. Petersburg."

"I am very grateful," I replied joyfully.

"Then I will play the role of this Negro."

"But what will you sing?"

"I've put in a Russian song which I learned long ago," he said. "*Vo Piru, Vo Besyedushki*."

The participation of Aldridge in the vaudeville and particularly his singing of a Russian song gathered for my benefit so many people that there wasn't a place you could drop an apple in. . . . Aldridge sang the Russian song with gusto, and its characteristic peculiarities, which he had evidently well studied, he conveyed in a way that was killing. The public encored without end. He repeated the song more than ten times.[8]

We now give in full an unedited letter from a Theatre Manager in Kharkov which gives some idea of the terms and conditions which Aldridge was able to command. It is dated 21st March 1863, and is addressed to Aldridge in care of Anson, Esq., Theatrical Agency Office, Bow Street, Covent Garden, London. The month before, he was in Kharkov. Now he is in England for a brief reunion with Margaret, who is very ill, and in April he is back again in Poltava, which is pretty fast travelling for those days:

Forgive me please that I did not give you any answer about your coming or your not coming to Kharkov but the reason was that I could nothing decide before I was sure I would become the

Theatre house at Poltava. Now I have taken the house notwithstanding the large sum I will be obliged to pay for it, being sure of the great income you will bring. I ask you then, my dear Sir, to come to Kharkov, Ekaterinoslav and Poltava, but I fear that our arrangements require a little change. It will be utterly impossible to perform more than 6 times in Kharkov (I mean the 5th as your half benefit) and I ask of you to arrive for the 29th or 30th of May. For every performance I propose to you 200 r. (as we arranged it before) and Ekaterinoslav 7 performances your half benefit the 5th time every evening 100 rbls. At Poltava 10 performances (the 7th evening your half benefit). I am afraid I am not able to propose to you more than 200 rbls. every performance as money matters are bad and the expenses are too great, as I am obliged to pay for the house 2,750 rbls. Forgive my changing our last arrangements but you will find yourself that I act so on the utter impossibility. If the houses are full every evening we may perhaps add a few performances on those or other conditions. Give me an answer to this letter by telegraph and write if you are bringing new pieces as you wanted to do.

Goodbye, my dear Sir, and receive mine and my whole family's cordial salutations.

Yours truly and devoted,
LEONIDE MANGENKANIHOFF.

On 27th November he writes a letter to his son, now about sixteen:

MY DEAR SON,—I arrived here the night before last, fatigued but pretty well, thank God. I received a letter from your Mamma just as I was leaving Moscow. She was as well as could be expected.

I still at times feel the effect of my illness after leaving you, but none from the attack of the madman; if he had had a knife he could have killed me, as the attack was so instantaneous and unexpected.

Present my compliments to your Governor and his Lady, as also to Mr. Nethersole and Mr. Dick. Do you go home at Xmas, if so kiss Mamma for me, get your clothes changed, say I will pay the difference on my return—it is the establishment at the corner of Tottenham Court Road, you know it.

How are you progressing in French and your other studies? Well, I hope. Write to Mamma when you have time, tell her you have heard from me.

When you go there see that the gardener properly attends to the garden, and that it is well stocked with vegetables. Write me; I send you an envelope with kisses.

> Affectionately yours,
> IRA ALDRIDGE, K.S.

We have no information about the attack alluded to, who made it and what the circumstances were. But one thing is certain, poor Ira Aldridge had to put up with many things, not barring danger to his life, in his mission of pioneering realistic Shakespeare to the uninitiated.

Contemporary sources, newspapers, histories of Old Russian towns give further insight into the significance of Aldridge to the theatrical and cultural life of their people. The historian of the Nizhni-Novgorod Theatre writes:

Some three or four weeks ago a rumour spread through the town that it appears the famous actor, Ira Aldridge, would be visiting us. We must admit that at first we didn't believe this rumour, remembering the indifference of the Nizhni-Novgorod public to the art of the theatre: why then should Aldridge come to Nizhni? Our pessimistically inclined imagination began to sketch a picture of the empty auditorium, the dreamy physiognomy of the *kapeldieners*,* who no doubt with good reason, ask themselves the question, "For what use does a theatre exist in Nizhni?" (or more probably not even asking themselves such a head-splitting question), the somnambulent acting of the artistes—quite natural, in view of the lack of any interest paid to it, and the sleepy, drooping cabmen waiting at the theatre entrance. But, we thought, all these sad pictures will not come into the head of Aldridge, who has never lived in Nizhni: *ergo*, he most probably will come. The rumours about Aldridge's arrival turned out to be quite true; when he appeared on our stage for the first time in the role of Othello, the theatre had a full house. The fame which Aldridge had earned was completely merited by his highly artistic and, above all, most sensitive acting. In watching him as Othello, Lear, or Macbeth, one saw before you not Aldridge, but Othello, Lear, and Macbeth.[9]

The proof of an actor's popularity is not in the reviews but in the box-office. Aldridge played always to full houses, with prices

* Doorkeepers.

much above normal. In the town of Kaluga in 1864 he "gave two performances with the participation of the Kaluga theatrical company, and all the tickets, despite their disgracefully high prices, were sold out completely".[10]

"The visit of Aldridge to Kazan completely reversed 'normal' procedure. The theatre became too small for its audience. Twenty performances were given with prices doubled and an average house of 1,000 roubles a performance."[11]

"The arrival of Aldridge in Odessa [1866] brought the whole theatrical world into action. Despite the increased prices, the first night was not only filled, but overfilled. Many purchased tickets for the stalls at five times the original cost; families crowded into boxes, which were reserved well in advance."[12]

"In Rybinsk he played in the Market Theatre, an old warehouse with oil lamps. After the play a banquet was arranged in honour of the illustrious actor. On the table were sturgeons, ducks, geese, cold and roasted porkers, and different brandies and wines. Aldridge made a speech translated by a secretary. The Impresario, flattered with the presence of the eminent guest, regaled Aldridge so abundantly that he almost died. At night in the hotel, Aldridge felt spasms of the stomach and lost consciousness. Physicians were immediately summoned. At this time Rybinsk was ravaged with cholera and death was feared. However, Aldridge recovered and appeared in his next play, *King Lear*."[13]

After Aldridge's appearances at the theatres in Odessa in February and March 1866, the local Press carried the following:

The Chevalier Ira Aldridge, our distinguished guest, has now arrived at his tenth representation, and the furore, so great at his early performance has, if possible, increased. Certain it has in no wise diminished, as exemplified by the announcement that he would appear in that wonderful creation of the world's poet, *King Lear*. For some days previous to the representation not a seat was obtainable, and we hear that many were bought up by speculators, to the prejudice and injury of the public. This is not as it should be. There were rumours that more than ordinary care had been bestowed in the production of *Lear*, and certainly we were not wholly disappointed, although there was a lack of decoration in particular parts of the play which should not be apparent in an establishment holding the prominent rank of the Odessa Theatre. But to the play. From the previous efforts of

Mr. Aldridge, we were prepared for an intellectual banquet, his Othello and Shylock standing pre-eminent and unequalled in the annals of our dramatic history. The only approach in our day was the lamented Karatygin; he was excellent in certain portions of the play of *Othello*; in Shylock he excelled the great Mochalov, but they both, as is admitted, lacked the intensity, the impulsiveness, the artistic blending of the passions, portrayed in the Shylock and Othello of our swarthy guest, whose genius and natural taste certainly entitle him to be classed as one of our greatest living actors. Mr. Aldridge's appearance as the irritable monarch was imposing in the extreme, the feebleness and assumption of age being maintained throughout with great truth and fidelity. Mr. Aldridge gives us Lear from the English State Edition, which differs from the original in parts very materially, particularly the omission of the fool, the Attic Salt of this great work; again, the substitution of Edgar as the lover of Cordelia, instead of the King of France. Monsieur Aldridge's malediction of Goneril at the close of the first act was an artistic study; it was truly a climax. Kneeling bareheaded, his entire frame quivered with agony, that impassioned, natural fierceness which the genius of the artist never allowed to merge into rant produced an effect which never can be forgotten. The audience were evidently astounded and sat there spellbound for some seconds; then, as awaking from a dream, they simultaneously arose and summoned the artist no less than six times to express their wonder and delight and, amid substantial tokens of approbation showered upon the actor, a young lady in her enthusiasm threw a beautiful bouquet from one of the private boxes, attached to which was a most magnificent gold bracelet. . . . The Governor-General, Constantinoff, and suite, assisted at the presentation, and frequently applauded the talented African.[14]

The journal, *Entracte*, said:

The famous tragedian, Aldridge, pleased with the glad hospitality he has received in Russia, does not wish to leave, despite an invitation from the Director of the Drury Lane Theatre in London. At the present moment he is touring our western provinces with a Russian company (under the direction of Kostrovsky). Recently he gave some performances in Zhitomir. Despite the high prices, there was no lack of spectators. The Zhitomir public, where there are a great number of Jews, like above all *The Merchant of Venice*. The tragedy was repeated three times. *Othello* was given twice.[15]

One Press report told of a procession of Jews headed by the Rabbi coming to the theatre to thank him for his interpretation of Shylock. For the first time in Russian theatre history, Shakespeare's Jew became a human being.

The general practice was to put on a play for one or two nights, for which there might be sufficient audience, but when Aldridge came, unprecedented runs took place even in the smaller towns. In Penze, for instance, in December 1864 *Macbeth* ran for one week, followed by repeat performances of the *Merchant* and again *Macbeth*, and, finally, by demand of the public, *Othello* for three performances.

Davydov tells of Aldridge's great success in Tambov, where he, as a young actor, participated in the performances: "He played, I remember, without any advertisements, yet gathered a full house. All the landlords came with their families from the farthest corners of the province, and the gossip in those days was entirely about the black tragedian, and wild rumours spread round the town that he ate raw meat, washed down with brandy, and that he played with such passion and temperament that in *Othello* he had choked more than one Desdemona."[16]

Many people, to be sure, came not only to enjoy Shakespeare, but to see this "phenomenon" of a black tragedian. However, those who were attracted by the more vulgar elements of theatre stayed to enjoy the higher. And it should be remembered that Aldridge was playing in English all the time. The critic of Rostov-on-Don said that it would have made no difference if he had played in Chinese.[17]

In Tambov Aldridge had been so successful with his Shylock, Othello, and Lear that the public clamoured to see *Macbeth*, but the local company had neither the cast nor the sets to do *Macbeth*, so the local amateurs undertook to support Aldridge in this role. The local critic points out that without them "our public would not have had the possibility of seeing *Macbeth*, with all its difficulties and complexity of production. And what was extraordinary, despite these difficulties, was the fact that the whole production was performed with great artistry." These enthusiastic amateurs guaranteed Aldridge the sum of 300 roubles for his participation in this production. "The usual heavy expenses of a new production were considerably added to by the complexities of this effective play, the numerous new settings, military music, magic effects, etc. The gentlemen amateurs were therefore naturally apprehensive that, apart from the amount they had already sacrificed for costumes, exceeding 500 roubles, they would still have to pay out of their own resources the guarantee to Aldridge. But, thanks to the interest of the public, this fear did not come to pass; the box-office takings spoke louder than words—808 silver roubles, so that after paying Aldridge his agreed 300 roubles, and the stage expenses of 425 roubles, there yet remained 83 roubles 39 kopeks, which was given over for the benefit of the poor of the city of Tambov."[18] Durylin points out that 800 roubles was indeed a very large sum for an average-sized provincial theatre of that day.

But what was even more interesting was the artistic result of this effort, of which we have an unimpeachable witness, Davydov: "The amateurs . . . strove with all their might and, to tell the truth, this production, by its smoothness, the thoroughness with which the roles were learnt, and by its production, was much better and more interesting than productions with professional actors."

One can imagine how much work Aldridge put into that production, and how much love and affection, of which Davydov goes on to say: "At his farewell, local society brought the artist bread and salt on a silver plate, in the old Russian style, with a silver salt-cellar, and a hand-embroidered napkin decorated with Russian motifs. It was touching to see how the artist, when replying to the address, took the bread in his hands, pressed it to his heart and covered it with kisses. As souvenirs he distributed lithographs and photographs with tender inscriptions and his autograph. Long afterwards in the provinces one could see both in the albums and on the walls, faded with time, pictures of the talented artist whom the Russian public loved, and whom Fate brought to lie in Russian soil."[19]

That Aldridge was not forgotten when he left the provinces is attested to by the many letters written to him, letters from children, from lovesick young ladies, and from whole families writing together.

The younger generation took to Aldridge with keen delight. On the day of his benefit, the Amateur Circle of Dramatic Art presented him with a bouquet, bound with blue ribbon, with a Latin inscription which translates as follows:

The undersigned students of the Imperial University of Kazan feel bound to express their deep gratitude and veneration for the greatest actor of our time, the Master, Ira Aldridge, for the happy moments afforded them by his genius and artistic skill. They are aware that the great tragic actor is above all praise, but, convinced that their words are altogether too feeble to express his merit, they are desirous of proving by this address that they will ever cherish the memory of him who first taught them to understand the immortal works of the British poet.

At one of his last performances they brought him a laurel wreath with the same inscription, this time in Greek, and a special deputation was sent to express their gratitude for the boundless pleasure that he had given by his acting, revealing in Shakespeare new, hitherto unrevealed beauties. Aldridge received the deputation with outstretched arms. "Believe me, gentlemen," he said, "your gift will ever remain dear to my heart. Your ribbon, with the inscription, which is priceless to me, I shall preserve as a pledge of your love to me. Your bouquet of flowers will always remind me of these happy days, and I am under obligation to save for myself if but one petal of a flower that will fade; it will always remind me of the students of Kazan, so dear to my heart." And repeatedly he said, *"Wir sind alle Studenten."*[20]

And he kept his promise. Though all his valuable gifts and decorations have long since been sold, and his medals gone into the melting-pot, his presentation scrolls from the Russian actors and the students of Kazan have been preserved. For his students he not only played *Othello* and *Lear*, but also *Macbeth* and *Richard III*, which not even Petersburg had been able to see.

CHAPTER XVII

Family Life

IN the autumn of 1863 Aldridge applied for British citizenship. In a note to him dated merely "Hull, Monday", Sheahan said:

> I got my son last night to make a fair copy of my draft of the Memorial, and today I got four persons (myself included, Melbourne being out of the way) to sign it. You will have to go before any Solicitor in London, who is also a *Commissioner to Chancery* and make your declaration before him, then *seal* the letter and *take it to Whitehall yourself*. This course I am advised to tell you to take.
>
> I had to pay 12/- for taking the declarations here, and a couple of shillings for brandy to the witnesses. I have no more to say. I write in haste. Please send me the *Era* when you have done with it.

The other three witnesses were John Tessyman, John Symons, and Edward Short, all of Hull, who testified that they had known Aldridge not less than twenty-five years.

The document quoted below is one of the most conclusive in the matter of Aldridge's place and date of birth, and also clarifies to a degree some hitherto puzzling aspects of his personal life:

> The Memorial of Ira Frederick Aldridge to the Right Honorable Sir George Gray, Baronet, her Majesty's Principal Secretary of State, for the Home Department:
>
> Showeth that your Memorialist was born in the City of New York, United States of America; that he is the lawful son of the late Reverend Daniel Aldridge of that city, a man of colour; that he is 56 years of age, is a tragedian by profession and has long been known as the African Roscius; that he has resided in the United Kingdom of Great Britain and Ireland for 39 years, is married to an English lady, that he has no legitimate issue, that he now resides at Luranah Villa, Hamlet Road, Upper Norwood,

near London, and intends to reside there permanently; that being about to purchase some property in that neighbourhood, he has just been made acquainted with the necessity of seeking and obtaining the right and capacities of a natural born British subject to enable him to hold the said property and to bequeath it to his heirs; and that he most humbly and respectfully petitions that a certificate of naturalization be granted to him in pursuance of Statute 7 and 8 Victoria, cap. 66 entitled "An Act to amend the laws relating to aliens". And your Memorialist hereby declares that the statements contained in this memorial are all correct.

On 7th November 1863 Aldridge was granted British citizenship. This official document alone removes all doubt that Ira Aldridge was born in New York in 1807 and that he came to England in 1824. It further establishes that his son, Ira Daniel, and the children Luranah and Fred (Fritz), mentioned in his letter to Amanda, were not "legitimate issue". Obviously he had started a family with the young Swedish woman while Margaret was still living.

As has already been said, all efforts to establish Margaret's parentage have been fruitless, mainly because her maiden name was unknown to us. Aldridge's younger daughter, Amanda Ira (the "little stranger" of his letter from Semperkoff), told us that her father's first wife was the daughter of a London merchant, but beyond this, and the fact that "she made him work hard and was like a mother to him", and that "he was deeply grieved by her death", she knew nothing about her. The Census Report of 1861, when the family was living in Kentish Town (a district of London), gives Margaret's birthplace as Northallerton, Yorkshire, but does not give her maiden name. A careful examination of the parish records of all female infants born in Northallerton and christened "Margaret" in the appropriate period failed to trace her.

Margaret Aldridge died on 25th March 1864 in Luranah Villa at the age of sixty-six. The death certificate gave the cause of death as "asthma and general debility" and the "informant" as Ira Daniel Aldridge. The boy she had raised as her own and who called her "Mama" was at her bedside when she died. Whether Aldridge was in London at this time is not certain. He had spent the greater part of 1863 touring in Russia. In October and November of that year, when he applied for and received his British citizenship, he was in London, but in December he is already in St. Petersburg, and we find no further record of him until he attends the Actors' Shakespearean Supper in London in April 1864, so it cannot be stated whether or not he was present at his wife's funeral the previous month.

Just when and where Aldridge met the young Swedish woman who became his second wife we do not know. One would assume that it was in the summer of 1857, when he made his one and only visit to Stockholm, but Amanda Aldridge, while unable to give precise information on this point, said that they met somewhere on the Continent, "probably in Germany". She was emphatic that it was neither England nor Sweden. The first child of this union was a little girl born on 29th March 1860. Working backwards from that date, Aldridge was in England for the entire year 1859, and in 1858 we place him as follows:

January	. .	Saxe-Meiningen
July	. . .	London
August	. .	Brighton
September	. .	Prague
November	. .	Reval
December	. .	St. Petersburg

Aside from his visit to Stockholm in June 1857, we do not place him outside of England at any time during 1855, 1856, or 1857. During his extensive Continental tour of 1852-4 he was accompanied by Margaret and Ira Daniel. The likelihood, therefore, is that if they did in fact meet in Germany, it was in Saxe-Meiningen in January 1858.

All we know about Amanda Pauline von Brandt★ is that she was born in Sweden on 2nd March 1834, was left motherless at an early age, and after her father's remarriage left home and joined an operatic group. If 1858 was in fact the year of her meeting Aldridge, she was then twenty-four years old and he twenty-seven years her senior. It is significant that they waited a full year after Margaret's death before legalizing their union. The marriage took place on 20th April 1865 in the parish church of Penge, St. John the Evangelist, according to the rites and ceremonies of the Established Church, and was witnessed by J. J. Sheahan and his wife, Mary.

★ Amanda Aldridge gave her mother's name as "Paulina Ericksson Brandt".

According to the marriage certificate, Amanda was the daughter of Uloff von Brandt, a Baron of Sweden, but, according to information received from the Archivist of Stockholm, his name is not to be found in the printed genealogies of the nobility of Sweden or in the registers to wills and inventories, Census rolls, and church records in the city archives. The address of both bride and groom was given as Luranah Villa, which means that Amanda and the two children moved into the house soon after Margaret's death. Before that Aldridge had been maintaining two establishments, which accounts for his remarks to Amanda about the need to economize and his intention of selling his equipage.

Ira Daniel is now eighteen. How he takes the death of Margaret, his father's remarriage, and the sudden acquisition of a little sister and brother may be seen from two letters which he writes from Luranah Villa on the day of the marriage:

MY DEAR FATHER,—I write to congratulate you on the occasion of your marriage and to wish you and my dear stepmother every joy and happiness in your new relationship.

I am sure that you will find in Madame a true and loving wife, and one who will fill the lonely void so recently left in your home and your heart.

I shall use my best endeavour to continue to deserve your love and shall strive to the utmost of my power to win that of my stepmother by deference to her wishes and brotherly kindness to her children.

That you may be long spared to enjoy ever-increasing happiness is the most earnest wish of

Your dutiful and affectionate son,

IRA DANIEL ALDRIDGE.

The letter to his stepmother was neatly tied with blue silk ribbon:

MY DEAR MADAM,—It is with great pride and happiness that I feel now able to address you as Step-mother and I hope most sincerely that you may be long spared to us. I am sure that in you my father will possess a true and faithful wife, and that I myself shall be able to look upon you as a loving mother, worthy of replacing in my affection her whom I so recently lost.

As I have before assured you in conversation on the subject, I shall be very much grieved if you were to feel any apprehension respecting my conduct towards my brother and sister. I again desire you to be convinced that I shall love them as only a brother can love, and that nothing shall ever be wanting on my part which may tend to increase their welfare.

In conclusion I pray that God may bless and prosper you both, granting you many years of enduring happiness.

Such is the most earnest and heartfelt desire of your affectionate
Stepson,
IRA DANIEL ALDRIDGE.

When Aldridge died in August 1867 he left his widow with three small children—Luranah, seven, Ira Frederick, five, and Amanda (the first child to be born in Luranah Villa), seventeen months old. Four months later, on Boxing Day, another little girl was born. So we see that the two older children were born during Margaret's lifetime, but whether or not she knew about them we have no way of telling. At no time was there a separation between Aldridge and Margaret, although one may imagine that his feelings for the young and attractive Swedish woman were very different from his devotion to his first wife. More than two years after her death, on 24th July 1866, he writes in his diary: "My fifty-ninth birthday, in health, thank God, dream pleasantly of my Margaret." Nor is there any indication that the younger woman at any time tried to bring about a separation. Indeed, her regard for Margaret may be seen from the fact that the post-humous child was christened Rachael Margaret Frederika, and when this baby died of an intestinal disease shortly before her second birthday, she was laid in Margaret's grave in West Norwood Cemetery. So the childless Margaret had loved and raised her husband's first-born, and after death received in eternal rest his last-born.

Luranah, christened Irene Luranah Pauline, remembered her father, and used to relate how he would stand her at his knee and teach her little acts and songs, singing with her in his beautiful, deep voice to the accompaniment of the guitar. Both girls were sent to a convent school in Ghent, Belgium, Les Dames de l'Instruction Cretienne, a school for girls preparing to go into the professions. Luranah was there from the age of fifteen to nineteen, and Amanda from nine to eleven. Being one of the little girls, Amanda "played Cupid for the older girls in love". Luranah was

converted to Roman Catholicism, and Amanda might also have
adopted that faith, but her mother insisted she was not old
enough to know her own mind. Amanda recalled the great fête
at the convent: "all the front of it lit up with little lights. I rushed
out with pockets bulging with sweets. Luranah was very much
the saint, but I got all the sweets."

After Ghent, Luranah was sent to private schools in London,
Paris, and Berlin, and a good deal of the family money was spent
on her education. She developed into a beautiful and talented
woman possessing a glorious contralto voice which Charles
Gounod, after hearing her sing in Paris, described to Sir Augustus
Harris of Covent Garden as "the most beautiful voice I ever
heard". For many years she lived in Paris, where she was much
admired and sought after in the literary and musical circles in
which she moved. George Sand was one of her many friends.
When she participated in the Festival at Bayreuth in 1896, she
lived in Richard Wagner's home and became a close friend of his
daughter, Eva. She was a strong-willed, dominating and pleasure-
loving woman, and led a full, active, and gay life. She never
married. She appeared in most of the principal opera houses on
the Continent, and also gave concerts in England, France, and
Germany, always with favourable Press notices. The latest
programme in our possession is of a performance of *Hansel und
Gretel* at Covent Garden on 14th May 1901, in which she took
the part of the Witch.

In May 1890 Luranah travelled to Lodz to participate in a
concert in memory of her father, in which some of the most
prominent German and Polish artists took part. The concert was
a great success, and the proceeds were used to erect a tombstone
on her father's grave, which still stands, despite German occupation in both world wars.*

At the height of a successful career, and when she was enjoying
life to the fullest, Luranah became completely incapacitated and
spent almost twenty years in a wheel-chair, crippled with
rheumatism. She was bedridden when Roland Hayes, Lawrence
Brown, and Marian Anderson visited her in London. Although

* The same cannot be said of Shevchenko, for one of the first acts of
the Nazis on entering the Ukrainian town of Kanev during the Second
World War was to desecrate Shevchenko's tomb and to destroy his
memorial.

her suffering was "bravely borne", as her sister put it, the constant and severe pain endured for so many years without hope of cure or even relief, and the frustration of enforced withdrawal from a full and active life proved too much for her. In November 1932 the two sisters were living at 2 Bedford Gardens in Kensington. Their mother had died in that house on 18th February 1915 of acute bronchitis and heart failure at the age of eighty-one. Amanda was upstairs writing a letter when the daily woman who attended Luranah called up to her to come down quickly, as Luranah had been taken violently ill. When she came down, Luranah told her in French to call the doctor, that she had swallowed a bottleful of aspirin tablets. She was taken to the hospital in an ambulance, and died within an hour. She was buried in Gunnersbury Cemetery, just outside London, in the county of Middlesex. Thus, in 1932, Amanda was left entirely alone in the world, her brother Frederick having met a similarly tragic death many years before.

Ira Frederick Olaf Aldridge—Fred, as he was called—was born in 1862. When his parents made their final tours of the Continent in 1866 and 1867, this little boy was deposited in a boarding school in Paris. He was extremely unhappy there, and pleaded to be taken home, saying that he was mistreated by the other children, but the parents nevertheless left him there. Amanda was of the opinion that his extreme ill-health later on was the result of the hardships and mistreatment endured "as a little black boy", away from home and loved ones. One may wonder why the mother chose to accompany her husband on his tours when three small children, one a tiny infant, needed her care. The only explanation is that Aldridge himself was in failing health, and his wife must have been a comfort and help to him in his travels.

Fred, like his sisters, was highly gifted musically, and developed into an accomplished pianist, and later a composer. He was a pupil of Oscar Beringer, and at a student's concert received special commendation from Hans von Bülow. He accompanied Amanda at all her vocal recitals and was her "second self". He suffered from a serious heart and lung ailment and was advised not to live in the English climate. The circumstances of Fred's tragic death are summarized in a news item in the *Scarborough Gazette* of 2nd September 1886:

Shocking Death of a Musician at Scarborough

A very sad occurrence took place on Thursday evening last, resulting in what may be said to be the somewhat premature death of a young man named Frederick Ira Aldridge. The deceased was a professional musician of considerable ability. He visited Scarborough a few weeks ago in the capacity of orchestral conductor and pianist, with the "Manteaux Noirs" company, fulfilling an engagement at the Spa Theatre. Shortly afterwards he left the company above-named on the completion of their tour, and while at Sheffield he accepted an engagement to return to Scarborough as pianist at the Aquarium here. He had been a long time in a delicate state of health; and before he had been in Scarborough a fortnight, he was obliged to give up his duties through illness, and at once take to his bed. His symptoms were those of advanced consumption and an affection of the heart. He was attended by Dr. Cross from the 19th August, from which date he became much worse, and on Wednesday last it was thought he was rapidly sinking. Deceased's wife and mother were in attendance upon him, having been sent for on Thursday last. Dr. Cross was sent for, and he found the patient in a very feverish state, and occasionally delirious. Dr. Cross told Mrs. Aldridge that the deceased must not be left alone, as it was not improbable that he might at any time run out into the street or jump out of the window. In the early evening of the same day his wife and mother were sitting by him at the open window of his bedroom. He was gasping for breath; and suddenly, before the women could possibly restrain him, he groaned heavily, jumped from his seat and threw himself out of the window. He was taken up by some men in the street [James Street], and carried to his bedroom. Dr. Cross was immediately sent for and was promptly in attendance, arriving just in time to witness the man's death. An inquest of the circumstances was held by Robt. Collinson, Esq., Borough Coroner, at the Town Hall on Friday evening last, when the foregoing circumstances were deposed to in evidence by Mrs. Aldridge (deceased's wife), and Dr. Cross, the latter expressing the opinion that the immediate cause of death was concussion of the brain produced by the fall from the window taken by the deceased when in a state of febrile delirium. The verdict of the jury was in accordance with the medical opinion. Deceased was 25 years of age when he died. He was a "man of colour" and was, we are informed, the son of the late Mr. Ira Aldridge, whose dramatic talent caused him to be known as "The African Roscius". Very sad to say, the wife and mother of deceased are in almost destitute circumstances. Through the kindness of professional friends in Scarborough, a subscription was at once started for them, and it still remains open in charge of Mr. C. S. Clarke, Manager of the Aquarium. We understand that from the commencement of the poor man's illness, Lady Sitwell* has continued to manifest the kindest interest in this melancholy case.

At the inquest, the young woman who gave her name as Florence Aldridge testified: "The deceased was my husband. We have been married about two years. He was twenty-five years old when he died. He was delicate in constitution. He suffered from disease of the lungs from my first knowing him. A week ago yesterday I was telegraphed for at Huddersfield to come to Scarborough as my husband was ill. . . ." Searches in Huddersfield and advertisements in the Press have been unavailing in tracing this woman's identity. On a programme of *Les Cloches de Corneville*, an operetta which young Aldridge produced and conducted, we find a Florence Morton in the cast, and it is probable that she is the woman in question. A year after Fred's death, a song of his entitled "Luranah", the only composition which has come to light, was published by Novello, Ewer & Co. of London and New York, and was dedicated to "Florrie". Amanda Aldridge was quite certain that the couple were not married, and that there was no progeny. However, the attachment must have been a very deep one, and Florence, unable to recover from the shock and grief, took to drink. She called at the Aldridge home several times in such a state that she was finally refused admission.

Amanda attended the funeral, but Luranah was on the Continent and could not return in time. Because of the family's inability to purchase the grave space, Fred was buried in a multiple grave in the Dean Street Cemetery in Scarborough. Shortly before her death, Amanda expressed the hope that she would be able to "put up a nice stone on Fred's grave". This wish is about to be fulfilled through the kind efforts of Frederick O'Neal of New York, prominent Negro actor of stage and screen, who is arranging for a suitable monument to be placed on the grave. One of the main reasons for the family's financial straits was

* Grandmother of Dame Edith, Sir Osbert, and Sir Sacheverell Sitwell.

that the widow "had no head for business", as Amanda put it. Aldridge had left a certain amount of property, and the builder and solicitor took advantage of the widow's inexperience in these matters, with the result that she lost everything, but not before the medals and decorations which she had offered as security in meeting a mortgage payment had been, without her knowledge, melted down for the gold.

The story of Ira Daniel, the first-born son of whom Ira Aldridge had been so proud, is also a sad one. We have already seen the letters he wrote to his father and stepmother on their marriage in April 1865. Between that date and his emigration to Australia almost two years later, he lived with the family in Luranah Villa. He had received a good education and gave promise of developing into a fine man. He was interested in the theatre, and a letter from N. W. Hill in the October 1919 issue of *Notes and Queries* says: ". . . I do not know what became of the older son, though I can recall his acting very effectively in an amateur representation of *Box and Cox*." A change seemed to have come over the boy almost immediately after Margaret's death and after the young Swedish woman and the two children moved into Luranah Villa. He became wild, pleasure-loving, and irresponsible and, with his father being away most of the time, his stepmother, who was only about thirteen years his senior, could not manage him, and in February 1867 he left England for Australia. During the entire month of February Ira Aldridge was on a tour of the Continent—Geneva, Chalon, Dole, Dijon—and there is no way of knowing whether he knew when the boy left, but on 9th May he makes an entry in his diary: "Arrived Boulogne, very hoarse indeed. . . . Melancholy reflection respecting my poor Ira. He left for Melbourne this day eleven weeks." The last record we have of Ira Daniel is the following pathetic letter which he wrote to his stepmother from Melbourne on 24th October 1867:

MA CHERE MADAME,—I scarcely know how to commence my letter. To say that I am deeply grieved is not sufficient. I can hardly believe that it is true my dear, dear father is no more. Oh Madame! I have indeed a great deal to blame myself with, for I feel I have not acted as I ought to have done towards so good a parent.

Now truly I lament it now it is too late. I hope he forgave me for all the uneasiness and trouble that I caused him. I have never received a line from him or you since I left England for here. My father promised me that he would write; perhaps he was too ill. Was it so? How is it, my Dear Madame, that neither Mr. King or anyone did not write and let me know of my Dear Father's death. I should have been ignorant of it had it not been for the newspapers.

Now Madame, what I am about to say, believe me, comes from my heart. I have deeply wronged you and have always taken your good advice as hatred towards me, in fact, I did not understand the full meaning of your kindness. Mind, my Dear Stepmother, I am not asking you to call me back to England, far from it; but if you think that I could be of any service whatsoever to you or the Poor Children, say so, and if I do not get the money to return I will work my passage over. I can assure you I am quite altered and with God's assistance will never go wrong again. I have not been at all fortunate since I have been here for I was doing nothing for eleven weeks and now have only obtained a situation as money taker at the Haymarket Theatre at one Pound a week. I am indeed very thankful for even this. I hope soon to get something better.

How are you, my Dear Madame, and how is Luranah, Fred and the Baby? Please kiss them for me and tell them not to forget that they have a Brother who often thinks of them and who will also be their protector. Will you write to me? Yes, I am sure you will. I do not know where you are at present, therefore send this to Mr. King's care. Let me know all respecting my dear Father, did he leave me any particular message or not? If He did, I will do his bidding and shall feel happy to think that I have strictly obeyed his commands once. Was he long ill? Did he suffer much; I see by the papers that you, my Dear Step-mother attended him the whole time. I am glad that you were with him. I had no idea that he was going to Russia again as I also saw in the papers that he was going to visit America shortly. I know what a fearful blow this must be to you, but I think, my Dear Madame, it is a debt one must all pay sooner or later. Do you intend remaining at Norwood or going to France? If you have any pity for me, Madame, I am certain you will write, and let me know your whereabouts.

I really cannot understand why I have never had a letter from someone to tell me of my Dear Father's death. Why, I cannot tell. I see it occurred on the 7th of August at Lodz in Poland. Well, the Mail did not leave England for here until the 26th, surely there was sufficient time to write. I hope though next mail will bring me some news. I have though begun to despair for so many mails have already arrived, with no news for me. I have not much to write except, my Dear Madame, to condole and sympathize with you in your and my heavy loss, for indeed a better or kinder Father I know never existed. Try and bear up in this indeed great trial, and think if possible that you have a Stepson who although he may have wronged you is truly penitent and will ever as long as he lives do his best to atone for the injury he has already done you.

In conclusion, I again ask you to write me, pray do not keep me in suspense, and if you only say that would like me to return I will do so instantly. So God bless you, my Dear Madame, and the Children whom you, I pray, kiss for me. I cannot scarcely realize that the past is all true. Would to Heaven it were not. Good-bye, my Dear Stepmother, and believe me,

Ever your affectionate Stepson,

IRA D. ALDRIDGE.

The sad truth is that the stepmother did not ask him to return. She had been advised against it by friends, and in later life regretted this decision. Advertisements in the Melbourne Press and extensive searches by the Government Statist of Melbourne have not yielded any information about him. However, efforts are still being made to find out whether he ever married and, if so, whether there were any offspring. Ira Daniel offers the only hope and possibility that this family is not entirely extinct.

And now we come to Amanda, the only child with whom personal contact was possible during the preparation of this book.

Amanda Christina Elizabeth Aldridge was born on 10th March 1866 in Luranah Villa. Like Luranah and Fred, she showed great musical promise from early childhood. The mother raised all the children in a musical atmosphere and did everything possible to foster their talent. They attended most of the musical performances at the Crystal Palace, which was close by, and at fifteen Amanda made an appearance there, singing Handel's Creations Hymn and a ballad, with Sir August Mann conducting the orchestra.

Amanda played the piano "from the time my fingers could reach the keyboard", and, she reminisced, "At a concert in the convent school at Ghent I played the piano with another girl. I was only playing the accompaniment, but I was much more powerful, so they changed over and made her play the tenor. I was much younger than she was, but I made the most noise." She said that she owed her good diction to one of the teachers at this school, all of whom were of very high calibre. The most unforgettable years of her life were those spent as a student of Jenny Lind. On 20th April 1883, just turned seventeen, she found herself at the Albert Hall, nervously singing Beethoven's *"Die Ehre Gottes aus der Natur"* (which has been used as a hymn) before the Board of Examiners of the Royal College of Music, competing for a Foundation Scholarship. She won, and became one of nine pupils to study solo-singing under the supervision of that immortal artist. Her second study at the College was the piano. To her very last days she expressed great pride in being the only pupil for whom Jenny Lind ever wrote a testimonial of her musical gifts, and being recommended as a master of singing. After Miss Lind's retirement, she was placed under the tutelage of Sir George Henschel, and studied harmony and counterpoint with Sir Frederick Bridge and Dr. F. E. Gladstone. And then she had the further good fortune of studying with Dame Madge Kendal, who later wrote in her autobiography: "Madame Jenny Lind did me the honour to ask me to teach her pupils how to speak. When I called the first roll I found the name of Miss Aldridge at the top of the list. She told me that she was the daughter of the gentleman with whom I had played Desdemona at the Haymarket and naturally I at once took the greatest interest in her."

For many years Amanda was very successful on the concert platform as a contralto. In June 1905, after one of her recitals at Steinway Hall, the London *Times* wrote: "Miss Ira Aldridge held the attention of a large audience on Saturday afternoon. . . . So good an effect as that achieved by Miss Aldridge in Dvorak's gipsy songs calls for the exercise of a great deal of art. . . . Miss Aldridge's style is excellent, her voice warm and mellow, and her intelligence far beyond dispute; the combination may well serve to explain the measure of her success." When her public career was cut short by a severe attack of laryngitis, which permanently affected her voice, she remembered that Jenny Lind had once said, "Never mind what happens to your throat, Amanda. You can always earn a livelihood as a singing teacher, because you have a good insight into voice theory and practice," and turned to the teaching of voice-production and diction. Among her pupils have been some of the most distinguished professional singers, Marian Anderson, Paul Robeson, and Roland Hayes among them, and in more recent years the very popular and talented Muriel Smith and Ida Shepley.

Amanda was in her thirties when she first began to compose, and adopted the name "Montague Ring" to separate her work as composer from that of singer and instructor. She always "thought musically", and her mother encouraged her to write down the melodious phrases that she was always humming or playing. Many dozens of her piano and vocal compositions have been published, perhaps the most widely known being her *Three African Dances* and *Four Moorish Pictures*, which are played all over the world and have been recorded, broadcast, and used as incidental film music.

She had a very strong sense of duty and loyalty to her mother and sister, both of whom she dearly loved and cared for in their ill-health, to the sacrifice of her own personal happiness. She never married. "But don't you get the impression, young man," she said to Edward Scobie, "that Cupid stayed away from my door. On the contrary, it was at Steinway Hall that a young Jamaican doctor came into my life. A group of Negro singers from America were out front, and after the concert Mr. Plowden, their Manager, brought them to my dressing-room. In the company was Dr. David Phillips, a surgeon who had recently completed his studies at a London hospital and was returning to the West Indies. We fell in love and would have been married, but added to my work I had my mother and bedridden sister Luranah to care for."* Dr. Phillips did not marry either, and they corresponded regularly until his death in 1937, at which time he was Chief Medical Officer of Kingston.

Some idea of Amanda's personality and activities may be had from the following two letters she wrote to Mrs. Marguerite Downing in America, the first written from Henley-on-Thames on 19th March 1944, and the second from Chiswick in August 1945:

... I am just fairly well, frequent fits of depression which I try to ward off and I hope that with the coming spring good weather I

* Article in *Chicago Defender*, 8th March 1952.

will be my old self again. Yes—"old"—78 a few days ago. I tried
not to cry on that day because superstition has it that if you cry on
your birthday it is not good. All the same, I *did* drop one or two—
but nowadays, when so many are lonely, it is not unusual. I still
enjoy a hearty good laugh and only wish we could have one
together. . . . Friends tell me that they heard on the radio (from
New York) a long and appreciative talk on my father. I wonder if
you heard it. I have received press clippings from U.S.A., papers
with articles and portraits from various people (Clarence White,
Lawrence Brown and others). I go to London quite often to give
lessons at Weeks Studios in Hanover Square. I have two specially
good singers; Ida Shepley is one. She often broadcasts. She is
coloured, a little darker than me. Such a lovely voice, contralto,
and so intelligent and very good-looking. The other is English,
high soprano, also very intelligent, but has not yet made her
début. . . .

MY DEAREST LITTLE LADY!—Behold my new address! Yes, I'm
back in London—and oh! So glad. One of my pupils, my very
dear Ida Shepley, and her husband have bought this home and
offered me the top flat—(at a rental that I can afford). I moved in
on Friday and am very happy and comfortable. All my own old
furniture and belongings around me. And as you know, the
neighbourhood is very healthy and within easy bus ride from
Oxford Circus and other centres. The journey by train three and
four times a week from Henley and back was most tiring and I
hardly think I could have gone through another winter. So when
I was offered this flat I accepted promptly and thankfully.

All around—this area has been terribly bombed, but fortunately
this home escaped with shattered windows and a certain amount of
damage which has all been repaired—and so I hope Providence
will be kind and let me live to enjoy this peace. I still give some
lessons in Hanover Street studios besides having the use of the
drawing room here—where my grand piano is (I have Ida's small
piano up here in my flat).

And now, my dearest friend, I trust that you are getting
stronger and that your hand has quite recovered. I would have
written more often these last years but I was not often in the
mood—Henley depressed me. I daresay it was the effects of never
having the *sun* in my (top) room! Many people were charming
and friendly but *very few* had any music in them. So no wonder
I am rejoicing at being in town again and in an artistic atmosphere.

I met, by accident, Coleridge Taylor's daughter. She recognized me. I would not have known her after so many years. She told me that her composition—a symphony—was to be played, under her conductorship, at Bournemouth. She was very charming and good-looking. I inquired after her mother and brother—both well. When I introduced my pupil, Ida Shepley, she expressed her great pleasure, for she had heard Ida sing one of her father's songs on the wireless, only a week or so ago and had written to Stanford Robinson (the conductor) asking him to thank her (Ida) for her beautiful rendering.

Ida Shepley is in private life Mrs. Charles Skilbeck Smith. Her husband is English. I hear from dear kind Mrs. Caseley Hayford* at intervals. In her last letter she told me that Dr. Easmon and his wife (at one time a pupil of mine) are coming to London. I hope they will come to see me. Ida Shepley is partly West African and on her mother's side Canadian (white).

I must stop now. I hope I have not bored you, but it is so peaceful here, although the weather might be better! It is *pouring* with rain.

I hope, dearest, that you are comfortably settled with sympathetic neighbours and that your health is much improved. My fond love and I pray God's blessing on you. Many thanks for the paper with pictures of the beloved President.

Yours affectionately,
AMANDA IRA ALDRIDGE.

PS.—I am not far from Gunnersbury where you used to live. Also the cemetery where Luranah is buried.

Miss Aldridge spoke with love and tenderness about her American students and hoped she would see some of them again. Although she was almost ninety, and occasionally lapsed into vagueness, she knew about Paul Robeson's difficulties relating to his passport, referring to it as "hellish" and "shocking", and then added comfortingly: "It will take a little while yet before things get as they should be in your country."

Amanda died on 9th March 1956, one day before her ninetieth birthday.

It is sad to reflect how this family, so loving and united in life, were scattered in death. Ira Aldridge lies in Lodz, Poland. Margaret and the posthumous baby lie together in West Norwood Cemetery. The ashes of the second wife were strewn by her

* A friend in Sierra Leone.

younger daughter in Highgate Woods. Luranah lies in Gunnersbury Cemetery, Frederick in a multiple grave in Scarborough,
and Amanda in Streatham. Only Ira Daniel is unaccounted for.

★   ★   ★

Since the above was written, some of the long-sought information about Ira Daniel and Margaret Aldridge has come to hand.
We now have a certificate showing that on 10th January 1868,
scarcely three months after writing the pathetic letter to his stepmother, to which he received no answer, Ira Daniel Aldridge,
bachelor, tutor, of Lillydale, and Ellen Huxley, spinster, seam-
stress, of Lillydale, were married at the Registrar's Office, Fitzroy,
County of Bourke, Colony of Victoria. They each recorded their
birthplace as London.★ Ellen gave her age as twenty-two, and
Ira Daniel gallantly gave his as twenty-three, though he had not
yet reached his twenty-first birthday. Ellen's parents were Francis
Huxley, carpenter, and Harriet Huxley, maiden name Bedford.
Ira Daniel's parents were Ira Frederick Aldridge, actor, and
Margaret Aldridge, maiden name Gill. Thus, for the very first
time, do we learn Margaret's surname! !

Their first child, a little girl christened Margaret, was born on
20th January 1869. By the time the second child, Ira Frederick
Francis, was born on 12th March the following year, the
first baby had died. The third child, James Ira, born 27th July
1872, also died in infancy, and John Edward, the fourth and last
child (according to the birth certificates in our possession), was
born 27th July 1875. At this time Ira Daniel records his age as
twenty-seven, and his occupation as "teacher of languages". All
the children were born in Melbourne. Ira Frederick Francis died
at the age of twenty-four in a way curiously reminiscent of the
death of Ira Frederick Olaff in Scarborough eight years earlier. He
died on his way to the hospital in Melbourne, and according to
the *post mortem*, the cause was "pulmonary haemorrhage—ulcera-
tion of the right bronchus". He was married, but particulars
were not known, nor was anything known of his parents at the
time his death was registered.

We have not been able to obtain a death certificate for Ira
Daniel, which rather suggests that he left Australia, but efforts

★ On the second child's birth certificate Ellen's birthplace is given as Melbourne, and on the third and fourth children's as Sydney, New South Wales.

are still in progress to find out what happened to him. The only possibility, therefore, of any direct living descendant of Ira Aldridge, is John Edward Aldridge, born eighty-three years ago, or his offspring.

With the knowledge, at last, of Margaret's surname, it was possible to trace her origin. From information given by Margaret herself in a Census report, we knew that she was born in North-allerton, Yorkshire, and from her death certificate we knew her age. C. K. Croft Andrew, the County Archivist of Yorkshire, was kind enough to make a personal search in the parish records, and we now have a copy of the entry in the Baptismal Register of the Parish Church of Northallerton showing the birth of Margaret Gill on 17th December 1797, daughter of William Gill, stocking-weaver, and Ann Richardson Gill. It can, therefore, now be stated on the most reliable documentary evidence that Margaret Gill Aldridge was not "the natural daughter of a Member of Parliament from Berks", as the story goes.

This new light on Margaret's origin raises some very interesting questions which, regrettably, cannot be dealt with in the confines of this first biography, but must be left to future researchers and writers who may wish to go into these aspects of the Aldridge story. While there was a strong Abolitionist movement in England in that period, interracial marriages were rare. Interest-ingly, Mr. Andrew informed us that such a marriage took place in March 1795 between "John Thomas a Negro from the Coast of Africa but now resident in this Parish & township of Northaller-ton, batchelor (having been lately baptized) and Jane Cunningham of the township of Helperby but now resident in this town-ship, spinster". What was the public sentiment toward such marriages in those years? How did Margaret's parents feel about hers?

What were the educational opportunities for a child of a stocking-weaver, especially a female child, in northern England in the beginning of the last century? When and in what circum-stances did Margaret leave Northallerton for London, and how did she find her way into the circles where she could meet the young actor, already somewhat of a celebrity? Dr. James McCune Smith, who met her in Liverpool in 1832, described her as "an intelligent lady of fine accomplishments and great conversa-tional talent". From other accounts throughout the years, from entries in Aldridge's diaries and from correspondence with contemporaries, it would appear that she was a woman of education, culture, and ability. She accompanied her husband on his first Continental tour, lasting three years, dealing with "the rascals in the box-office", and handling most of his other business.

As we know, in 1847, after twenty-two years of marriage, her husband had a son by another woman. This child she brought up as her own. In 1860 her husband started a family with the Swedish woman whom he later married, and this, too, she apparently accepted with dignity and understanding. What was there in Margaret Gill's background that prepared her so well for the strange life in store for her? Perhaps one day we shall know.

CHAPTER XVIII

The Last Years

THE last few years of Aldridge's life were spent mainly in tours of Russia and the Continent, with occasional visits back to England. On 22nd April 1864 he at last receives public recognition and honour from fellow-actors in London—not of the kind he had for so long been receiving from his Continental colleagues, but recognition nevertheless. This was at a function held at the Freeman's Tavern on the Tercentenary of Shakespeare's birth. Tallis's *Illustrated Life in London* commented:

> Mr. Ira Aldridge, who has lately returned from Russia, is now in England, but is on the point of starting again for that Empire. He was present at the Actors' Supper given in celebration of the Tercentenary of Shakespeare's birth; and it is, perhaps, some consolation that this exponent of the great bard, who has been so much honoured in every country but Shakespeare's own country —his presence on the English stage being, by the immutibility of the canons governing things theatrical just now, it seems, out of the question—was thus enabled to participate in the festival to the honour of him he has done so much to make popular.

G. V. Brooke proposed the toast "To the British Drama"; J. V. Buckstone responded to it and proposed "The health of Mr. Ira Aldridge", who briefly responded and proposed the health of the Chairman. It is interesting to note that the really great luminaries of the day were not in attendance, but whether by design or accident we do not know.

Buckstone, Aldridge's old friend and professional colleague from his very first Coburg days, was now Manager of the Haymarket Theatre, and a year after the Shakespearean Supper he invites Aldridge to appear at the Haymarket. So, in the summer of 1865, thirty-two years after Covent Garden, seven years after the Lyceum, he achieves an engagement at the Haymarket and is again in the West End.

Buckstone, a prolific writer as well as a first-class comedian, took over the management of the Haymarket in 1853, and it was he who introduced the then unknown dramatist, T. W. Robertson, whose later plays were the forerunners of the modern drawing-room drama. It was Robertson's young sister, Madge Robertson (later Dame Madge Kendal), who was Aldridge's Desdemona at the Haymarket. Aldridge was now fifty-eight, with a background of forty years of uninterrupted work as actor and producer, and Madge Robertson was seventeen, probably the youngest actress ever to play the role, yet she already had thirteen years' stage experience, having made her début at the Marylebone Theatre at four! She made her first adult appearance in London as Ophelia to Walter Montgomery's Hamlet at the Haymarket on 29th July. He did not please the public, but the young, handsome, and appealing Miss Robertson did. Three weeks later came Aldridge's Othello.

The Press as a whole was favourable, the *Athenaeum*, which had been so appalled in 1833 by Henry Wallack's black servant pawing Ellen Tree, now saying:

Mr. Ira Aldridge was reluctantly accepted at the West-End. In Russia and the Continent Mr. Aldridge has been more successful. He plays with feeling, intelligence, and finish. We were glad that he was well received on Monday, and that his merits were acknowledged by a numerous audience. We may claim this black, thick-lipped player as one proof among many that the Negro intellect is human, and demands respect as such. The tragedy was remarkably well performed. . . . Madge Robertson an excellent Desdemona. . . . Altogether we have seldom witnessed a representation of this great tragedy which pleases us more.

The *Illustrated Times* wrote:

Despite the weather, despite the absence from town of everybody—except policemen, actors, loungers, and other unfortunates compelled to remain in it—despite the quantity of Shakespeare the British Public has witnessed during the past theatrical season, the Haymarket Theatre has been well filled every night since

Mr. Walter Montgomery opened it for the production of accepted legitimate drama only. . . .

Mr. Aldridge plays Othello with great care and conscientiousness. His whole performance is intelligent and energetic; he attempts no new readings, but treads in the beaten path, marked out for all Othellos since days of Edmund Kean. The same remark applies to Mr. Montgomery's Iago. Miss Madge Robertson was a most graceful, interesting and pathetic Desdemona.

On the other hand, *Bell's Messenger* said, ". . . And, as most of Othello's action was novel, the temptation scene had an air of originality. Miss Madge Robertson excelled as Desdemona and had to undergo some new business in the bed-scene which added to her murder some incidents that were extremely striking." The publication had prefaced these remarks by saying: "Now Mr. Aldridge, though a Negro, is a good actor, but with one exception has not hitherto been able to achieve an appearance at the West End. It may indicate a decay of the prejudice against colour that he was received by the audience with applause and that this performance was a legitimate success."

In her memoirs, Mrs. Kendal describes some of these "striking" incidents:

Mr. Ira Aldridge was a man who, being black, always picked out the fairest woman he could to play Desdemona with him, not because she was capable of acting but because she had a fair head. One of the great bits of "business" that he used to do was where, in one of the scenes he had to say, "Your hand, Desdemona," he made a very great point of opening his hand and making you place yours in it, and the audience used to see the contrast. He always made a point of it and got a round of applause, how I do not know. It always struck me that he had some species of—well, I will not say genius, because I dislike that word as used nowadays—but gleams of real intelligence. Although a genuine black, he was quite *preux chevalier* in his manners to women. The fairer you were the more obsequious he was to you. In the last act he used to take Desdemona out of the bed by her hair and drag her around the stage before he smothered her. I remember very distinctly this dragging Desdemona about by the hair was considered so brutal that he was loudly hissed.

It appears that in the smothering scene he made Miss Robertson wear stockings with painted toes, so that she would appear to be really undressed when he dragged her around! So much for the *Illustrated Times's* statement that Aldridge trod the beaten path in his treatment of Othello.

With her performance of Ophelia and Desdemona this season, it may be said that Madge Robertson began her long and successful career. For Aldridge it was his last performance in London but it was, at last, in a theatre royal and in the West End.

★   ★   ★

Throughout the years there are references to Aldridge's ill-health, and the "*Ich bin sehr Krank*" in his letter of 20th April 1855 indicates serious illness, but nowhere is there any clue as to the nature of the ailment. At no time does he curtail his activities; on the contrary, they are considerably increased. In the winter following his Haymarket appearance he is once more in Russia, certainly the very worst time for touring, but, though he suffered physical hardships unknown to the modern actor, he was free from many of the annoyances of present-day travel—passports, visas, currency restrictions, screening, red tape, and so on.

The last two years are probably the most crowded of his life. Even in these days of air travel, most actors would hesitate to cover the territory that he did. And all this time his responsibilities are growing. His money is invested in property which he cannot look after personally, so this and other matters are turned over to an agent Mr. Ray, who sends him the following report in the autumn of 1865:

HON'D. SIR,—I trust before this reaches you, you will have received a letter from me, for not knowing your address I wrote to the Bankers at Moscow and therefore have good reason to suppose it has preceded you—the principal contents relate to my having received the rents of Mount Pleasant House and Odessa House and having paid with the proceeds Messrs. Cramer's account for the piano at the Baroness's request. . . . Also paid to Mr. Staiger one year's ground rents for the Lees and Ashley House and Mr. Woodward's bill. . . . I am very sorry to have to inform you that we have suffered this week from an unusually severe gale which has done much damage in the country generally, also in London and the southern suburbs more particularly—a quantity of slates blew off at Luranah Villa, Odessa House and Mount Pleasant House—the others escaped damage, all were very much shaken by the wind—the houses in the wood received the fierce onslaught of the Gale—it blowing from the south-west. . . .

The Baroness . . . requests me to say all is well at Luranah Villa in case her letter miscarries. I called on Mr. Grist and have furnished him with two envelopes bearing your Moscow address. He promised to write to you this day and report fully about Master Ira.

In Odessa he was most cordially received and entertained by local society and by members of the diplomatic corps. E. C. Grenville Murray, the British Consul-General in Odessa, wrote him the following letter:

> *Dannenberg House, Odessa.*
> *Feb. 2, 1866.*
>
> DEAR MR. ALDRIDGE,—I called yesterday to congratulate you on your beautiful performance of Shylock. I like Othello better my-self as a play; but your reading of the character of the semi-Oriental Jew of the middle ages was a masterpiece of art. Some of the language of the part, however displeasing it may be to the prosperous Jews of our time, masters as they are of the secrets and councils of the world, must have required no common courage and large-heartedness to write in the time of Shakespeare.
>
> I should have liked to have seen you to talk about it, and am sorry you were out. Pray let me know when you will breakfast with me, though I hardly dare ask you out of town during this unfavourable weather.
>
> With the most sincere congratulations on your great success here, and unfeigned personal admiration, believe me to remain,
> Yours very faithfully,
> E. C. GRENVILLE MURRAY.

So, while the oppressed Jewish communities of Russia were grateful to Aldridge for his presentation of Shylock as a human being and not as a monster, the local British Consul-General, natural son of the second Duke of Buckingham and Chandos, attributes his own anti-Semitic sentiments to Shakespeare.

The local American Consul, however, is interested in Aldridge's head from the phrenological point of view! A cutting, undated and unidentified except for the heading "Our Annual" (seen in the Theatre Collection of the New York Public Library), is of interest, and the first sentence amusing:

Perhaps his best role is Othello, whom he is said by our Consul in Odessa to resemble much in character and demeanour.

The head of this eminent coloured man is very much larger than the average size for a white man which, as is generally known, is above the Negro type of head. According to the measurements sent us by the American Consul at Odessa, this is about 23 and a half inches in circumference. Referring to our portrait, we find the indications of an excellent combination of the organs, a fair balance of the intellectual faculties. The Knowing organs are predominant, Individuality, Eventuality, Language, Form, Locality and Time are large, and give his mind the tendency to inquire, examine, observe, and hold in memory tenaciously whatever he deems worthy of attention. The high forehead denotes a sympathetic nature and considerable ability to read character. Large Nature and very large Imitation qualify him to enter into the spirit of dramatic impersonation and assume with unusual facility the various phases of human character as he understands them. He has also much force, resolution and positiveness; more fire and pluck than is a dispositional characteristic of his race. The width between the ears exhibits a large degree of Destructiveness, while the facial indications of Combativeness show a good degree of it. His social nature is strong, evincing warmth of affection for friends, children and home. His interest in women is far from weak. In fact, we are led to believe that he excels most in those plays which represent life as associated with the domestic circle, or wherein earnestness of affection and vigour of action should characterize the performance. He evidently possesses large approbativeness; but his secretiveness and caution being also strongly marked, render him prudent, careful, and shrewd in the prosecution of whatever ambitious designs he may cherish. Commendation—the applause of the world—is acceptable to him, but he would court public sentiment in such a manner as not to manifest any special desire or appetite for it. He picks up information rapidly in his association with the world, and has much facility in adapting what he learns to his needs and purposes. He does not go through the world blindfold, but keeps his eyes and ears open, gathering much from experience that is profitable. He has good recuperative powers, an ample chest, free circulation, and excellent digestion, consequently his large brain is well nourished and sustained. The Negro is physiognomically striking and evidences the directness of his origin. His superior talents furnish strong testimonial in favour of those who advocate Negro equality, but unfortunately his, like that of Fred Douglass, is an isolated case and proves only rare possibilities or outcroppings from the common stock. Morally considered, Mr. Aldridge possesses a very happy organization, such as is desirable in the case of anyone, white or black.

On 3rd February he writes to his wife from Odessa, sending £20 in £5 Bank of England notes, saying: "I have been most enthusiastically received by four houses at double prices. I acted Macbeth last night with great success. I sent a box containing a splendid Timepiece and two branches." And now we have a few more extracts from his diary:

15th March (*1866*): Telegram, Herman from Constantinople. I leave against my inclination Saturday, pray God send me a safe and good passage.

16th March: Borrowed 200 silver roubles from S. Horowitz. Expect to leave tomorrow for Constantinople. Saw Schultz. Things not yet arrived. Called at Roffalavitch, Doctor Smith. Rain, Rain. Robinson called.

17th March: Write to Amanda, Ray and Ropere, sending invoices for goods, clock, etc., this afternoon. Sail, God permitting, for Constantinople. Sailed at 4 o'clock this afternoon on board the *Grand Duke Michael*, a beautiful vessel built by Mitchell & Co., Newcastle on Tyne. Two principal cabin passengers besides myself, lady and gent. Weather very mild in Black Sea. God preserve us. Weather still beautiful. Met rich man, a Tartar, killing vermin on his person. Disgusted with sight of it—he not ashamed.

19th March: Arrived at Constantinople (Pera) at 9 a.m. after an excellent passage, lodging at Mesara's Hotel, D'Angleterre, 24 frcs. daily including lodging and eating for self and Hermann. Mr. Carlton called, dined at *table d'hôte*.

20th March: Visited Mr. Morris the American Minister who received me very kindly, also U.S. Consul-General, John Holmes Goodenow, U.S. Vice-Consul Alex Thompson, David H. P. Brown, Dragoman, and John B. Brown, Secretary of Legation, Lord Lyons, British Minister, Mr. McCone, editor of *Levant Herald*, Editor of *La Turque*, L'Etoile, D'Orient, Miss Walsh, Mr. Guaraccino, British Vice-Consul and Mr. Loggie, Judge and Consul-General, visited the British Consular Court.

21st March: First rehearsal of Othello, with the French Artistes, went very well; visited the director (an American). Monsieur

Managre, Monsieur Rolland, an Irishman but a regular French-man whose name is Prendergast, all very friendly.

From Constantinople he writes to his wife:

MY DEAR AMANDA,—I arrived here on Monday morning nine o'clock. I am acting for the first time on Monday and Othello for the first time with the French. After I have finished here I am going back to Russia, where I am only acting three or four times. I have to commence my engagement at Easter. I hope you are over your trouble.* I should be so glad to see you if it were possible, but I must wait patiently.

I hope the boxes will arrive safe and also that the four bank-notes may come to hand. Tell Ira I have received Mr. Grist's letter and am satisfied with it. I wrote in a former letter to you respecting his clothes and anything he may require.

I am very busy at present but will write by the next mail. This is a curious place, all nationalities are represented. The Turkish women go veiled or wrapped up about the head, the eyes only supposed to be visible. It is dangerous to go out at night for there is robbery attended with murder very often, so I keep to my hotel.

Kiss the children for me. I will write a longer letter by the next mail, and believe me,

Your own affectionate
IRA.

PS.—Write to Poste Restante, Odessa. The weather here is quite warm, and the fruit trees are all in blossom.

If the Europe that Aldridge travelled through was a land of ferment following the 1848 revolutions and the liberation of the serfs in Russia, Turkey was by far the most backward land in which he had set foot. It had never been visited by an English theatre company, although there was considerable goodwill between both countries, especially after England had entered the Crimean War on the side of Turkey against Russia. Ira Aldridge was the first actor to present Shakespeare in English in the capital of the Ottomans, though the rest of the cast spoke French!

He presented *Othello*, the *Merchant of Venice*, and *Macbeth*, and his leading lady was Mlle. Desterbecq, a very competent French actress. No write-ups of his Turkish tour are to be found, but,

* Their second daughter, Amanda, was born on 10th March.

317

oddly enough, *Our Annual*, the same unidentified cutting that gave the phrenological report, said, *inter alia*: "In the Ottoman capital theatrical celebrities rarely appeared. Ristori,* who was there some time since, was considered to have made the greatest hit, but it fell very short of Ira Aldridge's success, as was attested by the crowded houses that witnessed his performances up to the last. This was a striking appreciation of the force of his genius from a very mixed population such, in fact, as is only to be met with in the city of the Sultan." The last photographs we have of him were taken in Constantinople. It was here that he first played with a French company, and this may have led him to the theatrical circles through which he finally arranged to go to Paris, the only capital of Europe where he had not yet played.

In July he is back in Kiev, and we have a few more diary entries:

5th July (1866): Bathed this morning as usual. Met one of the proprietors of the Château des Fleurs who invited me to dinner but I declined, preferring to dine quietly at a restaurant. Visit from a Jewish student requesting me to undertake an enquiry in England respecting property. Went with Mr. Rees to visit Miss Ainsworth, after to the Château des Fleurs, met the one-legged dancer Donati. Heard of Churbinoff.

6th July: Bathed this morning as usual. Letters from Sachse with engagements for Hermanstadt, one from Garpinchenko. Heat dreadfully oppressive, dangerous to go in the sun. Letters from my dear Luranah and Fred, also from Mr. Ray telling me of the successful let of Astrakhan House to a Mr. Hugh Fraser for £110 yearly.

7th July: Bathed this morning at 6 o'clock, drank at the shrine of the Sainted Prince Vladimir, the first Sovereign Christian Prince in Russia. He was baptized in the river Dnieper. Koch called, rehearsed Lear and after lunched at Madame Melcosky. Wrote to Luranah and Fred, also to Sachse and Garpinchenko. Acted Lear to a very brilliant house and great applause.

8th July: Bathed this morning and drank of the holy well water.

9th July: Bathed this morning, water better after the rain. Wrote Achembach and Colley, Moscow. Dined yesterday Château des Fleurs. Wrote to Missorie respecting Abdullah, also Achembach Moscow. Raining heavily. Rehearsed Macbeth, rain affects the

* Adelaide Ristori (1822-1906), Italian actress of tragic parts, played extensively throughout Europe, England, and the United States, rivalling Rachel.

sale of tickets. Acted Macbeth notwithstanding the inclement weather. The house very good indeed. I did not act with my accustomed spirit though the public were very much pleased and applauded loud and frequent.

10th July: Bathed this morning, water fresh and agreeable. Sent through Horowitz of Odessa 1,200 roubles to Mr. Bone and cheque for £90 to Mr. Ray to meet payments, my life insurance, piano, etc. Wrote also to Lyon, Horowitz, Bone, Ray, Benot, at the Governor's Rasia York, photographers, dined with M. Leclerc, Madame fond of dogs. Kastrofsky called to coffee at . . . evening Château. Present diamond ring.

11th July: Bathed this morning. Met General Mouravieff who invited me to visit him. Wrote Ray, Miss K. Doukoffsky, Captain Grofely, Vice-Consul Rochester, Kertch respecting the box sent to London by him. Wrote Stern Micolaieff. C. called and I got another acknowledgment from him respecting the 100 roubles. Dined Château, came into contact Neketan, the dirty yellow. Telegram from Poltawa.

24th July: On board the *Kusevi* on the Volga between Kyantzen and Saratov, my fifty-ninth birthday, in health, thank God, dream pleasantly of my Margaret.

From a Press item[1] we learn that during the night of 30th July in Kiev he was robbed of a large sum of money. In August he was in Zhitomir, and from there, at the invitation of Anastazy Trapszo, a leading Polish actor, who had acted Iago to Aldridge's Othello in Warsaw in 1862, and was now Director of the Lubelsk Theatre, he went to Lublin. He played Othello, Mungo, and Shylock to crowded houses, despite greatly increased prices of tickets. Trapszo again played Iago, and Desdemona this time was the lovely Joanna German (1843-1900), whose autographed photo was found among Amanda Aldridge's collection of her father's souvenirs. He could not play King Lear and Macbeth because of a previous ban of the Tsarist censors. One publication, in writing of Shylock, observed: "It is quite a different role from that of the savage son of hot scalding Africa. One would think only anger, wildness and fanaticism could exist for this famous tragedian and that all other feelings are completely foreign to him. But the character of Shylock was not at all outlined with savagery, and thereby Aldridge has shown us that he has not developed his talent in one direction only."[2]

He was given a farewell dinner by the local dramatic company at which mutual admiration and appreciation were expressed, and after a stop-over in Warsaw, with the same success, he left for London on 25th August.

★   ★   ★

Aldridge does not remain stationary for long. He is passionately fond of his family and is delighted with the new baby, but two months later he is opening in Versailles with *Othello*. "There is also this evening", said *Le Figaro*, "a most curious presentation, but if you wish to be present you must go to Versailles. . . . It is at the Theatre of Versailles that this strange affair will take place."[3] To *Le Figaro* a Negro actor is a very curious and strange affair, but the English *Theatrical Journal* reported: "Mr. Aldridge has been playing *Othello* at the Grand Theatre, Versailles, speaking, as is his wont, on such occasions in English, while the rest of the performers spoke French. His advent caused some sensation in Paris and the verdict of a portion of the French Press has been very favourable. Among those present, we are informed, were many of the greatest celebrities in Paris, including Alexander Dumas and Guizot."[4] This was Guizot of the Académie Française, whose translation of *Othello* was being used by the French company of the impresario, M. Kuschnick, with whom Aldridge was playing. It was here that Alexander Dumas, *père*, repeatedly embraced and kissed the cheeks of *"mon confrère,"* proudly declaring, *"Je suis aussi un Negre!"*

In November he is back home, and the next month he receives a letter from T. G. Clark of Versailles, one of the many friends he made on his tour of France:

> The tidings of your heavy loss* which found their way into the newspapers, and your personal illness have awakened my deepest sympathy. By this time I trust that you are again well and able to resume the honourable discharge of your professional duties not always discharged with so much dignity as by you. If I can do anything whatever in your interests here, always command my services. . . . Thank God that your Hope is not wholly in this world, but that He has imparted to you the sense of a better Treasure. May His blessing ever rest on you and yours. Believe me, with the highest esteem. . . .

* Probably a reference to the robbery in Kiev.

In February 1867, the month in which his son emigrates to Australia, Aldridge returns to the Continent. On the 8th he plays *Othello* at the Grand Theatre in Geneva, and then visits some of the French towns—Lyons, Chalons, Dole, Dijon, Havre, Cherbourg, Bordeaux, and many others. A Dijon newspaper reprinted the following remarks of *Salut Public* of Lyons, adding: "The success attained at Lyons is a guarantee of that which awaits the Negro tragedian in our town":

The playing of Mr. Aldridge is such as to surprise the spectators accustomed as they are to the routine and well-known intonations of our dramatic actors. One feels himself "stabbed" by the violence, the hate and the action of the black player. Here is an actor who is always in keeping with the action of the play, and he occupies himself entirely with his own business. I have never seen an actor so completely identified with his role. The illusion is complete.[5]

So great was the crush to see him that latecomers lost their reserved seats and the box-office had to refund money to many fashionable but disappointed patrons who could not get even standing-room. This was something new to them. They had always come late and their seats were always waiting. One local paper remarked: "Tonight, at his farewell performance at Dijon, people will not be late."

Despite explicit public announcements, many were taken by surprise to hear the actor hold forth in a foreign language. At first there was some disappointment, but this disappeared as soon as the play got under way and the action began to develop. "He has rent apart his soul by the playing of such a nature that it could be understood by any human being. He raised himself in the different levels of emotion to a height palpitating with interest, because he was completely identified through and through in his love and in his jealousy. Terrible in his fury and his vengeance, he was really marvellous and brought unanimous applause."[6]

The upper classes, as in England, did not approve, judging by the tone of their organ, *Le Figaro*, and in the provinces, also as in England, his basic audiences consisted of the ordinary people, who did approve: "The lower classes, generally little lettered, came with an enthusiasm that surprised us. But our upper class, no doubt tired by excursions and soirées, was conspicuous by its absence."[7]

In France, Aldridge had a good supporting company in the Troupe of Kuschnick, and his Desdemona, Mademoiselle Deborah, was highly praised, as also was Emilia and Iago. The Press was unanimous that Aldridge's presentation would leave, from many points of view, a lasting trace in the annals of the French theatre. One journal, reviewing *Othello*, raised an important question: "Why should not the provincial producers, instead of falling behind their colleagues in Paris, seek to lead the public into their deserted theatres, seek new elements of success for their deserted theatres in the so varied works of Shakespeare?"[8]

So here, too, his influence is felt. And it is in the *Album Dolois* that we read one of the last notices penned for a performance of Ira Aldridge, that of 2nd March 1867: ". . . We can affirm, without fear of contradiction by competent judges or by disgusted fans, that the presentation of Ira Aldridge is one of the most impressive Dole has ever beheld. What verisimilitude of passion! What warmth of sentiment! What elegance and naturalness of speech! Certainly Mr. Aldridge is a consummate tragedian and an outstanding artist."

In April he suffers another loss—all his boxes miscarry, including some of his most precious possessions. That same month he receives a letter from a friend in Odessa: "Here still remains the small box of flowers from the one Rouble Lady with the unpronounceable name at Izum about which you have sent no instructions and which does not look as if it would be worth the steam freight to England, not to speak of the jealousies that might arise from that 'Language of flowers'. As Easter time is now approaching, please say on whose tomb they are to be hung."

In April, he is back in London and the next few entries in his diary show how energetic he still is, despite his poor health:

8th April, 1867 (Monday): Met by accident Mr. G. Waters, an old acquaintance. He is manager for the London Chatham & Dover in Paris. Dear little Kitty very ill. Left at 7 p.m. for London. Interview with M. Bagiere, Director Italian Opera.

(Mr. George Waters later witnesses Aldridge's will, when he draws it up in Paris on 25th June.)

9th April: Arrived Victoria early this morning, saw Selman skulking. Went down to Norwood, passing the Cemetery. Kind reception from Mr. M. King. Called at the villa. Pleased with appearance at Sheffield.

(Selman is an actor who had played with Aldridge at various times. The cemetery is the West Norwood Cemetery where Margaret lies. The villa is Luranah Villa, the family home on Hamlet Road in Upper Norwood.)

10th April: At the Wells, and saw young Warner and his Father, who gave me Billets for the Japanese. At Tom Robertson and heard particulars of little Maggie.

("Young Warner" is John Lawrence Warner, who beat Ira Daniel to the first prize in elocution at the Collegiate School of Camden Town. A few months after this entry, Warner played Hamlet at the Sadler's Wells for his father's benefit, but according to the contemporary Press, he made little impression. "Little Maggie" is Margaret (Madge) Robertson, Aldridge's Desdemona at the Haymarket.)

One of Aldridge's last letters extant is the one he wrote on 17th April from Montpellier to Claude Henri Rouget, Editor of *L'Orchestra* in Paris:

MY DEAR SIR,—It seems that I am fated not to hear from you, and only at uncertain intervals. I think I told you of the arrival of the Diary and the two Almanacs, but I have not had a single paper, and what would I not give to see one. I am working very hard indeed, the weather is cold for the Midi. I hope to see you in three weeks time or thereabouts. I have visited from thirty-five towns in France, Rouen, Havre, Caen, Cherbourg, Nantes, Tours, Bordeaux, Toulouse, and received great applause for France, where the audiences are not at all noted for enthusiasm. I am going to Toulon, Nice and Marseilles, then return to Paris. I send you a notice from the *Journal de Toulouse*. Send me, I beg you, *Orchestra* and a few penny papers to Poste Restante, Marseilles. Madam joins me in best respects to yourself and amiable lady, and in the hope of hearing from you immediately, if possible, I remain

Your obliged,

IRA ALDRIDGE.

The next diary entry we have is for 9th May, when he says: "Arrived Boulogne, very hoarse indeed. Lodged at the British Hotel. A Mr. Daniels called. Melancholy reflections respecting my poor Ira. He left for Melbourne this day eleven weeks. Letters from Sheffield, Sachse, Waters, and Pontifex. Mr. Morgan called of the *Sporting World* and *Gloworm*."

In April, two great men, kindred spirits, meet in Paris—and let us read what Hans Christian Andersen says in his autobiography:

1867. The World Exhibition in Paris had just opened and people were pouring in from all countries of the world. . . . By April 11th I was in the train hastening to Paris. . . . One day as I was walking along, a smartly dressed woman came up with her husband, a Negro, and accosted me in a mixture of Swedish, English, and German. She had been born in Sweden, but had spent many years abroad. She said that she knew me from my portraits and wished to present her husband, who proved to be that excellent Negro actor, Ira Aldridge, then drawing the Parisians to the Odeon Theatre, where he was playing Othello. We shook hands and exchanged a few politenesses in English. I admit that it pleased me to have one of the Afric's gifted sons hail me as a friend. There was a time when I would not have ventured to say such a thing, but my friends have now understood that it is not vanity, but pleasure at all that God vouchsafes me, "the boy of fortune", and my friends farther off will also understand that it is so.[9]

Regrettably, the sections of Aldridge's diary in our possession are so fragmentary that we are left without any expression from him about this historic meeting. These two men had several things to bind them together. They were born in the humblest circumstances, they reached the heights in their fields of endeavour, ending up with the patronage of royalty and, at the same time, greatest popularity with the common people, the oppressed, with whom they were ever in sympathy, as revealed in their work. But they had still another thing in common—the friendship and admiration of Jenny Lind.

Andersen had a special interest in the colour question. He relates that the very first time he went to a theatre (surreptitiously)

he saw *Paul and Virginia*, the anti-slavery play in which Aldridge
had so often played: "He lived every moment of the story on the
stage; when the lovers parted, he burst into such violent crying
that all the audience in the poor people's boxes turned to look at
him. Some women tried to console him, saying it was only a
play."[10] Many years later, when Andersen decided to write a
play, he chose the plot of a French short story about a mulatto
who, after great struggle, marries the white Countess he has always
loved! This play, *The Mulatto*, his only successful one, remained
in the repertory of the Theatre Royal, Copenhagen, for ten
years.

Then this strange, ugly, little man who wrote such beautiful
fairy tales fell in love with the Swedish Nightingale! His love
was unrequited, but they became good friends, and though the
voice of Jenny Lind can never more be heard, she has been
immortalized by this greatest of story-tellers in *The Emperor's
Nightingale*:

> It begins very simply, a beginning that is often quoted as one of
> the most perfect in all literature: "In China, you know, the
> Emperor is Chinese, and all the people are Chinese . . ." and goes
> on to tell of the nightingale who sang in the wood and how the
> Emperor learned to prize his free little brown bird, with the
> throbbing living song in its throat, more than the glittering
> jewelled one with its clever musical box. "I can't make my home
> in the palace," said the nightingale, "but let me come when I
> want to; then I'll sing of an evening on this branch by the
> window, and my singing can make you both gay and thought-
> ful. I shall sing of those that are happy, and of those that suffer;
> I shall sing of the good and the evil that are here lurking about
> you."[11]

This was Hans Christian Andersen's tribute to the Swedish
Nightingale. When he died and his possessions became the
property of the nation, there was one album in which he kept
souvenirs of his life, and in it was a picture of Jenny Lind at her
loveliest—the same photograph that she presented to Ira Aldridge,
who preserved it as carefully as Hans Christian Andersen, for
to her he was "the greatest Othello of them all".

★   ★   ★

Aldridge may by this time have realized how seriously ill he was, or he may have had a premonition, for it seems more than mere chance that on 25th June, seven weeks before his death, he made his last will and testament, of which we give the text:

THIS IS THE LAST WILL AND TESTAMENT of me Ira Frederick Aldridge of Luranah Villa Hamlet Road Upper Norwood. Firstly I desire that all my just debts funeral and testamentary expenses be paid and satisfied by my Executors hereinafter named as soon as may be after my decease. Secondly I give devise and bequeath to my son Ira Daniel Aldridge the sum of five hundred pounds sterling absolutely on his attaining the age of twenty five years and thirdly I give and bequeath to my most respected friend Mr. John G. Bout of 2 Copthall Court City London five guineas for the purchase of a memorial ring for his own use and lastly I give devise and bequeath to my beloved wife Amanda Pauline of Luranah Villa Upper Norwood all and every my jewellery linen books plate pictures furniture glass horses carriages carts and also all and every sum or sums of money which may be at my house or about my person or which may be due to me at the time of my decease and also all other my monies invested in the stocks funds and securities book debts money or bonds bills notes or other securities and every other my estate and effects whatsoever and wheresoever both real and personal whether in possession conversion remainder or expectancy to and for her own use and benefit absolutely irrespective of any future coverture and her receipt alone shall be accepted as a sufficient discharge and I do nominate constitute and appoint my said wife Amanda Pauline Aldridge of Luranah Villa Hamlet Road Upper Norwood and John G. Bout, Esq. of 2 Copthall Court City London aforenamed to be the executors of this my last Will and hereby revoking all former or other wills by me at any time made I declare this to be my last Will and Testament in witness whereof I the said Ira Frederick Aldridge have to this last Will and Testament set my hand this twenty fifth day of June One thousand eight hundred and sixty seven—IRA FREDK ALDRIDGE, K.S. Signed and declared by the said Ira Frederick Aldridge the Testator on and for his last Will and Testament in the presence of us present at the same time who at his request in his presence and in the presence of each other have hereunto subscribed our names as witnesses—Geo. Waters Agent London Chatham & Dover Railway 30 Boulevard des Italiens Paris—Henry Davis, Clerk L.C. & D. Ry. 30 Bould. des Italiens Paris

PROVED at London 4th Nov. 1867 by the Oaths of Amanda Pauline Aldridge widow the Relict and John George Bout the Executors to whom administration was granted.

This is the first and only time we meet "the most respected friend, Mr. John George Bout", and so far we have no clue as to the significance of this bequest.

And now we have the last entries of his diary:

5th July (Friday): Rehearsed Marchand de Venice, Padlock. Dined at Grags Restaurant with Director Trebsko and Mad. Z. with Amanda, after rehearsed Lear.

6th July: Rehearsed and acted Shylock and Mungo, fair house and enthusiastic.

Three weeks after making his will he is being invited to America by several different parties, and already an announcement appears in a New York newspaper. The Civil War is over in the United States, and conditions are more favourable for the Negro emigrant to return to his homeland in triumph.

8th July: Last night gave last performance of Shylock and just received another letter from Messrs. Gibbons dated 19th June with three other propositions for America. Wrote to Gov. Besak respecting my robbery, also to Mrs. Rees. Received letter from Mrs. King from Milnthorpe. Wrote Gibbons, N.Y.

(Robert H. Gibbons and his brother, Thomas Francis Gibbons, agents, located at 446 Broome Street, New York, according to *Trow's Business Directory of New York City* for the year 1867-8.)

In the Ira Aldridge scrap-book in the Theatre Collection of the New York Public Library is to be found a small sheet printed in brown ink on white paper with no identification, but appearing to be a page out of a catalogue. It reads:

Dramatic

3. Aldridge (Ira, Baron, Celebrated Negro tragedian). Six A.L.S. (one with initials), and one A.L. not signed; dated Paris, Berlin, Warsaw, etc., Apr. 19-Aug. 4, 1867. To F. H. Gibbons & Company of New York concerning his proposed professional tour through U.S. With photo, Portrait with his signature.

Also L.S. by J. G. Methua on same business, 24 pages 8vo (9). Interesting correspondence respecting his terms, plans for tour, parts, etc. "My terms in the Imperial and Royal Theatres of the Continent are from fifty to seventy-five pounds sterling. . . . I will engage for five months . . . three representations weekly . . . receiving seventy-five pounds sterling and my individual expenses. The expenses of the Baroness Aldridge would be borne by me." Aldridge was born in the U.S. in 1804; played in Shakespearean and other parts with great success in England and the Continent. Played Othello to Kean's Iago.

From this document it will be seen that Mrs. Aldridge was to accompany him, and if the tour had materialized their little daughter, born in December, would have been born on American soil!

9th July (Tuesday): Rain. Telegrams from Astrakhan and newspaper from New York with announcement. Wrote Kuschnick, Ray, King and Waters. Heard more of the murder of Maximilian by that brute Friarery.

This is an obvious reference to Ferdinand Maximilian (1832-67), Emperor of Mexico, who was executed three weeks before. We know nothing of Aldridge's political opinions. He was, of course, a staunch fighter for racial equality, and we know he owned a copy of the *Letters of Junius*, which were highly critical and abusive of the British Government, but there is no indication that he had any "radical" tendencies. His list of patrons alone would attest to his acceptance of the *status quo*, with the exception of his interest in the advancement of his people, though now he is obviously emotional about the fate of Maximilian, who was a brother of Emperor Franz Joseph, from whom Aldridge had received two decorations. One would have imagined Aldridge's sympathies to have been with the Mexican Juarez (counterpart of Rolla), as against Maximilian (counterpart of Pizarro, the white invader attempting to subdue a coloured people), and they probably were, despite his expression about Maximilian, which may seem like a contradiction.

10th July: Rain, and more rain. Sent letter to Ray, Fred and Luranah, Jamar, and Jansens at Arderlecht (Bruxelles), Kuschnick, Waters, bought Tea, Sugar. Sent to Konsky for tickets pour concert. No one came to the Concert, which was for the benefit of the Poor.

11th July: Konsky called decorated and invited us to the Professors Lavenni, took refreshment, went in the evening to hear Konsky who had a few persons, very much surprised at his extraordinary execution, but to my mind it lacked feeling and expression. He was much and deservedly applauded; he wore all his decorations.

12th July: Left this morning at nine Radom en route to Petrokov by Warsaw arriving at this latter place about eight and lodged Hotel d'Angleterre where not a word of English is spoken, dined and fatigued to bed.

13th July: Went to Frankel Bunimer. The hamper sent from Paris not arrived. Paid to Lilly's* acct. 52 francs; left Halperin's acknowledgment with them but do not expect to get a farthing of my 800 roubles. Went in the evening to the theatre, saw King's Musketeers, immoral in the extreme. Lupinska played well and Rakiewicz looked well.

14th July: Leave this morning, please God, for Petrokov. Remitted 52 francs for Lilly. Bought machine for looking.

(This "machine for looking" is probably a stereoscope, a popular Victorian toy by means of which two photographs are merged to give an illusion of depth. Actors and scenes from plays were among the many slides available. Or it may have been a simple magic lantern, which, already in the 1850s, had a series of slides illustrating *Uncle Tom's Cabin*.)

15th July (Warsaw): Last night in the Theatre Warsaw. Saw the *Musketeers* by Dumas indifferently played. Disappointed in the train yesterday and today. At the opera *Robert the Devil* very indifferently played. The Stage Ballet bad, altogether different from what I expected.

16th July (Petrokov): Bought mustard and vegetable cakes. Paid bill R. and departed for Petrokov. Arrived about 7 p.m. Lodged at the principal hotel which is very dirty, received letters from Gibbons and Corbyn of America.† Letter from Penza, the former agreeing to give what I asked, one hundred pounds sterling for 20 weeks, three weekly. Also one from a M. W. Corbyn of New York at present in Paris. Wrote to

* Pet name of the youngest child, Amanda.

† Corbyn and Wall, dramatic agents, 649 Broadway, New York, N.Y.

Gibbons, Corbyn, Waters, sent P. Mask Radom Photo! Disappointed in Theatre a Saloon. All is dirty, hope to travel south soon, please God. Amanda unsettled in her stomach.

(This last is a reference to his wife's pregnancy; the baby, Rachael Margaret Frederika, was born in December.)

This ends the last diary entry so far traced.

In Petrikau (near Lodz) he played with the Trapszo Company, the same troupe that he used since his first arrival in Poland and with whom sympathetic ties and friendships had developed.

At about the time that he received the letter from Penze agreeing to his terms, he received the following letter from St. Petersburg:

> *Theatre's Direction,*
> *Nevsky Prospect,*
> *St. Petersburg,*
> *July 5, 1867.*

DEAR SIR,—The Count Boreh, the director of the Imperial Theatre, let me inform you that it is perfectly impossible to admit presently your proposition and to allow you any rights in the Imperial Theatres for the future season. Occupied as the totality of our Russian Company will be every day with the representation of the new tragedy of the Count Tolstoi and of others, it will remain no players to participate with you. This impossibility, the perfect trueness of which I can warrant, is me particularly sorrowful, because you know how much am I fond of your remarkable talent and how much do I like your amiable personal qualities and I appreciate your friendship to me. But—what cannot be, must not be. Notwithstanding I don't lose the hope to see you once in Russia, and in this hope I have the pleasure to be

Your most obedient servant,
PR. N. NASAROUR.

PS.—I belong now to the direction of the Imperial Theatres as the Secretary of the Director. My lady and my old aunt send you their most cordial compliments.

It is difficult to say whether the reasons given for this politely-worded rejection were genuine, or whether it was another case of "I am not allowed in St. Petersburg", as he wrote to Amanda from Kybrusk in May 1864, but certain it is that it was a disappointment to him.

We have seen from the catalogue item offering his letters for sale that as late as 3rd August, four days before his death, he wrote to Gibbons of New York about his tour. Into whose possession these valuable letters found their way we do not know, but perhaps one day they will come to light. The last letter of which we have the text is the one he wrote from Lowica, about fifty miles from his final destination, on 29th July, but again the addressee is unknown:

MY DEAR SIR,—We arrived here on Saturday comfortably accompanied from Blotuski by the station-master of Leutch* who speaks English very well. The Director met us with his carriage and we were most comfortably lodged at Paradis, a most beautiful place; the theatre is not very large but nicely appointed and so very clean.

I write to ask if the hamper has yet arrived, and to beg of you if it has, or as soon as it does, to send it to me as the Deutsch book of the vaudeville is in it, and I purpose giving it here. I hope to be enabled to leave here as early as possible in the next week. Will you further take the trouble to write me a few lines. I remain,

Very faithfully yours,

IRA ALDRIDGE.

PS.—Every place is sold for my first and second representations at double prices. Madam presents her compliments.

I.A.

Accompanied by his wife, Aldridge came to Lodz at the invitation of August Hentschel,† proprietor of the leading hotel and the local German Theatre. Mr. Hentschel announced in the Press that Aldridge's first performance would take place on 25th July at the German Theatre in Paradise (now 175 Piotrkowska Street), and added the following notice:

* Probably transliteration of the local pronunciation of the city's name, spelled "Lodz", although the actual sound was more like "Wooj".
† Father of Carl Hentschel, co-founder of the Playgoers Club of London, and grandfather of Irene Hentschel, producer and director.

THEATRICAL ANNOUNCEMENT

The famous tragic cavalier of Europe

IRA ALDRIDGE—NEGRO

son of the wealthy king of an African tribe, born on the shores
of the Senegal, Court Artist of Her Majesty, Queen of England,
and His Majesty, the Emperor of Austria, decorated with many
Orders of foreign palaces, and declared by all the foreign newspapers to be the only one who can portray in all its full beauty
and strength the most difficult role of the great Shakespeare,
Othello, for which he has received from the hands of His Highness, the Emperor of Austria, awards which are only presented to
those of the highest talent in old Germany, Grand Order of
Leopold. On his way from Paris to Petersburg, has consented to
make three appearances.

A. HENTSCHEL.

Lodz at that time, though only a small city of 35,000, was the
Manchester of Poland and rivalled even Moscow in the textile
markets of Europe. It was also, and still is, a stronghold of
cultural activity. The attempts to Russify Poland, and the suppression of the revolts against Tsarism, only served to intensify
the striving for national cultural expression and to stimulate
support for all struggle for freedom. Ira Aldridge represented that
struggle, merely by being a Negro working on an equal basis with
white colleagues. In addition, as we know, in his interpretations
he brought out not only the personal tragedy of Othello or
Shylock, but the social implications as well, and this would be
appreciated not only by the Poles, but by the large Jewish community of Lodz.

On the day of his scheduled opening performance, the Press
announced that "The failing health of Mr. Ira Aldridge prevented today's performance, but as soon as he recovers the show
will go on." But he did not recover, and the performance did
not go on.

He had arrived in Lodz in very ill health, but proceeded
nevertheless with the scheduled rehearsals, but these had to be
discontinued as he grew worse, and the opening performance
was postponed. On 7th August he died.

In the Lodz Register of Deaths appears the following certificate
(translated from the Polish):

332

In Lodz on the eighth of August in the year eighteen hundred and sixty-seven at ten o'clock in the morning, there came August Hentschel, a thirty-three-year-old hotel-owner, and August Michel, forty-nine-year-old sexton, both of Lodz, to intimate that IRA FRYDERYK ALDRIDGE, a dramatic artist temporarily living in Lodz, had died at five o'clock on the previous day. He was born in New York and at the time of his death was fifty-nine years old. His late parents were Daniel and Lurona Aldridge. He left a wife, Amanda, maiden name Brandt, and four children. After the death of IRA FRYDERYK ALDRIDGE had been personally satisfied and the certificate made out, it was read and signed by the Priest of the Parish [signature illegible], August Hentschel, and August Michel.

The *Warsaw Courier*, reporting this tragic event, said that "in two days a boil on the breast opened up, which proved fatal to him, and though they called in seven of the most eminent doctors in the city, they could not save him". There is no precise medical information as to the cause of death. Other material examined refers to a "boil on the lungs". Considering the length of time in which there was evidence of ill health, the likelihood is that he died of a serious lung condition of long standing, and that his arduous life hastened his death. The *Warsaw Courier* continues with its account:

On the 7th at 5 p.m. the life of Ira Aldridge passed away peacefully and painlessly. Mr. Hentschel did his utmost to save him. . . . The body of the deceased remained in one of the lower rooms of the Hentschel Hotel, where his life ended. His body was draped as if in a chapel. The features changed little after death. The day before the burial the Choir of the Society of Singers, over 100 people, sang the song of *Abfurung* (Farewell). On the day of the burial the same song was repeated. The Minister Pastor Ronthaler said the prayer. A Military Band accompanied the funeral, which played the hymn from Haydn's Oratorio, as well as the Society of Singers, the Orchestra of the Society of Soldiers, in uniform, and the Society of Dramatic Artists under the direction of Mr. N. Hentschel. On front of the coffin were carried his Orders on a cushion, and the deceased was decorated with a laurel wreath.

Behind the hearse followed the President of the City of Lodz, a Military Guard of Honour, and Guilds with their banners.

The widow rode in a carriage at the end of the procession. At the grave the Rev. J. X. Ronthaler made an obituary speech to the gathering of citizens.

Two days after his death, Ira Aldridge was buried in the Evangelical Cemetery in Lodz, in the plot of a family named Moes.

The tombstone, a great cross, erected in 1890, still stands, and to this day the grave of the African Roscius is cared for by the Society of Polish Artists of Film and Theatre.

Obituary notices appeared in far-flung corners of the world, considerable space being given in the cities and towns that had seen him. Ira Daniel learned of his father's death from the Melbourne Press. On 12th August the *Chicago Times* told its readers on the front page about the Great Fire at Bordeaux, about the issuance by Turkey of a circular note respecting the Cretan War, and, under a London dateline: "Ira Aldridge, the celebrated African Roscius, is dead. His death occurred while he was on a professional tour in Poland." Oddly enough, that newspaper on the previous day had the following announcement in its column on theatrical activities: "Ira Aldridge, Negro Tragedian, is to play in the Academy of Music soon", and listed his honours and decorations. The only reference we have seen of an appearance in the Academy of Music (presumably in New York) was in the *New York Herald* advertisement of 19th August 1858, quoted in Chapter XII.

*   *   *

So with the victory of the Civil War, fought for the emancipation of the slaves, Aldridge was at last returning to play in his native land. And proud he would have been, for was he not like Heine a soldier in the struggle for the liberation of mankind? He too had never lowered his standard in any of his battles for the same cause—the basic equality of all men under heaven.

Thus ended a career unique in the annals of world theatre, that of a little black boy from the Negro community of Lower Manhattan in New York, a product of the first African Free Schools and the first African Theatre; who, whatever the truth of his descent from a princely line, was certainly the son of a straw-vendor and lay-preacher, and who, emerging from an enslaved people, became a world artist, a scholar and a gentleman in the finest sense of that word, moving in the highest and most exclusive circles of the civilized world. Indeed, the title "Knight of Saxony" was bestowed upon him by the small but proud state of Saxe-Coburg-Gotha, whose Almanac was the most exclusive aristocratic social register ever known, beside which the New York Social Register would have been considered plebeian. His patrons, his orders and decorations are unparalleled by any other actor before or since. Yet his greatest support came from the common people, and Aldridge himself was conscious of that balance: for all his life his portrayal of the proud and tragic general of the Venetian Republic was inevitably followed by the songs and humour of the Negro slave, mixing protest with the eternal comedy of the oppressed.

As a pioneer in laying the foundations of that still-to-come theatre of the human race, Ira Aldridge was the first to show that a black man could scale any heights in theatrical art reached by a white man—and recreate with equal artistry the greatest characters in world drama. And he did this alone, without the aid of any social or political organizations such as abound today to help "backward peoples", without any subsidies or scholarships, on his own two feet, with his own skill, versatility and talent.

He did this in a white world, and showed that if a white can blacken his skin to represent Othello, then a black man can whiten his skin to represent Lear, Macbeth, or Shylock with equal artistry. A simple fact—but even today not wholly accepted in this democratic age. Nevertheless, the coloured peoples are now beginning to achieve, in fact, the equal rights he always made his basic theme. Perhaps the very fact of this book is itself a reflection of that upsurge, and perhaps at no other time would it have been so propitious. Perhaps the name of the African Roscius, lost for nearly a hundred years, once more will shine bright in an even wider world than the one in which he struggled.

And one day, for sure, there will be professional African theatres in South Africa, Ghana, and Nigeria, and Negro theatres for black and white in Alabama, South Carolina, and Georgia, and some of these theatres and companies will be named after Ira Aldridge, and the great dramas of the world, including their own, will be played by black companies for their own people, and they will tour the same countries Aldridge toured, and similarly triumph.

For Ira Aldridge, the African Roscius, there could be no greater tribute.

In bringing to the world an unrecognized star in the firmament of the dramatic art, a dark star whose brilliance has been dimmed by sins of omission and commission of the white world, we hope we have, in some measure, paid the debt we owe to the people who gave this great man to the world.

A few lines of his own Farewell Address are a fitting Epilogue to the drama of his life:

> Othello's occupation's gone—'tis o'er,
> The mask has fallen, I'm your actor here no more,
> But still your pupil, protégé, whate'er
> Your kindness made me, and your fostering care . . .
> You, who espousing injured Afric's cause
> First cheered my efforts by your kind applause,
> O'erlooked my errors, taught my mind to soar
> And ope'd my path to England's genial shore.
> Though we must part, my best protectors, still
> My heart will cherish, till its fount is chill
> That proudest record—the fresh memory
> That here the sable African was free!
> From every bond—save those which kindness threw
> Around his heart, and bound it fast to you.

References

CHAPTER I

1. *On the Stage*, Dutton Cook. Sampson Low, Marston, Searle, and Rivington, London, 1883.
2. *Curiosities of the American Stage*, Laurence Hutton. Harper and Brothers, New York, 1891.
3. *The Works of Théophile Gautier*, translated and edited by Professor F. C. de Sumichrast, Department of French, Harvard University. George C. Harrap, London, 1900 (24 vols.).
4. *Annals of Covent Garden Theatre from 1782 to 1897*, Henry Saxe Wyndham. Chatto & Windus, London, 1906.
5. *Fifty Years of an Actor's Life*, John Coleman. Hutchinson & Co., London, 1904.
6. *Leben und Kunstler-Laufbahn des Negers Ira Aldridge*. Allgemeine Deutsche Verlage-Anstalt, 1853.
7. *Ira Aldridge: Zyciorys*. Drukarni Czasu, Krakow, 1854.
8. *Negern I. Aldridge, Lefnadsteckning med portratt*. Minne af hans upptradande i Stockholm, sommaren, 1857.
9. *Ira Aldridge: Biographicheski Ocherk*. K. Zvantsev, St. Petersburg, 1858.
10. *Vie du Nègre Ira Aldridge*. Agence Kuschnick, Paris, 1866.

CHAPTER II

1. *The American Revolution in New York*, prepared by the Division of Archives and History of the University of the State of New York, 1926.
2. *The Souls of Black Folk*, Dr. W. E. B. DuBois. A. C. McClurg & Co., Chicago, 1903.

CHAPTER III

1. *History of the African Free Schools*, Charles C. Andrews. Mahlon Day, New York, 1830.

CHAPTER IV

1. *Annals of the New York Stage*, George C. D. Odell. Columbia University Press, New York, 1928 (Vols. 3, 4).
2. *Memoirs of Charles Mathews*, edited by Mrs. Mathews. Richard Bentley, London, 1839 (4 vols.).
3. *A Glance at the Life of Ira Aldridge*. Fountain Peyton, Washington, D.C., 1917.

4. *The Drama*, November 1825.
5. Coleman, *op. cit.*

CHAPTER V

1. *Sheridan to Robertson: a Study of the Nineteenth-century London Stage*, Ernest Bradlee Watson. Harvard University Press, Cambridge, Mass., 1936.
2. *Saunders's News Letter*, Dublin, 24th December 1832.
3. Letter of Maurice Lenihan in *Notes and Queries*, London, 14th September, 1872.
4. *History of the Theatres of Brighton from 1774 to 1885*, Henry C. Porter. King and Thorne, Brighton, 1886.

CHAPTER VI

1. *Leben und Kunstler-Laufbahn, op. cit.*
2. *Old Odessa*. A. de Ribas, 1913. Quoted by Durylin.
3. "Aldridge on the Moscow Stage", B. Almazov. *Russki Vestnik* (Russian Herald), October 1862, No. 40, pp. 12-13.
4. *Belfast News Letter*, 10th July 1829.
5. *Hull Advertiser and Exchange Gazette*, 12th June, 1829.
6. *Dramatic Magazine*, 1st July 1829.
7. *The London Theatre in the Eighteen-thirties*, Charles Rice. Society for Theatre Research, Annual Publication No. 2, London, 1950.
8. *Some Account of the English Stage, from the Restoration in 1660 to 1830*. John Genest, H. E. Carrington, Bath, 1832 (10 vols.).
9. *Blood and Thunder*, Maurice Willson Disher. Frederick Muller, London, 1949.

CHAPTER VII

1. *A History of the City of Dublin*, John Warburton. T. Cadell and W. Davies, London, 1818.
2. *Memoirs, 1843-1863*, E. F. Yunge. Sphinx, St. Petersburg, 1913 (in Russian).

CHAPTER VIII

1. *Edmund Kean*, Harold Newcomb Hillebrand. Columbia University Press, New York, 1933.
2. *Letters of Mr. and Mrs. Charles Kean Relating to Their American Tours*, edited by William G. B. Carson, Washington University, St. Louis, 1945. Letter from E llen Kean to Miss Marianne Skerrett, 1866.)

CHAPTER IX

1. *The Cambrian*, 3rd August 1833.

References

CHAPTER X

1. *Northern Whig* (Belfast), 1st May 1838.
2. *Era*, 26th March 1848.
3. *Theatrical Journal*, 17th April 1841.
4. Quoted in the *Cambrian Weekly*, 6th April 1844.
5. Coleman, *op. cit.*
6. Quoted in the *Era*, 2nd May 1846.
7. *Northern Whig*, April 1846.
8. *Theatrical Times*, 30th December 1836.
9. *Northern Whig*, 26th October 1847.
10. *Theatrical Times*, 5th, 12th, and 19th February 1848.
11. *Era*, 4th November 1843.
12. Coleman, *op. cit.*
13. *Notes and Queries*, 17th August 1872; letter from J. J. Sheahan.
14. *Ibid.*, 25th May 1872; letter from J. M.

CHAPTER XI

1. *Pantheon*, 1852 (Russian publication), quoted by Durylin.
2. *Theatrical Journal*, 8th December 1852.
3. *Czasu* (Times), 9th November 1854 (Crakow, Poland).
4. *The Negro in Our History*, Carter G. Woodson. Associated Publishers, Washington, 1922.
5. *Information Bulletin of Saratov*, No. 141, 1864 (Russian).
6. *Czasu*, 3rd November 1854.

CHAPTER XII

1. *The Black Man, His Antecedents, His Genius, and His Achievements*, William Wells Brown. James Redpath, Boston, 1863.
2. "Centenary of Negro Drama", Archibald Haddon. *The Crisis*, New York, February 1934.
3. *Lectures on Dramatic Art and Literature*, Augustus William Schlegel: translated by John Black. Baldwin, Cradock and Jay, London, 1815, Vol. 2, p. 198.

CHAPTER XIII

1. *Ira Aldridge, Biographicheski Ocherk* (A Biographical Essay), K. Zvantsev. St. Petersburg, 1858, pp. 3-34.
2. "Notes of a Poet: St. Petersburg Life", I. Panayev. *Sovremennik* (Contemporary), St. Petersburg, 1858, Vol. 72, Book 6, pp. 257-78.
3. "Social Events", M.Z. (Zotov). *Sin Otyechestva* (Son of the Fatherland), 30th November, 1858.
4. Almazov, *op. cit.*

339

5. Cited in the *Anglo-African Magazine*, February 1859.

6. *Voyage en Russie*, Théophile Gautier. Charpentier and Fasquelle, Paris, 1895, pp. 254-6.

7. *Pisma* (Letters), A. F. Pisemsky. Academy of Science, U.S.S.R., Moscow-Leningrad, 1936, p. 128.

8. *Perepiska M.A. Balakireva so Stasovym* (Correspondence of M. A. Balakirev with Stassov). St. Petersburg, 1917, p. 40.

9. "The Little Bee's Newspaper Notes". *Severnaya Pchela* (Northern Bee), 1858, No. 259, p. 1089.

10. *Sochinyeniya i Perevody* (Collected Works and Translations), A. I. Bazhenov. Moscow, 1869, Vol. 1, pp. 178-86.

11. Zvantsev, *op. cit.*

12. *Zhizn i Trudy M. P. Pogodin* (Life and Works of M. P. Pogodin), N. Barsukov. St. Petersburg, 1902, Vol. XVI, pp. 192-6.

13. *Northern Bee, op. cit.*

14. *Ibid.*, 31st December 1858, No. 287.

15. Barsukov, *op. cit.*

16. Panayev, *op. cit.*

17. *Dyed Russki Tseny* (Grandfathers of the Russian Stage), S. Bertenson. St. Petersburg, 1916, p. 147.

18. *Sin Otyechestva*, 14th December 1858, No. 50.

19. *Teatralny i Muskalny Vestnik* (Theatrical and Musical News), K. Zvantsev. St. Petersburg, 1858, No. 51, pp. 602-3.

20. *Durylin, op. cit.*, p. 37.

21. Article in *Yuni Chitatel* (Russian children's magazine), St. Petersburg, *c.* 1903-4. Quoted in *Ira Aldridge, American Negro Tragedian and Taras Shevchenko, Story of a Friendship*, Marie Trommer. New York, 1939.

CHAPTER XIV

1. *Brighton Gazette*, 2nd September 1858.

CHAPTER XV

1. *Moskovski Zhurnal Iskusstvo* (Moscow Journal of Art), November 1862.

2. "Iz Dalekovo Proshlovo" (The Distant Past), A. F. Kon. In the anthology, *Sto Lyet Malomu Teatru* (A Hundred Years of the Maly Theatre), Moscow All-Russian Theatrical Society, 1924, pp. 96-8.

3. "U. M. S. Shchepkina" (with M. S. Shchepkin), M. V. Lentovsky. *Moskovsky Listok* (Moscow Bulletin), 1895, No. 116.

4. *Vospominaniya Aktyera* (Memoirs of an Actor), A. A. Alekseyev. Moscow 1894, pp. 138-9.

5. *Vospominaniya i Pisma* (Memoirs and Letters), P. A. Strepetova. Academia, Moscow, 1934, pp. 167-8.

6. "Zapiski" (Notebooks) of G. N. Fedotova, unpublished; quoted by Durylin, p. 218.

7. *Razkaz o Proshlom* (Tales of the Past), V. N. Davydov. Academia, Moscow, 1930, pp. 97-105.
8. *Vstryechi i Vospominaniya* (Meetings and Memories), I. N. Zakharin (Yakunin). St. Petersburg, 1903, p. 317.
9. *Vospominaniya o Perezhitom i Vidyennom v 1864-1909* (Memories of What I Have Experienced and Seen from 1864-1909), I. I. Yanzhul. 1st Series, St. Petersburg, 1910, p. 52.
10. Bazhenov, *op. cit.*
11. "Aldridge-Othello", letter to the Editor, with notes, I. A., *Dyen* (Day), 29th September 1862, No. 39, pp. 17-18.
12. *Sin Otyechestva*, 1858, No. 40; quoted by Durylin.
13. *Ibid.*, 7th December 1858, No. 49, quoted by Durylin.
14. *Klochki Vospominaniyi* (Fragments of Memories), A. A. Stakhovitch. Moscow, 1904, pp. 99-100.
15. *Put Provincialnoy Actrisy* (The Path of a Provincial Actress), M. I. Belizary. Iskusstvo, Leningrad-Moscow, 1938, pp. 14-15.
16. *Stati, Pisma, Vospominaniya* (Articles, Letters, Memoirs), A. I. Urusov. Moscow, 1907, Vol. 1, p. 64.
17. "Correspondence of Aksakov and N. S. Sakhonskaya (Kokhanovskaya)'', compiled by O. G. Aksakov (1862). *Russkoye Obozreniye* (Russian Review), June 1897.
18. Almazov, *op. cit.*

CHAPTER XVI

1. *Staraya Odessa* (Old Odessa), A. de Ribas. Odessa, 1913, p. 121.
2. "The Black Tragedian and White Public", I. Goltz-Miller. *Odessky Novosti* (Odessa News), 3rd February 1866.
3. *Moyemu Chitatelu* (To My Readers), A. Verbitskaya. 1st Edition, Moscow, 1908, p. 15.
4. *Spravochny Listok Gorod Saratova* (Information Bulletin of the Town of Saratov), 1864, Nos. 128, 129.
5. *Vospominaniyakh Aktyera* (Memoirs of an Actor), P. M. Nadimov-Shamshenko. Manuscript in Bakrushin Theatre Museum, Moscow, No. 1,016.
6. Davydov, *op. cit.*
7. "In Saratov", essay. *Volga*, 5th September 1864, No. 40.
8. Alekseyev, *op. cit.*
9. *Nizhegorodskyi Teatr, 1798-1867* (Nizhni-Novgorod Theatre), A. S. Gatsisky. Nizhni-Novgorod, 1867, pp. 68-9.
10. *Russkaye Tsena* (Russian Stage), 1864, No. 12, p. 187.
11. *Ibid.*, 1865, Nos. 4-5, pp. 247-8.
12. *Odessky Novosti* (Odessa News), 18th January 1866, No. 12.
13. "Ira Aldridge in Russia", Sergius Kara-Mourza. *The Crisis*, New York, September 1933.
14. *Odessky Novosti, op. cit.*
15. *Entracte*, 4th September 1866, No. 34.
16. Davydov, *op. cit.*

17. "Aldridge on the Rostov Stage", letter to the Editor, *Russkava Tsena*, 4th September 1864, No. 34.

18. "Aldridge in Tambov", *Tambovsky Gubernskiye Vedemosti* (Tambov Provincial Chronicle), 24th October 1864, No. 53, "Local News".

19. Davydov, *op. cit.*

20. *Russkaye Tsena*, 1865, Nos. 4-5, pp. 247-8.

CHAPTER XVIII

1. *Kurier Warszawski*, 3rd August 1866.
2. *Lublin Courier*, 10th August 1866.
3. *Figaro*, 23rd November 1866.
4. *Theatrical Journal*, 5th December 1866.
5. "L'Union Bourguigonne", *Journal de Dijon*, 20th February 1867.
6. *Ibid.*, 22nd February 1867.
7. *Publicateur de Dole et du Jura*, 28th February 1867.
8. *Journal de Marne*, 13th March 1867.
9. *The Mermaid Man: Autobiography of Hans Christian Andersen*. Arthur Barker, London, 1955, p. 30.
10. *Hans Christian Andersen*, Rumer Godden. Hutchinson, London, 1955.
11. *Ibid.*

Index

AARON (*Titus Andronicus*), 171-3
Abbey Theatre (Dublin), 98
Aberdeen, 108-12
Aberystwyth, 140
Academy of Music (New York), 334
Actors' Shakespearean Supper, 293, 310
Adams, W. Davenport, 8
Afghanistan War, The (play), 170
"African Apollo", 119, 139
African Company, *see* African Theatre
African Free Schools (New York), 23-7
African Grove, *see* African Theatre
African Theatre (New York): African
  Grove, 33; arrest of the cast, 34-6;
  Brown's Tea-garden, 24, 31; Brown's
  Theatre, 32; closing, 34-6; Pantheon, 34;
  partition for whites, 32; ridicule in Press,
  32-6; visit by Charles Mathews, 40
African's Vengeance, The (play), 94-5
Aix-la-Chapelle (Aachen), 177
Aksakov, I. S. (Editor, *Dyen*), 265, 272, 273
Alambra (*Paul and Virginia*), 87
Album Dolois, 322
Aldridge, Amanda Christina Elizabeth
  (Amanda Ira), (daughter): 2, 5, 6, 12,
  184; birth, 302; schooling, 302; pupil of
  Jenny Lind, 303; adopts name "Mon-
  tague Ring" as composer, 304; romance,
  304; letters, 304-6; death, 306; burial,
  307
Aldridge, Amanda Pauline (second wife):
  184; I.A. letters to, 276-8; 292; birth,
  293; death, 297; 306
Aldridge, Daniel (father), birth, 15-20;
  name, 19; occupation, 20-1; second
  marriage, 24; 20, 26, 31n., 46, 291
Aldridge, David (nephew), 250
Aldridge, Ellen Huxley (eldest son's wife),
  207
Aldridge, Florence Morton (alleged wife of
  younger son), 299
Aldridge, Ira, ancestry, 15; white blood,
  19; birth, place and date, 16, 18, 23, 291;
  pupil at African Free School, New
  York, 23; death of mother, 23; awarded
  prizes for declamation, 24; sails on a
  brig, 24; intended for church career, 28;
  develops passion for theatre, 28; inspired by James Hewlett of African
  Theatre, 28; plays Rolla (*Pizarro*) at
  African Theatre, 39; attempts Romeo,
  39; Charles Mathews's impersonation of
  I.A. as Hamlet, 40-3; I.A.'s denial, 43-4;

obtains employment as dresser to Henry
Wallack, 45; alleged attendance at
Schenectady College, 46; sails for England on same ship as James Wallack, 47;
attendance at Glasgow University, 48;
early theatrical activities in England, 51;
first known major engagement in London, 53; first starring role, Oroonoko,
53; "unprecedented success", 58; stage
names and designations, 54-5; second
starring role, Gambia (*The Slave*), 58;
engagement at Coburg Theatre extended, 65; marriage to an English-
woman, 66; early repertoire, 70; first
provincial engagement, Brighton, 66;
first singing and comic role, Mungo
(*The Padlock*), 70; second comic role,
Ginger Blue (*Virginian Mummy*), 75;
American tour, plans for, 78, 142, 153,
176, 218, 327-8; biographical memoir
distributed to audience, 78; plays with
John Vandenhoff, 79; first official
honour, Republic of Haiti, 79-81; sings
"Opossum Up a Gum Tree", 81; plays
with Charles Kean, Belfast, 81-2; song
"The Negro Boy", written for I.A. by
J. Bisset, 83; "Farewell Address", 78,
83; search for new roles, 85; first non-
Negro role, Rolla (*Pizarro*), 87; first
white European role, Captain Dirk
Hatteraick (*Guy Mannering*), 88; second
white European role, Bertram (*Bertram*),
90; Shylock, Macbeth, Richard III and
other new roles, 94; attempts writing
poetry, 97; engagement at Theatre
Royal, Dublin, 98; impresses Edmund
Kean with his "wondrous versatility",
103; successful engagement at Bath, 107;
poor supporting cast, 110; tour of
Southern Ireland, 111; engagement at
Theatre Royal, Covent Garden, 115;
threats and attacks in Press, 117; circulation of "Crito" handbill calling for fair
play, 118; repeats Othello by popular
demand, 129; engagement abruptly terminated, 130; long run at Surrey
Theatre, 136; inflammatory attacks in
Press, 137; hoax of I.A.'s accidental
death, 140; testimonials from Miss
O'Neill and Madame Malibran, 142,
143; patrons, 145; establishes bona fides
as gentleman, 145; criticized for bowdlerizing Shakespeare, 147; introduces

343

Ira Aldridge—The Negro Tragedian

Aldridge, Ira—*cont.*

"A Grand Classic and Dramatic Entertainment", 147; gives lecture on the drama, 148; joins the Freemasons, 152; first appearance in *Black Doctor*, 155; birth of a son, 157; impact on provincial box-offices, 158; inadequacy of repertoire, 160; offer from Surrey Theatre, 161; gift from brother actors in Scotland, 167; search for new roles, 170; adapts *Titus Andronicus*, 170; reaches impasse in career, 175; first continental tour, accompanied by wife and son, 177; recognition by fellow-artists in Germany, 178; presented to Duchess of Saxe-Coburg-Gotha, 179; performs for H.M. Frederick IV of Prussia, 182; receives Prussian Gold Medal for Art and Science, 182; meets Jenny Lind in Dresden, 183; receives Medal of Ferdinand from Franz Joseph, Emperor of Austria, 185; plays with Hungarian and German theatre companies in Budapest, 185; negotiates for tour of France, 193; contributes to abolitionist cause, 197; returns to England, 200; indications of severe illness, 201; alleged performance of Hamlet in Sheffield, 203; invitation to Stockholm, 206; Chevalier Ira Aldridge, Knight of Saxony, 210; introduces Shakespeare to Serbia, 211; engagement at Lyceum Theatre, London, 212; *New York Herald*, 19th August, 1858, announces tour of U.S., 219; first visit to Tsarist Russia, 220; Gautier's critique of I.A. as Othello and King Lear, 229; bi-lingual performances commented on in Press, 229-31; rivalry and antagonism of Samoilov, 236; honoured by fellow actors at Benefit in St. Petersburg, 238-41; meets Shevchenko at home of Count and Countess Tolstoy, 242; first performance of *King Lear* in England, 245; buys property in Upper Norwood, 253; second tour of Russia, Moscow, 1862, 255; plays with Russian company, 255; Shchepkin's criticism, 258; meeting with Sadovsky, 260; influence on Russian actors, 260; attack by Kokhanovskaya in Russian Press, 265; hostility in Moscow, 268-70; defence by prominent writers, 271-2; brings Shakespeare to outlying Russian provinces, 275; hailed as "strolling missionary of art", 275; Jewish community appreciate his interpretation of Shylock, 288; British naturalization, 291; Margaret (first wife), 292, 308-9; Amanda Pauline (second wife), 293-4; children, 295-308; Actors' Shakespearean Supper,

319; *Othello* at the Haymarket, with Madge Robertson as Desdemona, 311; phrenological analysis, 315; tour of Turkey, Russia, Poland, France, 313-22; meeting with Hans Christian Andersen, 324; last will and testament, 326; final negotiations for American tour, 327-8; stricken in Lodz, Poland, 332; death, 332; funeral, 333

Aldridge, Ira, by S. Durylin, 12
Aldridge, Ira, Memorial Chair, 1
Aldridge, Ira, Memorial Collection, 4
Aldridge, Ira, Society, 4
Aldridge, Ira Daniel (son), 101; birth, 157; appearance, 158; illness, 187; 192, 200, 209, 249; letter to father, 253; 278, 284, 292; letters to father and stepmother on their marriage, 294-5; emigrates to Australia, 300; letter to stepmother from Melbourne, 300-2; marriage and children, 307-8
Aldridge, Ira Frederick Francis (grandson), 307
Aldridge, Ira Frederick Olaff (son), 277, 278, 292; birth, 297; illness, death and burial, 298-9
Aldridge, Ira Lewis (great grand-nephew), 250
Aldridge, Irene Luranah Pauline (daughter), 277, 278, 292; education, 295-6; musical career, 296; illness, death, burial, 296-7
Aldridge, James Ira, (grandson), 307
Aldridge, John Edward (grandson), 307
Aldridge, Joshua (brother), 18, 23, 28, 250
Aldridge, Lurona (mother), 18, 19
Aldridge, Margaret (first wife), 66, 112, 113, 134, 153, 157; accident, 174; ill health, 179; 187, 189, 190, 191, 192, 200, 207-9, 219, 278, 283; death, 292; burial, 295; 306-9
Aldridge, Margaret (granddaughter), 307
Aldridge, Rachael Margaret Frederika (posthumous daughter), 295, 306
Aldridge, surname, 19
Aldridge, Staffordshire, 19
Aldridge in Moscow—A Lyrical Scene, 266
Alekseyev, A. A. (Russian actor), 260, 283
Alexander II, Tsar of Russia, 221
Alexander, John Henry, 113, 134
Alexandrinsky Theatre (St. Petersburg), 222, 256
Alexandrova (Russian actress), 281
All God's Chillun Got Wings, by Eugene O'Neill, 157
All Union Theatrical Society, Moscow, 12
Almazov, S. (Russian critic), 272, 273
Alonzo of Castille, see The Revenge
Amateur Circle of Dramatic Art, Kazan, 289

354

KING ALFRED'S COLLEGE LIBRARY